W9-ABP-928

A publication of

THE WRIGHT INSTITUTE

a center for interdisciplinary research,
graduate training, and social action

Berkeley, California

Sanctions
for Evil

Sources of
Social Destructiveness

nevitt sanford
craig comstock
& associates

BAUM

SANCTIONS FOR EVIL

 Jossey-Bass Inc., Publishers
615 Montgomery Street • San Francisco • 1971

SANCTIONS FOR EVIL
Sources of Social Destructiveness
                Nevitt Sanford, Craig Comstock, and Associates

Jossey-Bass, Inc., Publishers
615 Montgomery Street
San Francisco, California 94111

Library of Congress Catalog Card Number 79–129769

International Standard Book Number ISBN 0–87589–077–6

Manufactured in the United States of America
                Composed and printed by Hamilton Printing Company
                Bound by Chas. H. Bohn & Co., Inc.

JACKET DESIGN BY WILLI BAUM, SAN FRANCISCO

FIRST EDITION

Code 7104

THE JOSSEY-BASS
BEHAVIORAL SCIENCE SERIES

General Editors

WILLIAM E. HENRY, *University of Chicago*

NEVITT SANFORD, *Wright Institute, Berkeley*

Preface

Most social destructiveness is done by people who feel they have some kind of permission for what they do, even to the point of feeling righteous, and who commonly regard their victims as less than human or otherwise beyond the pale. In *Sanctions for Evil* we trace the process of destructiveness, showing how dehumanization occurs, how sanctions for evil come to exist, and how people cooperate in doing harm or in failing to prevent it. Drawing on sociology, psychiatry, political theory, psychology, and related fields, the authors sort out the complexity of the sanctioning process and suggest ways to impede or prevent it.

In showing how specific types of social destructiveness are related to others and to the process of sanction-giving, we have sought to make *Sanctions for Evil* useful to a number of groups who encounter social destructiveness in their work and must cope with it, seek to prevent it, or inform others about it.

Although *Sanctions for Evil* has been in preparation for several years, it began rapidly to take its present shape soon after we first heard of the My Lai massacre. At that time the staff of

The Wright Institute decided to hold a public symposium on "The Legitimation of Evil," on the kind of event that had occurred at My Lai and was soon to occur at Kent State University in Ohio and at Jackson State College in Mississippi. We prepared an introduction to the concept of social destructiveness and an outline of topics to be covered. We then asked various scholars and scientists to write papers which they would read and discuss at the symposium and later revise for publication.

Widespread interest in this approach to the vexing topic of destructiveness was indicated by the warm response of colleagues to our invitations; by the decisions of public television to carry the symposium live on KQED, San Francisco, and Pacifica Foundation radio to rebroadcast the proceedings; and not least by the stimulating reaction of the audience, which included representatives of all the groups for which *Sanctions for Evil* was written.

Discussion at the symposium itself and further conferences among the authors helped to improve the organization of *Sanctions for Evil* and also assisted the authors in preparing their chapters —a task which in most cases led to a considerable revision or expansion of what had been offered at the symposium. (Perhaps the most notable instance of expansion is the far-ranging essay by Charles Drekmeier, which began as some brief remarks and became what is now Chapter Thirteen.) In order to complete our general plan we meanwhile asked Philip P. Hallie to prepare a chapter based on his remarks from the floor at the symposium, and we arranged to include distinguished papers written by Robert Jay Lifton, by George De Vos, and by Viola W. Bernard, Perry Ottenberg, and Fritz Redl. Apart from these three, all the chapters were written for this book by authors who not only knew what their fellows were saying but had the benefit of their criticism.

Most of the authors of *Santions for Evil* have been concerned with social destructiveness for some time. For example, our interest in anti-Semitism and authoritarianism was revived in 1966 when we were asked by Norman Cohn to undertake some studies in collaboration with his newly founded research center in the University of Sussex, England—at that time called the Centre for Research in Collective Psychopathology but since renamed The Columbus Centre. Cohn and his group were making a fresh

attempt to understand the phenomenon of Nazism or, more generally, all those forms of collective destructiveness in which the victims are seen as less than human. Their approach has been mainly
psychoanalytic and historical. With the help of a grant from the
Columbus Trust, the British foundation which also supports
Cohn's research, and with the advice and counsel of Cohn and
his group, we together with Jan Howard were able in 1967 to begin theoretical and observational studies of what we called destruc-
tivness and dehumanization. These studies were later assisted by
a grant from the Foundation's Fund for Research in Psychiatry
and are continuing with a greater empirical accent with the support of the National Institutes of Mental Health (Grants #5 K05
MH 12829–02 and #3 K05 MH 12829–01S1). These several
sources of support are gratefully acknowledged.

We express our warm thanks also to the Acquinas Foundation for a grant which, made on short notice, enabled us to hold
our public symposium; to Stanley Rodgers of Grace Cathedral,
San Francisco, and to his staff for providing an auditorium and
excellent arrangements for the occasion; to radio station KUOP
of the University of the Pacific for recording all the proceedings
and making the tapes available to us; and to the Society for the
Psychological Study of Social Issues, which at a critical time provided funds for the transcription of these tapes. Harvey Glasser,
chairman of the board of The Wright Institute, and Wendy Turn-
bull brought talent and devotion to the task of planning the symposium, and they had the able assistance of Myra Engelman of
The Wright Institute, whose quiet efficiency made the final days of
preparation seem far less hectic than they really were.

Various individuals helped us in important ways in the
preparation of *Sanctions for Evil*. We owe a special debt of grati-
tude to Herman Blake, David Daniels, Marshall Gilula, Thomas
Harriman, Stanley Milgram, Steven Perryman, and Edwin Shneid-
man for speaking from the platform at the symposium and thereby
influencing the content of our book although their words do not
appear within it.

In organizing the book we had the wise counsel of William
E. Henry. Edward Opton, Jr., contributed valuable ideas and
suggestions at all stages of the editing. Patience Merian typed and

retyped much of the manuscript with serenity and high competence and rendered many other valuable services. We also thank
Pamela Fischer of Jossey-Bass for her expert editorial work.

NEVITT SANFORD
CRAIG COMSTOCK

Berkeley
January 1971

Contents

Contents

The Authors

Robert N. Bellah, *chairman of the Center for Japanese and Korean Studies and Ford Professor of Sociology and Comparative Studies, University of California, Berkeley*

Viola W. Bernard, *professor of psychiatry, Columbia University College of Physicians and Surgeons*

Craig Comstock, *research associate, The Wright Institute; doctoral candidate, Stanford University*

George De Vos, *professor of anthropology, University of California, Berkeley*

Bernard L. Diamond, *professor of law and of criminology and clinical professor of psychiatry, University of California, Berkeley and San Francisco*

Charles Drekmeier, *professor of political science, Stanford University*

Troy Duster, *associate professor of sociology, University of California, Berkeley*

Philip P. Hallie, *Griffin Professor of Philosophy and Humanities, Wesleyan University*

Jan M. Howard, *research sociologist and lecturer, University of California Medical Center, San Francisco*

Irving L. Janis, *professor of psychology, Yale University*

Robert Jay Lifton, *professor of psychiatry, Yale University*

Edward M. Opton, Jr., *senior research psychologist, The Wright Institute*

Perry Ottenberg, *professor of psychiatry, University of Pennsylvania School of Medicine*

Fritz Redl, *professor of behavioral sciences, College of Education, Wayne State University*

Nevitt Sanford, *scientific director, The Wright Institute*

Neil J. Smelser, *professor of sociology and associate director of the Institute for International Studies, University of California, Berkeley*

Robert H. Somers, *research sociologist, Family Research Center of the Langley-Porter Neuropsychiatric Institute, and The Wright Institute*

Sanctions
for Evil

*Sources of
Social Destructiveness*

CHAPTER 1

Sanctions for Evil

Nevitt Sanford, Craig Comstock

~~~~~~

W hen the My Lai massacre was finally reported, many of us saw the fate of that hamlet not as an isolated atrocity distinct in its effect from the rest of the war but as an emblem of the larger destructiveness to which our country was contributing in Vietnam. Apart from the moot question of which soldier did what on that day in 1968, we asked (in Telford Taylor's phrase) "how far what they did departed from general American military practice in Vietnam as they had witnessed it." [1]* While taking issue with critics who argue that the United States purpose in Vietnam has been genocidal or that our society is now fascistic, we do find certain disturbing similarities

* Notes for this chapter start on p. 337.

1

between the mass victimization of another people in Vietnam and the way black people in our country have been treated as if they were things or even of the way the Nazi regime set out to eliminate "inferior races." The similarity to which we mainly refer lies not in the intentions of the dominant group in each case—here especially the differences are obvious—but rather in the creation of what Philip P. Hallie calls a "cruel relationship." [2] In each of these situations members of one culture hold the power of death or grievous harm over a people regarded as inferior and sometimes as subhuman, as material to be acted upon.

Harm of this magnitude and duration does not happen by accident or inadvertence, nor is it done by solitary individuals violating the common practice of their organization or society. Most of the large-scale destructiveness is done by people who feel they have received some kind of permission for what they do—as we call it, a sanction for evil. [3]

Not all destructiveness is lethal or even physical in its agency; much of it happens through the medium of words or other symbols, in the relations which people establish or into which they find themselves forced. Television watchers may glimpse racism in the "overresponse" of officers who spray with bullets a dormitory at a black college or a tenement block in a northern ghetto, but even if the inevitable commission ventures some criticism of the police, most people appear to regard these "incidents" as mistakes at worst, not as marks of a widespread relationship between peoples. In fact, however, the most pervasive effects of racism occur in the lives of millions who are conscious of being routinely denigrated or exploited. Thus, in speaking of social destructiveness, we have in mind not only occasions of gross and visible cruelty, but also the pattern of social relations whose deep effects are described in *Black Rage,* a psychiatric account of the despair and hatred which racism may arouse in its victims. [4] We feel it is worth exploring similarities between the routine oppression experienced by black men and the sharp often fatal violence suffered by the inhabitants of Vietnam.

In defining social destructiveness, we distinguish this process from such behaviors as "violence" and such motives as "aggression." Although few students of violence have devoted enough attention to physical injury inflicted by agents of the state, whether abroad or at home, research in the category has nonetheless covered a broad range of evils, including riots and looting, rapes and assault, damage of property by "militants," as well as assassinations and the less factual violence so popular still on television. Work done on topics such as these often bears on social destructiveness, but we wish to examine the process as a whole, not only in terms of spectacular acts or a single motive. We begin, in fact, with the observation that not all social destructiveness is violent in the ordinary sense, nor is a given act which contributes to it necessarily motivated by aggression. The motive, for example, may be simply the fear of disobeying a superior, and the harm may be a violation of human dignity accomplished without intent to inflict physical injury to people or to damage property.

The destructiveness on which we focus is social both in the sense that it occurs among people (though sometimes through the medium of technology) and in the sense that those who do it receive a sanction from other people for their acts. They do not act alone, nor do they act merely against things. Third, the destructiveness we study is also social in that it often involves a judgment of one group by another, a negative valuation of people, sometimes an outright denial of their humanity. Finally, we emphasize that social destructiveness can harm not only its immediate victims but also the society in which it occurs or by which it is sustained—a pattern considered further in Chapter Sixteen.

All four of these characteristics of social destructiveness appear, for example, in racism. The victims are people, not a form of property or labor or material to be used. Although a single racist can exist in a tolerant or integrated population, racism is usually a group phenomenon. We are reminded of the cabaret joke current in the early 1930s in Germany: "Show me one Nazi." "What do you mean? Here is a whole room full of Nazis." "Yes, but show me *one* Nazi." Racism is also social in the sense that it expresses the feelings of one group toward another (or toward what it imagines that other to be). And, finally, as many Americans are coming to feel, racism directed against black people or other

racial minorities hurts our society as a whole. It corrupts our admirable values, leads to a widespread sense of insecurity, and induces first the pain of guilt and then the damaging defenses that
people erect against that guilt.[5] In this sense, the victimizers also
suffer, while remaining ignorant both of the damage suffered by
the victims and of the psychic warping undergone by the dominant
group. Some critics stress the severity of this process by describing
it as violence, but racism is not necessarily violent in the behavioral sense.

We can further distinguish social destructiveness from violence. Whereas the former by definition proceeds from what we
call a sanction for evil, many acts of violence are done without any
kind of permission. For example, a private citizen who attacks or
kills another person, except when acting reasonably in self-defense,
can seldom claim an exemption from the criminal code, although
his act may never come to the attention of the authorities and,
even if it does, he may never be brought to trial. Questions such
as these, however, fall in the field of criminology. Here we focus
instead on those acts of violence (and other harmful acts) which
are done with some permission, often by organizations or by people variously acting together. Examples abound. During a war
people are taught to kill other people and are ordered to do so
under pain of punishment. During civil disorder, officers may find
they can use harsh methods without being severely disciplined,
and some local leaders have even told them to shoot to kill. In any
given case, the nature of the sanction is a matter for empirical
inquiry, but except in the case of an individual officer who truly
goes berserk in defiance of orders, we may assume that police or
guardsmen who use unnecessary force probably feel they have
permission for what they are doing, if only from one another. Similarly, those people who for a political cause band together to bomb
buildings, kidnap officials, highjack planes, or snipe at police do
not regard their acts as wrong; on the contrary, they often feel
pride. They, too, claim permission or justification for what they
are doing.

In each case, we ought to ask how the impression arose that
the violence enjoys a sanction. To do so need imply no moral judg-

ment of the claims made by "defenders of law and order" or by "liberation fighters"; nor do we have to imply, in advance, that all violence is equally wrong. Nonetheless, as the title of this book indicates, we define our topic in terms common to moral discourse. In using the word *evil*, we mean not that an act or pattern of life is necessarily a sin or a crime according to some law, but rather that it leads to damage or pain suffered by people, to social destructiveness of a degree so serious as to call for use of an ancient, heavily freighted term.[6] Several of our contributors discuss this term in historical and philosophic context, especially in Chapters Twelve, Thirteen, and Fourteen.

For the moment, though, consider a very simple case, reported in a San Francisco paper of a century ago: "Some citizens of this city, while hunting in Marin County yesterday, came upon a large group of miserable Digger Indians. They managed to dispatch thirty of the creatures before the others ran away."[7] We may assume that those hunters had not been appointed by the law to hunt down Indians. Yet we are not told that these early San Franciscans felt it was wrong to shoot Indians as if they were coyotes. Seemingly, the law against murder did not apply, even though the victims were obviously helpless, not aggressive. The hunters undoubtedly felt they had a social sanction to dispatch certain kinds of people, a sanction which might take the abstract form of "the only good X is a dead X." Whether X is an Indian, a "nigger," or a "gook," the phrase serves as a sanction for acts which a person would not with clear conscience commit against a member of his own group.

Thus, social destructiveness as we see it exhibits the following features: People do harm to other people or act in such a way as to sustain a pattern of harm. (Damage to things, in itself, is not included.) Those who do the harm are forbidden to do it to a member of their own group. They act not separately on their individual initiative but with the permission or favor, or even under the command, of their group or a leader or at least certain peers. They see the victims as less than human or falsely regard them as aggressive or both. At one extreme social destructiveness is done by a mob or by some other unstable aggregation which engages in what sociologists call collective behavior. As we have seen, however, violent forms of social destructiveness may also be enacted by a highly disciplined group such as an army or police force (although we would not argue that all violence used by such groups leads necessarily to social destructiveness).

In its less violent forms, social destructiveness is done or is sanctioned by a wide variety of groups. In the simplest paradigm, X tells Y that he may act in such a way that Z is harmed (a relation considered in detail in the Epilogue). In complex situations, the sanction may take the form not of a direct statement but of a subtle, disguised, or even unconscious offer of permission to a person who then acts upon it. Although some sanctions are given for acts openly defined as destructive, the form of most sanctions in some way disguises their probable or intended result. In such a case, a sanction is given for a verbally defensible purpose, which, however, participants may recognize as a cover for destructive acts. Sometimes, nobody but the victim may appreciate the harm being done, as when policy makers decline to look at destructive side effects (so-called) or when officials remain innocent of the life experiences of those with whom they deal. In these cases, selective perception itself becomes a sanction. The official may intend no harm, but neither does he notice its occurrence; and if complaints are made, he may show considerable imagination in defining the harm away.

Events of the past few years suggest that we need to know much more than we do about this process of sanction-giving. In fact, we need a comparative study of the variety of ways in which people come to feel sufficient social approval to participate in acts which harm or degrade other people and of ways in which we fail to notice or understand the harm suffered by others. For example, what kind of sanctions sustain the pattern of social relations known as institutional racism? (Contributors discuss this question in Chapters Eleven and Fourteen, and we return to it in the Epilogue.) Unhappily, once racism becomes embedded in a society, even along with a variety of decent traditions, it may persist long after many people condemn it or reject inherited forms of prejudice against the oppressed group. Racism may persist in part because its years of ascendency have put the victims in such a bad position and have structured social institutions in such a way that, apart from exceptional individuals, the oppressed group is left to confirm the fear or denigration of it which was common in the dominant culture. The ironic result is a renewed sanction for business as usual, which leads to further dehumanization of the victims.

We regard dehumanization as both a cause and an effect of social destructiveness. Dehumanization of others, as noted above, is an element in the sanctioning process—a topic discussed at length in Chapter Eight—and some loss of what is distinctively human occurs in the person who carries out destructive acts (and, to some degree, in those who condone such acts). It has often been remarked that because most cultures prohibit killing people or enslaving them, the process of defining some people as subhuman (lacking will or feelings) is necessary in order to justify what would otherwise be murder or involuntary servitude. From the annals of social destructiveness we may glean an enormous catalogue of names people have been called in order to strip away their humanity.[8] Whether people are seen as devils or monsters, germs or vermin, pigs or apes, as robots, or as abstract menaces, they are thus removed from the company of men and exposed to the defenses we employ against those threats. In a war, for example, dehumanization often affects not only the image of the enemy but also the character of soldiers. When a patrol in Vietnam kidnaps a native girl, gang rapes her, and then kills her to remove the evidence,[9] we call the patrol members brutalized, meaning that they seem to have become insensitive to the suffering of others or to have lost their capacity for empathy—the topic of Chapter Nine—and that they have found the means for direct release of their most primitive impulses.

In exploring the process which leads to this range of results, we do not mean to imply that destructiveness is the monopoly of a single country or race or political persuasion. We draw many of our examples from American experience and often find fault in government actions, but we do not wish to imply that only a government or "the establishment" can offer sanctions for destructive-

ness; nor do we feel that this country is implicated more deeply
than various others. However, our analysis of social destructiveness
had better begin at home if we are to avoid the error of deflecting
attention from our own wrong-doing to that of an outsider, an
enemy, a scapegoat—an error which itself so often serves as a
sanction for evil. In preparing to consider the culpability of those
who have wronged us, we would do well to ponder what a legal
scholar wrote in reaction to the trial of Adolf Eichmann: "In a
deep sense one becomes competent to judge not by proving that
he differs completely from the defendant, but by his awareness of
what it is that he shares with him." [10] Conversely, in discussing the
war in Vietnam, we do not mean to suggest (as some critics have)
that because United States actions there have been dubious at
best, or immoral, the actions of other participants must be fault-
less. In fact, we regard that assumption as merely a reversal of the
hawkish argument that anything we do there is permissible, no
matter how destructive the effect, because the other side is evil.

In editing this book, however, our purpose has been less
to cover such topics as the war or racism or the psychology of the
arms race or other forms of institutional evil than to show how
these topics and many others can be linked as aspects of social destructiveness. The book therefore is organized not according to
various types or examples of destructiveness but according to several ways of approaching the process as a whole: through its social
forms, through its psychological background, and through its cultural matrix.

In considering the range of acts described as social destruction, we look first at the social or political processes through which
such destruction occurs. Neil J. Smelser sketches them in general
terms, providing theoretical distinctions useful throughout the
book. Troy Duster discusses the identification sometimes made
between the welfare of society or of the state and the power of its
arms of force, as when people urge that the police be given a free
hand or the military be unleashed. Robert Jay Lifton and Edward
M. Opton, Jr., both analyze aspects of the sanctioning process,
using the My Lai massacre as an extreme case of general patterns

in the Vietnam war. As American involvement in that war decreases, many would prefer to forget it as soon as possible, but the lessons suggested by our experience there ought to be clearly drawn, for they may apply to situations that lie ahead and not only to a particular war. Lifton focuses on the situation of the soldier in Vietnam; Opton, on the reactions of citizens at home. In his analysis of "groupthink" among the makers of foreign policy, Irving L. Janis shows how forms of distortion and irrationality common in cohesive small groups helped produce such fiascos as the Vietnam war with its attendant dehumanization.

Behind the social interactions lie psychological and cultural dynamics. Whether one conceives of culture as broader than society or personality as deeper, neither field can replace social analysis but both can enrich it enormously, in part by suggesting certain long-range remedies for destructive patterns. In Part Two, Fritz Redl examines a number of the excuses that people offer for taking part in destructive acts and ways in which the superego is relieved of its normal duties. Viola W. Bernard and her colleagues show how dehumanization, regarded here as a composite psychological defense, works to increase the danger of mass social destructiveness, as in nuclear war. Bernard L. Diamond discusses an extreme type of dehumanization, one in which an inability to identify with other people may lead to sociopathic behavior. Nevitt Sanford, one of the authors of *The Authoritarian Personality*, describes the relation between the psychological syndrome called authoritarianism and the social phenomenon of destructiveness. In explaining the expressive function of systems of social segregation, George De Vos explores some of the motives of racism other than economic exploitation. His analysis also provides a bridge from personality to culture, the subject of Part Three.

Here Robert N. Bellah shows how traditional American understandings of evil may accelerate social destructiveness. In looking to the future he sketches a new image of man—a theme to which Sanford later returns. In a long chapter that deals with many of the themes so far raised in the book, Charles Drekmeier explores preconditions for and failures of moral sensitivity, asking how men come to see one another as things to be used or destroyed. In his discussion of two ways of knowing and their relation to destructiveness, Drekmeier offers a variety of perspectives —phenomenological, behavioral, and philosophical—not often found in a single author. He asks whether a form of reason has emerged which impedes, perhaps makes impossible, our ability to see destructive behavior for what it is.

After having shown how social structure, psychic process, and culture can conspire to sanction evil, we turn in Part Four to some types of resistance, of awareness, and of social change in addition to those suggested or implied in previous chapters. Philip P. Hallie considers resistance from the viewpoint of the direct victim (in his dominant example, the slave who rebels); Jan M. Howard and Robert Somers, from the viewpoint of the organization member who is led toward participation in destructiveness; and Craig Comstock, from that of the citizen, the everyman in whose name so much violence is being done or prepared. In particular, Comstock examines how systems are often harmed by their own defenses and how awareness of this process may reduce reliance on self-defeating responses to danger. Picking up this theme, Nevitt Sanford tells how sanctions for evil are prevented in the long run not only by specific counter-measures but by a positive vision of what men and their society can become and by broad efforts toward personality development which can sustain such a way of life.

In the Epilogue, we draw together some of the major themes by discussing how to study social destructiveness further. Noting that the way we approach the problem governs the kind of knowledge we can find, we outline not yet another new field, but a way of approaching problems with which many of us are concerned, a way which centers less on how destructive acts are done than on how they are defined as legitimate or acceptable and how destructive effects are ignored by those who could help to prevent them. By concluding with a program of education and an outline for research, we do not wish to imply that immediate and sustained political action is unnecessary or that we can wait until we bring in more findings or help prepare a new generation to make use of them. In fact we believe that efforts at change are a necessary part of learning about social process, for, as in psychoanalysis, a study of resistances may illuminate the dynamics of a system as nothing else can.

Part I

━━━━━━━━━━━━━━━━━━━━━━━━━━━━━━━━━━━━━━━

In considering the range of acts described as social destruction, we look first at the social or political processes through which such destruction occurs. Neil J. Smelser sketches them in general terms, providing theoretical distinctions useful throughout the book. Troy Duster discusses the identification sometimes made between the welfare of society or of the state and the power of its arms of force, as when people urge that the police be given a free hand or the military be unleashed. Obviously many groups other than political leaders or agents of the state can sanction destructiveness, but as a complement to violence commissions, which emphasize crime, riots, and other unofficial violence, we here draw attention to violence and other harm that is done, encouraged, or tolerated by officials. Robert Jay Lifton and Edward M. Opton, Jr., both analyze aspects of the sanctioning process, using the My Lai massacre as an extreme case of general patterns in the Vietnam war. As American

DESTRUCTIVENESS AS SOCIAL PROCESS

involvement in that war decreases, many would prefer to forget it as soon as possible, but the lessons suggested by our experience there ought to be clearly drawn, for they may apply to situations that lie ahead and not only to a particular war. Lifton focuses on the situation of the soldier in Vietnam; Opton, on the reactions of citizens at home. In his analysis of "groupthink" among the makers of foreign policy, Irving L. Janis shows how forms of distortion and irrationality common in cohesive small groups helped produce such fiascos as the Vietnam war with its attendant dehumanization. Since the state may enjoy the force not only of the law but also of an immense military and police apparatus, the destructiveness that it sanctions is no less urgent a problem than are private kinds of violence properly denounced by government commissions. Here we examine the breakdown of humane controls among the agents of official violence (Chapter Four), the citizenry (Chapters Two and Five), and the leadership (Chapter Six).

Some Determinants of Destructive Behavior

Neil J. Smelser

T he problem of evil is so ancient, so intractable, and so complex that it is scarcely possible to utter the phrase without evoking dozens of connotations—connotations which are simultaneously biological, psychological, social, moral, and theological. For this reason, discourse on the subject is likely to run afoul; because the term *evil* taps so many meanings, we stand a good chance of talking past one another at all times. In this chapter I address the problems of why and by what mechanisms evil becomes socially acceptable and therefore likely to be perpetrated. But because the term *evil* is such an ambiguous one,

15

I begin by setting forth a few definitions and distinctions that are intended to frame the universe of discourse within which I operate here.

Initially it is essential to draw a distinction, as was done in Chapter One, between evil on the one hand and force and violence on the other. In some situations the exercise of force and violence are universally agreed not to be evil, even though these situations may be regarded as regrettable necessities of the human condition. As an illustrative situation I have in mind the right—even the duty—of a parent forcibly to restrain a child from walking into traffic, even though this act may do some physical and psychological violence to the child. As another I have in mind the right—even the duty—of a police officer to exercise force and violence to prevent one citizen from forcibly abducting another. It seems ill advised to regard such situations as perpetrations of evil.

What meaning, then, ought we to reserve for evil, considered in its social context? I think the term is most appropriately applied to situations when force, violence, and other forms of coercion exceed institutional or moral limits. By this definition the following kinds of situations qualify: (1) When individuals or groups not empowered by a legitimately accepted order to exercise coercion do so—for example, in armed robbery or wanton mob destruction. (2) When individuals or groups legally and institutionally empowered to exercise coercion exceed the legitimate limits of that exercise—for example, a parent who tortures his child, a policeman who brutally beats a citizen, a military unit which massacres civilians. However, because the goodness of the institutionalized order cannot always be assumed, a third situation must be added: (3) When the institutionalization of the exercise of coercion offends some higher standards of humanity or morality that we feel ought to be observed—for example, the police state, which is solidly institutionalized, to be sure, but which may be regarded as evil because it assaults the freedom, dignity, and civil liberties of its subjects.

Like the other contributors to this book, I am interested in the causes of these kinds of evil. I concentrate here especially on the cultural and social determinants. In particular, I ask four related but distinguishable questions: (1) How is evil legitimized?

What kinds of shared values or beliefs or sentiments are appealed to in order to render the prosecution of evil permissible or desirable? (2) How is evil authorized? The question of legitimization refers mainly to cultural values or standards. The question of authorization refers to the social context of the behavior. What persons or agencies authorize evil? Who gives it the green light? These questions suggest the importance of identifying the roles people in authority play in the genesis and prosecution of evil. (3) How are people mobilized for evil actions? The question of authorization refers to the degree to which organized social arrangements permit or encourage evil. In addition to gaining permission, however, people must often be positively stimulated, organized, and led to perpetrate evil. The question of mobilization concerns especially the role of leadership. Sometimes those who authorize destructive actions are also instrumental as leaders, but not always. For this reason, it is important to distinguish between authorization and mobilization as separate social determinants of evil actions. (4) How is evil rationalized? This question arises by virtue of the fundamental fact that even if evil actions are legitimized and authorized, they invariably occur in the context of other, competing values and standards that define them as illegitimate and, indeed, evil. Evil invariably occurs, that is, in a context not only of its own legitimization but also of a contrary set of values that label it illegitimate. A tension is thus created between two standards of conduct. Rationalization refers to the shared cognitive processes by which people attempt to smooth over and otherwise come to terms with that tension.

In the remainder of the chapter I identify some of the processes that are involved in legitimizing, authorizing, mobilizing for, and rationalizing evil. I consider these processes both in relatively spontaneous, unstructured situations and in institutionalized, structured situations.

One of the most profound aspects of evil is that he who does the evil is typically convinced that evil is about to be done to him. He regards the world or at least part of it as dangerous or bent on destruction and therefore something justifiably to be destroyed. Sometimes this belief appears fleetingly in a moment of crisis. I have in mind the inexperienced National Guardsmen, called in periodically to quell ghetto disturbances in 1967, who, upon hearing or thinking they heard shots, literally panicked and began shooting in various directions. This reaction seems to have happened also in the Kent State tragedy. I also have in mind the rumors of atrocities—sometimes justified and sometimes unjustified—that typically run through the ranks of both rioting citizens and those who are attempting to put the rioters down. These fleeting beliefs and rumors identify an enemy and pave the way for his destruction.

Sometimes these beliefs develop over long periods of time. During the winter of 1968 I did some consulting work for the staff of the National Advisory Commission on Civil Disorders. As part of this work I examined some fairly detailed data on the racial disturbances in Plainfield, New Jersey, in July 1967. It was both instructive and saddening to see the sequence of incidents— the unmet demands, the miscommunication between racial leaders and town leaders, the death of a policeman—that led to the buildup of two inflexible sets of beliefs, one held by blacks and one by the police. Both sets were identical in structure: they portrayed the other side as vastly more deliberate, organized, cunning, premeditated, and malicious than the other side actually was. These sets of beliefs had several consequences. They provided for each side a cognitive framework within which almost any kind of behavior could be regarded as evidence of malevolence. For example, black demands for a public meeting were interpreted by the police as evidence of the blacks' intention to mobilize for attack; if they did not demand a public meeting, the police suspected that they were meeting secretly to mobilize for an attack. And the blacks interpreted police behavior in similar ways. Furthermore, these beliefs justified preventive attacks on the part of both sides, attacks which further confirmed and consolidated the beliefs themselves. And, finally, as these beliefs became more and more rigid and stereotyped, the behavioral options left to either side—other than lashing out in rage at the other—were progressively diminished. Such social-psychological dynamics often lead to destructive behavior; the external world, or some part of it, is regarded as an incarnation of evil, and this perception leads to the perpetration of evil.

In still other cases the belief in the enemy becomes part of a developed ideology and may become institutionalized in the sense that it legitimizes continuous destructiveness. The rumors that often preceded lynchings in the post-Restoration South were that a black had assaulted a white man or raped a white woman— thus confirming the general belief that the black was a dangerous, uncontrolled animal and thus making his destruction, in the minds of the whites, both legitimate and imperative. The stereotype of the Jew in Nazi ideology and the stereotype of the Japanese in America in World War II, although differing in content, legitimized destructive behavior which would have been regarded as evil under other circumstances.

One legitimizing ingredient of destructiveness, then, is to hold a belief that some enemy is simultaneously evil, intelligent, and omnipotent. Furthermore, because these beliefs have such a strong component of anxiety, they are likely to be very volatile, generalizing and switching from object to object, particularly in times of danger or crisis.

The instances I have just cited constitute the negative side of the belief system that legitimizes evil. But they are only half the story. In addition, the perpetrator of evil typically holds fast to a corresponding belief in his own omnipotence and moral superiority. To believe that one is an indestructible saint or crusader makes it easy to spread destruction in the world. Indeed, that belief often demands that one stamp out evil.

In those unstructured situations I mentioned, these beliefs often appear only in embryo. They may be as simple as the brief but exhilarating sensation of omnipotence that the soldier experiences when plunging a bayonet or shooting a bullet into a hated enemy. Or they may emerge as that momentary surge of magical thinking that runs through a crowd when it stones a hated political leader who has been publicly executed. These fleeting moments of omnipotence that accompany destructive actions make these actions both easy and attractive.

The legitimizing function of these beliefs is seen clearly in religious and political ideologies. Consider, for example, the righteous and crusading spirit of the church militant with its Christian soldiers—a spirit which has infused the Christian tradition in various ways and which has been employed on numerous occasions to legitimize excesses of violence. Or consider the other side of the coin—Nazi anti-Semitism: a firm belief in the racial and moral purity and superiority of the Aryan race, by virtue of which the evils of the world were to be overcome. Or, to bring the illustrations perhaps closer to home, consider one strand of the traditional cultural myth of American masculinity, particularly as it is manifested repeatedly in folk heroes such as Superman, the Lone Ranger, and Batman. Here is the one-man vigilante, who, by sheer dint of his hypermasculine qualities, his cleverness, and, above all, his moral superiority, brings the evil forces at least to justice and perhaps to their destruction. (This myth reveals the moral ambivalence often concealed by beliefs in moral righteousness. The mythical superman must be above the law. Usually, moreover, the official representative of the law—the sheriff or the police commissioner—must sit on the sidelines, helpless, and be rescued by the extralegal but superhuman and supermoral stranger who takes the law into his own hands and saves the day.)

I do not mean to equate all these illustrations in every way or to assert that they all have an equal potential for erupting into destructive behavior. And although arguing that these cultural myths help to bring people to the threshold of destructive behavior, I do not assert that the beliefs automatically manifest themselves in such behavior. Indeed, such cultural myths enjoy a more or less universal and permanent existence and tend to be activated only under certain historical conditions. Some of these historical conditions come into existence, moreover, when destructive behavior is authorized and rationalized. I turn now to a few brief illustrations of these other conditions.

Above and beyond the cultural beliefs that predispose people to perpetrate the kinds of actions we have been considering lies the separate question of the social milieu. The literature on collective behavior is replete with theories of the group mind, the anonymity that the crowd provides, and the magic of the demagogue. Rather than review these theories—most of which are rather too general to be helpful—I focus specifically on a few examples in which authority and leadership are likely to facilitate or impede destructive behavior.

Let me begin with a simple, hypothetical, but, I am certain, typical example. The coach of a college or high school football team is, in one respect, supposed to be a model of discipline and self-control for the athletes on his team. After all, the maximization of these qualities presumably contributes much to winning games. Traditionally, too, coaches have taken an interest in the general conduct of the players—their grades, their dietary habits, their general moral conduct. Yet this authority is often exercised with a mock severity or, indeed, permissiveness. An example is the coach's remark, made with a grin and a wink, to his players on a road trip, "O.K., boys, remember, no whoring around before the game tomorrow." A prohibition on the face of it, the remark is actually an informal authorization of a visit to the brothel and an indication that no sanctions will be invoked. And although the mock prohibition does not mobilize the boys for the adventure, it increases the probability that they will mobilize themselves.

Consider the role of authorization now in relation to destructive behavior and in situations other than the informal, unstructured illustration I have given. The likelihood of rampages of destructiveness is greatly heightened when some person or agency in authority condones or at least permits these rampages. The most naked form of authorization is that in a totalitarian state which establishes mass destruction, concentration camps, or slave labor camps as a matter of official policy. But this form is not the only one. Consider the military policies in Vietnam of search and destroy, free-fire zones, and using whatever means are necessary to destroy the enemy. These policies say, in effect, that anything goes and, although not ordering civilian massacres, set the normative climate that encourages miltary units to exceed whatever limits on destructiveness may otherwise be observed. Or, finally, consider the political or military authority that simply remains silent, thus establishing an atmosphere that does not oblige troops to destroy but does not oblige them not to either. Furthermore, if effective counterauthorizing agencies—for example, courts capable of handing down severe penalties for brutality —do not exist or are feeble, the probabilities are increased that evil may be authorized or quasiauthorized with impunity.

In some cases those who authorize evil also mobilize men

and resources into a destructive apparatus. A totalitarian government bent on mass extermination and an army girded for total war are instances of simultaneous authorization and mobilization. In other cases, however, authorization involves a posture of permissiveness or ambiguity on the part of authorities, a posture that does not openly and positively sanction—and thereby guarantee the perpetration of—destructiveness. In these cases the mobilization for evil develops through independent social mechanisms.

Consider again my hypothetical example of the athletes away from their home institution for a road game. After the mock admonition from the coach, which sets the stage for a sexual adventure, a number of athletes, rooming in the same motel, are sitting around, bored and waiting. One of the athletes suggests that they go out and find prostitutes. The idea is discussed, and after a while the informal leader of the group says he is not in the mood; the project dies. Or, after the suggestion is made and discussed, the informal leader says he thinks it is a good idea. One of the others protests, saying he is not interested. One of his buddies says, "What's the matter, are you a fairy or something?" He gives in, and they all leave.

The latter situation illustrates how the several determinants I have outlined combine to produce an episode of behavior. The action—going to a brothel—is legitimized by the appeal to some ideal of masculinity. The ideal invoked is that it is important to be a man (and not to be its obverse, a homosexual). The action is given authorization by the mock admonition by the coach. And it is mobilized by invoking norms and personal influence in the small group. None of the determinants alone is sufficient to produce the episode; but when all combine, it is very likely to occur.

Although one hesitates to generalize too much from this situation, some of the lynchings, massacres, and rapes of history must be written according to this script. A military unit, fatigued after battle, perhaps demoralized and angry after its own partial decimation, finds itself in an isolated situation, away from many usual social controls. The sport of killing a few "goons" arises as a collective assertion of some vague but strongly held ideal of masculinity (and possibly a collective denial of in-group rivalry and homosexuality). The event may be triggered, moreover, by the critical initiative taken by a formal or informal group leader.

As I indicated, the rationalization of evil is similar to but distinct from its legitimization. By rationalization I mean the ways in which the perpetrators of evil come to terms with their own consciences and with the value systems that condemn their behavior as illegitimate. Much can be learned about rationalization by studying the familiar psychological mechanisms of defense—projection, denial, displacement, intellectualization, and rationalization itself. The study of individual reactions to the My Lai massacre reported in Chapter Five is striking confirmation of the defensive lengths to which people go to protect themselves from their consciences, even when they have not been directly involved in the evil act itself.

As though individuals were not good enough at making rationalizations on their own, society and its language provide us with dozens of ready-made homilies and proverbs by which we may build bridges between our consciences and our reprehensible behavior. Consider the following: "All's fair in love and war." "Done in the line of duty." "It was either them or us." These utterances are simple reassurances that the actor need not bear all the guilt for the deed because special circumstances justify it. Insofar as these reassurances are readily available and commonly accepted, deeds of evil are rendered easier to execute.

Much of what I have written in this chapter strikes a somewhat pessimistic note with respect to the prevention and control of evil. After all, man is very ingenious and prolific at legitimizing, authorizing, and rationalizing almost anything, evil included. Furthermore, many of the forces that go into the legitimization and rationalization of evil are very firmly rooted in the depths of man's impulse life, his social and political conflicts, his ideological and religious traditions, and his situational vicissitudes. As a result, they are likely to be very impervious to modification by deliberate social policy.

However, it does seem possible and plausible to dedicate social energies to the reform of systems of authorization. I have in mind new legislation at all levels restricting the excesses that military and police personnel perpetrate. I have in mind the

widespread institutionalization of civilian review boards for check-
ing police and military conduct. I have in mind new policies that
honor people by public citation for the exercise of restraint and
control in explosive and violent situations—medals for refusing
to kill instead of medals for killing. I have in mind programs for
the mass media that portray bravery and courage as the capacity
to refrain from destructiveness when the opportunity allows. I
expect that none of these measures or even a combination of all
of them will bring an end to evil and destructiveness. As I indicated, evil is an intractable problem and to attack it is like attempting to assault a granite boulder with one's bare hands.
However, the most promising line of attack is on those very structures that are institutionalized around the issues of violence and
destructiveness. What is required is an attempt to shape them as
institutional structures that are vitally necessary for social existence, to be sure, but at the same time to regard them as necessary
evils rather than as holy instruments designed to stamp out evil.
To tailor legislation, policy, and procedures in line with this
rationale seems to me the most feasible means to break into and
deflect those cumulative and seemingly irreversible sequences of
behavior that end in destructive excesses.

CHAPTER **3**

Conditions for Guilt-Free Massacre

Troy Duster

Several years ago Harold Garfinkel wrote a short essay entitled "Conditions of Successful Degradation Ceremonies."[1*] The purpose of the essay was not to offer a recipe for those who would like to degrade a fellow human but to explain the process of degradation through a novel device. Garfinkel has long held that a good method for clarifying a process is to tell how to make it happen. In his exposition, he details eight conditions which he argues must be present for the successful public degradation of a man. In general, the man must come to be seen as a symbol of something totally contrary to what others in the community regard as the communal good.

* Notes for this chapter start on p. 338.

Using Garfinkel's paper as a suggestive model, I attempt
here an exposition of guilt-free massacre. Such an exposition is
not undertaken lightly. If I thought that I were exposing new
thoughts and strategies for such an outcome to an audience now
unaware of them, I would abandon the task. My purpose is quite
the opposite, and it is important that it be stated clearly.

Subtly and almost imperceptibly to some, this nation developed all the conditions for guilt-free massacre of Vietnamese
and neighboring peoples and is now well on the road with respect to the Black Panthers. Thus, in explaining the process I
point to various conditions which already exist but which are too
seldom recognized as parts of a pattern. The purpose of the exposition is threefold: to understand clearly the process itself by
saying out loud how to do it; to alert others who may be the next
victims of the process; and to offer some suggestions for disman-
tling or intercepting the process.

At least three forms of guilt must be distinguished before
we proceed to a discussion of guilt-free massacre: Guilt can refer
to the commission of an act regarded as reprehensible, immoral,
illegal, or the like. In such cases, men are characterized as guilty
or innocent with reference only to whether the act was committed,
and guilt in this sense is independent of retribution or redress.
Guilt can also refer to the subjective feeling state of actors. This
sense of guilt can result from matters of omission as well as commission. Men can feel guilt for being silent and inactive as they
passively observe injustice. On the other hand, one may actually
commit an act that others would call immoral but lack a sense of
guilt. (For a further discussion of this possibility, see Chapter
Nine.) Finally, guilt can refer to the pronouncement of culpability by men formally empowered to make such pronouncements, as in the case of the judiciary, review boards, and juries.
In this usage what is called guilt can be independent both of the
commission of the act and of any feeling of guilt. Innocent men
have been found guilty. Obversely, one can be guilty of the commission of the act but be characterized as not guilty by a police
review board, a court-martial, or the judiciary.

In this chapter, I am concerned with a particular configuration of these three forms of guilt, in which commission of a mas-

sacre (actual guilt) would lead neither to a sense of guilt nor to a pronouncement of guilt. I attempt to specify what conditions must typically prevail in a society for such a configuration to occur.

One further distinction is in order. Whole societies or whole armies do not commit massacres. Certain men are always singled out to do the work, and this commission of the act is the easiest of the three forms of guilt to pinpoint. The men do their work, however, in the name of the society, the nation, the army, the police, or the church. The subtle problems come in determining final culpability and the location of conscience. Can whole societies sense guilt? If organizational structures are to be blamed, then what is the culpability of individuals within those structures? Does it make any sense, indeed does it make any difference, to talk about the location of guilt in the Germany of the Third Reich? Although I am not able to answer many of these questions of culpability in this chapter, I hope some purpose is served by raising the issues and setting forth the conditions for guilt-free massacre.

The most general condition for guilt-free massacre is the denial of the humanity of the victims. You call the victims names like gooks, dinks, niggers, pinkos, and Japs. The more you can get high officials in government to use these names and others like yellow dwarfs with daggers or rotten apples, the more your success. In addition, you allow no human contact. You prevent travel, or you oversee the nature of contact if travel is allowed. You prevent citizens from going to places like China, Cuba, and North Vietnam, so that men cannot confront other men. Or on the home front, if contact is allowed or if it cannot be prevented, you indicate that the contact is not between equals; you talk about the disadvantaged, the deprived. You make sure that the culture and customs of the target population are seen as having no value to your own group, and you inculcate this attitude either by laughing at those cultures and customs or by destroying them.

Since other contributors to this volume deal with the dehumanization of the victims (as in Chapter Eight) and some with resistance to this process (as in Chapter Fourteen), I emphasize other conditions for a guilt-free massacre. However, I ought to

mention the role of race and racism in the dehumanization process. Massacres clearly have occurred within racial groups: whites
have massacred whites as in centuries of European war, blacks
have massacred blacks as in the Nigerian civil war, and the Far
East has witnessed internecine slaughters on a large scale. It is
foolish to treat race, therefore, as a necessary condition for massacre. Nonetheless, the existence of racial groups in structurally
superior positions, exploiting and oppressing other racial groups
—the pattern discussed in Chapter Eleven—is one of the most
conducive settings for massacre.

In such a setting, as in others where race may play no role,
we can isolate a number of social conditions which lead to guilt-
free massacre. The first is the soldering of a *connection* between
faith in the well-being of a society and faith in its organizational
arm of violence. (Externally, this organization is the army; internally, the police.) France during the Dreyfus affair offers an example of soldering such a link. Toward the end of the affair even
the generals of the French army knew of Dreyfus' innocence. Yet
they had come to believe that to acknowledge his innocence would
be to undermine the faith of the French people not only in their
army but in France as a nation. And among many citizens, too,
an attack on the army was seen as an attack on France. The cry
was "treason."

Once the connection is made between the well-being of
the state and the actions of its army or police, citizens may soon
conclude that the army or the police can never be wrong. Title II
of the Omnibus Crime Control Bill of 1968 provided for wiretapping of suspects and the use of this evidence in court without
the consent of the accused. When some of us pointed out that
wiretapping could be used against anyone, its defenders argued
that the police would use it only against criminals. If you are not
a criminal, so goes the argument, then you have nothing to fear
from the police. If our primary aim is to make the work of the
police easy, then we should give the police access to our houses,
our mail, our telephones, our office desks, our private dresser
drawers, and our closets. If we have nothing to hide, then who
could object to opening all aspects of our lives to surveillance by

the police? Surely, they would use such investigative powers only for our good—namely, not against us but against others. That has been the reasoning of the defenders of no-knock police investigation. On reflection, the line of argument seems to come out of a nightmare, but such men exist, and they establish the first condition for guilt-free massacre. "Why would the police harm innocent men?" they ask, discounting both the fallability and corruptability of humans given latitude and power made legitimate by the state—a problem considered further in Chapter Sixteen.

In defining the second condition, we observe that groups such as the police or the army treat organizational grounds for action as superior to individual grounds for action. Individuals in a society sometimes have the nerve to stand up to organizations and claim that they, as individuals, are better and truer carriers of the values of the society than are the organizational arms. For example, those individuals who opposed slavery before 1860 often argued that the state was wrong. They argued that, in terms of the Declaration of Independence and the Constitution, slavery violated the basic values of the republic and ought, therefore, to be opposed or no longer tolerated by the various institutions of society. In this way the abolitionists asserted the legitimacy of their actions while casting doubt on the legitimacy of institutions that helped to perpetuate slavery. That same claim was made by individuals who, in the old Civil Rights movement, refused to comply with police orders that interfered with their right to register to vote. And the same claim is often made now by those who refuse induction into the army.

However, those who equate the well-being of the state with the actions of its coercive arms effectively ignore the claims of individual moral superiority. For such people, the police and the army are right by definition, and the will of individuals must be subordinated to these organizations, which set internal standards of conduct in an attempt to stamp out individuality. In the military, uniforms are required and discipline is deified; insubordination becomes a most serious offense. In order to reinforce the notion of the superiority of organizational will to individual will, the army and the police regulate personal choices and social and political choices (such as where one can go, the content of one's speech, and even whom one can meet).

In subordinating their will to that of the organization, members gain protection for all but the most egregious actions in the line of duty. As long as the individual is acting as a policeman or as a soldier, his actions are not individual but organizational. We can see these mechanisms when a policeman shoots a young black boy in the back and is excused on the ground of justifiable homicide. The same mechanism may operate on a larger scale.

The third condition for guilt-free massacre is a connection between whatever fragment remains of individual responsibility and the organization with its rules. Loyalty to the organization takes precedence over every other consideration, every other loyalty, every other morality, and individuals are ostracized for violation of this loyalty. In the Dreyfus case, Picquart was the subject of hatred and rebuke by army colleagues who saw him as one who placed the innocence of Dreyfus over loyalty to the army. At first, the army and the police require that individuals be subordinate only within the ranks. Next, however, they may define individual differences as suspicious at best and possibly traitorous.

This means that individuals in the army begin to believe that their actions alarm or please the army authorities only insofar as they relate to organizational rules. This begins to free them for otherwise illegal activity. They come to understand that they can even indulge themselves in personal ways as long as they do not cross the organization. They can intimidate homosexuals, harass and sometimes molest women, or act rowdily in places of business, and the authorities look the other way. In fact, members may pick up cues that the authorities even approve. This approval begins to seal loyalty to the organization, for it protects the member from the discipline he would receive if he were a civilian. The individual police officer, for example, starts to conclude that the force gives him latitude and protects him. He can saunter into restaurants for free meals and into stores for free clothes. His primary identification shifts to the police, whose vision of the larger society he comes to adopt.

People outside these organizations, people of privilege who are not policemen or soldiers, find it easy to understand this primary identification. They begin to say, "Of course policemen are more upset by the murder of a policeman than they are about the murder of a young black teenager. Of course," they begin to say, "we will offer twenty-five thousand dollars reward for the murderer of a policeman, but not one penny reward for the murderer of Fred Hampton, a leader of the Black Panthers." Who offered twenty-five thousand dollars reward for the murderer of James Rector? Was his life less significant? When policemen begin to think of themselves more as policemen than as members of a people and when men of power and privilege tacitly agree, the third condition for guilt-free massacre is met, the merger of individual responsibility with the organization and its fate. When men see themselves and are seen only as members of an organizational arm, even their illegal actions cannot be charged as guilty, for that would reflect upon the organization; and this charge is avoided at all costs because of the original connection between faith in army or police and faith in the nation.

Fourth, just as the individual policeman or soldier can avoid blame by obtaining organizational cover for his actions, organizations have their strategies for avoiding blame. Of these, the most important and the most effective are secrecy and isolation, usually in combination. Both the army and the police claim that secrecy is crucial to their operations. Public scrutiny and control are avoided on the grounds both of inexpertise ("the generals know best") and of subversion (enemies of the people are among the people). The police are increasingly isolated from the communities that they police, both by patterns of geographical and residential recruitment and by the increasingly closed kinship network of recruitment.[2] Citizen control in the form of civilian police review boards is opposed on the grounds of mistrust and bad faith. And any military action or document that may be incriminating can be classified top secret in the national interest.

When outside investigations reveal a scandal and blame

must be located, top officials claim total ignorance. The culprits, the lower level actors who did the dirty deeds, "did so on their own," always. In the Chicago and Denver police scandals of the last decade, in the My Lai massacre, in the price-fixing conspiracy in the electrical appliance industry, in almost every case where public scrutiny reveals the necessity for locating blame in organizations, top officials always claim no knowledge of the activity.

Up until this point I have discussed several preconditions for a guilt-free massacre, conditions which can be understood as processes. The next two conditions refer instead to settings or contexts for the perpetration of acts accompanied by guiltlessness ensured through processes already described.

The fifth condition is the existence of what we can literally call a target population. There has to be a population to massacre, a vulnerable population, a population that has inferior firepower (or better, no firepower at all). What do I mean by firepower? It is not peculiar that the Mau Mau, known always in the Western press as Mau Mau terrorists, killed a few hundred British, while the British killed several thousand blacks in Kenya. Nor is it peculiar that the number of Algerians killed by the French army far exceeded the number of French colonists killed by Algerian rebels, commonly called terrorists in the Western press. The same pattern is true for the Portuguese massacres of black Angolans and for countless other cases. Does anyone need to be reminded that this nation massacred so many native American Indians that only a fraction remain? In each instance, the target population was vulnerable to outside firepower. Nations with megaton bombs are left alone. However much you may want to turn the firepower there, you prudently choose a more vulnerable population. In 1962 government officials were telling us that there were only a few thousand Communists in Vietnam. Officials of that same government now admit gleefully that the United States is responsible for the deaths of perhaps 350,000 Vietnamese people. Similarly now, we are told that there are only a few hundred (or perhaps a thousand) Panthers. The rest are "good Negroes." Just as in Saigon, where every angry Vietnamese has become a potential Viet Cong to be shot now and questioned later, we may soon approach the day when in Harlem every angry black is a potential Panther

to be shot and then questioned. As I said in the beginning, this
is no revelation, for we are well practiced in the techniques of
guilt-free massacre and have come a long way in the designation
of a new target.

The sixth and final condition is the simplest, and the most
complex. You have to develop the motivation to conduct a massacre. In the United States, it seems that all you have to do is to
get high government officials to repeat over and over again, "it is
in the national interest, in the national interest, the national interest." Many, many people seem to become mesmerized. For example, the director of the FBI took it upon himself to proclaim
the Panthers as a subversive group working against the national
interest, thereby making them a target population and helping to
set the stage for what followed. When police in Chicago raided a
residence occupied by Panthers and killed Hampton, nobody
even bothered to ask which officer had fired the fatal shot. It was
enough to say the police had done it in the line of duty; individual
responsibility had disappeared. Nor was the department as a
whole reprimanded. Whenever Panthers have been shot by police, all but a thoughtful few of the public have yawned and
glibly concluded that, well, they must have deserved it—a type of
reaction considered further in Chapter Five. We are well down
the road to guilt-free massacre, and few even raise the question
of blame, much less initiate any vigorous pursuit of the individuals who do the dirty work.

There are many strategies for intercepting the process and
preventing it from developing to the point where the massacre
finally occurs. The Panthers tried to eliminate the vulnerability of
the black population to the armed force of the police. They armed
in self-defense. The California legislature responded swiftly by
stripping the population of firearms. The strategy that the Panthers chose could be effective but only if a considerable proportion of the black population began to bear arms. To try to disarm
a large proportion of the black population would be civil war, a
price few would want to pay. After the murders of the black students at Jackson State in the spring of 1970, Whitney Young
urged blacks to pick up the gun. That put the Urban League
only three years behind the Panthers. However, to disarm a few

hundred members of a militant organization infiltrated by government agents is not a large or difficult problem for federal,
state, and local police acting in concert.

Others have tried to use the strategy of persuasion, reason,
and concerted moral pressure to the point of civil disobedience
in the effort to convince those in positions of political power that
the national interest is not served, for example, by the slaughter of
thousands of Vietnamese people per month. But such methods of
resistance usually concern the larger issues of the war itself, its
immorality and illegality. Some argue that since the economic
basis for exploitation of Third World populations is fundamental
to all other processes, a discussion of massacre is so limited that
it can at best illuminate only a fragment of the issues. While I
agree that we must have understanding of the basis for war and
poverty as well, the degree of such an exclusionary concern is
probably related to how close one is to the target population.

Another approach emphasizes organizational strategies,
working within the army and the police to produce attitudes that
separate the notion of individual responsibility from organizational goals. But the reward and punishment systems of organizations, especially military organizations, are so powerful that this
is a long-range task. A promising direction is the alteration of
the reward system itself, and that suggestion leads to the next approach.

Somehow, in order to prevent guilt-free massacre, we must
separate the connection now made so firmly between the well-
being of the state and the infallibility of its arm of violence. It is
important, but it is not enough, to demand civilian control of
the military and local control of the police. I do not have the
answer, but a suggestion or two is in order. C. Wright Mills
talked about the "higher irresponsibility." The army and the
police are authoritarian organizations. Orders come from the top
and go down. The tight authoritarian line of control makes possible very effective internal accountability. Men at lower levels
do not organize to redress their grievances and to hold the top
accountable. The fact that authority and responsibility are relatively clearly defined means that the immediate superior officer

can either prosecute the violations of men under his command or face being prosecuted himself.

It is not enough for the highest level officers to be held accountable to civilian authorities merely in the sense that the latter hire and fire the former. In addition, officers should be found guilty for failing to prosecute violations by any lower level personnel. Prosecution of high level police and army personnel would make the violations themselves very visible, an important element in separating the dangerous connection between commitment to the well-being of the state and belief in the infallibility of the police and the military. It is now regarded as trivial when Marines in San Diego beat up a few homosexuals. It would not be trivial if generals were prosecuted for not court-martialing those Marines. We could rid ourselves of some of the higher level irresponsibility, for generals and police captains would have to stop claiming ignorance and then dropping the case. To an extraordinary degree, the military and the police claim the right to discipline their own ranks without interference, but when violations of human rights and the public trust go unpunished, we need ways either to prod the internal process or, when necessary, to override it. If the officials responsible drop the case, they are to be found guilty. If they take the case, they must explain why they failed to control their subordinates or must face prosecution. There would no longer be a problem of tracing blame back to persons who act on order.

If we remain with structures already available, the civilian judiciary is the most logical place to bring top level military and police personnel to account. However, the courts act very slowly. Moreover, there is a problem getting personnel at a lower level to act as prosecution witnesses or as plaintiffs because of fear of reprisals or a general reluctance to play the role of informer. And, as was revealed in the Dreyfus affair, generals are hardly going to aid in the prosecutions of other generals. Finally, collusion may exist between the military and the political powers.

Thus, it is both necessary and desirable to develop new institutional arrangements for obtaining that accountability. A good way to begin would be the creation of the office of ombudsman totally independent of the army and the police. The ombudsman and his staff should be generously funded by the state and should have subpoena powers and the authority to investigate even top secret documents in the pursuit of alleged violations, for otherwise the coercive arms of the state may cloak their violations by restricting the relevant information. While the ombudsman should develop safeguards to ensure the protection of those civilians and military persons who provide information about such violations as murder, rape, theft, and massacre, incentive to place evidence with the ombudsman should come from the creation of significant public and personal rewards. By allowing for the prosecution of top officials, we can encourage these officials to prosecute violations by their subordinates instead of trying to conceal them. At the same time, we may break through the protective wall of silence now so effectively operating on soldiers and policemen when they see violations by other soldiers and policemen, violations that may otherwise reach the level of massacre. We have enough decorations for bravery in slaughter. We should establish a few for those brave enough to prevent slaughter.

Existential Evil

Robert Jay Lifton

~~~~~~

The American invasion of Cambodia and the killings at Kent State, Augusta, and Jackson State dramatically accentuated a national emergency that has actually been with us for so long as to be virtually chronic. That emergency includes at least three terrifying dimensions: the possibility of nuclear war resulting from our provocative military adventurism in Southeast Asia; a state of spiritual degradation and conflict more extreme than any in recent memory; and a pervasive sense of extreme incompetence and instability in the country's political and military leadership. In the face of all this, can we view My Lai as past history, overtaken by new and more immediate threats?

This chapter is based in part on a review published in the *New York Times,* June 14, 1970 (© by the New York Times Company; reprinted by permission) and in part on a statement presented to the Senate Subcommittee on Veterans' Affairs, January 27, 1970 (both parts reprinted by permission of Robert Jay Lifton, c/o International Famous Agency, Inc.).

I think not. My Lai, in fact, is the essence of the American problem. When we take a good look at the significance of what happened there—as the fine books by Richard Hammer and by Seymour M. Hersh help us to do—we meet our present situation head on.[1]* We recognize in much of American behavior and inclination something that can only be called existential evil. And that evil is deeply bound up with illusion.

Everything about My Lai speaks of death—and not only death but the most absurd and unacceptable forms of death. There were the more than four hundred people herded together and systematically shot by the now notorious Charley Company of the American Division on March 16, 1968, in the hamlet listed on American maps as My Lai 4, in the village of Son My in Quang Ngai Province; and at least one hundred more people killed at a nearby subhamlet (as Hammer makes clear) by a sister unit known as Bravo Company. The slaughter took place midst the generally indiscriminate killing of Vietnamese civilians by American air bombing and artillery and small-arms fire, especially but not exclusively in such "free-fire zones" as the Son My area. And there were the deaths of members of Charley Company itself, preceding the group's entry into My Lai—six killed and twelve severely wounded by mines on February 28 and then a similar death on March 14 of a popular and much respected noncommissioned officer, Sergeant George Cox.

Captain Ernest Medina's "pep talk" on the night prior to the massacre was actually a funeral oration for the fallen sergeant. There is some dispute as to exactly what Medina said, but most of the men seemed to agree that, as one of them later put it, "Medina meant for us to kill every man, woman, and child in the village." Another GI recalled hearing Medina say that when the company left the area "nothing would be walking, growing, or crawling." Referring to the pained emotions the men felt about Cox's and others' deaths, Medina was said to have told the men to "let it out, let it go." Which they did.

More symbolically, one may speak of the death of responsibility within the American military. A distinguished West Point

* Notes for this chapter start on p. 338.

Existential Evil

graduate and former Congressman, speaking at a conference on
war crimes, emphasized the terrible "slippage" in morality and
group pride that seems to have developed throughout the army's
structure of command. And one senses a much more general
death of American moral authority. My Lai was not the cause
but the result of these symbolic deaths—of the pattern of "rule
by nobody" (in Hannah Arendt's phrase) or the "system of nonresponsibility" (in Masao Maruyama's) that has prevailed in Vietnam. There has been no clear point of responsibility for all of
the dying and killing, bodily or symbolic.

There were of course identifiable men who fired the bullets, but they had received orders as a group to do so, not only
from Medina but from their immediate leader in the field, Lieutenant William Calley, and both officers apparently set clear personal examples of how to go about the matter. Medina himself,
it also appears, was under orders from field grade officers who, for
their part, were doing no more than carrying out standard policy
in a *permanent* free-fire zone. That policy, according to Hammer,
"in essence . . . meant that any Americans operating within it
had, basically, a license to kill, and any Vietnamese living within
it had a license to be killed."

One must then raise questions about the responsibility of
William C. Westmoreland, then commanding general in Vietnam,
of the top generals in the Pentagon, the secretary of defense, and
the President—for creating the policies that legitimate this indiscriminate killing and indeed for insisting that we intervene violently in a revolutionary civil war in Southeast Asia, at such
appalling cost to the Vietnamese (and now the Laotians and
Cambodians) and to Americans as well. But such men are far
away and, moreover, have "good reasons" for doing what they do
—helping the South Vietnamese to repel an "outside invasion"
or to live under a "democratic government." Never mind the
fact that both contentions are illusory, as is the American-style
program for propping up an unwilling army and an even more
unwilling people to resist a relatively popular and much more
efficient revolutionary force, through a program named (the irony
is strictly unconscious) "Vietnamization."

Such illusions in turn derive from a still extant cold-war

cosmology characterized by a sense of absolute American virtue
and equally absolute Communist depravity—along with a peculiarly American brand of technological pragmatism which views
the whole situation in Vietnam as no more than "a job to be
done" with the help of "American know-how." So that although
ultimate responsibility must be assigned to our military and political leaders, their distance from the events together with their
cosmology enhance their psychic numbing—their inability to *feel*
what really goes on in a free-fire zone, what it is like to be a peasant in a premodern culture victimized by the incredible firepower released by advanced American technology of destruction,
or, for that matter, how it feels to be a terrified, profoundly confused, and depersonalized GI doing the firing.

Then add to this deadly system of nonresponsibility Hammer's shocking disclosure that My Lai was a mistake—Americans
had meant to go into a different subhamlet where Viet Cong
were really active. You are left with a sense of the profound
alienation—the lost bearings and unconnectedness—of our combat units. The American presence in Vietnam becomes that of a
hideous blind giant, skilled at killing but unable to "see" what
he kills. My Lai now permits us to take a good look.

And My Lai *is* America in Vietnam—no more, no less. Of
the more than fifty GIs I have talked to about such matters, the
only surprise I heard expressed about My Lai was about the fact
that so much fuss was made of it. Of course more people were
killed there than is usual, but to claim that My Lai is in any way
unique is to insult our intelligence and to distort history. Both
books on the massacre make this absolutely clear, to the credit of
the two authors, Hammer and Hersh.

All that we do in Vietnam is characterized by a spurious
sense of mission. The murderous behavior of GIs is a direct result
of the contradictions of their situation, which derives in turn from
the illusory American cosmology mentioned before (and its related
insistence upon geopolitical and economic "commitments"). The
GI, then, is victim no less than executioner. Thrust into this alien
revolution in an alien culture, assigned an elusive enemy who is
everyone and no one, sent into dangerous nonbattles in a war

lacking the most elementary rules or structures of meaning, what do we expect him to do? He in fact finds himself in exactly the situation Jean-Paul Sartre has described as inevitably genocidal— troops from an advanced industrial nation engaged in a counter-insurgency action in an underdeveloped area, against guerrillas who merge with the people.[2]

The books by Hammer and by Hersh not only confirm that thesis but give us the basis for understanding the individual-psychological state of false witness directly contributing to the indiscriminate killing. The GI sees his buddies killed and feels overwhelmed by the survivor's need to find meaning in his death encounter by acting significantly upon it. Unable to locate an enemy on whom to take revenge and thereby "bear witness," he must find his "meaning" by victimizing the innocent. One of the men, Terry Reed, made this pattern of false witness quite explicit: "To me the war was being ambushed every three to five days, being left with scores of wounded GIs. Then come right back at the enemy by going into an innocent village, destroying and kill-ing the people."

What I believe to be the ultimate form of false witness that took place at My Lai was a momentary illusion on the part of GIs that in gunning down at point-blank range babies, women, and old men, they were finally involved in a genuine military action— their elusive adversaries had finally been located, made to stand still, and annihilated—an illusion, in other words, that they had finally put their chaotic world back in order. The other side of that illusion was that those they were shooting were not people at all but were, as one GI put it, "like animals." Or, in Hammer's words, "some subhuman species who live only by the grace of the Americans [so that] to kill them is no more a crime than to spray DDT on an annoying insect."

This dehumanizing of all Vietnamese is not merely racist but a product of the degrading role Americans have constructed for the people of the South—an inefficient military dictatorship which cannot get its army to fight (because there is nothing to fight for), a sea of corruption in which rich Americans become targets for petty cheating of all kinds—and with a resulting mutual hatred between Americans and South Vietnamese probably much greater than any which exists between Americans and Viet Cong or North Vietnamese.

False witness leads to the rule of death—to what Hammer calls "the contagion of slaughter." Hersh makes clear the GIs engaged in slaughter not because they were combat weary but because they were combat hungry—or at least hungry for a more structured and "clean" form of combat, as compared to their terrifyingly exposed situation (they had in fact run from their first brush with the Viet Cong). The point about the rule of death, however, is that its very violence eliminates distinctions, especially distinctions between false and true witness, between spurious and authentic mission.

That pattern was made clear to me during an interview of my own with a GI who had been at My Lai, in which he explained: "If it's dead, it's VC—because it's dead. If it's dead, it *had* to be VC. And of course, a corpse couldn't defend itself anyhow." The same sentiment was expressed by a GI "joke" quoted by Hersh: "If it's dead and isn't white it's a VC."

A related sense of killing as a solution to chaos was expressed by Jay Roberts, a GI journalist present at the scene: "It's just that they didn't know what they were supposed to do; killing them seemed like a good idea, so they did it." The American ritual of the "body count," which has been used as the criterion for our "progress" in the war, thus becomes a grotesque epitome of false witness. Again My Lai is a source of wisdom: the official army report spoke of 128 "enemy" dead. The body count is thus exposed for its combination of lie and gruesome competition (companies vied with each other for higher body counts). It also contains an equally gruesome technicizing (as long as there is a *count*, there must be some progress).

That official "report" of a nonexistent combat engagement was of course again consistent with the logic of false witness and the rule of death, as was the subsequent military suppression of the real details of My Lai. We need not go into the mixture of conscious lies, half-conscious distortions, and routine body-count manipulations. We can accept Hammer's indisputable point that "the military did not want to find out officially what had hap-

pened . . . did not want to learn the details . . . and made no
real effort to learn the truth." How could it have been otherwise?
To have opened oneself to the truth of My Lai would have meant
confronting the vast web of deadly falsity surrounding the Vietnam war and America's relationship to it. Nor [was] anything approaching fundamental truth being sought by the military in its
. . . prosecutions of participants at My Lai or in its actions against
higher-ranking officers for their part in the cover-up. These [were]
in fact diversions from the murderous deceptions at the core of the
entire American project in Indochina.

Do you wonder now about our body counts in Cambodia?
Do you see any relationship between My Lai and Kent State—not
in any literal sense but in the two situations involving young
Americans in uniform, confused about their mission and fearful
about their own safety, acting in that obscure area between orders
and unchanneled emotion, and ending up applying inappropriate
and deadly force at the expense of the innocent? Do you see any
relationship between phrases used by GIs, such as "Indian country" (to describe areas in which Viet Cong reside), or "the only
good dink is a dead dink," and earlier historical patterns of American racism? or to the more recent words of a Mississippi State
trooper: "Better get an ambulance. We just killed some niggers."
Does the easy killing of Vietnamese have something to do with
the difference between the national outcry over Kent State and the
relatively quiet response to Jackson State and Augusta?

When I talk to students about My Lai, some simply shrug
and say, "What can you expect?" From the war, they mean—but
also, from America. I for one, enraged as I am—and that is the
only proper mental state for anyone who has read these two books
—still expect more. My feeling about My Lai is the same as
that of one of the GIs who described it as "just like a Nazi-type
thing." It is indeed just the kind of thing we were supposed to be
fighting *against* in World War II. I think the young really expect
more from America too, as they are showing in the vast effort they
are leading to turn the country around, to demonstrate, above all
to themselves, that there is more to America than My Lai.

This demonstration assumes a special complexity for their
friends and brothers who have been sent to fight in Indochina.

For veterans of any war there is a difficult transition from the "extreme situation" of the war environment to the more ordinary civilian world. This was noted after World War I, World War II, and the Korean War, but only recently have we begun to appreciate the problem from the standpoint of the psychology of the survivor. The combat veteran of any war has survived the deaths of specific buddies, as well as the deaths of anonymous soldiers on his and on the enemy's side. He survives the general war environment, within which he was taught that killing was not only legitimate but proper and necessary.

Upon returning to civilian life the war veteran faces several important psychological tasks in relationship to the deaths he has witnessed. He must, first of all, struggle with anxiety he continues to feel, often in association with the indelible images of death, dying, and suffering that constitute the survivor's "death imprint." He must also struggle with feelings of guilt and shame resulting directly from the war experience. These guilt feelings can relate simply to the fact that he survived while so many others died, or they may focus upon the specific death of one particular buddy who in some way, he feels, was sacrificed, so that he, the veteran, could go on living. His sense of guilt may also relate to his having killed enemy soldiers or having done various other things in order to stay alive. But his overall psychological task is that of finding meaning and justification in having survived and in having fought and killed. That is, as a survivor he must, consciously or unconsciously, give some form to the extreme experience of war, in order to be able to find meaning in all else he does afterward in civilian life.

These psychological tasks are never perfectly managed, and as a result the veteran may experience anything from a mild readjustment problem to disabling forms of psychiatric impairment. Typically, the returning veteran manifests a certain amount of withdrawal from civilian life, a measure of distrust of the civilian environment—a feeling that what it offers him may well be counterfeit—and some confusion and uncertainty about the meaning of his wartime experience and of his future life. His overall adjustment is greatly influenced by the extent to which he can become inwardly convinced that *his* war and *his* participation in that war had purpose and significance.

All of this is true for the Vietnam veteran. But in addition his psychological experience is influenced by certain characteristics of the war in Vietnam. The average Vietnam GI is thrust into a strange, faraway, and very alien place. The Vietnamese people and their culture are equally alien to him. Finding himself in the middle of guerrilla war in which the guerrillas have intimate contact with ordinary people, the environment to him is not only dangerous and unpredictable but devoid of landmarks that might warn of danger or help him to identify the enemy. He experiences a combination of profound inner confusion, helplessness, and terror.

Then he sees his buddies killed and mutilated. He may experience the soldier-survivor's impulse toward revenge, toward overcoming his own emotional conflicts and giving meaning to his buddies' sacrifices by getting back at the enemy. And in an ordinary war there is a structure and ritual for doing just that—battle lines and established methods for contacting the enemy and carrying out individual and group battle tasks with aggressiveness and courage. But in Vietnam there is none of that—the enemy is everyone and no one, never still, rarely visible, and usually indistinguishable from the ordinary peasant. The GI is therefore denied the minimal psychological satisfactions of war, and, as a result, his fear, rage, and frustration mount.

At the same time he notices that the South Vietnamese fight poorly or not at all; and rather than ask himself why this is so, he tends to associate them with the general corruption and deterioration he sees all about him. Any previous potential for racism is mobilized, and he comes to look upon Vietnamese as inferior people or even nonhuman creatures.

This dehumanization of the Vietnamese by the individual GI is furthered by his participation in such everyday actions as the saturation of villages with bombs and artillery fire and the burning of entire hamlets. Observing the deaths and injuries of Vietnamese civilians on such a massive scale and the even more massive disruptions of village life and forced relocations, he cannot but feel that the Vietnamese have become more or less expendable.

That is why Vietnam veterans I have talked to were not really surprised by the recent disclosures of atrocities committed by American troops at My Lai and elsewhere. Virtually all of them had either witnessed or heard of similar incidents, if on a some-what smaller scale. Sometimes these killings have been performed with the spirit of the hunter or the indiscriminate executioner— pot shots at random Vietnamese taken from helicopters, heavy fire directed at populated villages for no more reason than a command-ing officer's feeling that he "didn't like their looks." In addition there have been many accounts of such things as the shoving of suspects out of helicopters, the beheadings of Viet Cong or Viet Cong suspects, and of various forms of dismembering the bodies of dead Vietnamese.

Actions such as these require an advanced state of what I have called psychic numbing—the loss of the capacity to feel—and of general brutalization.[3] Where such actions are committed in a direct face-to-face fashion—without even the psychological protec-tion of distance that is available to those who drop bombs from the sky or direct long-range artillery fire—the psychological aber-ration and the moral disintegration are very advanced indeed, for while there is little ethical difference between killing someone far away whom one cannot see and looking directly into the victim's eyes from five or ten feet away while pulling the trigger, there is a considerable psychological difference between the two acts.

The Vietnam GI also is profoundly affected by atrocities committed by the Viet Cong, by South Vietnamese soldiers, and by South Korean forces. All of these contribute both to his numb-ing and his brutalization. But it is one's own atrocities that haunt one most. And no one can emerge from that environment without profound inner questions concerning the American mission in Vietnam and the ostensibly democratic nature of our allies there —even if, as is often the case, the GI resists these questions and keeps them from his own consciousness.

Whatever kind of adjustment the returning Vietnam vet-eran appears to be making, he must continue to carry images of these experiences inside of him. Survivors of a special kind of war, these men constitute a special kind of veterans' group. Murray Polner, a historian who has now interviewed more than two hun-dred Vietnam veterans as part of an investigation of their experi-ences, has found that none of the men he talked to—not one of them—was entirely free from doubt about the nature of the American involvement in Vietnam. This does not mean that all of them actively oppose the war but rather that as a group they have grave difficulty finding innner justification for what they have experienced and what they have done.

That is exactly what former army Captain Max Cleland, a triple amputee, meant when he told the Senate Subcommittee on Veterans' Affairs in December 1969: "To the devastating psychological effect of getting maimed, paralyzed, or in some way unable to reenter American life as you left it, is the added psychological weight that it may not have been worth it—that the war may have been a cruel hoax, an American tragedy, that left a small minority of young American males holding the bag." It is also what a nineteen-year-old Marine who had lost part of his leg and was awaiting medical discharge meant when he told Polner: "I think any other war would have been worth my foot. But not this one. One day, someone has got to explain to me why I was there." [4] This inability to find significance or meaning in their extreme experience leaves many Vietnam veterans with a terrible burden of survivor guilt. And this sense of guilt can become associated with deep distrust of the society that sent them to their ordeal in Vietnam. They then retain a strong and deeply disturbing feeling of having been victimized and betrayed by their own country.

As a result many continue to be numbed as civilians, the numbing now taking the form of a refusal to talk or think about the war. Some become almost phobic toward television broadcasts or newspaper reports having anything to do with the war. A number of those I spoke to could only take jobs permitting them to remain isolated from most of their fellow Americans, often night jobs. One Vietnam veteran told me, "I worked at night because I couldn't stand looking at those nine-to-five people who sent me to Vietnam." Yet these men are also affected by the deep ambivalence of the general American population about the war in general, an ambivalence which extends to those who have fought it. It is difficult for most Americans to make into heroes the men who have fought in this filthy, ambiguous war, and if they try to do so with a particular veteran there is likely to be a great deal of conflict and embarrassment all around. There is in fact an unspoken feeling on the part of many Americans that returning veterans carry some of the taint of that dirty and unsuccessful war.

From work that I and a number of others have done on related forms of war experience and survival, we can expect various kinds of psychological disturbance to appear in Vietnam veterans, ranging from mild withdrawal to periodic depression to severe psychosomatic disorder to disabling psychosis. Some are likely to seek continuing outlets for a pattern of violence to which they have become habituated, whether by indulging in antisocial or criminal behavior or by, almost in the fashion of mercenaries, offering their services to the highest bidder. Similarly, many will hold on to a related habituation to racism and the need to victimize others. Any of these patterns may appear very quickly in some but in others lie dormant for a period of months or even years and then emerge in response to various internal or external pressures.

What I have been saying is that we cannot separate the larger historical contradictions surrounding the American involvement in Vietnam from the individual psychological responses of our soldiers. Indeed the Vietnam veteran serves as a psychological crucible of the entire country's doubts and misgivings about the war. He has been the agent and victim of that confusion—of on the one hand our general desensitization to indiscriminate killing and on the other our accumulating guilt and deep suspicion concerning our own actions. We sent him as an intruder in a revolution taking place in a small Asian society, and he returns as a tainted intruder in our own society. Albert Camus urged that men be neither victims nor executioners.[5] In Vietnam we have made our young men into both. . . .

CHAPTER 5

It Never Happened and Besides They Deserved It

Edward M. Opton, Jr.

A few years ago most Americans associated war crimes, military atrocities, and state-sanctioned murder only with Adolf Hitler, Hideki Tojo, and a few other evil dictators and evil dictatorships. A small number of historians and moralists knew better, and their statements to that effect can be found by a diligent search of scholarly journals. But almost without exception, even those of us who were aware of the four-

This chapter grows in part from work done with Robert Duckles and other students and staff of the Wright Institute.

hundred-year atrocity of the treatment of the black minority in the United States, of the genocide of the native Americans, of the Northern and Southern Andersonvilles of the Civil War, of the two hundred thousand Filipinos slain when the United States decided to replace Spain as the colonial owner of the Philippines— even those who knew this history thought of it as thankfully remote and not as continuous with the present policy of the government. Past history does not call for present action to stop atrocities.

The American war in Indochina radically changed the perspective of many Americans. This chapter is addressed primarily to that large minority who are at least able seriously to entertain the possibility that the cruelties we fought against in Germany and Japan must be faced within our own country as well. The lessons of My Lai are, I hope, the basis for a small part of the learning from history that will be required if we are not to repeat that history endlessly.

The public reaction and nonreaction to My Lai are particularly rich in lessons for those who may want to act to prevent its frequent repetition. I here link the public reaction to My Lai with broad aspects of the massacre in five main conclusions. First, most of the explanations that were advanced for the massacre are seriously lacking in credibility. They explain away rather than explain; they say in one way or another that My Lai does not count rather than acknowledge its significance. Almost all public speculation on the massacre began with the assumption that it was an isolated, uncharacteristic incident. (For a further discussion of the facade of shocked surprise, see Chapter Seven.) The speculation therefore was on what exceptional circumstances could have resulted in such a deviation from normality. "They must have gone berserk" is the most oversimplified example of this speculation.

Explanations in terms of the hard fighting and casualties the men had experienced fall into this category. But the fact is that many units have fought harder and longer, have suffered more casualties, and have lived under worse conditions than Company C, 1st Battalion, 20th Infantry, both in this and other wars. Uncomfortable and dangerous as the war in Vietnam is for our men, it is a great deal less uncomfortable and a great deal less dangerous for the typical soldier than was the Korean War or World Wars I and II.

Efforts to find an explanation of the massacre in the personalities of the officers and enlisted men involved are similarly misdirected. Undoubtedly these men have their quirks and oddities, but so do we all. No one reported behavior of the officers or enlisted men before or after My Lai that smacks of abnormality. Parents of the men did not complain that their sons returned from Vietnam in any abnormal psychic state. The men were reported to have gone about their gruesome work for the most part with cool efficiency and tragic effectiveness. The fact that the accused officers and men did nothing to draw special attention to themselves in the months before and after the massacre indicates that they were not remarkably different from run-of-the-mill soldiers. Genuine explanations of My Lai require us to pay attention to the factors that lead ordinary men to do extraordinary things. The American tradition is to locate the source of evil deeds in evil men. We have yet to learn that the greatest evils occur when social systems give average men the task of routinizing evil.

Another kind of speculation on the causes of My Lai is the reverse of those discussed above. "This kind of thing happens in war," it is said. "It's terrible, but you have to expect excesses in combat." Not so. There have been excesses in combat in every war, but American soldiers have not carried out any comparable, large-scale, public shooting and bayoneting of infants, women, and old men since the campaigns against the Indians, as far as I know. This massacre is most emphatically not the kind of thing that has happened in recent American wars. The question for investigation is In what ways is My Lai the kind of thing done as a matter of routine in Vietnam?

Instead of trying to explain away this tragedy, we must recognize that although the pattern of violence at My Lai was not a riot or the result of a mass psychosis, it does have its counterparts in certain American traditions: genocidal attacks on American Indians in the nineteenth century and mass lynchings, which persisted until the 1930s. In both these cases, as at My Lai, the victims were of a different race. In addition, scientific studies of lynch mobs have shown that the members of such mobs are by no means berserk; rather, theirs is an all too rational response to the encouragement, spoken or unspoken, of their community leaders. The attitudes of elected officials and leading members of the community are crucial in permitting lynchings; rarely if ever has a mob carried out a lynching when the community leadership truly opposed it.

Second, the My Lai massacre was only a minor step beyond the standard, official, routine United States policy in Vietnam. This official policy is to obliterate not just whole villages but whole districts and virtually whole provinces. This policy has been eulogized in polished academic prose by Samuel P. Huntington, professor of government at Harvard: "If the 'direct application of mechanical and conventional power' takes place on such a massive scale as to produce a massive migration from countryside to city, the basic assumptions underlying the Maoist doctrine of revolutionary war no longer operate. The Maoist-inspired rural revolution is undercut by the American-sponsored urban revolution." [1]* This description of the most massive bombing and scorched-earth operation in the history of the world as an "American-sponsored urban revolution" must be one of the most panglossian rationalizations of the murder of civilians since Adolph Eichmann described himself as a coordinator of railroad timetables.

At first, efforts were made to remove the inhabitants before "saving" the regions by destroying them, but the pressure of the vast numbers of refugees thus created—at least one-third of the entire population of South Vietnam—led to policies even more genocidal. Jonathan and Orville Schell, writing in the November 26, 1969, *New York Times* observed:

Experience in Quang Ngai Province as journalists has led us to write this letter in hopes of dispelling two possible misapprehensions: that such executions are the fault of men like [William] Calley and [David] Mitchell alone and that the tragedy of Son My (My Lai) is an isolated atrocity. We both spent several weeks in Quang Ngai some six months before the incident. We flew daily with the FACs (Forward Air Control). What we saw was a province

* Notes for this chapter start on p. 338.

*utterly destroyed. In August 1967, during Operation Benton, the
"pacification camps" became so full that Army units in the field
were ordered not to "generate" any more refugees. The Army com-
plied. But search-and-destroy operations continued. Only now
peasants were not warned before an air strike was called in on
their village. They were killed in their villages because there was
no room for them in the swamped pacification camps. The usual
warnings by helicopter loudspeakers or air-dropped leaflets were
stopped. Every civilian on the ground was assumed to be enemy
by the pilots by nature of living in Quang Ngai, which was largely
a free-fire zone. The pilots, servicemen not unlike Calley and
Mitchell, continued to carry out their orders. Village after village
was destroyed from the air as a matter of de facto policy. Air
strikes on civilians became a matter of routine. It was under
these circumstances of official acquiescence to the destruction of
the countryside and its people that the massacre of Son My occurred. Such atrocities were and are the logical consequences of
a war directed against an enemy indistinguishable from the people.*

The genocidal policy is carried out in other ways as well.
I have personally accompanied a routine operation in which Cobra
helicopters fired twenty-millimeter cannons into the houses of a
typical village in territory controlled by the National Liberation
Front. They also shot the villagers who ran out of the houses. This
action was termed *prepping the area* by the American lieutenant
colonel who directed the operation. "We sort of shoot it up to
see if anything moves," he explained, and he added by way of
reassurance that this treatment was perfectly routine.

It is official policy to establish free-fire zones and kill zones,
where anything that moves is fired upon. Although in the original
theory these were zones from which civilians had been removed,
they now include many inhabited villages. It is official policy to
destroy the Vietnamese stockpiles of rice in National Liberation
Front areas, thus starving the women and children (the armed
men, we may be sure, provide themselves with the undestroyed
portion of the rice harvest). I have personally observed this policy
carried out and reported through official channels as if such destruction were as routine as the weather report—which indeed it

is. It is also official, though secret, policy to destroy rice and other crops with chemical defoliants. "In some instances entire villages are suspected of being Viet Cong sympathizers; killing their food crops prevents their use as a staging area for any sort of military operations and has in some instances led to complete abandonment of the village." [2]

We seem long ago to have given up the idea of gaining the allegiance of the people of Vietnam. "Winning the hearts and minds" is now maintained only as a public relations slogan for consumption on the home market. In Vietnam itself the policy is, as explained to me by a Marine officer, "If you've got them by the balls, the hearts and minds will follow." Getting the villagers by the balls means bombing and shelling them from their villages, assassinating their leaders, breaking up their families by removing the men, and removing the rural population to concentration camps euphemistically called refugee camps. All these official policies involve killing and on a large scale. The furor over the My Lai massacre must have seemed grimly illogical to the troops in the field. As satirist Art Hoppe put it, "The best way [to kill civilians], it's generally agreed, is to kill them with bombs, rockets, artillery shells, and napalm. Those who kill women and children in these ways are called heroes." [3] How is it, the foot soldier must wonder, that to kill women and children at less than five hundred paces is an atrocity, at more than five hundred paces, it is an act of heroism?

The official policy that results in large-scale killing of civilians through impersonal, long-distance weapons is matched by an official practice of not trying to reduce the cumulatively large-scale killing of civilians in thousands of individual, personal atrocities: dropping civilians out of helicopters and killing civilians by torture during interrogations; picking off civilians in their rice paddies in the large areas where anything that moves is officially considered an enemy; killing civilians for sport; plinking at them from passing air and land vehicles.

While in Vietnam I was surprised by the frequency of stories of civilians dropped from helicopters. Since I did not inquire about war crimes among soldiers and officers I met casually, it seemed that the men had some inner pressure to talk. Jonathan Schell observed the same phenomenon.[4]

"No one has any feelings for the Vietnamese," said Sproul, a private from Texas. "They're lost. The trouble is, no one sees the Vietnamese as people. They're not people. Therefore, it doesn't matter what you do to them." "We interrogate our prisoners in the field, and if they don't cooperate, that's it," said Brandt. "Our prisoners are usually people that we have just picked up in a hamlet that should've been cleared. But there are insufficient facilities for the people in the refugee camps, so they come back, and they're automatically considered V.C. Then we give it to 'em." "Those V.C.s are hard to break," said Sproul. "One time, I seen a real vicious sarge tie a V.C. upside down by the feet to the runners of a chopper and drag him three thousand feet in the air. . . . Another time, I seen them get a bunch of V.C.s in a chopper. They push out one first, and then tell the others that if they don't talk they go out with him. And they talk."

The half boasting of soldiers about dropping people out of helicopters seems to be an uncomfortable probing of the listener and of the storyteller by himself, a queasy assertion that the helicopter murders and the other war crimes which they epitomize are acceptable. In this vein, Schell quotes a group of pilots discussing the bombing of schools and orphanages:

At dinner . . . the pilots began to make jokes in which they ridiculed the idea that the bombings they guided were unnecessarily brutal by inventing remarks that might be made by men so bloodthirsty that they took delight in intentionally killing innocents. The joke tellers appeared to bring out their remarks with considerable uneasiness and embarrassment, and some of the pilots appeared to laugh unduly long in response, as though to reassure the tellers. . . . "Bruce got a bunch of kids playing marbles," said Major Nugent. The group laughed again. "I got an old lady in a wheelchair," Lieutenant Moore said, and there was more laughter. . . . Lieutenant Moore was so severely racked with laughter that he could not swallow a mouthful of food, and for several seconds he was convulsed silently and had to bend his head low with his hands over his mouth. Tears came to his eyes and to Major Nugent's. "Oh, my!" Lieutenant Moore sighed, exhausted by all the laughing. Then he said, "I didn't kill that woman in the wheelchair, but she sure bled good!" Nobody laughed at this joke. A silence ensued. Finally, Captain Reese suggested that they find out what movies were playing on the base that night.

Of course, not all military personnel participate in this banter. For example, nineteen nonaviation junior officers aboard the aircraft carrier *Hancock*—half the junior officers assigned to the crew—lodged an official protest against the war with the captain of the ship. As an example of the symbolic importance and the ambivalent attitude toward helicopter killings in particular consider the following account.[5]

Fred Sedahl, now a reporter for the Savanah Morning News, *said he has been buried with telephone calls since his story appeared yesterday. Sedahl described, among other incidents, a 1965 act in which a Viet Cong prisoner was thrown out of a helicopter to "certain death" by a South Vietnamese interpreter in full view of Marines in the helicopter. "You ought to take a helicopter ride with me," a man who called yesterday said. "I know just exactly what to do with guys like you. You should be the one taken up and dropped out."*

These small-scale war crimes have become so common that our reporters seldom report them; they are no longer news. They have become routine to many of our soldiers, too, and the soldiers, to preserve their equilibrium, have developed the classical psychological methods of justifying what they see happening. They come to think of the Vietnamese not as humans like themselves or even, as the army indictment for the My Lai massacre put it, as "Oriental human beings," but as something less than human. It is only a small further step to the conclusion that "the only good dink is a dead dink," as Specialist 4 James Farmer, Company C, 4th Battalion, 3rd Infantry, 198th Infantry Brigade, American Division, expressed it to the *New York Times*.[6]

The foot soldier in Vietnam sees Farmer's conclusion acted out daily, in air bombings, in artillery action, in napalm holocausts, in foodless and waterless refugee camps, and in the actions of his unpunished fellow soldiers who cut down a civilian here or a family there. The only good dink is a dead dink is in the wind in Vietnam, and our soldiers receive plenty of training in bending before that wind. In such an official and quasiofficial climate the My Lai massacre logically represents no major deviation. Because the massacre was a minor embellishment on established policy and practice, it is hypocritical self-righteousness to condemn the men who committed it without condemning those who set the criminal policy itself.

Therefore, my third conclusion is that the major responsibility and guilt for the massacre lie with the elected officials who make policy in Vietnam and with the high military officials who have misled both elected officials and the general public as to what they have been doing under the authorization of those policy directives. Our elected officials and their appointed advisers have special knowledge and considerable freedom of choice. We have the right and the duty to hold them personally responsible for the ignorance, insensibility, lack of human understanding, and poor judgment they have displayed in shaping our Vietnam policy. Especially deserving of blame are those officials who knew that policies were wrong but found it expedient to remain silent rather than endanger their careers or risk the ill will of their teammates. (On the problems of "groupthink" see Chapter Six.)

High officials in our government have participated fully in the practice of portraying the other side as an aggregate of evil demons. This imagery was at one time so prominent and routine in official pronouncements and in the media that only people with some determination to think for themselves could resist adopting it as a matter of course. Among high officials, as among the general public, the dehumanization of the enemy tends to spread, so that now those who dare to demonstrate against our Vietnam policy are called "bums" by Richard Nixon and "parasites," "goats," and

"creeps" by Spiro Agnew. Readers of *The Authoritarian Personality* [7] recognized in Agnew's "impudent snob" speech a text book
manifestation of modern totalitarianism. It is common enough
for a hard-hitting political speech to contain numerous references
to tendencies the speaker's constituents are known to be against,
but it is decidedly uncommon in America for a high official to
display the whole characteristic pattern of authoritarian ideas and
images—a pattern further described in Chapter Ten. The implications of public utterances like those of the vice-president are not
far to seek. "I think," a nineteen-year-old infantryman told Helen
Emmerich, "someone ought to kill those long-haired, queer bastards back in the world. Anyone who demonstrates against the war
ought to be lined up and killed, just like any gook here." [8] I know
from personal experience that this sentiment is not uncommon.

Fourth, American citizens share in the responsibility for My
Lai, for there has been available to all ample evidence that the
United States has been committing large-scale war crimes in Vietnam. A will to disbelieve, a self-serving reluctance to know the
truth, just plain indifference, as well as failings in our ethics and
in our educational system, have prevented our electorate from
influencing politicians whose policies allow for crime against
humanity. If some of us are disposed to blame our elected officials
for the wrong policies in Vietnam, these officials are quick enough
to pass the responsibility back to the general public, pointing to
opinion polls and silent majorities who favor these policies. These
officials have a good point. We as a people do bear much of the
responsibility for My Lai. The guilt is in large part collective.
The massacre may not have happened had our soldiers not been
brought up in a culture in which racism and a good-versus-evil,
Manichean approach to international relations are deeply rooted.
A large number, perhaps a critically large number, of the soldiers
would possibly have refused to take part in the massacre had they
not been raised on a psychic diet of television violence, which almost every day of their lives impressed its lesson of the cheapness
of life. Few of us have done much that was personally incon-
venient to discover or to fight against either the root sources or the
proximal causes of My Lai. Yet those citizens who opposed the
war are in a position different from those who favored it; and

those who reluctantly gave assent are in a psychological situation different from that of those who participated vicariously in the killing and the victories. There are, in other words, different degrees of responsibility and of potential for feeling guilt.

Some light is shed on these matters by a survey of reaction to My Lai carried out by students and staff members of the Wright Institute in December 1969. As far as we know, this study was the first ever attempted on American responses to alleged American war crimes. Our conclusion was that the impetus to an emotional cop-out that produces complacent members of a silent majority is surprisingly strong in almost all of us, young as well as old, liberal as well as conservative, interviewer as well as interviewee. The sample was not a large one—most of our data came from forty-two long interviews with randomly selected telephone subscribers in Oakland, California, plus four in-person interviews—but the results are consistent with larger, less intensive surveys by the *Wall Street Journal*,[9] the *Minneapolis Tribune*,[10] the Harris Poll,[11] and *Time*.[12] *Time* reported that 65 per cent of its sample of 1,608 individuals denied being upset by the news of the alleged massacre. Our intensive interviews throw some light on how those 65 per cent assimilate My Lai into the expected, normal routine or disbelieve that any massacre took place or do both simultaneously.

Anyone who would understand how people defuse the potential emotional chaos that would logically follow from knowledge of monstrous atrocities committed in their name must begin with the Germans. I do not mean to imply that the war crimes of the Americans or our reactions to those crimes are any more or less monstrous than those of the Germans. If data were available comparisons might be made with the French, the Russians under Joseph Stalin, the Belgians in the Congo, the Turks in Armenia, the Indonesians in the mid-sixties, the Sudanese in 1970. The comparison of American with German reactions to war crimes is made because only for the Germans is documentation of popular reaction readily available. After 1945 the Allies carried out an active de-Nazification program which included massive attempts to educate the German people about what they and their government had done on the theory that a Germany ignorant of its history would be condemned to repeat it. The effort was a failure. Our propagandists found it almost impossible to induce people to think about what they prefered to forget. With few exceptions, Germans interviewed during the de-Nazification campaign stood at an emotional distance far from the Nazi crimes, feeling personally and morally uninvolved and unconcerned, or they denied the facts or they projected the guilt on others or they rationalized and justified the atrocities or they simultaneously engaged in several or all of these mental maneuvers, little inhibited by logical consistency.

Straight-out denial of the facts and the meaning of the German genocide in World War II was by no means confined to the Germans. Arthur Koestler was among the few who spoke from many platforms in the early 1940s trying to rouse the English-speaking public to the horror of the German extermination policy. Commenting on the British and American reaction to his efforts, Koestler writes:

There is a dream which keeps coming back to me at almost regular intervals; it is dark, and I am being murdered in some kind of thicket or brushwood; there is a busy road at no more than ten yards distance; I scream for help but nobody hears me, the crowd walks past, laughing and chattering. I know that a great many people share, with individual variations, the same type of dream. I have quarreled about it with analysts, and I believe it to be an archetype in the Jungian sense: an expression of the individual's ultimate loneliness when faced with death and cosmic violence and his inability to communicate the unique horror of his experience. I further believe that it is the root of the ineffectiveness of our atrocity propaganda. For, after all, you are the crowd who walk past laughing on the road; and there are a few of us, escaped victims or eyewitnesses of the things which happen in the thicket, . . . who, haunted by our memories, go on screaming on the wireless, yelling at you in newspapers and in public meetings, theaters, and cinemas. Now and then we succeed in reaching your ear for a minute. I know it each time it happens by a certain dumb wonder on your faces, a faint glassy stare entering your eye; and I tell myself: now you have got them, now hold them, so that they will remain awake. But it only lasts a minute. You shake yourself like puppies who have got their fur wet; then the transparent screen descends again, and you walk on, protected by the dream barrier which stifles all sound.[13]

Koestler would have found the responses of our Oakland citizens painfully familiar. For example, an airline stewardess was asked during the interview to inspect the *Life* magazine photographs of My Lai.[14] As she viewed the mangled bodies and the contorted faces of those about to die she trembled and her chin dropped to her chest. Her eyes closed to shut the pictures out. For several seconds she seemed unable to move. But she recovered immediately, for I then asked, "You said before that you weren't surprised. Do you have any other reactions besides that?" She responded: "No, I don't. . . . It—when people are taught to hate, it doesn't surprise me how they react, particularly when they are given a weapon; it just seems to be one of the outcomes of war." The contrast between the distress and shame apparent in her bodily reaction and the bland detachment she tried to put into her words could not have been more striking. The shakiness of her posture of "it doesn't surprise me" became evident less than a minute later when she said: "And it amazes me how a group of individuals can follow such a command."

Both emotional detachment and logical self-contradiction seem to serve a common purpose, namely, self-centeredness. The need to exclude from one's thinking such potentially troublesome matters as American war crimes was stated explicitly by some subjects. For example, one said: "I can't take the responsibility of the world on my shoulders too strongly myself. . . . It upsets me. I'm having my own problems and can't take this stuff too seriously since it causes me worries and problems." Another subject, one who declined to be interviewed, said: "Well, I don't know, you see, I can't get upset about all these things, so I can't give you an opinion one way or another. Okay?" The seemingly paradoxical emotional detachment makes sense on the premise that emotions signal a need to do something, to be involved, even to take responsibility. The spectators who listened to Kitty Genovese scream as she was slowly murdered outside their New York apartments reported afterward a similar, seemingly paradoxical emotional detachment. The two instances are comparable, and in both the emotional detachment makes it possible to center one's attention and effort on oneself, one's own needs and problems, and, hence, not to get involved with external matters.

Most of the Americans we approached would have felt at home in the emotional climate of postwar Germany. In 1946 Moses Moskowitz reported on a survey of German opinion: "The most striking overall impression is the absence in the German of any emotional reaction toward Jews, be it positive or negative. It was shocking at times to listen to people decrying the evils of Nazism, reciting the horrors of concentration camps . . . without one word of sympathy for the victims." [15] Similarly, Morris Janowitz found that when the Germans were informed about the concentration camps, they "seldom or never spontaneously offered to help rehabilitate the inmates. This reaction is consistent with the reports that there was no humanitarian move by the Germans in the neighborhood of the camps to assist in alleviation of the suffering . . . until they were ordered to do so by the military commanders." [16]

Partial or complete denial of the fact of the massacre at My Lai was common. One might expect the extreme forms of denial from such people as Mitchell, one of the accused, who has said: "I can recall no such case where I know of anyone being hurt. . . . It is my opinion that what they say happened did not happen." And one might expect the same reaction from Alabama Governor George Wallace: "I can't believe an American serviceman would purposely shoot any civilian. . . . Any atrocities in this war were caused by the Communists." [17] But total denial is by no means confined to those implicated in the alleged massacre and to superpatriots. A man who felt that the United States should, but could not, get out of Vietnam told us: "Our boys wouldn't do this. Something else is behind it."

Another complete denial came from a woman who, like the man above, was ambivalent about the war. At one moment she advocated withdrawal by the end of 1970; however, she also endorsed the idea of escalating and winning the war, no matter what the consequences, but without killing innocent people. As for My Lai, she said: "It's too unbelievable that they would do something like that." Another person, asked if he believed the massacre really happened, first gave a strong endorsement of Nixon's policy, then said: "I can't really and truly. No. I don't. I think it could have been a prefabricated story by a bunch of losers."

Strong doubts served the same purpose as complete denial for some people. "Anything could happen. How do we know what's going on?" asked a man who wanted the war escalated; and one of several individuals who felt so threatened by the subject that they cut off the interviews in the middle said: "No, sometimes I don't [believe that the massacre happened]. Sometimes I think that our newspapermen get a little bit wild." Implicit in the words of some respondents seemed to be a plea, a desire to find a way not to have to believe in the reality of the alleged massacre. A sixty-six-year-old grandmother described her family's reaction: "My foster daughter doesn't believe it. She thinks it never happened. Finally [she] admitted to me that she doesn't want to believe it happened. She doesn't want to believe it. She knows in her heart but refuses to face facts." Apparently the ability to wish away the unpleasant is prevalent in both Germany and America: An elderly German woman said: "The only thing I do know is that if such a good, kind people as the Germans are capable of killing millions of human beings, as you say they did, humanity is fundamentally beastly." [18] A Los Angeles salesman said: "I don't believe it actually happened. The story was planted by Viet Cong sympathizers and people inside this country who are trying to get us out of Vietnam." A Lakewood, Ohio, mother said: "I can't believe that a massacre was committed by our boys. It's contrary to everything I've ever learned about America." Marvin Sandidge, a Memphis contractor, said: "I can't believe anyone from this country would do that sort of thing." [19]

Justification was the other most prevalent means of coping with the unwelcome news. One of the principal justifications our respondents offered was the idea that orders must be followed. Even some of the dovish respondents gave statements like this: "What would their punishment have been if they had disobeyed? Do they get shot if they don't shoot someone else?" And another moderate dove said: "They were given an order to do something. They will shoot you if you don't. They had no choice." And a woman who wanted all United States troops out of Vietnam by the end of 1970 said: "They have to follow orders, too, or go to jail." Only a few respondents recalled that some of the GIs had refused to shoot. One of those few was asked what the men should have done. He said: "What a lot of them did, refuse. Quite a few of them refused. Fact is, I even read where one of them shot himself in the foot so he would be evacuated, so he wouldn't have any part of it." The idea that one must follow orders was more acceptable to men than to women; when asked what they would have done if ordered to line people up and kill them, 74 per cent of women said they would have refused, but only 27 per cent of men said so. Perhaps ominously, youth were no more independent of spirit than their elders; those over thirty-six more often favored putting the enlisted men who did the shooting on trial than did those under thirty-six, and slightly more of the older group expressly said that the men should have disobeyed orders to kill civilians.

The idea that the men were justified by the orders they received implies placing the guilt on someone higher up, and a number of our respondents made this explicit. Germans, similarly, tended to blame the war crimes on Hitler, their leaders, the National Socialist Party, the SS, or military fanatics. But the idea that Germans, as individuals, might have been in turn responsible for selection and toleration of their leaders was steadfastly rejected. While the question of the responsibility of the American public was not specifically asked of our predominantly dovish sample, no one extended the scope of responsibility to himself in particular or to the American people in general. Encouragingly, however, in a follow-up questionnaire three months later several respondents did say they believed Americans, including themselves, were ultimately responsible for My Lai. Just as Janowitz found in Germany, so in America someone higher up is often held responsible but almost never those ultimately responsible for the government: the people.

Another popular justification was that the alleged victims were not civilians but enemies: "Now had these civilians, had these women set booby traps for these people?" Another man who felt he was a dove ("I'd hate to say I'm a hawk"), yet who advocated that the United States "let out the stops," said, "These little bastards are devious," implying in context that the women and children were not innocent bystanders.

None of the respondents said that My Lai was justified as revenge for National Liberation Front actions, but many seemed to think so: "I understand that the Viet Cong, from the start, have bombed schoolyards, schoolhouses, movie theaters, restaurants . . . just worthless bombing, and it's killing innocent people by the score. And these are their own people." And a hawk said: "Our boys have been castrated by the VC and no one stood up for them. There was no sensation made of this."

If this kind of justification is common among civilians, it is not surprising that four sergeants in Vietnam wrote to the *San Francisco Chronicle* (December 31, 1969) to explain their approval of My Lai: "You know that this is a VC village, they are the enemy, they are a part of the enemy's war apparatus. Our job is to destroy the enemy, so kill them; a war can be won only when the enemy forces are destroyed or too demoralized to fight effectively. . . . I want to come home alive, if I must kill old men, women, or children to make myself a little safer, I'll do it without hesitation."

Although the four sergeants speak bluntly of killing the enemy, an army officer in our sample who had just returned from Vietnam justified the massacre in terms of its presumed psychological effect:

I could see the possibility that it was an order from higher up, just as a deterrent to the other people in the area not to harbor the VC. . . . And this is really a very good tactic if you stop to think about it, in a war. If you scare people enough they will keep away from you. [Interviewer: You feel this is a good tactic in a war?] Yeah, if you want to fight a war. Aw . . . I'm not saying that I approve of the tactic. [Interviewer: But you think it's an effective tactic?] Yes, definitely. I think it's an effective tactic. And people who are running wars probably think the same way: that this is an effective tactic.

However, we did not hear one justification reportedly used by postwar Germans. The respondents, with one exception, did not tell us that the victims were members of an inferior race. This is not to say that people were unaware of the role of overt racism in making My Lai possible. Both hawk and dove respondents often said that GIs tend to look on Vietnamese civilians as subhuman, as gooks, slopes, and dinks. One man, a Vietnam veteran, gave several specific examples from his own experience to back up his opinion that our lower-level officers and enlisted men typically treat the Vietnamese people as nonhumans, speak of them as nonhumans, and think of them as nonhumans. But, with the one exception, every subject coupled this awareness of racial prejudice in others with an abstinence from publicly subscribing to it himself.

The exception said that the typical GI's view of the Vietnamese is that "they're subnormal." Moreover, he said, "I think it's true." He then went on immediately to add, "I think that the GIs are very sympathetic toward the Vietnamese people as a whole. . . . The GIs over there are trying to educate and help these people." This individual's forthright racism seems in line with his statement later that "the German Nazis were a superior race eliminating a—what they thought was a threat to their existence."

I remember that in Vietnam, among those responsible for the activities on which the citizens of Oakland were commenting, justification of war crimes by dehumanization of the victims was very common indeed. The Vietnamese are turned into debased abstractions—gooks, slopes, dinks—or are spoken of in zoological terms. "Look," a captain told Jonathan Schell after directing the bombing of a group of Vietnamese houses, "those villages are completely infested with VC, just like rats' nests." [20] But it all comes down to racism in the end: "A lot of these people wouldn't think of killing a man," Michael Bernhardt said of Company C. "I mean, a white man—a human so to speak." [21]

Usually the dehumanization of the Vietnamese has little intellectual or ideological content; the shift from human to subhuman is easiest if not thought about. There are openly ideological exceptions though; for example, while covering a search-and-destroy operation near Hue, in August 1967, I met a college student who had received a fellowship to spend the summer in Vietnam as a reporter for a college newspaper news service. The conversation turned to killings of civilian prisoners under torture. The student-reporter stoutly defended the practice: "It's not like killing people," he maintained. "These are Communists."

Along with the dehumanization of the enemy (and of friendly civilians) goes a dehumanization of the self, in psychiatric terminology *dissociation*, a sense of eerie or even ludicrous detachment:

Bernhardt says he was not moved by compassion as he watched the slaughter but by a sense of how ridiculous and illogical it all seemed. "I wasn't really violently emotionally affected. I just looked around and said, 'This is all screwed up.'"... What he does remember best are a few gruesome vignettes—one soldier, in particular, who laughed every time he pressed the trigger. ("He just couldn't stop. He thought it was funny, funny, funny.") [22]

A final important justification or mitigation was that other evils have been worse. A young woman, asked if the Son My massacre resembled Nazi atrocities, said: "Oh, it's not the same as their dirty cruelness. I guess it's similar in a way. . . . They killed women and children. It doesn't make sense. . . . Like, the Nazis, they used showers with acid in the water or something like that, and that was really horrible. Our men are just shooting people." However, it was usually very difficult to induce people to make comparisons of any kind. The first comparative question, "Do you know of any incidents from other wars, whether or not this country was involved, that can be compared with My Lai?" produced many avoiding answers: "I can't think of any." "No." "None at all that I can recall." Only when Germany or Lidice were mentioned did painful comparisons begin to emerge, often with strained efforts to find differences.

I have argued that most people responded to the My Lai massacre with one or both of two main propositions, "It never happened" and "besides, they deserved it," and that both propositions prop up the conclusion that "I need not concern myself with

68

Sanctions for Evil

it." This argument should come as no surprise to students of the silent majority.

But what of the nonsilent minority, the above-average, articulate citizens and the intelligentsia? An informal analysis of newspapers, letters to editors, and the *Congressional Record* convinces me that politicians and intelligentsia were much less reluctant to concern themselves with My Lai than was the man in the street. Some (not all) Congressional supporters of the Vietnam war acknowledged they were appalled by the massacre, and William Buckley, a leading conservative and hawk, wrote: "Thus far [My Lai] looks like simple barbarism, like blood-lust sadism. The trouble with that explanation is that it does not easily reconcile with what we know about typical Americans. . . . The prosecution of the guilty will, then, tell us a lot about them and not a little about us." [23]

Discomfort over My Lai was not, however, universal among the intelligent, and they, too, were able to conclude that it never happened, and, besides, that they deserved it. For example, a Connecticut man, in a letter drawing together quotations from several sources, wrote:

What facts? There are some accusations, of the type regularly used by the Viet Cong, and some photos. Of these photos, Senator Pete H. Dominick, Republican-Colorado, said: "Not one picture in the Life *story showed anyone committing an atrocity." He also said that the photographs do not jibe with the actual geography around the village of Son My [My Lai]. . . . The campaign to crucify our fighting men for doing their duty is strangely reminiscent of the "police brutality" issue.*[24]

The best example of an intelligent denial-defense of the My Lai massacre that I have seen is a lawyerlike treatise by Rouben Chublarian, a former officer in the Soviet Army, former lecturer at Central Asia University, and winner of awards from the Freedoms Foundation of Valley Forge, Pennsylvania, and from the government of Spain. Chublarian's paper is too detailed to summarize, but two quotes give the central theme: "The statesmen of South Vietnam, who have thoroughly investigated the Son My incident, have found that the GIs 'have not committed a crime.'" And, besides, savagery and excessive shooting were justified, a conclusion Chublarian supports by quotations from Nikolai Lenin, Mikhail Sholokhov, William T. Sherman, and Woodrow Wilson: "The drive to revenge is connected with the drive to win the battle, and 'to be victorious you must be brutal and ruthless.'" [25]

These various ways of defusing the emotional potential of My Lai were used by hawks and doves alike, though not in equal proportions. Hawks, more than others, tended to justify the alleged massacre. Both hawks and doves argued in one way or another that no massacre happened. The doves tended to comfort themselves with the thought that My Lais happened in every war, hence one need not be upset. Regardless of the method, the effect was the same: emotional disengagement. I believe the general nonresponse to My Lai by our random sample of Oaklanders was not fundamentally different from the nonresponse of Kitty Genovese's neighbors. Whether it is Vietnamese peasants or one's neighbor, emotional detachment makes it possible to keep one's attention and concern focused on Number One, me, myself, I. No malignant evil intent is necessary for men to tolerate or even reluctantly to applaud war crimes; all that is required is self-centeredness. This focus on the self need not imply any pathological egotism but only impotence to affect the course of events. Milton Mayer explained the phenomenon in his analysis of the Germans' passive acceptance of Nazism: "Responsible men never shirk responsibility, and so, when they must reject it, they deny it. They draw the curtain. They detach themselves altogether from the consideration of the evil they ought to, but cannot, contend with. Their denial compels their detachment." [26]

My fifth conclusion regarding public reaction to My Lai is that little is to be gained, and perhaps much lost, by attempts to force recognition of responsibility on those who completely wash their hands of the blood of My Lai. But, if we assume that no one can be stirred to action by such atrocities or if we fail to press for full and frank application of social science to American war crimes, we participate by passivity in the horror of My Lais, past and future. We must make sure that as many people as possible know the truth and are guided by it. Unless a substantial number of people who can speak and write with authority strive to keep the evil of My Lai and of the larger policy of which it is an expression before the public, it is difficult to see what will prevent our military from persisting in genocide in Vietnam and in future Vietnams.

But dealing with this guilt-laden subject will not be easy, for guilt that is on the edge of consciousness can lead to further destructiveness more easily than to contrition. Charles Manson, the alleged leader of the group accused of the Sharon Tate murders, seeing that his followers were shaken after their work, reportedly insisted that they commit more murders the next night. This psychological stratagem was used regularly in the Nazis' training of the SS. Efforts to induce consciousness of guilt in people who lack the inner strength to bear it can backfire, evoking behavior that relieves queasiness by demonstrating that what is feared can be done, even more and worse, without catastrophic consequences to oneself.

Public breast-beating, whether self-flagellation or condemnation of everyone except oneself, is probably futile at best and a dangerous indulgence at worst. Constructive handling of feelings about My Lai requires paying attention to what we can do to prevent future atrocities and to block the next Vietnam.

Social scientists in particular need not be part of a silent majority as, with rare exceptions, we so far have been. Psychologists can investigate what makes some killing psychologically close and shocking while the same death by bomb or shell is a matter of indifference. Sociologists have not yet reported on the structural aspects of the military reward system that ensures that almost all war crimes remain unreported. Survey researchers, psychiatrists, and clinical psychologists could assay the extent of long-lasting alienation and anomie among returned Vietnam veterans, as Robert Jay Lifton does in Chapter Four. The social sciences could join together in examining the pervasive distortion in information as it passes up and down the chain of military and civilian command and how this distortion is used to justify and rationalize mass murder. Funding such work will be difficult, but if social scientists think the work is important enough, they will find the means of sponsorship and support. At times to know and to remain silent is to be an accomplice. One of the lessons of My Lai is that silence in the face of such human disaster can no longer be an acceptable response.

CHAPTER **6**

Groupthink Among Policy Makers

Irving L. Janis

$\mathbf{O}$ther chapters in this volume emphasize the authorization for dehumanizing actions that stems from policy decisions by government officials. It is this policy-making process that I talk about here.[1]* I have been studying a series of notorious decisions made by government leaders, including major fiascos such as the Vietnam escalation decisions of the Lyndon B. Johnson administration, the Bay of Pigs invasion plan of the John F. Kennedy administration, and the Korean Crisis decision of the Harry Truman administration, which unintentionally provoked Red China to enter the war. In addition, I have examined some fiascos by European governments, such as

* Notes for this chapter start on p. 340.

the policy of appeasement carried out by Neville Chamberlain and his inner cabinet during the late 1930s—a policy which turned over to the Nazis the populations and military resources of Austria, Czechoslovakia, and other small countries of Europe. In all these instances, the decision-making groups took little account of some of the major consequences of their actions, including the moral and humanitarian implications.

When we examine how each of these decisions was made, we find that it was rarely the work of just one man—even though historians may refer to it as the President's or the Prime Minister's decision. Rather, the decision was a group product, resulting from a series of meetings of a small body of government officials and advisers who constituted a cohesive group of policy makers. For example, when we look into the way the Vietnam policies of the Johnson administration were arrived at, we discover very quickly that the key decisions were made by a small cohesive group. In addition to the President, the group included McGeorge Bundy, the special White House assistant (later replaced by Walt Rostow); William Moyers, press secretary (later replaced by George Christian); Robert McNamara, secretary of defense (replaced during the last months of the Johnson administration by Clark Clifford); and Dean Rusk, secretary of state (who managed to remain in Johnson's policy-making group from the bitter beginning to the bitter end). For several years George Ball, who was undersecretary of state, also participated in the meetings. The group also included Earle Wheeler, chairman of the Joint Chiefs of Staff, and Richard Helms, director of the Central Intelligence Agency.

It was surprising for me to discover the extent to which this group and other such small groups of policy makers displayed the phenomena of social conformity regularly encountered in studies of group dynamics among ordinary citizens. For example, some of the phenomena appear to be completely in line with findings from social psychological experiments showing that powerful social pressures are brought to bear by the members of a cohesive group when a dissident begins to voice his objections to a group consensus. Other phenomena I describe are reminiscent of the shared illusions observed in encounter groups and friendship cliques when the members simultaneously reach a peak of group-y feelings. Above all, numerous indications point to the development of group norms that bolster morale at the expense of critical thinking.

To begin, I mention here the main sources for the Vietnam case study. One is an insightful article by James C. Thomson, Jr.,[2] a historian at Harvard, who spent many years as a participant observer in the government, first in the State Department and then in the White House as an assistant to Bundy. Another is a book by David Kraslow and Stuart H. Loory,[3] two journalists who interviewed many government officials involved in forming policies concerning the Vietnam war. The third is a book by Townsend Hoopes,[4] who was acting secretary of the air force in the Cabinet. Hoopes's book is especially valuable for understanding the social and political pressures put on McNamara, Clifford, and other high officials who, toward the end of the Johnson administration, became disillusioned and began to favor deescalation of the war. Using these and several other references, we can get some idea of the forces that enabled intelligent, conscientious policy makers to make the series of grossly miscalculated decisions that had such destructive effects on the people of Vietnam and such corrosive effects within our country.

One of the first things we learn from these accounts is that when the in-group of key advisers met with Johnson every Tuesday (they sometimes called themselves the Tuesday Luncheon Group), their meetings were characterized by a games theory detachment concerning the consequences of the war policies they were discussing. The members of this group adopted a special vocabulary for describing the Vietnam war, using terms such as body counts, armed reconnaissance, and surgical strikes, which they picked up from their military colleagues. The Vietnam policy makers, by using this professional military vocabulary, were able to avoid in their discussions with each other all direct references to human suffering and thus to form an attitude of detachment similar to that of surgeons. But although an attitude of detachment may have functional value for those who must execute distressing operations, it makes it all too easy for policy makers to dehumanize the victims of war and to resort to destructive military solutions without considering their human consequences.

Thomson, who has reported this tendency from close at hand, recounts a memorable meeting in late 1964 when the policy planners were discussing how much bombing and strafing should be carried out against Vietnamese villages. The issue was resolved when an assistant secretary of state spoke up saying, "It seems to me that our orchestration in this instance ought to be mainly violins, but with periodic touches here and there of brass." Thomson, in retrospect, came to realize that he had himself undergone attitude changes, that he had acquired the same sense of aloof detachment that pervaded the war policy discussions of Washington bureaucrats. Back at Harvard, after leaving his post in the White House, he was shocked to realize that the young men in front of him in the classroom were the human beings in the manpower pool he had been talking about so detachedly when discussing problems of increasing the number of draftees with the policy makers in Washington.

This dehumanization tendency is closely related to another characteristic of Johnson's policy-making group: reliance on shared stereotypes of the enemy and of the peoples of Asia. Their grossly oversimplified views overlooked the vast differences in political orientation, historic traditions, and cultural patterns among the nations of Asia. Their sloganistic thinking about the North Vietnam Communists overlooked powerful nationalistic strivings, particularly North Vietnam efforts to ward off Chinese domination. As a historian, Thomson was shocked to realize the extent to which crudely propagandistic conceptions entered into the group's plans and policies. The policy makers, according to Thomson, were disposed to take a very hard-nosed, military stance partly because of these stereotyped notions. Here we have a prime example of the rigid and stereotyped thinking that Neil J. Smelser, Jr., Robert Jay Lifton, and others discuss elsewhere in this volume. The dominant view demonized the enemy as embodying all evils, which legitimized the use of relentlessly destructive means. These stereotypes were evidently incorporated into the norms of the policy-making group, so it was very difficult for any member to introduce a more sophisticated viewpoint.

In a cohesive group that adopts such norms, what happens when a member starts expressing his mild doubts and says, "Let's sit back for a moment and think this over; don't we need to make some distinctions here?" or "Shouldn't we talk about some of the consequences we may have overlooked?" Such questions must often go through the minds of the participants before they agree on a policy that has some obvious drawbacks. But as soon as anybody starts to speak about his doubts, he discovers, often in subtle ways, that the others are becoming somewhat irritated and that he is in the presence of powerful group pressures to be a booster, not a detractor.

Typically, a cohesive group, like the in-group of policy makers in the Johnson administration, develops a set of norms requiring loyal support of past decisions. Each member is under strong pressure to maintain his commitment to the group's decisions and to support unquestionably the arguments and justifications they have worked out together to explain away obvious errors in their judgment. Given this shared commitment, the members put pressure on each other to continue marching to the same old drum beat and to insist that sooner or later everyone will be in step with it. They become inhibited about expressing doubts to insiders as well as outsiders with regard to the ultimate success and morality of their policies.

Whenever a group develops a strong "we feeling" and manifests a high degree of solidarity, there are powerful internal as well as external pressures to conform to the group's norms. A member of an executive in-group may feel constrained to tone down his criticisms, to present only those arguments that will be readily tolerated by the others, and to remain silent about objections that the others might regard as being beyond the pale. We can surmise from studies of work teams, social clubs, and informal friendship groups that such constraints arise at least partly because each member comes to rely upon the group to provide him with emotional support for coping with the stresses of decision-making. When facing any important decision, especially during a serious crisis, a group member often develops feelings of insecurity or anxiety about risks that could adversely affect the interests of the nation or organization and that could damage his own career. Moreover, most policy decisions generate conflicts between different standards of conduct, between ethical ideas and humanitarian values on the one hand and the utilitarian demands of national or organizational goals, practical politics, and economics on the other. A platitudinous policy maker is likely to reassure his colleagues by reminding them that you can't make an omelet without breaking some eggs. Nevertheless, each man's awareness that moral and ethical values are being sacrificed in order to arrive at a viable policy can give rise to distressing feelings of shame, guilt, depression, and related emotional reactions associated with lowering of self-esteem. Given all the uncertainties and dilemmas that arise whenever one shares in the responsibility of making a vital decision, such as war policies affecting the welfare and survival of entire nations, it is understandable that the members of a decision-making body should strive to alleviate stress.

Some individuals in public office are extraordinarily self-confident and may not need the support of a cohesive group when their decisions are subject to public criticism. I think, for example, of the spirited symphony orchestra conductor Thomas Beecham, who once said, "I have made just one mistake in my entire life and that was one time when I thought I was wrong but actually I was right." Not everybody who is accustomed to putting it on the line as a decision maker is able to maintain such unassailable self-confidence however. So, not surprisingly, most members of a cohesive policy-making group strive to develop a sense of unanimity and esprit de corps that help them to maintain their morale by reaffirming the positive value of the policies to which they are committed. And, just as in friendship cliques, they regard any deviant within the group who insists on calling attention to the defects of the policies as objectionable and disloyal.

Social psychologists have observed this tendency in studies of students' clubs and other small groups. Whenever a member says something out of line with group norms, the other members increase communication with the deviant. Attempts to influence the nonconformist member to revise or to tone down his dissident ideas continue as long as most members of the group feel reasonably hopeful about talking him into changing his mind. But if they fail after repeated attempts, the amount of communication they direct toward the deviant goes down markedly. From then on, the members begin to exclude him, often quite subtly at first and later more obviously, to restore the unity of the group. A social psychological experiment conducted by Stanley Schachter in America and replicated in seven different European countries showed that the more cohesive the group and the more relevant the issue to the goals of the group, the greater the inclination of the members to reject a recalcitrant deviant.

During Johnson's administration, when any member of the in-group began to express doubts—as some of them certainly did—they were treated in a rather standardized way that strongly resembled the research findings just described. At first, the dissenter was made to feel at home—provided that he lived up to two restrictions: that he did not voice his doubts to outsiders, which would play into the hands of the opposition; and that he kept the criticisms within the bounds of acceptable deviation, not challenging any of the fundamental assumptions that went into the prior commitments the group had made. Thomson refers to such doubters as domesticated dissenters. One domesticated dissenter was Moyers, who was described as Johnson's closest adviser. When Moyers arrived at a meeting, we are told, the President greeted him with, "Well, here comes Mr. Stop-the-Bombing." But Moyers and the other domesticated dissenters, like Ball, did not stay domesticated forever. These men appear to have become casualties of subsequent group pressures; they resigned long before the entire Johnson administration became a casualty of the Vietnam war policy, long before that startling day when Johnson appeared on television and tearfully explained why he was not going to run again.

Given the series of cautionary examples and the constant reaffirmation of norms, every dissenter is likely to feel under strong pressure to suppress his doubts, misgivings, and objections. The main norm, as I have already suggested, becomes that of sticking with the policies on which the group has already concurred, even if those policies are working out badly and have some horrible consequences that may disturb the conscience of every member. The main criterion used to judge the morality as well as the practical efficacy of the policy is group concurrence. The belief that "we are a wise and good group" extends to any decision the group makes: "Since we are a good group," the members feel, "anything we decide to do must be good."

In a sense, loyalty to the policy-making group becomes the highest form of morality for the members. That loyalty requires them to avoid raising critical issues, to avoid calling a halt to soft-headed thinking, and to avoid questioning weak arguments, even when the individual member begins to have doubts and to wonder whether they are indeed behaving in a soft-headed manner. This loyalty is one of the key characteristics of what I call groupthink.

I use the term *groupthink* as a quick and easy way to refer to a mode of thinking that people engage in when they are deeply involved in a cohesive in-group, when concurrence-seeking becomes so dominant that it tends to override critical thinking. *Groupthink* is a term of the same order as the words in the newspeak vocabulary George Orwell presents in his dismaying world of *1984*, where we find terms like *doublethink* and *crimethink*. In putting groupthink into that Orwellian class of words, I realize that it takes on an invidious connotation. Exactly such a connotation is intended since the term refers to a decline in mental efficiency and in the ability to test reality and to make moral judgments. Most of the main symptoms of groupthink arise because the members of decision-making groups avoid being too harsh in their judgments of their leader's or their colleagues' ideas. They adopt a soft line of criticism, even in their own thinking. At their meetings, all the members are amiable and seek complete concurrence on every important issue, with no bickering or conflict to spoil the cozy atmosphere.

Paradoxically, however, soft-headed groups can be extraordinarily hard hearted when it comes to dealing with out-groups or enemies. In dealing with a rival nation, policy makers in an amiable group atmosphere find it relatively easy to resort to dehumanizing solutions, such as authorizing large-scale bombing attacks on large numbers of harmless civilians in the noble cause of persuading an unfriendly government to negotiate at the peace table. An affable group of government officials is unlikely to pursue the ticklish, difficult, and controversial issues that arise when alternatives to a harsh military solution come up for discussion. Nor is there much patience for those members who call attention to moral issues, who imply that this "fine group of ours, with its humanitarianism and its high-minded principles," may be capable of adopting a course of action that is inhumane and immoral. Such cohesive groups also tend to resist new information that contradicts the shared judgments of the members. Anyone, no matter how central a member of the group, who contradicts the consensus that has already started to emerge is regarded as a deviant threatening the unity of the group.

Many other sources of human error, of course, can impair the quality of policy decisions. Some errors stem from psychological factors in the personalities of the decision makers. Also, special circumstances can create undue fatigue and other stresses that interfere with adequate decision-making. In addition, numerous institutional factors embedded in the social structure may make for inefficiency and may prevent adequate communication from knowledgeable experts. The concept of groupthink puts the finger on a source of trouble that resides neither in the single individual (as when a man's judgments suffer from his prejudices) nor in the institutional setting (as when an authoritarian leader has such enormous power over the individuals who serve on his policy-planning committees that they are intimidated into becoming sycophants). Along with these well known sources of defective judgment, we must consider what happens whenever a small body of decision makers becomes a cohesive group. We know that group psychology has its own dynamics and that interactions within a friendly group often are not conducive to critical thinking. At times, the striving for group concurrence can become so dominant that it interferes with adequate problem-solving, prevents the elaboration of alternative courses of action, and inhibits independent judgment, even when the decision makers are conscientious statesmen trying to make the best possible decisions for their country or for all of humanity.

In my case studies of cohesive policy-making committees I have repeatedly noted eight main symptoms of groupthink, several of which I have already illustrated in the foregoing discussion: (1) a shared illusion of invulnerability, which leads to an extraordinary degree of overoptimism and risk-taking; (2) manifestations of direct pressure on individuals who express disagreement with or doubt about the majority view, making it clear that their dissent is contrary to the expected behavior of loyal group members; (3) fear of disapproval for deviating from the group consensus, which leads each member to avoid voicing his misgivings and even to minimize to himself the importance of his doubts when most of the others seem to agree on a proposed course of action; (4) a shared illusion of unanimity within the group concerning all the main judgments expressed by members who speak in favor of the majority view (partly resulting from the preceding symptom, which contributes to the false assumption that any individual who remains silent during any part of the discussion is in full accord with what the others are saying); (5) stereotyped views of the enemy leaders as evil, often accompanied by the assumption that they are too weak or too stupid to deal effectively with whatever risky attempts are made to outdo them; (6) an unquestioned belief in the inherent morality of the in-group, which inclines the members to ignore the ethical or moral consequences of their decisions; (7) the emergence of self-appointed mind guards within the group—members who take it upon themselves to protect the leader and fellow members from adverse information that may prevent them from being able to continue their shared sense of complacency about the effectiveness and morality of past decisions; and (8) shared efforts to construct rationalizations in order to be able to ignore warnings and other forms of negative feedback, which, if taken seriously, would lead the members to reconsider the assumptions they continue to take for granted each time they recommit themselves to their past policy decisions.

When most or all of these interrelated symptoms are displayed by a group of executives, a detailed study of their deliberations is likely to reveal additional symptoms that are, in effect, poor decision-making practices because they lead to inadequate solutions to the problems under discussion. Among the main symptoms of inadequate problem-solving are the following:

First, the discussions are limited to a few alternative courses of action (often only two alternatives) without an initial survey of all the various alternatives that may be worthy of consideration.

Second, the group fails to reexamine the course of action initially preferred by the majority of members from the standpoint of nonobvious risks and drawbacks that had not been considered when it was originally selected.

Third, the group fails to reexamine any of the courses of action initially rejected by the majority of members from the standpoint of nonobvious gains that may have been overlooked and ways of reducing the seemingly prohibitive costs or risks that had made these alternatives appear to be inferior.

Fourth, little or no attempt is made to obtain information from experts within the same organization who may be able to supply more precise estimates of potential losses and gains to be expected from alternative courses of actions, particularly on matters about which none of the members of the group are well informed.

Fifth, selective bias is shown in the way the group reacts to factual information and relevant judgments from the mass media or from outside experts. The members show positive interest in facts and opinions that support their initially preferred policy and take up time in their meetings to discuss them, whereas they tend to ignore facts and opinions that do not support their initially preferred policy.

Sixth, the members of the group spend little time thinking about how the chosen policy or set of plans may be unintentionally hindered by bureaucratic inertia, be deliberately sabotaged by opponents, or be temporarily derailed by common accidents that happen to well laid plans; consequently, they fail to work out contingency plans to cope with setbacks that could endanger the overall success of the decision.

All six of these defects are products of groupthink. These same inadequacies can arise from other causes such as erroneous intelligence, informational overloads, fatigue, blinding prejudice, ignorance, panic. Whether produced by groupthink or by other causes, a decision that suffers from these defects has little chance of long-run success. When the group members try to implement their poorly worked out plans, they are soon shocked to find themselves caught in one new crisis after another, as they are forced to work out from scratch the solutions to vital questions about all the obstacles to be overcome—questions that should have been anticipated beforehand. Their poorly constructed decision, like a defective old auto that is starting to fall apart, is barely kept running by hastily patching it up with whatever ill-fitting spare parts happen to be at hand. For a time, the owners may loyally insist that they are still operating a solidly dependable vehicle, ignoring as long as possible each new sign that another part is starting to fail. But only extraordinary good luck can save them from the ultimate humiliation of seeing the whole thing fall so completely to pieces that it has to be abandoned as a total loss.

I am not implying that all cohesive groups necessarily suffer from groupthink. All in-groups may have a mild tendency toward groupthink, displaying one or another of the symptoms from time to time, but it need not be so dominant as to influence the quality of the final decision of the members. The term *groupthink* also does not imply that there is anything necessarily inefficient or harmful about group decisions in general. On the contrary, a group whose members have properly defined roles, with methodical procedures to follow in pursuing a critical inquiry, is probably capable of making better decisions than is any individual in the group who works on the problem alone. However, the great gains to be obtained from decision-making groups are often lost because of powerful psychological pressures that arise when the members work together, share the same set of

values, and, and, above all, face a crisis situation where everyone is
subjected to a high degree of stress. In these circumstances, as
conformity pressures begin to dominate, groupthink and its attendant deterioration in the quality of decision-making set in.

Time and again in the case studies of major historic fiascos,
I have encountered evidence that like-minded men working in
concert have a great many assets for making adequate decisions
but also are subjected to group processes that have serious liabilities. Under certain conditions, which I believe we can start to
specify, the liabilities can outweigh the assets. A central theme
of my analysis then can be summarized briefly in a somewhat
oversimplified generalization, which I offer in the spirit of Par-
kinson's laws. The main hypothesis concerning groupthink is
this: The more amiability and esprit de corps among the members of an in-group of policy makers the greater the danger that
independent critical thinking will be replaced by groupthink,
which is likely to result in irrational and dehumanizing actions
directed at out-groups.

Since this groupthink hypothesis has not yet been tested
systematically, we must regard it as merely a suggestive generalization inferred from a small number of historical case studies.
Still, one should not be inhibited, it seems to me, from drawing
tentative inferences—as long as we label them as such—concerning the conditions that promote groupthink and the potentially
effective means for preventing those conditions from arising.

Can we specify the conditions that help to prevent groupthink? Certainly not with any degree of certainty at present. But
strong indications from comparative studies of good versus poor
governmental decisions suggest a number of relevant hypotheses.
So far, I have had the opportunity to examine only a small number of policy decisions, contrasting several major fiascos with two
major decisions that provide counterpoint examples. One of the
latter was the course of action decided upon by the Kennedy
administration in October 1962, during the Cuban missile crisis.
This decision involved the same cast of characters as the Bay of
Pigs fiasco in 1961. My study of the Cuban missile crisis suggests
that groupthink tendencies can be prevented by certain leader-

ship practices that promote independent thinking. Another such counterpoint example I have looked into is the work of the small planning committees in the Truman administration that evolved the Marshall Plan in 1948. Like the White House group that developed the plan for coping with the Cuban missile crisis, these groups made realistic appraisals of how the Soviet Union and other out-groups were likely to respond to the various alternatives being considered, instead of relying on crude stereotypes and slogans.

One fundamental condition that appears to have an adverse effect on the quality of many vital decisions is secrecy. Frequently, only members of a small group of high-level officials are allowed to be in on a decision concerning the use of military force. The decision-making group is insulated from the judgments of experts and other qualified associates who, as outsiders, are not permitted to know anything about the new policies under discussion until after a final decision has been made. In the United States government there is a rule that even among men who have the highest security clearance, no one should be consulted or informed when a secret policy is up for discussion unless it is absolutely essential for him to know about it.

Small groups are highly susceptible to concurrence-seeking tendencies that interfere with critical thinking during crisis periods, especially if they restrict their discussions to the group itself. The chances of encountering effective, independent evaluations are greatest when the decision is openly discussed among varying groups who have different types of expertise, all of whom examine the decision and its probable outcomes from the standpoint of somewhat different value orientations. But when a decision is closed—confined to a small group—the chances of encountering anyone who can break up a premature emerging consensus is reduced. Similarly, insulation of the decision-making group greatly reduces the chances that unwarranted stereotypes and slogans shared by members of the group will be challenged before it is too late to avert a fiasco.

The problem of isolation from out-groups has been mentioned as a condition for guilt-free destructive behavior in Chapter Three. Here I am speaking of more than isolation from out-groups. It is a matter of isolation from other potential in-group members, such as respected associates in high positions within the government who are not members of the specific policy-making group. If brought into the meetings, these nonmembers may be capable of presenting a fresh point of view and of raising critical questions that may be overlooked by the in-group. Their comments may induce members of the group to reconsider their assumptions.

If group isolation promotes groupthink, with its consequent mindless and dehumanized policies, then we should see what may be done to help prevent insulation of the members of a policy planning group. First, each member of the planning group can be expected to discuss the deliberations with associates in his home office—assuming that he has associates who can be trusted—and then to report back to the planning group the reactions obtained from this source of relatively independent thinkers.

A second safeguard is to invite to each meeting one or more outside experts or qualified colleagues who are not core members of the policy-making group, including representatives from other branches of the government who are known to be critical thinkers, sensitive to moral issues, and capable of presenting their ideas effectively. Such outsiders were, in fact, deliberately brought into the Executive Committee meetings during the Cuban missile crisis and were encouraged to express their objections openly so that the group could debate them. This atmosphere was quite different from the one that prevailed throughout the Bay of Pigs planning sessions, which were restricted to the same small group of advisers and were dominated by the two CIA leaders who had developed the ill-fated plan. On one occasion, Chester Bowles was present as undersecretary of state to replace his chief, Rusk, who had to attend a meeting abroad. But Bowles was never asked about his reactions. He sat there silently, listening with horror to a discussion based on what he regarded as incredibly foolish and dangerous assumptions. After he left the meeting, he wrote down his objections in a memorandum to Rusk, who promptly buried it in the State Department files. In this instance, Rusk took on the role of what I call a self-appointed mind guard.

Third, a multiple-group procedure can be instituted so that instead of having only a single group work on a given major policy problem from beginning to end, responsibility is assigned to several planning and evaluation groups, each carrying out its deliberations, concurrently or successively, under a different leader. At times, the separate groups can be brought together to hammer out their differences, a procedure which would also help to reduce the chances that the decision makers will evolve a consensus based on shared miscalculations and illusory assumptions.

Now we turn to factors other than isolation that determine whether groupthink tendencies will predominate in a cohesive policy-making group. In the light of my comparative case studies, the following additional prescriptions can be added to the three already mentioned as possible antidotes for counteracting groupthink.

Fourth, new leadership procedures and traditions may be established so that the leader abstains from presenting his own position at the outset to avoid setting a norm that evokes conformity before the issues are fully explored by the members. For example, the leader may deliberately absent himself from the initial policy-making discussions, as Kennedy did when the White House Executive Committee began to meet during the Cuban missile crisis. In order to introduce this corrective procedure, of course, the leader has to be willing to renounce some of his traditional prerogatives.

Fifth, at every general meeting of the group, whenever the agenda calls for evaluation of policy alternatives, at least one member can be assigned the role of devil's advocate, to function like a good lawyer in challenging the testimony of all those who advocate the majority position. During the Cuban missile crisis, Kennedy gave his brother, the attorney general, the mission of playing devil's advocate, with seemingly excellent results in breaking up a premature consensus. When this devil's advocate's role is performed well, it requires the members of the group to

examine carefully the pros and cons of policy alternatives before
they agree upon the best course of action.

Sixth, throughout all the group meetings, each member
can be assigned the primary role of critical evaluator of policy
alternatives, a role which takes precedence over any factional loy-
alties and over the traditional forms of deference or politeness that
often incline a man to remain silent when he objects to someone
else's cherished ideas. This proposed practice, which could not be
instituted unless it were wholeheartedly approved, initiated, and
reinforced by the President and other top executives in the hierarchy, can help to counteract the spontaneous group pressures for
concurrence-seeking. It should certainly prevent an illusion of
unanimity from bolstering a premature consensus.

Seventh, whenever the policy issue involves relations with
a rival nation or organization, at least part of a session can be devoted to surveying recent warning signals from the rivals, using
special audiovisual techniques or psychodramatic role-playing, to
stimulate the policy makers to construct alternative scenarios regarding the rival's intentions. In order to counteract the members'
shared illusions of invulnerability and tendency to ignore or explain away any warning signals that interfere with a complacent
outlook, this special effort may be required to induce them to
become sharply aware of the potential risks and the need for making realistic contingency plans.

Eighth, after a preliminary consensus is reached concerning
what seems to be the best policy alternative, a special session can
be held at which every member is expected to express as vividly
as he can all his residual doubts and to rethink the entire issue
before making a definitive choice. This second-chance meeting
should be held before the group commits itself by taking a final
vote.

Two main conclusions are suggested by the case studies of
foreign policy decisions: along with other sources of error in
decision-making, the symptoms of groupthink are likely to occur
from time to time within cohesive small groups of policy makers;
and the most corrosive symptoms of groupthink are preventable
by eliminating group insulation, overdirective leadership prac-

tices, and other conditions that foster premature concurrence-seeking. Awareness of these tentative conclusions can be useful to those who participate in policy-making groups if it inclines them to consider introducing one or another of the antidote prescriptions just listed—providing, of course, that they are aware of the costs in time and effort and realize that they must also watch for other disadvantages before they decide to adopt any of the prescriptions as standard operating procedure. A collaborative team of practical-minded men who know their organization from the inside, working with social scientists who know operations research from the inside, may find a relatively painless way to carry out field studies on the feasibility of the most promising procedures and to assess their overall effectiveness. The objective evaluations made by a team of administrators and social scientists ought to be able to weed out the ineffective procedures and provide solid evidence to keep the good ones going.

Sometimes it may even be useful for one of the policy makers to ask at the right moment, before a decision is definitely made, "Are we allowing ourselves to become victims of groupthink?" I am not proposing that this question should be placed on the agenda or that the members should try to conduct a group therapy session, comparable to parlor psychoanalysis. Rather, I have in mind enabling some policy makers to adopt a psychological set that inclines them to raise critical questions whenever there are signs of undue complacency or premature consensus. One such question has to do with the consensus itself. A leader who is aware of the symptoms of groupthink, for example, may say, "Before we assume that everyone agrees with this proposed strategy, let's hear from those who haven't said anything yet, so that we can get all points of view onto the table." In addition to this common sense application, some ingenious procedures may be worked out or spontaneously improvised so that the symptoms of groupthink are counteracted by participants who know about the groupthink hypothesis without constantly having to remind the group of it.

With these considerations in mind, I suggest that awareness of shared illusions, rationalizations, and other symptoms fostered by small-group interaction may curtail the influence of groupthink in policy-making groups, including those that meet in the White House. Here we may apply George Santayana's well known adage: "Those who cannot remember the past are condemned to repeat it." Perhaps with a better understanding of group dynamics we can avoid repeating the history of the Vietnam war, with its indiscriminate destruction of native villages and its My Lai massacres.

PART II

A*fter the social inter-
actions that lead to social destructiveness we next explore
some of its psychological and cultural dynamics. Whether one
conceives of culture as broader than society or personality
as deeper, neither field can replace social analysis, but both
can enrich it enormously, in part by suggesting certain long-
range remedies for destructive patterns. Opening this part of*
Sanctions for Evil *with a speculative and informal essay, Fritz
Redl examines a number of the excuses that people offer for
taking part in destructive acts and ways in which the superego is
relieved of its normal duties. Viola W. Bernard and her colleagues
show how dehumanization, regarded here as a composite psychological defense, works to increase the danger of mass social destructiveness, as in nuclear war; and Bernard L. Diamond
discusses an extreme type of dehumanization, one in which an
inability to identify with other people may lead to sociopathic*

90

PSYCHOLOGICAL
SOURCES

behavior. (In the Epilogue we return to the complex issue of dehumanization.) In the remaining chapters of this part, contributors consider in detail the links between personality and society, in particular some patterns which subvert democratic values. Nevitt Sanford, one of the authors of The Authoritarian Personality, *describes the relation between the psychological syndrome called authoritarianism and the social phenomenon of destructiveness. In explaining the expressive function of systems of social segregation, the psychological advantage that dominant groups take over their "inferiors," George De Vos explores some of the motives of racism other than economic exploitation, the kind emphasized in Marxist theory. The examples used in this part of* Sanctions for Evil *include a massacre, sociopathic crimes, caste systems, authoritarian political appeals, and the possibility of nuclear war; what ties them together is a complex of psychological dispositions that encourage social destructiveness.*

CHAPTER 7

The Superego in Uniform

Fritz Redl

I know nothing about the military, about political strategy, about economics, or about political science, and I have no firsthand data on massacres such as the one at My Lai. All I am using as a basis for this chapter are the clinical vapors arising from the behavior of delinquent or sick kids —or of normal kids in the grip of growing pains. By clinical vapors I mean basic unconscious human characteristics and cramps, which may not be visible to the naked eye but which underlie human motivation often beyond recognition. I am discussing here the puzzle of group psychology and its impact on the personality of the individual, especially under unusual circumstances. This topic bears not only on massacres but also, as my ex-

93

amples will suggest, on many other occurrences, some of them familiar to everyone.

Let us first consider how the initiatory act can serve as a kind of magic exculpation. Just to make sure we get together on what I have in mind, let me present three vignettes:

Slide 1. Schoolboy, dragging his feet on the way home. He got himself into trouble by some silly mischief, some prank that was supposed to be funny but did not quite turn out that way. His first defense, when confronted by his old man is "honest, I didn't start it! It was Teddy who did it first!" Now, if his old man is on his toes, he will not let him get away with it, for Teddy's initiatory act is no excuse. However, when the old man talks it over with Mama in the evening, he suddenly realizes that although it is no excuse, it is an explanation. And worse, since it is their kid, both agree that "the trouble is that our nice little kid runs around with bad company. We better forbid him to play with that Teddy kid." The lesson is that in a psychological sense, the fact that somebody else did it first is more than a thin alibi. It is a guilt-assuaging fact. Had Teddy not done it first, the parents would have been able to assume that their son's superego would have been good enough to keep him out of it altogether.

Slide 2. In the Middle Ages, or so some historians seem to have told me, if a bunch of thieves was caught red-handed, the leader was hanged on the spot, but the rest of them got away with minor punishments. They only had a hand chopped off or something of that sort. Even the law accepted the fact that the others were less guilty. The one who does it first therefore fulfills three services for the rest of the gang: He sets the example. By his own behavior he justifies to the others what is being done; they are then exempt from guilt up to a point. And he promises that, if caught, he will take all responsibility upon himself, not only all the risks; they can get away with less punishment, and they can even blame him for having started it to begin with.

Slide 3. Adolf Hitler had a way of saying things which to the liberals and intellectuals of his time seemed downright idiotic. Repeatedy, when threatening the whole world with conquest, he declared, "I take the responsibility upon myself." What a silly statement, we used to say. And how easy to talk that way when nobody could take him up on it. However, Hitler was right, we were wrong. By declaring himself the all-responsible leader and instigator, he did, psychologically speaking, legitimize whatever anybody else under his command did, and the others could thus consider themselves exempt from guilt. He did make it possible for their private superegos to go to sleep and thereby to participate in whatever action he demanded. And, moreover, he gave them the implicit right to blame him for everything if things went wrong.

If we make just one slight modification and change temporal priority (did it first) to rank-and-power priority (being in command), the reality of human unconscious motivation is that the initiatory act does in fact relieve the individual supergo of its bothersome task, no matter how irrational this may seem. This relief is not logical, but it is psychologically real. And it is about time for us to remember that psychological realities, crazy as they sound, are as real and fatal as the realities of our hardware world.

The supergo can be relieved of its task in another way, which I call depersonalization through the tribal dance. When tribal rituals are performed, the participants put on a uniform. Never mind that in our anthropological pictures and movies what we see does not look like what we would call a uniform at all. It may be face paint, a hairdo—even that uniform is not as new as you think—or preferably a mask. Besides the usual and well known reasons for donning this uniform it seems to serve two special purposes: to render the actors incognito and to make sure that everybody knows this behavior is acceptable only under temporary conditions and needs to be terminated when the show is over. For the duration of the religious rite or the carnival the actors are not themselves but primarily faceless members of a collective enterprise. In short, their civilian superegos do not have to be worried, ashamed, or embarrassed, or to make them feel guilty for whatever is done while the ceremony lasts. (Remember what people sometimes do when they go to a convention in another town or when they dress up as tourists and go to a faraway place.)

The mere puting on of a uniform creates a switch in the role of the personal superego. Behavior which otherwise would be guilt ridden is now OK. However, putting on a uniform brings additional burdens. The collective superego, which thus replaces the personal one, has some special demands too. Certain things which the id would be permitted to do if the superego had stayed in its civilian role are now out. The special limitations the collective superego imposes explain the rage of the very people who demand killings exculpated by the wearing of a uniform when killing occurs for which the uniform is not an official excuse.

For the war in Vietnam this point has special implications. If all the opponents in warfare and half of the allies are of a race different from ours, then the problem of the uniform gets confusing. Psychologically speaking, for the Vietnam warrior of American origin, at first sight all the native population wears the enemy uniform, even while they run around in their civilian roles.

Our example of tribal rituals provides another analogy to events in Vietnam. In the extremely cruel sacrificial rituals of some tribes—the Aztecs, for instance—the amount of terrible suffering imposed upon the victim seems hard to comprehend. Rites like the defloration and killing of an innocent virgin picked at random and prepared for the ordeal by a variety of ritualistic acts seem to us awful beyond comprehension. However, to the participants, the goal of the performance was not cruelty at all, although the act obviously also offered a chance for sadistic impulses to sneak their gratifications in. Both parties, the tormentor as well as the tormented, participated in one and the same performance, through what I call the sacrificialization of the victim. They were like actors on the same stage, the tormentor and his victim taking part in a script bigger than either of them. What happens to the victim in that situation is not just killing. In the process of being killed on an altar, the victim is elevated from the mass of ordinary members of the population at large and becomes something very special. Her death assumes a meaning way beyond the lives of the participants.

In an unusual mass slaughter of civilians occurring in times of war, the victims are no longer perceived as just that many people killed. Soldiers do get reduced to simple statistics under those conditions, but the victims have it better. From simple casualties, they become victims, their death is sacrificialized. They may be dead, but their death is different from just being run over by a car and for this reason seems incredible and unnatural to us. In the moment of death they become similar to the brave enemy soldier whom one wipes out but respects in the process. In short, in hand-to-hand combat of a sort, the basic symbolic meaning of behavior changes. The victim—unimportant and miserable though he may have been in civilian life—is elevated to having a role in regular warfare. And, although his naked body may lie distorted in a ditch, our image of him comes closer to that of the official representative of the enemy in uniform.

The implication is that our indignation and righteous wrath displayed in such cases are not entirely genuine or due to our pity and sympathy for the human suffering endured. I have a sneaking suspicion that some of the indignation displayed by otherwise quite hawkish people is due to anger at having the basic code of the uniform of the soldier violated and at having to accept the people killed in this way as enemy soldiers who deserve respect.

There is another and equally fascinating side to this picture. The very perpetrator of the massacre, the tormentor, usually, if things become official and public, ends up as the victim of a similar collective purification ceremony himself. It would be hard to call the My Lai tormentors innocent, and they may well deserve whatever punishment they receive. But they do not deserve to be made the sole carriers of a collective guilt. What happened to them was complicated. Their individual superegos had been knocked out or they would not have been ready to kill anybody at all, not even a soldier of the enemy force. In place of their individual superegos, the soldiers were governed by the collective superego, the superego in uniform. According to this authority, killing in war not only is permissible but is a duty to be done even when feelings of personal pity or qualms of conscience may tempt soldiers to get soft in special circumstances. And what makes the perpetrators of a civilian massacre so guilty in official eyes is not that they killed but that they committed a particular kind of killing forbidden by the uniform and did so in a situation where they were not ordered to and would not have been allowed to, even under a rather unsentimental behavior code. The soldiers are being punished by the very value system that taught them to kill.

So, there is not as much leeway for justified moral indignation at the individual perpetrators as there seemed to be at first sight. Why then the enormous delight of the collective in its display of punitive wrath? This response seems to me to indicate that when it comes to repairing the injustices done to the original victims of atrocities, we are engaged not so much in an expression of pity for them as in eagerness for another spectacle; we can now use the perpetrators as props in a separate justification rite. And even better than that, after they are duly punished and the victims are avenged, we can happily go back to legitimate warfare again with even less need to examine that part of the human tragedy than we felt before. In other words, it is not only the cruelty of the tormentors we want to punish; we also want to make sure that, by punishing them appropriately, we exempt ourselves from our contribution to the whole mess. Since we are lucky enough to find a deviant offender who can now safely be picked as a scapegoat for the community at large, the system is reconfirmed as righteous.

The reasons for angry indignation against the perpetrators can also be found in another phenomenon. Among the most serious casualties of all warfare is the clarity of human thought. Among the first signs of serious personality decay is an obvious decay of logic, the reprimitivization of thinking. From the many and too numerous forms of primitive thinking I illustrate only a few, using some of my adolescent toughies for examples, just to make the point. At a camp for delinquent kids, I am in session with one. "What made you steal that wallet from Bobby?" I say. "He has less money than you and you even admit you like him and have nothing against him personally." Kid (indignantly): "What are you talking about? I ain't mad at him! But somebody swiped my wallet two weeks ago, so of course I want one back!" Consider another example. Kid: "Boy, are we going to give it to those bastards of the Jefferson Intermediate next week! You just wait and see!" I: "But what have they done to you?" Kid: "Oh, not they, but two months ago a group of them beat up on one of ours." I: "What for?" Kid: "Oh, he was a fool. He went into their territory and started up with their girls. But we will take care of them, but good."

Need I go further into contemporary details or even remind you that not only delinquent teenagers can sink that low? Otherwise logical, self-respecting, and honorable people, in times of war or mayhem of any sort, take refuge in this form of reprimitivized thought. And although such thinking sounds illogical, it is quite satisfying to the participants at the time. Any usable cause can be substituted for the real cause, and the greatest advantage of such promiscuous causation is that you can change the personnel involved and switch to substitutes or even symbolic substitute targets. This concept of collective reprisal is the most vicious and irrational of many of the forms of primitive thought. In warfare, even in the most restrained and technicalized warfare, regression to this form of thought is collectively legitimized so much that even the civilian mind, not exposed to the stress and strain of danger situations, drifts into accepting it without experiencing the natural disgust with illogical thought.

In the process, we feel that anybody who made us be that illogical deserves to be punished for his deeds. It is my hunch that much of the angry indignation the intellectual liberal feels against the perpetrators of displaced revenge is, among other things, panic at the awareness of how close he could come to regressing into primitive thinking himself.

Let us now turn to the question of what lies behind the facade of "shocked surprise." I have run time and again into parents whose kids have "split" long ago and have not missed any of the most pernicious drugs or have even been forced into pushing them. They are running around in school and at home quite obviously under the influence, and nobody seems to be concerned. If they are seen in a school corridor with the visible signs of fever or whooping cough, nobody hesitates to send them to the doctor fast. But since it may be drugs, even the principal is afraid to interfere, for the parents may not like it, and how can he have proof?

Then, they turn up on stretchers. It may take a week or more, if we are successful at all, to bring them back to where the vegetables look more like kids again. At the stretcher point we meet with the most vehement shocked surprise, and not only from their parents. "How could it be possible? We thought this was just adolescence after all because they are honestly involved in a

good cause. And, besides, they are not just some unfortunate speci-
mens from the dregs of mankind! They are our own, most of
them intelligent, gifted, or unusually talented."

Whenever I meet this kind of shocked surprise, I become
suspicious. Nothing is wrong with surprise as such; the most
healthy reaction of the human mind is waking up to the fact that
maybe all is not as simple as we had assumed before. In heavy
overdoses, however, shocked surprise is often a way of warding
off the impact of new findings on theories that have begun to rot.
If we take our surprise seriously, we need to look at our premises,
which must have been outdated or wrong to begin with. If we
indulge in prolonged orgies of shocked surprise, we hope to hang
on to our wrong premises by making sure that the counter-evi-
dence remains the surprising exception which only reconfirms our
old assumptions after all.

For example, our shocked surprise at the My Lai incident,
so happily displayed in spite of mounting evidence to the contrary, means only one thing: We hope for dear life that we can
hang on to the assumption that nothing is wrong with organized
war itself; those unfortunate, occasional, and understandable
breakdowns of specifically vulnerable individuals are at fault. Violence Commission after Violence Commission has run into trouble
in defining violence in a desperate attempt to leave the phenomenon of war out of it. Even under the shadow of the nuclear bomb,
we still hang on to the belief that war can be an acceptable form
of problem-solving and that the push button dropping of the bomb
on Hiroshima or Dresden has nothing at all to do with a single
soldier who goes berserk and suddenly starts shooting women and
kids.

Behind the surprise maintained for too long lies the hope
that warfare with all the fancy new hardware maintained by the
official collective superego in uniform can remain a justifiable
means for the settling of collective disputes and that we can remain safe from misfiring outbursts such as the My Lai massacre,
viewing them as unfortunate exceptions where somebody's id suddenly went berserk, even though his superego was still in uniform.

Let's stop being surprised. The American human is not all
that different from other humans, and given emergency condi-

tions or miserable decay of organizational designs, his defense against human feeling and his mechanisms for legitimizing evil will obviously be as effective and terrific in their impact as they are anywhere else. The only surprising thing is our surprise itself. In the technological era we have entered, the whole phenomenon of good old war is out; the human species cannot afford it anymore. This is where the challenge lies, not primarily in the individual cases of breakdown of uniformed morale.

CHAPTER

Dehumanization

Viola W. Bernard, Perry Ottenberg,
Fritz Redl

We conceive of dehumanization as a particular type of psychic defense mechanism and consider its increasing prevalence to be a social consequence of the nuclear age. By this growth it contributes, we believe, to heightening the risks of nuclear extermination.

Dehumanization as a defense against painful or overwhelming emotions entails a decrease in a person's sense of his own individuality and in his perception of the humanness of other people. The misperceiving of others ranges from viewing them *en bloc* as "subhuman" or "bad human" (a long-familiar component of group prejudice) to viewing them as "nonhuman," as though they were inanimate items or "dispensable supplies." As such, their maltreatment or even their destruction may be carried out or acquiesced in with relative freedom from the restraints of conscience or feelings of brotherhood.

In our view, dehumanization is not a wholly new mental mechanism but rather a composite psychological defense which draws selectively on other well known defenses, including unconscious denial, repression, depersonalization, isolation of affect, and compartmentalization (the elimination of meaning by disconnecting related mental elements and walling them off from each other). Recourse to dehumanization as a defense against stresses of inner conflict and external threat is especially favored by impersonal aspects of modern social organization, along with such special technological features of nuclear weapons as their unprecedented destructive power and the distance between push button and victim.

We recognize that many adaptive, as well as maladaptive,[1]* uses of self-protective dehumanization are requisite in multiple areas of contemporary life. As a maladaptive defense in relation to war, however, the freedom from fear which it achieves by apathy or blindness to implication of the threat of nuclear warfare itself increases the actuality of that threat: the masking of its true urgency inactivates motive power for an all-out effort to devise creative alternatives for resolving international conflict. Dehumanization also facilitates the tolerating of mass destruction through bypassing those psychic inhibitions against the taking of human life that have become part of civilized man. Such inhibitions cannot be called into play when those who are to be destroyed have been divested of their humanness. The magnitudes of annihilation that may be perpetrated with indifference would seem to transcend those carried out in hatred and anger. This was demonstrated by the impersonal, mechanized efficiency of extermination at the Nazi death camps.

The complex psychological phenomenon which we call dehumanization includes two distinct but interrelated series of processes: *self-directed dehumanization* relates to self-image and denotes the diminution of an individual's sense of his own human-

Reprinted by permission of the publisher from V. W. Bernard, P. Ottenberg, and F. Redl, "Dehumanization: A Composite Psychological Defense in Relation to Modern War," in M. Schwebel (Ed.), *Behavioral Science and Human Survival* (Palo Alto, Calif.: Science and Behavior Books, 1965).
 * Notes for this chapter start on p. 340.

ness; *object-directed dehumanization* refers to his perceiving others as lacking in those attributes that are considered to be most human. Despite the differences between these two in their origins and intrapsychic relationships within overall personality development and psychodynamic functioning, both forms of dehumanization, compounded from parts of other defenses, become usable by the individual for emotional self-protection. These two forms of dehumanization are mutually reinforcing: reduction in the fullness of one's feelings for other human beings, whatever the reason for this, impoverishes one's sense of self; any lessening of the humanness of one's self-image limits one's capacity for relating to others.

It seems to us that the extensive increase of dehumanization today is causally linked to aspects of institutional changes in contemporary society and to the transformed nature of modern war. The mushrooming importance in today's world of technology, automation, urbanization, specialization, various forms of bureaucracy, mass media, and the increased influences of nationalistic, totalitarian, and other ideologies have all been widely discussed by many scholars. The net long-term implications of these processes, whether constructive or destructive, are beyond the scope of this [chapter], and we do not regard ourselves qualified to evaluate them.

We are concerned here, however, with certain of their more immediate effects on people. It would seem that for a vast portion of the world's population, elements of these broad social changes contribute to feelings of anonymity, impersonality, separation from the decision-making processes, and a fragmented sense of one's integrated social roles, and also to pressure on the individual to constrict his affective range to some machinelike task at hand. Similarly, the average citizen feels powerless indeed with respect to control over fateful decisions about nuclear attack or its aftermath.

The consequent sense of personal unimportance and relative helplessness, socially and politically, on the part of so many people specifically inclines them to adopt dehumanization as a preferred defense against many kinds of painful, unacceptable, and unbearable feelings referable to their experiences, inclinations, and behavior. *Self-directed dehumanization* empties the individual of human emotions and passions. It is paradoxical that one of its major dynamic purposes is protection against feeling the anxieties, frustrations, and conflicts associated with the "cog-in-a-big-machine" self-image into which people feel themselves pushed by socially induced pressures. Thus, it tends to fulfill the very threat that it seeks to prevent.

These pervasive reactions predispose one even more to regard other people or groups as less than human or even nonhuman. We distinguish among several different types and gradations of *object-directed dehumanization*. Thus, the failure to recognize in others their full complement of human qualities may be either partial or relatively complete. Partial dehumanization includes the misperceiving of members of "out-groups," *en masse,* as subhuman, bad human, or superhuman; as such, it is related to the psychodynamics of group prejudice. It protects the individual from the guilt and shame he would otherwise feel from primitive or antisocial attitudes, impulses, and actions that he directs—or allows others to direct—toward those he manages to perceive in these categories: if they are subhumans they have not yet reached full human status on the evolutionary ladder and, therefore, do not merit being treated as human; if they are bad humans, their maltreatment is justified since their defects in human qualities are their own fault. The latter is especially true if they are seen as having superhuman qualities as well, for it is one of the curious paradoxes of prejudice that both superhuman and debased characteristics are ascribed simultaneously to certain groups in order to justify discrimination or aggression against them. The foreigner, for instance, is seen at once as "wicked, untrustworthy, dirty," and "uncanny, powerful, and cunning." Similarly, according to the canons of race prejudice, contradictory qualities of exceptional prowess and extraordinary defect—ascribed to Orientals, Negroes, Jews, or any other group—together make them a menace toward whom customary restraints on behavior do not obtain. The main conscious emotional concomitants of partial dehumanization, as with prejudice, are hostility and fear.

In its more complete form, however, object-directed dehumanization entails a perception of other people as nonhumans

—as statistics, commodities, or interchangeable pieces in a vast "numbers game." Its predominant emotional tone is that of indifference, in contrast to the (sometimes strong) feelings of partial dehumanization, together with a sense of *noninvolvement in the actual or foreseeable vicissitudes* of others. Such apathy has crucial psychosocial implications. Among these—perhaps the most important today—is its bearing on how people tolerate the risks of mass destruction by nuclear war.

Although this communication is primarily concerned with the negative and maladaptive aspects of dehumanization, we recognize that it also serves important adaptive purposes in many life situations. In this respect, it resembles other mental mechanisms of defense. Some of the ingredients of dehumanization are required for the effective mastery of many tasks in contemporary society. Thus, in crises such as natural disasters, accidents, or epidemics in which people are injured, sick, or killed, psychic mechanisms are called into play which divest the victims of their human identities, so that feelings of pity, terror, or revulsion can be overcome. Without such selective and transient dehumanization, these emotional reactions would interfere with the efficient and responsible performance of what has to be done, whether it be first aid, surgery, rescue operation, or burial.

Certain occupations in particular require such selectively dehumanized behavior.[2] Examples of these include law enforcement (police, judges, lawyers, prison officials); medicine (physicians, nurses, and ancillary personnel); and, of course, national defense (military leaders, strategists, fighting personnel). Indeed, some degree of adaptive dehumanization seems to be a basic requirement for effective participation in any institutional process. Almost every professional activity has some specific aspect that requires the capacity for appropriate detachment from full emotional responsiveness and the curtailment, at least temporarily, of those everyday human emotional exchanges that are not central to the task at hand or which might, if present, impede it. The official at the window who stamps the passport may be by nature a warm and friendly man, but, in the context of his job, the emigrant's hopes or fears lie outside his emotional vision.

Margaret Bourke-White, the noted photographer, was at

Buchenwald at the end of World War II as a correspondent. Her account of herself at that time aptly describes the adaptive use of dehumanization, both self-directed and object-directed: "People often ask me how it is possible to photograph such atrocities. . . . I have to work with a veil over my mind. In photographing the murder camps, the protective veil was so tightly drawn that I hardly knew what I had taken until I saw prints of my own photographs. I believe many correspondents worked in the same self-imposed stupor. One has to or it is impossible to stand it." [3]

The only occasions to date on which nuclear bombs have been used in warfare took place when the "baby bombs" were dropped on the civilian populations of Hiroshima and Nagasaki. Robert Jay Lifton has reported on reactions among the Hiroshima survivors, as well as his own, as investigator.[4] His observations are particularly valuable to us since, as a research pychiatrist, he was especially qualified both to elicit and to evaluate psychodynamic data. According to the survivors whom he interviewed, at first one experienced utter horror at the sudden, strange scene of mass deaths, devastation, dreadful burns, and skin stripped from bodies. They could find no words to convey fully these initial feelings. But then each described how, before long, the horror would almost disappear. One would see terrible sights of human beings in extreme agony and yet feel nothing. The load of feeling from empathic responsiveness had become too much to endure; all one could do was to try to survive.

Lifton reports that during the first few such accounts he felt profoundly shocked, shaken, and emotionally spent. These effects gradually lessened, however, so that be became able to experience the interviews as scientific work rather than as repeated occasions of vicarious agony. For both the survivors and the investigator, the "task" provided a focus of concentration and of circumscribed activity as a means of quelling disturbing emotions.

In these instances, the immediate adaptive value of dehumanization as a defense is obvious. It remains open to question, however, whether a further, somewhat related, finding of Lifton's will in the long run prove to be adaptive or maladaptive. He learned that many people in Japan and elsewhere cannot bear to look at pictures of Hiroshima and even avoid the museum in which they are displayed. There is avoidance and denial of the whole issue which not infrequently leads to hostility toward the A-bomb victims themselves or toward anyone who expresses concern for these or future victims. May not *this* kind of defense reaction deflect the determination to seek ways of preventing nuclear war?

We believe that the complex mechanism of dehumanization urgently needs to be recognized and studied because its use as a defense has been stepped up so tremendously in recent times and because of the grave risks it entails as the price for short-term relief. This [chapter] represents only a preliminary delineation, with main attention to its bearing on the nuclear threat.[5]

Many people, by mobilizing this form of ego defense, manage to avoid or to lessen the emotional significance for themselves of today's kind of war. Only a very widespread and deeply rooted defense could ward off the full import of the new reality with which we live: that warfare has been transformed by modern weaponry into something mankind has never experienced before and that in all-out nuclear war there can be no "victory" for anyone.

The extraordinary complacency with which people manage to shield themselves against fully realizing the threat of nuclear annihilation cannot be adequately explained, we think, by denial and the other well studied psychological defense mechanisms. This is what has led us to trace out dehumanization as a composite defense, which draws upon a cluster of familiar defenses, magnifying that fraction of each which is most specifically involved with the humanness of one's self-image and the perception of others. It operates against such painful feelings as fear, inadequacy, compassion, revulsion, guilt, and shame. As with other mental mechanisms of defense, its self-protective distortions of realistic perceptions occur, for the most part, outside of awareness.

The extent to which dehumanization takes place consciously or unconsciously, although of considerable interest to us, is not relevant enough to this discussion to warrant elaboration. This also holds true for questions about why dehumanization as such has not hitherto received more attention and study in clinical psychiatry.[6] At least one possible reason might be mentioned, however. Most defense mechanisms were not studied originally in relation to such issues as war and peace, national destiny, or group survival. Instead, they came under scrutiny, during the course of psychotherapy, as part of the idiosyncratic pathology of individual patients. This could have obscured the recognition of their roles in widespread collective reactions.

In order to avoid confusion we should also mention that the term *dehumanization* as we are using it refers to a concept that is different from and not connected in meaning with the words *humane* and *humanitarian*. "Inhumane" cruelty causes suffering; maladaptive dehumanization, as we point out, may also lead to suffering. Yet even these seemingly similar results are reached by very different routes; to equate them would be a mistake. A surgeon, for example, is treating his patient humanely when, by his dehumanization, he blots out feelings of either sympathy or hostility that might otherwise interfere with his surgical skill during an operation.

No one, of course, could possibly retain his mental health and carry on the business of life if he remained constantly aware of, and empathically sensitive to, all the misery and injustice that there are in the world. But this very essentiality of dehumanization, as with other defenses, makes for its greatest danger: that the constructive self-protection it achieves will cross the ever-shifting boundaries of adaptiveness and become destructive, to others as well as to the self. In combination with other social factors already mentioned, the perfection of modern techniques for automated killing on a global scale engenders a marked increase in the incidence of dehumanization. Correspondingly, there is intensified risk that this collective reaction will break through the fragile and elusive dividing line that separates healthy ego-supportive dehumanization from the maladaptive callousness and apathy that prevent people from taking those realistic actions which are within their powers to protect human rights and human lives.

A "vicious cycle" relationship would thus seem to obtain between dehumanization as a subjective phenomenon and its objective consequences. Conscience and empathy, as sources of guilt and compassion, pertain to human beings; they can be evaded if the human element in the victims of aggression is first sufficiently obscured. The aggressor is thereby freed from conscience-linked restraints, with injurious objective effects on other individuals, groups, or nations. The victims in turn respond, subjectively, by resorting even more to self-protective dehumanization, as did the Hiroshima survivors whom Lifton interviewed.

One might argue, and with some cogency, that similar conversion of enemies into pins on a military map has been part of war psychology throughout history, so are we not therefore belaboring the obvious? The answer lies in the fundamental changes, both quantitative and qualitative, that nuclear weapons have made in the meaning of war. In fact, the very term *war*, with its preatomic connotations, has become something of an outmoded misnomer for the nuclear threat which now confronts us. "Modern war"—before Hiroshima—reflected, as a social institution, many of the social and technological developments which we have already noted as conducive to increased dehumanization. But with the possibility of instantaneously wiping out the world's population—or a very large section of it—the extent of dehumanization as well as its significance for human survival have both been abruptly and tremendously accelerated.

In part, this seems to be due to the overtaxing of our capacity really to comprehend the sudden changes in amplitudes that have become so salient. In addition to the changed factors of *distance, time,* and *magnitude* in modern technology, there is the push button nature of today's weaponry and the *indirectness* of releasing a rocket barrage upon sites halfway around the world, all of which lie far outside our range of previous experience. When we look out of an airplane window, the earth below becomes a toy, the hills and valleys reduced to abstractions in our mental canvas; but we do not conceive of ourselves as a minute part of some moving speck in the sky—which is how we appear to people on the ground. Yet it is precisely such reciprocal awareness that is required if we are to maintain a balanced view of our actual size and vulnerability. Otherwise, perceptual confusion introduces a mechanistic and impersonal quality into our reactions.

The thinking and feeling of most people have been unable as yet to come to grips with the sheer expansion of numbers and the frightening shrinkage of space which present means of transportation and communication entail. The news of an animal run over by a car, a child stuck in a well, or the preventable death of one individual evokes an outpouring of sympathetic response and upsets the emotional equanimity of many; yet reports of six million Jews killed in Nazi death camps or of a hundred thousand Japanese killed in Hiroshima and Nagasaki may cause but moderate uneasiness. Arthur Koestler has put it poignantly, "Statistics don't bleed; it is the detail which counts. We are unable to embrace the total process with our awareness; we can only focus on little lumps of reality." [7]

It is this unique combination of psychosocial and situational factors that seems particularly to favor the adoption of the composite defense we have called "dehumanization"—and this in turn acts to generate more and more of the same. The new aspects of time, space, magnitude, speed, automation, distance, and irreversibility are not yet "hooked up" in the psychology of man's relationships to his fellow man or to the world he inhabits. Most people feel poorly equipped, conceptually, to restructure their accustomed picture of the world, all of a sudden, in order to make it fit dimensions so alien to their lifelong learning. Anxiety aroused by this threat to one's orientation adds to the inner stress that seeks relief through the defense.

We are confronted with a *lag in our perceptual and intellectual development* so that the enormity of the new reality, with its potential for both destructive and constructive human consequences, becomes blurred in our thinking and feeling. The less elastic our capacity to comprehend meaningfully new significances, the more we cling to dehumanization, unable to challenge its fallacies through knowledge and reason. Correspondingly, the greater our reliance on dehumanization as a mechanism for coping with life, the less readily can the new facts of our existence be integrated into our full psychic functioning since so many of its vital components, such as empathy, have been shunted aside, stifled, or obscured.

Together, in the writers' opinion, these differently caused but mutually reinforcing cognitive and emotional deficiencies seriously intensify the nuclear risk; latent psychological barriers against the destruction of millions of people remain unmobilized and hence ineffective for those who feel detached from the flesh and blood implications of nuclear war. No other mechanism seems to fit so well the requirements of this unprecedented internal and external stress. Dehumanization, with its impairment of our personal involvement, allows us to "play chess with the planets."

Whether it be adaptive or maladaptive, dehumanization brings with it, as we have noted, a temporary feeling of relief and illusion of problems solved or at least postponed or evaded. Whatever the ultimate effects of this psychic maneuver on our destiny, however, it would seem to be a wise precaution to try to assess some of its dangerous possibilities. Several overlapping aspects of maladaptive dehumanization may be outlined briefly and in oversimplified form, as follows.

Increased emotional distance from other human beings. Under the impact of this defense, one stops identifying with others by seeing them as essentially similar to oneself in basic human qualities. Relationships to others become stereotyped, rigid, and, above all, unexpressive of mutuality. People in "out-groups" are apt to be reacted to *en bloc;* feelings of concern for them have become anesthetized.

George Orwell illustrates this aspect of dehumanization in writing of his experience as a patient.[8] His account also serves as an example of the very significant hazard, already mentioned, whereby professionally adaptive uses of this defense (as in medical education and patient care) are in danger of passing that transition point beyond which they become maladaptive and so defeat their original purpose.

Later in the day the tall, solemn, black-bearded doctor made his rounds, with an intern and a troop of students following at his heels, but there were about sixty of us in the ward, and it was evident that he had other wards to attend to as well. There were many beds past which he walked day after day, sometimes followed by imploring cries. On the other hand, if you had some disease with which the students wanted to familiarize themselves, you got plenty of attention of a kind. I myself, with an exceptionally fine specimen of a bronchial rattle, sometimes had as many as a dozen students queuing up to listen to my chest. It was a very queer feeling—queer, I mean because of their intense interest in learning their job, together with a seeming lack of any perception that the patients were human beings. It is strange to relate, but sometimes as some young student stepped forward to take his turn at manipulating you, he would be actually tremulous with excitement, like a boy who has at last got his hands on some expensive piece of machinery. And then ear after ear . . . pressed against your back, relays of fingers solemnly but clumsily tapping, and not from any one of them did you get a word of conversation or a look direct in your face. As a nonpaying patient, in the uniform nightshirt, you were primarily a specimen, a thing I did not resent but could never quite get used to.

Diminished sense of personal responsibility for the consequences of one's actions. Ordinarily, for most people, the advocacy of or participation in the wholesale slaughter and maiming of their fellow human beings is checked by opposing feelings of guilt, shame, or horror. Immunity from these feelings may be gained, however, by a self-automatizing detachment from a sense of *personal* responsibility for the outcome of such actions, thereby making them easier to carry out. (A dramatic version of the excuse "I was only carrying out orders" was offered by Adolf Eichmann at his trial.)

One "safe" way of dealing with such painful feelings is to focus only on one's fragmented job and ignore its many ramifications. By blocking out the ultimately destructive purpose of a military bombing action, for instance one's component task therein may become a source of ego-acceptable gratification, as from any successful fulfillment of duty, mastery of a hard problem, or achievement of a dangerous feat. The B-29 airplane that dropped the atomic bomb on Hiroshima was named Enola Gay, after the mother of one of its crew members. This could represent the psychological defense of displacing human qualities from the population to be bombed to the machine.

One of the crew members is reported to have exclaimed: "If people knew what we were doing we could have sold tickets for $100,000!" And another is said to have commented, "Colonel, that was worth the twenty-five-cent ride on the 'Cyclone' at Coney Island." [9] Such reactions, which may on the surface appear to be shockingly cynical, not only illustrate how cynicism may be used to conceal strong emotions (as seems quite likely in this instance); they also suggest how one may try to use cynicism to bolster one's dehumanization when that defense is not itself strong enough, even with its displacement of responsibility and its focusing on one's fragmented job, to overcome the intensity of one's inner "humanized" emotional protest against carrying out an act of such vast destructiveness.

Increasing involvement with procedural problems to the detriment of human needs. There is an overconcern with details of procedure, with impersonal deindividualized regulations, and with the formal structure of a practice, all of which result in shrinking the ability or willingness to personalize one's actions in the interests of individual human needs or special differences. This is, of course, the particular danger implicit in the trend toward bureaucracy that accompanies organizational units when they grow larger and larger. The task at hand is then apt to take precedence over the human cost: The individual is seen more as a means to an end than as an end in himself. Society, the corporation, the five-year plan—these become overriding goals in themselves, and the dehumanized man is turned into a cost item, tool, or energy factor serving the mass machine.

Even "scientific" studies of human behavior and development, as well as professional practices based on them, sometimes become dehumanized to a maladaptive extent.[10] Such words as *communicate, adjust, identify, relate, feel,* and even *love* can lose their personal meaningfulness when they are used as mere technical devices instead of being applied to specific human beings in specific life situations.[11] In response to the new hugeness of global problems, patterns of speech have emerged that additionally reflect dehumanized thinking. Segmented-fragmented concepts, such as "fallout problem," "civil defense," "deterrence," "first strike," "preemptive attack," "overkill," and some aspects of game theory, represent a "move-countermove" type of thinking which tends to treat the potential human victim as a statistic and to screen out the total catastrophic effect of the contemplated actions upon human lives. The content of strategy takes on an importance that is without any relation to its inevitable *results,* the defense of dehumanization having operated to block out recognition of those awesome consequences that if they could be seen, would make the strategy unacceptable. The defense, when successful, narcotizes deeper feelings so that nuclear war, as "inevitable," may be more dispassionately contemplated and its tactical permutations assayed. In the course of this, however, almost automatic counteractions of anxiety are frequently expressed through such remarks as "People have always lived on the brink of disaster," "You can't change human nature; there will have to be wars," and "We all have to die some day."

Inability to oppose dominant group attitudes or pressures. As the individual comes to feel more and more alienated and lonely in mass society, he finds it more and more difficult to place himself in opposition to the huge pressures of the "organization." Fears of losing occupational security or of attacks on one's integrity, loyalty, or family are more than most people can bear. Self-directed dehumanization is resorted to as a defense against such fears and conflicts: by joining the party, organization, or club, and thus feeling himself to be an inconspicuous particle in some large structure, he may find relief from the difficult decisions, uncertainties, and pressures of nonconformity. He may also thereby ward off those feelings of guilt that would arise out of participating in, or failing to protest against, the injustices and cruelties perpetrated by those in power. Thus, during the Nazi regime, many usually kindhearted Germans appear to have silenced their consciences by emphasizing their own insignificance and identifying with the dehumanized values of the dictatorship. This stance permitted the detached, even dutiful, disregard of their fellow citizens, which in turn gave even freer rein to the systematic official conducting of genocide.

Feelings of personal helplessness and estrangement. The realization of one's relatively impotent position in a large organization engenders anxiety [12] which dehumanization helps to cover over. The internalized perception of the self as small, helpless, and insignificant, coupled with an externalized view of "society" as huge, powerful, and unopposable, is expressed in such frequently heard comments as "The government has secret information that we don't have" or "They know what's right, who am I to question what they are doing?" or "What's the use? No one will listen to me."

The belief that the government or the military is either infallible or impregnable provides a tempting refuge because of its renunciation of one's own critical faculties in the name of those of the powerful and all-knowing leader. Such self-directed dehumanization has a strong appeal to the isolated and alienated citizen as a protective cloak to hide from himself his feelings of weakness, ignorance, and estrangement. This is particularly relevant to the psychological attraction of certain dangerous social movements. The more inwardly frightened, lonely, helpless, and humiliated people become, the greater the susceptibility of many of them to the seductive, prejudiced promises of demagoguery: the award of spurious superiority and privilege achieved by devaluing the full humanness of some other group—racial, religious, ethnic, or political. Furthermore, as an added advantage of the dehumanization "package," self-enhancing acts of discrimination and persecution against such victim groups can be carried out without tormenting or deterrent feelings of guilt since these are absorbed by the "rightness" of the demagogic leader.

In recent decades and in many countries, including our own, we have seen what human toll can be taken by this psychosocial configuration. It has entered into Hitlerism, Stalinism, U.S.A. "lynch-mobism." If it is extended to the international arena against a "dehumanized" enemy instead of an oppressed national minority, atomic weapons will now empower it to inflict immeasurably more human destruction and suffering.

The indifference resulting from that form of dehumanization which causes one to view others as inanimate objects enables one, without conscious malice or selfishness, to write off their misery, injustices, and death as something that "just couldn't be helped." As nonhumans, they are not identified with as beings essentially similar to oneself; "their" annihilation by nuclear warfare is thus not "our" concern, despite the reality that distinctions between "they" and "we" have been rendered all the more meaningless by the mutually suicidal nature of total war.

Although this type of dehumanization is relatively complete, in the sense of perceiving others as not at all human, it may occur in an individual with selective incompleteness under certain special conditions only, while his capacity for other emotional ties is preserved. This may prove socially constructive or destructive, depending on the purposes to which it is put. Thus, we have already noted how "pulling a veil" over her mind helped Bourke-White adaptively in her socially positive job of reporting atrocities. But it was compartmentalized dehumanization that also helped many to commit those very atrocities; they were able to exterminate Jews with assembly-line efficiency as the Nazi "final solution" while still retaining access to their genuine feelings of warmth for family members, friends, and associates.

These contradictory emotional qualities, often appearing side by side in the same person, are also evidenced—in the opposite direction—by outstanding deeds of heroic rescue by those who, under different circumstances, might well exhibit dehumanized behavior. Almost daily, the newspapers carry stories of exceptional altruism; individuals or whole communities devote their entire energies to the rescue of a single child, an animal, or, perhaps (in wartime), a wounded enemy soldier. What accounts for the difference between this kind of response to the plight of others and that of dehumanized callousness? How are the adaptive humanized processes released?

One research approach might consist of the detailed description and comparative analysis of sample situations of both kinds of these collective reactions, which have such opposite social effects. A case history of community apathy which could be compared in such a study with instances of group altruism already on record was . . . provided by A. M. Rosenthal, an editor of the *New York Times*.[13] At first glance, perhaps, his account of dehumanization, involving but one individual and in peacetime, may not seem germane of our discussion about nuclear war. But the macrocosm is reflected in the microcosm. We agree with Rosenthal that the implications of this episode are linked with certain psychological factors that have helped pave the way for such broad social calamities as fascism abroad and racial crises in this country, both in the North and South. It does not seem too farfetched, therefore, to relate them to the nuclear threat as well.

For more than half an hour, one night in March 1964,

thirty-eight respectable, law-abiding citizens in a quiet middle-class neighborhood in New York City watched a killer stalk and stab a young woman in three separate attacks, close to her home. She was no stranger to these onlookers, her neighbors, who knew her as "Kitty." According to Rosenthal, "Twice the sound of their voices and the sudden glow of their bedroom lights interrupted him and frightened him off. Each time he returned, sought her out, and stabbed her again. Not one person telephoned the police during the assault; one witness called after the woman was dead." Later, when these thirty-eight neighbors were asked about their baffling failure to phone for help, even though they were safe in their own homes, "the underlying attitude or explanation seemed to be fear [of] involvement—any kind of involvement." Their fatal apathy gains in significance precisely because, by ordinary standards, these were decent, moral people—husbands and wives attached to each other and good to their children. This is one of the forms of dehumanization that we have described, in which a reaction of massive indifference—not hostility—leads to grievous cruelty, yet all the while, in another compartment of the self, the same individual's capacity for active caring continues, at least for those within his immediate orbit.

Rosenthal describes his own reaction to this episode as a

peculiar paradoxical feeling that there is in the tale of Catherine Genovese a revelation about the human condition so appalling to contemplate that only good can come from forcing oneself to confront the truth . . . the terrible reality that only under certain situations and only in response to certain reflexes or certain beliefs will a man step out of his shell toward his brother. In the back of my mind . . . was the feeling that there was, that there must be, some connection between [this story and] the story of the witnesses silent in the face of greater crimes—the degradation of a race, children hungering. . . . It happens from time to time in New York that the life of the city is frozen by an instant of shock. In that instant the people of the city are seized by the paralyzing realization that they are one, that each man is in some way a mirror of every other man. . . . In that instant of shock, the mirror showed quite clearly what was wrong, that the face of mankind was spotted with the disease of apathy—all mankind. But this was too frightening a thought to live with, and soon the beholders began to set boundaries for the illness, to search frantically for causes that were external, and to look for the carrier.

As we strive to distinguish more clearly among the complex determinants of adaptive-maladaptive, humanized-dehumanized polarities of behavior, we recognize that stubborn impulses toward individuation are intertwined with the dehumanizing trends on which we have focused. Both humanization and dehumanization are heightened by interpenetrating social and psychological effects of current technological and institutional changes. The progress of the past hundred years has markedly furthered humanization: it has relieved much of human drudgery and strain and helped to bring about increased leisure and a richer life for a larger part of the world's population. Despite the blurring of personal distinctiveness by excessive bureaucracy, there are now exceptional opportunities, made possible by the same technology that fosters uniformity, for the individual to make rapid contact with, and meaningful contribution to, an almost limitless number of the earth's inhabitants. The same budgets, communication networks, transportation delivery system, and human organizations that can be used to destroy can also be turned toward the creative fulfillment of great world purposes.

Our situation today favors contradictory attitudes toward how much any individual matters in the scheme of things, both subjectively and from the standpoint of social reality. At one extreme a few individuals in key positions feel—and are generally felt to have—a hugely expanded potential for social impact. Among the vast majority there is, by contrast, an intensified sense of voiceless insignificance in the shaping of events. Objectively, too, there is now among individuals a far greater disparity in their actual power to influence crucial outcomes. More than ever before, the fate of the world depends on the judgment of a handful of heads of state and their advisers, who must make rapid decisions about actions for which there are no precedents. Ideas and events, for better or worse, can have immediate global impact.[14] A push button can set a holocaust in motion; a transatlantic phone call can prevent one.

In spite of humanizing ingredients in modern life and the fact that men of goodwill everywhere are striving ceaselessly toward goals of peace, freedom, and human dignity, we nevertheless place primary emphasis, in this [chapter], on dehumanization because we feel that the dangers inherent in this phenomenon are particularly pervasive, insidious, and relevant to the risk of nuclear war.

From a broad biological perspective, war may be viewed as a form of aggression between members of the same species, Homo sapiens. The distinguished naturalist K. Lorenz has . . . pointed out a difference, of great relevance to the relationship between dehumanization and nuclear warfare, in the intraspecies behavior of animals who live in two kinds of groups.[15] In the one, the members live together as a crowd of strangers: there are no expressions of mutual aggression, but neither is there any evidence of mutual ties, of relationships of affection, between individuals in the group. On the other hand, some of the fiercest beasts of prey—animals whose bodily weapons are capable of killing their own kind—live in groups in which intense relationships, both *aggressive and affectionate,* exist. Among such animals, says Lorenz, the greater the intraspecies aggression, the stronger the positive mutual attachments as well. These latter develop, through evolution, out of those occasions, such as breeding, when cooperation among these aggressive animals becomes essential to their survival as a species.

Furthermore—and this is of the utmost importance for survival—the greater the capacity for mutual relationships, the stronger and more reliable are the *innate inhibitions* which prevent them from using the species-specific weapons of predatory aggression, fangs, claws, or whatever, to maim or kill a member of their own species, no matter how strong the hostile urge of one against another. For example, when two wolves fight, according to Lorenz, the potential victor's fangs are powerfully inhibited at what would be the moment of kill, in response to the other's ritualized signal of immobile exposure to his opponent of his vulnerable jugular.

Man's weapons, by contrast, are not part of his body. They are thus not controllable by reflexes fused into his nervous system; control must depend, instead, on psychological inhibitions (which may also function through social controls of his own devising). These psychic barriers to intraspecies aggression—which can lead to our becoming extinct—are rooted in our affiliative tendencies for cooperation and personal attachment. But these are the very tendencies that, as this [chapter] has stressed, dehumanization can so seriously undermine.

Lorenz speaks of a natural balance within a species—essential to its preservation—between the capacity for killing and inhibition. In that sense, perhaps, man jeopardizes his survival by disturbing, with his invention of nuclear bombs, such a balance as has been maintained throughout his long history of periodic "old-style" wars. Such a dire imbalance would be increased by any shift on the part of the "human animal" toward a society essentially devoid of mutual relationships, for this would vitiate the very tendencies toward emotional involvement and cooperation which are the source of our most reliable inhibitions against "overkilling." Therefore, in terms of the parallels suggested by Lorenz, in order to protect ourselves against the doom of extinction as a species, we must encourage and devise every possible means of safeguarding the "family of man" from becoming an uncaring crowd. Not merely the limiting or halting but the reversing of maladaptive dehumanization emerges as a key to survival.

What can be done to counteract these dangers? Assuredly, there is no single or ready answer. The development of psychic antidotes of *re*humanization must involve a multiplicity of variables, levels of discourse, and sectors of human activity commensurate in complexity with the factors that make for *de*humanization. Our attempt in this [chapter] to identify this mental mechanism and to alert others to its significance, its frequency, and its interrelatedness to nuclear risk represents in itself a preliminary phase of remedial endeavor, for the very process of recognizing a psychosocial problem such as this, by marshaling, reordering, and inter-

preting diverse sets of facts to find new significances in them, is
a form of social action and one that is especially appropriate to
behavioral scientists. Beyond this initial posing of the problem,
however, any chance of effectively grappling with it will require
the converging efforts of those in many different professions and
walks of life.

Rehumanization as a mode of neutralizing the dangerous
effects that we have stressed should not be misconstrued as aiming
at the reestablishment of pre-nuclear age psychology—which would
be impossible in any case. We cannot set history back nostalgically
to "the good old days" prior to automation and the other changes
in contemporary society (nor were the conditions of those earlier
days really so "good" for the self-realization of a large portion of
the population). On the contrary, the process of rehumanization
means to us a way of assimilating and reintegrating, emotionally
and intellectually, the profound new meanings that have been
brought into our lives by our own advances, so that a much fuller
conviction than ever before of our own humanity and interdepen-
dence with all mankind becomes intrinsic to our basic frame of
reference.

The imperative for speeding up such a universal process of
psychological change is rooted in the new and *specific* necessity
to ensure survival in the face of the awesome irreversibility of
nuclear annihilation. The most essential approaches toward achieving this goal, however, lead us into such *general* and only seemingly unrelated issues as the degree of political freedom and social
justice; our patterns of child care and child-rearing; and our philosophy of education, as well as the quality of its implementation.
. . . The process of dehumanization, which eventuates in indifference to the suffering implicit in nuclear warfare, has its beginnings
in earlier periods and other areas of the individual's life. It is
through these areas that influences conducive to rehumanization
must be channeled.

We need to learn more and to make more effective use of
what is already known about how to strengthen people's capacity
to tolerate irreducible uncertainty, fear, and frustration without
having to take refuge in illusions that cripple their potential for
realistic behavior. And we urgently need to find ways of galvaniz-

ing our powers of imagination (including ways of weakening the hold of the emotionally based mechanisms that imprison it).

Imagination and foresight are among the highest functions of the human brain, from the evolutionary standpoint, and also among the most valuable. They enable us to select and extrapolate from previously accumulated experience and knowledge, in order to create guidelines for coping with situations never before experienced, whose nature is so far unknown.

Other kinds of learning ordinarily serve us well in the complicated process of establishing behavior patterns for meeting new life situations. We are able to learn by trial and error, for example, from our firsthand experiences and from successively testing the value of alternative approaches as similar situations arise. Also, we learn much by vicariously living through the reported experiences of others.

Through imagination, however, a completely new situation can be projected in the mind in its sensate and vivid entirety, so that the lessons it contains for us can be learned without the necessity of going through it in real life. This form of "future-directed" learning, which creative imagination makes possible, is therefore uniquely advantageous in dealing with the problematic issues of thermonuclear war; it permits us to arrive at more rational decisions for preventing it without having to pay the gruesome price of undergoing its actuality.

The fact is that the "once-and-for-all" character of full-scale nuclear war renders the methods of "learning through experience" —our own or others'—not only indefensible (in terms of the human cost) but also utterly unfeasible. The empirical privileges of "profiting" from an experience of that nature would have been denied to most if not all of humanity by the finality of the experience itself.

Accordingly, it would seem that whatever can quicken and extend our capacity for imagination, in both the empathic and conceptual spheres, is a vital form of "civil defense." It requires, to begin with, all the pedagogic ingenuity that we can muster to overcome the lag in our intellectual development that keeps us from fully comprehending the new dimensions of our existence. Yet, our endeavors to develop new modes of thinking can be canceled out by the constricting and impeding effects of dehumanization. The terrible potential of this subtle mechanism to facilitate the depopulating of the earth lies in its circumventing human restraints against fratricide. We are faced, therefore, with the inescapable necessity of devising ways to increase opportunities for meaningful personal relationships and maximum social participation throughout the entire fabric of our society.

CHAPTER 9

Failures of Identification and Sociopathic Behavior

Bernard L. Diamond

People resort to violence when they have or think they have no alternative, no other means of coping with a situation, or when they regard violence as an appropriate, legitimate, and approved method of dealing with a situation or (and less often) when they obtain some pleasure, satisfaction, or reduction of tension from the act. In all violent actions, criminal or legitimate, those of the sadistic rapist-murderer or those of the heroic soldier, these common attributes are found, and each act of violence can be understood in terms of the varying mix of these features. Surprisingly, the mixture is not in the proportion which conventional moral attitudes would assume. Not infrequently those who commit apparently sadistic and bizarre crimes believe that they are acting in wholly legitimate ways, compelled by the necessities of the situation; and they derive no particular satisfaction or pleasure from the criminal act. On the other hand, a policeman in the course of law enforcement activities may derive great sadistic pleasure from the brutality of his own actions. Killing enemy soldiers may be for some soldiers a harsh, fearful, and obligatory task; for others it may contain all the pleasures of the dangerous hunt and the sadistic revenge.

Individual differences such as these play a role in events of the kind under discussion in this volume. Chapter Eight and others stress the importance in such events of the dehumanization of the victim or victims. It is reasonable to ask: Are some individuals peculiarly disposed, or at least more disposed than others, to see other people as less than human? If the answer to this question is yes, then what are the sources in personality and background of this disposition? To throw some light on these questions let us examine a type of personality—the sociopathic personality—that is frequently seen by students of crime and delinquency. Knowledge of how such a personality develops may also help us to understand the processes by which dehumanization of the object—and of the self—takes place in extreme situations.

An essential element of all individuals suffering from so-called sociopathic personality disorders is the defective quality of their interpersonal relationships. Their capacity to love, in the sense of a true object relationship, is markedly impaired, and, as a consequence, they are deficient in the compassionate, ethical, and moral values intrinsic to a mature object relationship. Generally, this deficiency takes the behavioral form of asocial or antisocial acts, which quickly lead the individual into conflict with society. Hence, the diagnostic term *sociopathic personality*. Sociopathic behavior varies from committing impulsive crimes of great violence and cruelty through gradations of acting immorally to very subtly exploiting others so indirectly and over such long periods of time that the lack of human compassion and ethical values is not easily apparent.

Many current psychiatric explanations of sociopathic behavior, even though phrased in psychoanalytic terminology, tend to classify and to separate the delinquent from the normal in suspiciously unscientific ways. Even the most casual inspection of any large prison reveals the vast diversity of personalities for whom the only common denominator is that each has been apprehended for violating the criminal law. Without falling into the trap of searching for the one true explanation of crime, we must still look for mental mechanisms which are universal and which to some degree can be applied to all persons, in or out of prisons. In searching for such a mechanism, we may be wise to ask: Why do normal persons not commit more sociopathic actions than they do? What stops the average person from being cruel and sadistic toward others? Why does everybody not steal and lie and cheat?

One answer is the fear of shame and punishment, either externally administered by society or internally administered by the superego. Yet I cannot believe that ethical behavior—nonsociopathic behavior—is determined solely by the negative restraints of the fear of punishment. If this were so, punishment would be a much more effective deterrent than it is. Are there not ego mechanisms more closely related than is punishment to traditional ethical concepts?

A clue exists, I think, in the biblical law "love thy neighbor as thyself," emphasized so strongly both in the Old Testament (Lev. 19:18) and by Jesus (Matt. 22:39). To love thy neighbor as thyself is the essence of the ego mechanism of identification. To identify with another is a powerful psychological force of morality and civilized human conduct. It is a positive, libidinally driven force, mediated through the ego, and it represents a higher order (in the sense of being more mature) than the negative restraints of fear of external punishment or of guilt of the superego.

The emotional reactions of the sociopathic personality are usually described as superficial, shallow, and transient, lacking in permanence and in depth. But these descriptions are only figures of speech, for the affectual responses of the sociopath are fully as intense and as deep and often as permanent as the emotions of others. Frequently the sociopath, because of his poor control and instability, demonstrates emotions even more intensely than do normal persons. So what do we mean when we describe his reactions as shallow and superficial, callous or indifferent, lacking in compassion, human feeling, and remorse? These phrases obviously refer to defects in the nature of the interpersonal relationships of the sociopath. They are symptoms of deficient or faulty identification with others. To have a sense of compassion and ethicomoral feeling toward another, one must be able to identify with the other, to have a libidinal investment in the other person as a love object or at least as a narcissistic projection. To be unable to identify with others is to treat persons as things.

Even the most moral, righteous, and ethical person does not feel guilt or shame if he breaks a stick or burns a piece of paper. They have no human value, and their destruction is not an act of sadism or perversion. We regard the destruction of things as immoral only when we identify with their owners or when we treat the things as if they were human because of their special symbolic value. Thus, burning a book may be immoral because of the symbolic value of the contents of that book. The book becomes human, so to speak, and we experience it as something precious to the extent that we identify with it as being human. But a person who has no capacity to identify with others treats people and the objects people value as meaningless things that can be destroyed at will. We need not postulate sadism, perversion, or any defect of the superego to account for the destruction.

If we assume that the basic pathology of the sociopath lies in the area of identification—that he lacks the capacity for identification with others or that he identifies in only limited or circumscribed ways or that his identifications are shifting or transient —then a great deal of what the sociopath does, particularly his antisocial actions, can be accounted for. If the perpetrator of a seemingly cruel and sadistic murder has no capacity for identification with the victim, then he may regard the act as no more cruel or sadistic than the discarding of a simple object. In the absence of identification people become things to destroy or discard at will. And the prized possessions of others can be taken for one's own use with no moral compunction or remorse. In the absence of the ego mechanism of identification the biblical injunction of "love thy neighbor as thyself" and the Golden Rule—"Therefore all things whatsoever ye would that men should do to you do ye even so to them"—become completely meaningless and incomprehensible.

Examples of complete inability to identify with any other person are likely to be rare. Space does not permit full discussion of the factors in childhood which contribute to the development of the mechanism of identification. By and large, a child develops such capacity in direct proportion to the stability and depth of the interpersonal relationships to which he is exposed. Love by parents, expressed in terms appropriate to each level of the libidinal development of the child, is certainly the prime factor. But we also know that certain traumatic events can cause the child to regress, to abandon his attempts at identification, and to retreat into the narcissistic gratifications of earlier developmental levels. It would be extraordinary for a child to develop utterly without the capacity to identify with a meaningful adult without at the same time showing such marked ego defects that he would properly be classified as psychotic rather than psychopathic.

This conclusion is borne out by experience; the schizophrenic rather than the sociopath demonstrates the most profound disturbances in human relationships. A thirty-three year old schizophrenic male saw himself as an exalted messianic figure, the victim of unjust persecution in his childhood. Abandoned by his real parents, he had grown up in strictly religious foster homes and parochial schools. As a child he loved and was loved by no one. He was discharged from the army for homosexuality, committed grand theft, and was sent to prison. While in prison he conceived his plan of revenge on society: he would kill as often as he could to make up for the "thousand times" he had died as a child. He claimed to be a pacifist who hated violence. But he believed it necessary to conduct this one-man war against hypocritical Christian morality. On his release from prison he murdered at least eleven victims before he was again apprehended. His victims were either children or casual homosexual pick-ups. He hardly knew any of his victims, and with none did he have any significant relationship. He expressed not the slightest remorse or concern over his crimes and felt his conduct to be completely justified by the circumstances. He insisted that he was sane and looked forward with eagerness to the publicity of his trial, making elaborate plans to shock the public and the jury with revolting details of the murders. He refused to identify a number of the victims or to locate the bodies, insisting that he be paid five hundred dollars for information about each body. At no time did he express any emotional interest in his victims as persons. To him they were things to be destroyed as required in the fulfillment of his mission.

The typical sociopath is likely to show some capacity to identify with others but only in restricted, transient ways. Particularly, some sociopaths seem able almost instantly to withdraw any identification feelings when their psychological needs so demand. A young professional armed robber described an episode during which he and a close buddy, whom he highly regarded, robbed a service station. They were detected, and when chased by the police, his buddy was shot and killed. Despite his previous closeness to this friend, he experienced no sense of loss at his death. The friend was a sucker for getting himself killed—it was somehow his own fault. At the instant of his death, all feelings were retracted from the relationship, and the friend became a thing whose loss did not matter.

Even where there is true sadistic perversion, the carrying out of the destructive act seems to require a complete lack of any feelings of identification with the victim. A twenty-nine year old male discovered in adolescence that if he choked the girl with him whom he was having sexual relations he experienced an intense orgastic thrill. For a long time he only pretended to squeeze the girl's neck and released his hold when she complained. He had some concern about how the girl might feel and he did not want to frighten her. But as an adult on two occasions he had intercourse with women "who meant nothing to me." He could not resist the urge to carry the strangulation to completion. He left the first woman when she became unconscious, and he did not know that she subsequently died. He strangled the second woman until he knew she was dead. He regretted his impulsiveness because he knew that it was wrong to kill and that he must be punished. But he seemed to have no concern for the feelings or person of either woman. He thought of them as little better than dispensable prostitutes. In his earlier sexual experiences he had some real feeling for the girl, identifying with her at least to the extent of appreciating that she would not want to be hurt or frightened. But with the two murders, the victims meant nothing to him; they were things to be used to satisfy his sadistic urge.

These few cases are too brief to prove my thesis. But they do illustrate the principle involved. Further clinical experience will tell whether this disturbance in identification is as prevalent among offenders as I suspect it to be. I believe that, if confirmed, this ego mechanism will cut across diagnostic lines and be found in the schizophrenic, the neurotic, the sociopath, and the so-called normal offender, not only with crimes of personal violence but with property crimes as well.

However, I do recognize cases where the opposite holds true, cases where the crime results from pathological overidentifications either with the hated self or with a hated and incorporated love object. And there are crimes where violence results from other defense mechanisms. A murder may be a defense against a threatened psychotic disintegration. Or a slaying may result from a need to bring the punishment and wrath of society upon the murderer himself. Many different psychological mechanisms can result, under particular circumstances, in violence and crime. But I do believe that lack of identification with the victim is at the core of destructive sociopathic behavior.

A final word is necessary about the almost universal prevalence of this ego mechanism in relation to morality. The reader will be familiar with the ease with which all but a few exceptionally moral persons are able to rationalize cheating on their income tax or taking advantage of an error by a large store or corporation. People who would never dream of stealing from someone they know may feel no compunctions when the victim is impersonal —a large organization—or is too remote to personalize. Conventional morality breaks down completely in the absence of identification with the victim. In such a situation the most normal person may behave as does a psychopath. Perhaps this is the secret of war. We hate and degrade our enemies, thus blocking any emotional identifications with them as persons. We make them into something subhuman—things rather than people—so that we may destroy and kill with impunity. When there is no identification, we are all sociopathic.

But relationships among humans do not have to be in-hibited, neurotic, perverse, or destructive. On the contrary, they can be free, uninhibited, creative, and fulfilling, and so should the work of man be self-realizing, exhilarating, and deeply satisfy-ing. Freud, asked for his definition of complete mental health, replied "Lieben und Arbeiten"—love and work. The human ner-vous system and the human mind are quite capable of achieving mental health so defined. Whether our social, ethical, and politi-cal development can permit it is another matter.

We live in a world in which much destructive behavior either is legitimate or is at least tolerated with some degree of ap-proval by public officials, by groups, and by societies. Most people do not object to violence as such; they object only to illegiti-mate violence. Killing by the policeman, by the prison execu-tioner, or by the soldier at war is regarded as necessary and in no way immoral. Even the private individual is entitled to kill in defense of his life, his family, or his property. The police are en-couraged to engage in violent, and sometimes illegal, behavior in their war against crime with the rationalization that such behavior is necessary for social control. Civil disorders have been marked by repeated episodes of violence by police and militia, and there seems to be a growing use of violence by law enforcement agencies. Sometimes the agents of legalized violence express with impunity their own psychopathology in such activities.

Despite the apocalyptic proportions of the actual and poten-tial violence which surrounds us, most persons are able to go about their business with equanimity, shutting their eyes to any dis-asters which do not directly impinge on their personal welfare. To some, however, violence becomes a wholly acceptable act which is perceived by themselves and by others as the proper way of behaving. To kill, to burn, to destroy need not be experienced as bad or evil when such acts have been overtly or covertly autho-rized and thereby legitimated. Disturbed world and domestic con-ditions, with the ever present atmosphere of violence, undoubtedly have a powerful impact upon the marginal, the maladjusted, the psychotic, the embittered, and the alienated. The individual who is well integrated with society and with himself tends to leave vio-lence to those who are specifically designated by the society to do it. The marginal, the mentally ill, and the disaffected, however, are attracted like moths to a flame by the violence of the establishment. For example, capital punishment, instead of deterring crime, may make murder irresistible to the enraged and depressed man with suicidal ambitions. The paranoid psychotic with delusions of grandeur recognizes no authority but his own: Seeing that nations right their wrongs with violence, he believes that it is proper for him to do that also and proceeds to kill in response to his paranoid ideas. The alienated fanatic emerges from his insignificance and becomes a heroic figure by means of the assassin's bullet.

The right to be violent and destructive of human life can never be reserved for the proper institutions of society alone. The mentally ill, the socially maladjusted, and the marginal individuals always attempt to usurp such powers. Legitimate violence always provokes illegitimate violence. Whenever established authorities control by force and violence, then those persons outside the establishment, including the young, the mentally ill, the poor, and the segregated, tend to express their frustrations through force and violence. We cannot have a society in which some individuals, such as policemen and soldiers, are permitted to express their sadistic and violent urges, while the outcasts and marginal members of society are prohibited from expressing similar urges. Inevitably, the illegitimate will usurp the violence of the legitimate, and the tragic escalation of destructive forces will become unavoidable.

I do not subscribe to the thesis that violence and destruction are the natural lot of mankind. The current zoological theories of human behavior, such as those set forth in *African Genesis* [1]* and *The Naked Ape*,[2] are naive and pseudoscientific in their confusion of capacity with necessity. Even if one assumes genetically determined patterns of behavior, such as territoriality or intraspecies aggression (and evidence of such instincts in humans is very slight indeed), man is not necessarily doomed to follow such instinctual patterns. Whatever potential for behavior is determined by man's genes, his actual behavior is determined by what he learns, and what he learns is defined by his cultural heritage and his experiences.

* Notes for this chapter start on p. 341.

The violence, destructiveness, and dehumanization that are inevitable in war and not uncommon in peace are not the consequences of a biological structure which dooms us to catastrophe. And I think it equally incorrect to attribute violence and destructiveness exclusively to a defective personality structure—sociopathic or otherwise—or to a psychopathological condition. Despite the difficulties of diagnosis and of definition, I think we can recognize such a clinical entity as sociopathic personality, but instances of definite, well defined predisposition to violence are not common in my experience. More prevalent and more dangerous to society are those persons who are not psychopaths or schizophrenics yet who, under certain circumstances, can behave with the ruthless, dehumanized detachment of the sociopath.

What are the circumstances which can temporarily transform compassionate people into unfeeling sociopaths, willing, even eager, to abandon the Golden Rule? The following items constitute a very incomplete list of circumstances which may predispose to dehumanization and the legitimation of evil, but they illustrate how variable are the factors which can neutralize empathy and identification with others: (1) Propaganda which labels and portrays the victim in derogatory words and images, implying that he is subhuman, bestial, dangerous, and perverted; using racist names such as nigger, kike, gook, and honky—particularly effective are combinations of racist and political names such as Jew-communist. (2) Unfamiliar places where one must cope with persons who are different and strange, whose language one does not understand; soldiers fighting in foreign countries are especially vulnerable to this effect. (3) Fear, despair, grave uncertainty, and demoralization; seemingly, the effects are similar whether the cause is social and political oppression, economic deprivation, or participation in combat. (4) Exhilarated excitement associated with uninhibited group action, exemplified by the carnival spirit so often mentioned by participants in ghetto riots. (5) The willingness (or sometimes the necessity) to be blindly obedient to authority. The atrocities of war and of political oppression are experienced as being permissible when commanded by higher authority. (6) Physical factors—pain, fatigue, extreme hunger, drug or alcohol intoxication, the physical need to survive. (7) Appeals to higher, supernatural motives; violence and dehumanization in the name of religion, patriotism, nationalism, and ideology can supersede human compassion. The Golden Rule is suspended because the destruction of the victim is experienced as a sacrifice to the loftier goal. Paradoxically, as we achieve a greater identification with our fellow crusaders and other true believers, we lose all compassion for the heretic who does not share our convictions. As Erik Erikson has so well said: "In the name of high moral principles all the vindictiveness of derision, of torture, and of mass extinction can be employed." [3]

I, like most psychiatrists, am pessimistic about changing the behavior of those individuals whose lack of capacity to identify with others has been a lifelong, consistent pattern. Labeling and isolating may be all that can be done for the sociopathic offender who is dangerous to society. But the greater and more prevalent evil arises when the normal and ordinary person relinquishes his capacity for empathic identification, renounces the Golden Rule, and destroys his fellow man. The task is to study most carefully how his pattern develops and what makes it possible. To know well the psychological, social, political, and economic determinants may provide us with the means of preventing man from giving up his most human attribute: his ability to identify with his fellow man.

CHAPTER 10

Authoritarianism and Social Destructiveness

Nevitt Sanford

Confronted with an example of racism in our society, we may quite naturally be disposed to say that it was caused by racists. But, as some of the previous chapters suggest, a relatively decent person may be led by his social situation or organizational role to participate in what is coming to be recognized as institutional racism, and, conversely, a more liberal climate may cause another individual to suppress his racist tendencies. Clearly the relationship between personality and society is more complicated than a reflection of one in the other. What can

studies of authoritarianism in personality, which are not concerned primarily with social analysis, teach us about social destructiveness? What else do we need to know? What reformulations of
the original theory set forth in *The Authoritarian Personality* [1]*
are necessary now, after twenty years, and how may our knowledge
of authoritarianism in personality be integrated with contemporary social thought and research?

The role of personality in destructiveness is most clearly
observed when a single individual carries out a destructive act.
For example, in Gilroy, California, in April 1969, a young man
was arrested for trying to shoot a judge whose sentencing of a rapist he felt to be too lenient. He said the judge, who had a Jewish
name, was a "legal criminal, the worst kind." "The Jews don't like
anybody who's against the communist conspiracy. I've been threatened morally by the Jews by being called a queer. They threatened
me bodily too." [2] This young man apparently harbored in himself
a disposition to aggressive behavior, a set of persistent, irrational
beliefs about Jews and Communists, a punitive attitude toward
sex offenders, a doubtful feeling about his sexual adequacy, and
a belief that he was being victimized.

The authors of *The Authoritarian Personality* would not
have hesitated to say this young man exhibited, to an extreme
degree, the authoritarian personality syndrome, for they found
that all the traits just mentioned are closely related and that together they distinguish males who were high on a scale for measuring anti-Semitism. The authors also showed that various other
traits belong to this same pattern, and they accumulated evidence
and developed a theory on the ways in which all these traits are
related dynamically.

The young man in Gilroy was undoubtedly disturbed,
probably psychotic, at the time of the shooting, but according to
current conceptions of mental illness, he was not categorically different from other people. His psychopathology is best conceived
as a matter of degree; in groups of people chosen at random, each
of the traits noted in his case has been found to vary from little or
none to an extreme amount, and the whole pattern of traits, which

* Notes for this chapter start on p. 342.

can be conceived of as a more or less unitary structure, has been observed to vary in amount from one person to another. Personality looms large in the case of this young man because, apparently, so little in the way of external stimuli was required to trigger his destructive action. A newspaper item about the sentencing of the rapist was enough to start him ruminating, and he acted alone; he felt, apparently, no pressures to conform with the destructive inclinations and actions of a face-to-face group, no compulsion to obey some authority.

In most cases of overt destructiveness, particularly those in which the action is collective, the role of personality is not easy to define or estimate. Personality lies behind behavior and within the individual; it is an organization of dispositions, of readinesses, of susceptibilities. We infer personality from behavior, but since behavior always depends on the situation of the moment, we can rarely say much about personality on the basis of behavior in a single situation. We must depend, instead, on observation of the person in numerous, varied situations. Even if we have a chance to interview individuals who have taken part in a massacre or riot, diagnosis is difficult, for situational determinants such as danger, fatigue, group pressure, and orders from above are usually potent.

In many cases of social destructiveness such factors are sufficient to evoke the action regardless of the personalities of the participants, but in the case of the disturbed young man personality by itself was nearly sufficient. Probably in most cases of destructive action the role of personality lies somewhere between these two extremes. If we consider a company of National Guardsmen called to quell a disturbance on a campus, a company of soldiers assigned to "clean out" a village suspected of harboring enemy troops, or a company of policemen given the task of raiding a building from which sniping has been reported, we can reasonably assume that individuals in the company differ in their predisposition to take part in group destructiveness. Individuals who are most predisposed in this way will be among those who take the lead in any collective destructiveness that occurs; people less disposed will join in later as excitement mounts and the stimulus of what the others are doing becomes intense; and still others will fire into the ground or the air or refuse to participate at all. The greater the disposition to collective destructiveness the less the stimuli necessary to evoke destructive action.

The relations between personality and the social environment are more complicated than this however. Personality is not a closed system which is formed early in the individual's life and which thereafter cooperates with environmental factors in determining social effects without any change in itself. On the contrary personality exists within social systems. Not only is it very largely a product of past relations with such systems, but its state depend on what is happening in the surrounding social environment. At any given time there are transactions between aspects or features of the personality and processes in the environment. What we diagnose or measure in personality changes if critical features of the environment change; for example, a stable conscience breaks down if it loses all its external reinforcements, or an individual may adopt a mechanism of defense if this mechanism is widely used by members of a social group to which he belongs.

At the same time, the processes of a social group are, in part, expressions of the personalities of the individuals who constitute that group. The social processes involved in the legitimation of evil—such as dehumanization of victims, total belief in the justice of one's cause, obedience, and conformity—correspond to traits which were found, in dynamic relation one to another, in individuals scoring high on a scale for measuring authoritarianism. The question is, why do these processes and traits go together? Why is it, for example, that people who stereotype others are also over-obedient to authority? One could observe or read reports of a great many massacres or instances of institutional racism without arriving at the answer, for the relationship of these two tendencies is within the individual; it has to do with inner conflicts and deep personal strivings. Thus, the understanding of collective destructiveness is furthered by studies of authoritarianism in personality.

In order to increase such understanding here I first summarize some of the major findings and theories that we reported in *The Authoritarian Personality* and then discuss some research carried out since the publication of that volume. In the following brief summary I give attention only to findings and conclusions that have held up through two decades.

Data for the research were collected through questionnaires and interviews. The questionnaires, designed to yield measures of social attitudes such as attitudes toward Jews, were administered to over 2500 Americans in various walks of life. Interviews, conducted usually with people whose attitudes were extreme, served as a check on the validity of the questionnaires and as a means for exploring the characters and backrounds of key individuals. We directed attention first to anti-Semitism, then to attitudes toward a variety of other minority groups, and then to various opinions, attitudes, and values which appeared to be associated with anti-Semitism and other forms of prejudice.

Some of the first findings concerned the essential irrationality of anti-Semitism. People who are hostile toward Jews have over-generalized and frequently contradictory opinions of them; all Jews are said to have this or that fault, and any Jew who is found to be at fault in one respect is assumed to be at fault in all respects, even though some of the faults could not possibly coexist in the same person (for example, clannishness and a desire to push in where not wanted). Opinions so irrational could not derive from concrete experience with particular Jews, nor are they likely to be modified by anything that Jews, singly or in groups, do.

In appraising opinions and attitudes with respect to various other minority groups, we found that prejudice is highly generalized; a prejudiced person directs negative opinions and hostile attitudes not only toward racial or ethnic minorities but toward any group—social, economic, national, religious, or ideological—that he sees as different from his own. In this sense, anti-Semitism, apart from some special features, can be regarded primarily as an aspect of generalized prejudice.

Prejudice against various out-groups is so closely associated with bias in favor of the subject's own group (in-group) that we were led to regard the two as aspects of a single phenomenon. Reviving a term of W. G. Sumner's, we called it ethnocentrism and the scale for measuring it the E scale. The term *ethnocentrism* describes attitudes common to anti-Semitism, prejudice against people of color, jingoistic nationalism, religious bigotry, and ideological fanaticism. Anti-Semitism or any other form of prejudice is not an attitude toward a particular group developed through more or less rational processes out of experiences with members of that group, but is a way of thinking about groups and group relations. Those thinking in this way divide all people categorically into homogeneous groups or classes, infer the essential nature of a person from a knowledge of what group he belongs to, arrange all groups and all people within groups into hierarchies with the strong at the top and the weak at the bottom, and solve most moral questions by assuming that the good is what good people do—good people being those who belong to the same group as oneself. This way of thinking about groups and group relations is associated with characteristic views on politics, economics, religion, social relations, family, and sex.

    This outlook did not strike us as something that had been learned at school or taken over totally from any existing propaganda agency. Instead, we were led to the view that the ethnocentric outlook is generated and maintained primarily because it serves important needs within the individual personality. Our third attitude scale, the fascism, or F, scale, was therefore designed to test our hypothesis that the underlying character structure expressed in ethnocentrism is expressed in various other ways as well. Using this scale with our whole sample of 2500, we demonstrated close association between ethnocentrism and the following tendencies: rigid adherence to conventional values; submissive attitudes toward moral authorities of the in-group; readiness to punish the slightest violation of conventional values; opposition to the subjective, imaginative, or tender-minded; belief in primitive, hereditarian theories and in mystical determination of the individual's fate; inability or unwillingness to deal with the indefinite, the ambiguous, or the probable; preoccupation with the dominance-submission aspect of human relationships and exaggerated exertions of strength and toughness; cynicism with respect to human nature; and disposition to ascribe evil motives to people. A subject's score on this scale correlated highly enough with his score on the anti-Semitism scale so that for estimating anti-Semitism in a population the former may be substituted for the latter. Not every prejudiced person displays all these tendencies, but in general they are found together in a pattern we called authoritarianism. Instead of claiming categorically that some people exhibit the pattern while others do not, we preferred to think of authoritarianism as existing in different degrees in different individuals.

Since the publication of *The Authoritarian Personality* the measuring instruments described in that volume, particularly the E scale for measuring ethnocentrism and the F scale for measuring authoritarianism, have been used by numerous investigators with various groups of respondents. As R. Brown says: "On the level of covariation, of one variable correlated with another, the findings of *The Authoritarian Personality* seem to me to be quite well established. Anti-Semitism goes with ethnocentrism goes with antiintraception goes with idealization of parents and self goes with authoritarian discipline in childhood goes with a rigid conception of sex roles, etc." [3]

Many studies carried out since 1950 have widened the circle of covariation. They have shown high scores on the E or F scale to be associated with high scores on scales for measuring rigidity, misanthropy, dogmatism, traditional family ideology, restrictiveness toward the use of alcohol, and punitiveness toward alcoholic patients; with characteristic behavior in experimental situations (such as low tolerance for ambiguity of visual stimuli and, under some conditions, rigidity in problem solving); and with characteristic behavior in various social roles (such as dominance and possessiveness in mothers; autocratic, totalitarian behavior in schoolteachers; ineffectiveness in army officers; unreceptivity to psychotherapy in psychiatric patients; unwillingness to volunteer for psychological experiments and low tolerance for personal freedom in college freshmen).

These findings have strengthened the argument in favor of a central and relatively deep-seated personality structure which helps to determine prejudice and other behavior in a wide variety of situations. These findings, however, like those reported in *The Authoritarian Personality*, refer to general relationships, correlations between or among variables in populations of people. Although the coefficients of correlation are very high by ordinary standards, some people in the sample do not go with the majority. For example, the correlation between anti-Semitism and ethnocentrism, as reported in *The Authoritarian Personality*, is 0.80 (where 1.00 is perfect correlation in ranking), but this correlation leaves open the possibility that some people are prejudiced against Jews but not against Negroes and vice versa. Research has helped to define limits for the generalizations in *The Authoritarian Personality* and to reveal the complexity of the matters considered in that volume. N. Cohn, for example, has argued cogently, on the basis of historical studies, that traditional European anti-Semitism and contemporary anti-Negro prejudice in the United States have different psychodynamic sources, the former being a displacement of hostility toward the "bad" father of childhood, the latter largely a projection onto Negroes of reprehensible sexual and aggressive tendencies which the prejudiced person has to suppress.[4] G. Selznick and P. Steinberg have produced evidence that anti-Semitism is not always as total as *The Authoritarian Personality* suggested; they found in a nationwide study of anti-Semitism in the United States that whereas Negroes generally are a good deal less likely than whites to have discriminatory attitudes toward Jews, they hold strongly anti-Semitic views in the area of economics, a fact which the authors attribute to the Jews' unique place in Negro ghetto life.[5] Finally, being politically liberal or low in authoritarianism in the United States today is no guarantee that a person has no prejudice against Negroes; Marlynn May found among his sample of church members a number of anti-Negro beliefs and attitudes that were more characteristic of liberals than of conservatives or radicals.[6] Studies such as these are contributing to a more differentiated and more expanded picture of prejudice than that which we offered in *The Authoritarian Personality;* they do not, however, cast doubt upon the general findings reported in that volume.

    Less well established is the theory we worked out to explain the origins and development of ethnocentrism and authoritarianism within the individual personality. This theory was based largely upon differences in what individuals scoring at opposite extremes on our scales said about their backgrounds and histories, upon general psychoanalytic theory, and upon our clinical experience with highly prejudiced and relatively unprejudiced individuals.

    Most important, according to this theory, is the pattern of discipline to which the individual is subjected in childhood. An authority that is at once stern, rigid, unreasonable, and unloving arouses hostility, which, instead of being directed against the strong and (as the child must believe) "good" people who wield such authority, is suppressed and displaced onto substitutes and eventually, with some assistance from parents and educators, onto outgroups. Though submitting to this kind of authority, sometimes even protesting too much, the child does not accept it in the sense that it finds a place in the formation of his own conscience. Authority remains, as it were, out there—to be obeyed self-pityingly, if it is strong enough and unavoidable enough, and, to be ignored when it is possible to get around it. The individual who must submit to authority, regardless of its merits, because he lacks the moral resources to oppose it is left with a continuing sense of impotence, which is infuriating because its sources are unrecognized. He tends to strike out wildly, finding all manner of possible causes for his troubles: people are against him, he is being persecuted, "it's the Jews."

In attempting to overcome his sense of weakness he insists upon his superiority and presents himself to the world as a strong and hard-headed fellow. Since weakness is contemptible, he cannot admit it in himself or tolerate it in others. When the perceived weakness of others reminds him of his own, he becomes violent, the more so as his victim is pitiable and less able to strike back. The device of projecting onto others that which cannot be admitted in oneself is used not only for managing weakness but for putting from oneself various other unrecognized tendencies. This explains why a group, once placed in the role of out-group, may be seen as the embodiment of all manner of evil.

This formulation, unfortunately, has not so far been sufficiently tested by empirical research. The relationship of authoritarianism and pattern of upbringing still has to be based largely on retrospective accounts of childhood events. According to such accounts, discipline in the families of authoritarian men and women was characterized by relatively harsh application of rules in accordance with conventional values; and this discipline was commonly experienced as threatening or traumatic or even overwhelming. In the families of subjects low on authoritarianism, on the other hand, discipline was often for the violation of principles, and the parents often made an effort to explain the issues to the child, thus enabling him to assimilate the discipline.

In view of the more authoritarian subject's obvious inclination to put as good a face as possible upon his family and his childhood situation, we assumed that such negative features as appeared in his account were probably to be taken more or less at their face value—that is, we believed that the high authoritarians came, for the most part, from homes in which a rather stern and distant father dominated a submissive and long suffering but morally restrictive mother and in which discipline was an attempt to apply conventionally approved rules rather than an effort to teach general values in accordance with the perceived needs of the child. This view seems to be in accordance with the findings of a quantitative study by D. B. Harris and his colleagues,[7] who showed that in answers to a questionnaire the parents of prejudiced children tended to emphasize obedience, strict control, and the inculcation of fear significantly more than did the parents of relatively unprejudiced children.

Our original theory about the origins of authoritarianism calls for longitudinal studies in which developmental trends in children are observed against a background of events and practices in the home. The closest to this ideal so far is the work of Else Frenkel-Brunswik and her associates. These workers measured prejudice in children as young as ten years and obtained information on family background, handling of discipline, and childhood events by visits to the home and extensive interviews with the parents. Frenkel-Brunswik writes:

A preliminary inspection of the data supports the assumption made in The Authoritarian Personality *that warmer, closer, and more affectionate interpersonal relationships prevail in the homes of the unprejudiced children. . . . In the home with the orientation toward rigid conformity, on the other hand, actual maintenance of discipline is often based upon the expectation of a quick learning of external, rigid, and superficial rules which are bound to be beyond the comprehension of the child. Family relationships are characterized by fearful subservience to the demands of the parents and by an early suppression of impulses not acceptable to the adults.*[8]

Contrary to the emphasis in *The Authoritarian Personality,* however, personality formation is by no means due solely to experience in the home nor is it nearly completed in the preschool years; development in personality continues through school and college and beyond. Among the many studies carried out since 1950 that make this point, more than a few bear directly on social destructiveness. The E and F scales have been administered to large samples of students in all classes in various kinds of higher educational institutions. According to the summary of this work by Kenneth A. Feldman and Theodore M. Newcomb, ethnocentrism-authoritarianism is significantly reduced between freshman and senior years in most colleges.[9] This is a hopeful finding from the point of view of possible remedial actions. As I explain in Chapter Seventeen, educational procedures carried out in accord with current theory of personality development in college can have a marked impact on those predispositions that enter into the legitimation of evil.

In considering changes in E and F scale scores during a period in college we must take note of the possibility that these changes are due to superficial adaptation to the relatively tolerant campus culture, as well as—or, perhaps, rather than—to changes in the personality itself. Are ethnocentrism and authoritarianism not simply cultural norms for which individuals serve as carriers? This issue brings us back to the question raised earlier concerning the relations of personality and the social environment of the past and present.

Culture certainly seems to be a main determinant of the fact that mean E and F scale scores differ, in all college classes, from one institution to another, being higher, for example, in church-related colleges than in secular ones, higher in vocationally oriented institutions than in those in which the liberal arts are accented. Culture comes very much to the fore when these scales, properly translated, are used in different nations. University students in Germany, Egypt, and Lebanon, for example, obtain significantly higher scores than do their counterparts in the United

States. Cultural determinants also play a part in various studies in which ethnocentrism and authoritarianism have been found to be associated with low income, low education, and religious fundamentalism. In all these cases an individual can agree with items expressive of ethnocentrism or authoritarianism because he has learned this responese from his parents, teachers, or friendship group—he has, in other words, accepted a cultural norm. We can even conceive of a culture in which the whole set of dispositions expressed in the E and F scales go together to form a pattern.

However, we are now only transferring the question of what makes the dispositions go together. Why should racism be associated with anxiety about sex, with self-glorification, and with submissiveness toward authority? The question is the same whether we are talking about a culture or about an individual. In *The Authoritarian Personality,* we argued, as I do here, that the component dispositions are related dynamically; they constitute a working system in an individual or in a social group. In any culture the emotional impulses of individuals are shaped through shared experience in the social group, and ways of controlling these impulses are developed in order to form and to favor cultural values. Thus personality needs and dynamics help to shape culture, just as culture, once formed, influences personality development and individual behavior.

The idea of widely shared personality needs seems necessary to explain why the policemen alleged to have committed the murders in the Algiers Motel incident, like the uniformed murderers of civil rights workers in Mississippi, assumed that nothing very serious would happen to them as their cases moved through the local courts, and to explain why they even felt aggrieved at being singled out in a way that led to their suspension from the force. They had good reason to believe that they were doing what the general public wanted done. As E. Friedenberg has suggested, they were acting out the fantasies of the populace.[10] An idea of what some of these fantasies may be is suggested by the remark of an Ohio woman after the shooting to death of four university students by National Guardsmen—"they should have killed four hundred of them"—or the argument of the chairman of a subcommittee of the House of Representatives that gunfire should have been used against demonstrators who gathered outside the Justice Department in Washington and threw rocks.[11] In the prevailing culture of the United States aggressive impulses are strong though often unrecognized, and a viable way of handling them is to participate vicariously in the aggression of officials against people who have been defined as morally low—usually, today, people of color, though students are another prominent target. We know from the German experience something of what happens when people who represent this trend gain control of the press and educational system. Fortunately, this trend in our culture is opposed by others.

Personality and social processes also interact in organizations and institutions where, as we have seen, apparently ordinary people, even people who profess opposition to the general trend of the system, act in discriminatory or destructive ways merely by doing their jobs. (Chapter Fifteen outlines some alternatives to this kind of acquiescence.) Organizations are structures of roles more or less rationally designed to achieve stated purposes, but they are also collectivities of people who devise ways to make their lives meaningful and to cope with shared problems. In other words, organizations develop cultures. (A. L. Kroeber and Talcott Parsons suggest that the term *culture* be used for "transmitted and created content and patterns of values, ideas, and other symbolic-meaningful systems" and the term *"society*—or more generally, *social system*—be used to designate the specifically relational system of interaction among individuals and collectivities." [12]) It is proper and useful to study the cultures of particular organizations, such as factories,[13] colleges,[14] and medical schools,[15] and to examine whether the general relations of personality and culture noted earlier hold in these special cases. At the same time, individuals use the formal role structure itself for defensive purposes and for the gratification of their needs, including unconscious ones. This use of the structure becomes apparent when efforts are made to change an organization. Individuals vest much interest in things as they are; they put something of themselves into their work roles, so that changing the organization means changing individual personalities at the same time.

Finally, general principles govern the functioning of both organizations and individual personalities. Although it is improper to speak of an authoritarian organization or culture or person as if this rubric could embrace everything important about him or it —we may point to authoritarian trends in the organization or observe that the whole organization sometimes behaves in an authoritarian way. Such organizational behavior may occur in response to threats from outside. In response to the criticisms of parents or legislative bodies a school or a school system may define its roles narrowly, insist on rigid adherence to them, make many rules, and punish deviations from them in totalitarian ways—by treating small infractions the same as large ones or by punishing all for the mistakes of a few; it may, in short, create a situation in which behavior in all ranks is determined more by the need to ward off anxiety than by the rational requirements of tasks. Such a state of affairs arouses the authoritarian tendencies in individuals, and since authoritarian behavior is now rewarded, these tendencies are strengthened; moreover, since individuals who are decidedly non- or antiauthoritarian tend to leave the school or system, the fit between personality and organization becomes very close indeed.

But, however close the fit between personality and social structure or between personality and culture, we should never assume that personality is a mere reflection of the social environment of the present or a mere carrier of the social environment of the past. The social elements incorporated by the individual are not perfect copies of what exists outside. Each assimilation is a product of something from the culture and something already in the person.

In formulating the relations of personality, social structure, and culture we must think not of simple identities but of subtle, intimate, and complex interactions among the three systems. While these systems are open, they are nonetheless systems, each with some integrity of its own. To understand their interactions we must first be clear about the nature, functioning, component systems, and boundaries of each, which means that it is not a bad strategy to have some social scientists specializing in each of the three areas—personality, social structure, and culture.

The authors of *The Authoritarian Personality,* however, in focusing upon personality, accented the fixity of patterns formed early in the individual life and gave little attention to the influence of contemporary social events. This suggested that we would have to raise a new generation in the right way before we could expect much reduction in authoritarianism. This view was, and is, no doubt as unpalatable to the general public as it is to social scientists.

This pessimistic emphasis may help explain why public understanding of authoritarianism seems not much greater today than it was in 1950. People rarely are willing or able to distinguish between authoritarianism and the exercise of ordinary, legitimate authority. Many students tend to label as authoritarian anyone who undertakes to meet the requirements of a proper authoritative role. A second widespread error among those who make some use of the concept is to apply authoritarian personality to a sharply delineated category of people. Thus, they ask, "How many authoritarian personalities are there in our society? Is the number increasing?" This tendency, coupled with a negative evaluation of this personality disposition, resembles the stereotyping that is one of the main characteristics of authoritarianism itself. This stereotyping happens despite the efforts of researchers to define the authoritarian disposition as a complex dimension of personality which varies in amount from one extreme to another and never totally embraces a person. A third common error is neglect of the complexity of authoritarianism, particularly of the relationships between surface traits and underlying dynamic sources. Sometimes this error takes the form of failure to recognize subtle indications of true authoritarianism, and sometimes it takes the form of mistaking for authoritarianism, or labeling as authoritarian, a trait such as dogmatism or aggressiveness or anti-intellectualism, which though found along with authoritarianism is also commonly found with other personality dispositions.

This lack of understanding is no doubt due in part to the fact that the reading public and even social scientists in fields other than psychology have never had a fair chance to get at authoritarianism. The essentials of the subject have rarely if ever been presented in a form that had any appeal for the general reader or that could be widely used in schools and colleges. But the problem is greater than this: those scientists who have sought to inform the public about authoritarianism and the potential for fascism in America have met with a great deal of resistance.

"It can't happen here" was, as Sinclair Lewis noted, the prevailing American reaction to the rise of German and Italian fascism in the 1930s. Lewis suggested rather convincingly that it could happen here, but when fascism became the enemy in World War II and when its evils were fully exposed in the immediate aftermath of the war, the idea of anything of the sort happening here became more unthinkable than before. Words such as *Nazi*, *fascist*, *totalitarian*, *Hitlerism*, *authoritarian* acquired enormous emotional connotations of a negative sort and were soon being hurled at political enemies.

However, by 1950, when *The Authoritarian Personality* made its appearance, communism was the major political enemy, and national policy was to mobilize in the struggle against this enemy all the emotional and spiritual resources that had been effective in the fight against the Axis powers. In order to do this so soon after a struggle in which the communists and we had been allied in a fight against fascism, it was necessary to make the point that the real enemy was totalitarianism—of whatever variety—and that communism and fascism were essentially the same thing. Some intellectuals and social scientists joined in the effort to make this equation, writing about the irrelevancy of the right-left dimension in politics and about the end of ideology.

Not until the early 1960s did the right-left continuum begin to reappear in the social scientific literature and in the media. This reappearance followed the scaling down of the Cold War that had begun in the late 1950s. It became permissible to speak of the zealous anticommunists as a type and to regard authoritarianism, certainly the sort that we find in America, primarily as a rightist phenomenon. Clearly in a communist state, where the government is a well established bureaucracy, individuals who have authoritarian personality dispositions are inclined to support the government. But in the United States, where the communist parties have always been weak and despised, the appeals of communism have to be understood differently.

We may well believe that individuals to whom communism

appeals are troubled or rather desperate, but there is very little to suggest that in their underlying personality structures they have much in common with people who score high on the F scale. When American communists have been psychoanalyzed, as I have done in several cases, what stands out is their basic fight with the father and what most characteristically comes out in behavior is a tendency to see the "bad father" in all sorts of authorities and figures of the establishment. One may dramatize the basic differences in personality between the prototypic potential fascist and the prototypic revolutionary in the following way: A boy of five years comes upon a scene in which his father is attacking his mother verbally or physically. The little boy who is later to become attracted by fascism assumes that the mother must have done something wrong —that she should not have provoked the father—and he proceeds to ally himself with the stronger of the two. The boy who is later to become a revolutionary leaps to the defense of his mother and on the basis of this experience and others like it sees the world as a place in which the weak are forever being brutalized by the strong. When these themes are carried over into politics, the differences between the two are striking. I had a patient during World War II who fitted the case of the first boy mentioned above. He argued passionately that defeat would be inevitable. This outlook is dramatically different from that of the political radical who feels compelled to attack the powers that be, however legitimate their authority. This continuing fight with a stern father does not, however, seem to be a major theme in the lives of alienated students today. More important with many of them, it appears, is disappointment with a weak father—reactivated through betrayal by political and intellectual leaders—and a continuing search for someone worthy of respect and emulation.[16]

Radical elements highly visible in society (such as activist students and militant blacks) call our attention to the right-left continuum in politics, but many people still tend to accent the similarities of the extreme right and the extreme left and to define the enemy as extremist. Related to this tendency is the fact that fascism, a bad word, is used by leftists to clobber their political opponents; and it is used without much discrimination sometimes to refer to things which are not in fact fascistic. At the same time rightest politicians, fully aware of the emotional value of the old words, do not hesitate to call fascist or Hitleristic or McCarthyist whatever they wish to evoke sentiment against. For example, the governor of California has referred to student demonstrators as fascists and has likened their behavior to that of the Nazi street fighters. Some intellectual leaders, no doubt out of extreme exasperation, have indulged in the same tendency. The outgoing president of Harvard referred to students' interruptions of speakers as McCarthylike and was seconded by the chancellor of the University of California at Los Angeles. This is obscurantism of an exquisite sort, confusing as it does oppression by a powerful government authority with protest by people who may feel ignored, desperate, and vulnerable.

Such obscurantism on the part of political and intellectual leaders, faithfully passed along by the media, has a profound molding effect on the opinions of the general public, no matter what their predispositions. This effect is intensified, however, by the fact that any effort to enlighten the public about fascism involves telling them what they do not want to hear. As shown in Chapters Five and Eight, we possess a great variety of well established defenses against hearing that our actions in Vietnam or our attacks on militant blacks are like the most characteristic activities of the Nazis. Moreover the emotions to which authoritarianism and legitimized aggression appeal go very deep. Any one with the slightest inkling of the kinds of passions to which politicians appeal in their attacks on students and militant minority groups cannot help but feel anxious. That the people being appealed to are not anxious is due to the fact that they are unaware of their own impulses and of the implications of what is being said to them.

This situation gives us an indication of the enormous work that remains to be done. Despite its size, *The Authoritarian Personality* was only a start. In Chapter Eighteen Craig Comstock and I outline an approach to the continuing study of social destructiveness. We need not only to clarify concepts, as I have attempted to do in this chapter, and to conduct research, but also to find means to increase people's awareness of themselves and their situations. Merely presenting the facts is not enough. We must take into account the nature of resistance to understanding. Hence we must develop procedures and create educational situations in which people can be brought into close touch with their feelings and their authentic selves. At the same time there can be no letup in political activity aimed at counteracting the propaganda which perpetuates what Robert Jay Lifton calls the cosmology of the Cold War and which serves so well to legitimize for the ordinary citizen some of the great evils of our time.

CHAPTER 11

Conflict, Dominance, and Exploitation

George De Vos

In this [chapter] I juxtapose a consideration of several social and psychological processes in man which are involved in conflict and which are usually considered separately in different frames of reference. Compared with other animals, situations of dominance and conflict in man are compli-

This chapter first appeared in A. de Reuck and J. Knight (eds.), *Conflict in Society:* a Ciba Foundation symposium (London: J & A Churchill, 1968) under the title, "Conflict, Dominance and Exploitation in Human Systems of Social Segregation." It is reprinted here by permission of the author and publisher.

cated by his development of the psychological capacity to manipulate symbols internally and his capacity to constitute groups on the
basis of learned conscious experiences of self as a member of a
particular segment of a total social structure.

The issues I shall touch upon need more elaborate recapitu-
lation of previous theoretical expositions than I can permit myself
within the present limits. I can only refer to the principal sources
on which I draw. On the one hand, I have drawn freely on the
formulations of Emile Durkheim on the role of the sacred in man's
social life.[1]* On the other hand, I refer to psychological processes
formulated on the general psychoanalytical theory of mental development.[2]

Questions of dominance or conflict in man cannot be considered apart from questions of group membership and its symbolic representation in human thought. One of Durkheim's major
contributions to social anthropological theory was his analysis of
the nature of group religious beliefs and practices as they refer to
a sense of group, as well as individual identity as a source of the
experience of power within the individual. To these insights into
man's social nature must be juxtaposed what we are coming to
know of the developmental processes involved progressively in the
maturation of human thought from infancy to adulthood. Understanding conflict and dominance in man involves a thorough ex-
ploration of the psychological development of both his emotions
and his cognitive capacities. Man's social institutions serve to allow
him to express states of inner feeling symbolically in a social context as well as to organize his capacities to direct instrumental behavior toward the explicit realization of social goals.

In the course of cultural evolution man has created forms
of social organization with specialized occupational segments more
complex than those attained by any other animal form. He has
created systems of specialization or stratification that need continually to be maintained by processes of psychological internalization which are more readily disturbed by external events than
those found imprinted as instinctual patterns in other animals.

* Notes for this chapter start on p. 342.

Man's complex systems of social dominance remain uncertain and continually open to conflict.

Human history can be characterized not only by an ever-increasing pace of social evolution but also by an ever-increasing instability and recurrence of conflict from both without and within political or social groups. Dominance among men remains precarious and insecure. Man, throughout his history, has learned to live with more intraspecific violence and conflict than is normally found in the animal kingdom.[3]

In man, developed cultural traditions help to govern behavior and to remove potentials for intragroup conflict. Man's social relationships come to be organized both horizontally and vertically, in groups by sex and age, in generations, in systems of kinship, or, in more complex societies, by systems of informal and formal associations. The systems of social organization based on increased occupational specialization tend also to involve some form of group structure based on distinctions of class or caste. Social dominance in human society, therefore, becomes related to group identity—that is to say, an individual's dominant or subordinate status is defined by group membership even more than by individual prowess. Group status systems, which define how social dominance is stratified, tend to permit the emergence of forms of exploitation of one section of a society by another which can in time become sources of further conflict within the society.

To understand the sources of conflict within a society one must examine both psychologically and sociologically how human beings continue to cope with the potential instabilities of social stratification, either by internal psychological resolutions related to group identity or by social movements resolving overt conflict situations between groups.

When conflict is relatively rare in society, two conditions are operative. First, conceptually and symbolically there appears a stabilized attribution of force or power and hence dominance to individual members placed in particular social positions in the society which is not challenged by those in subordinate positions. Second, this system is not maintained simply by coercion but by the mutual internalization of constraint on each status level, as defined in accord with expected reciprocal group, as well as individual, role behavior among the members of the society.

From one psychological perspective, stabilized patterns of social dominance and prestige in human societies, from their simpler forms even to their more complex structures, are related to the development of a conscious symbolic attribution of the possession of power and potency to particular objects and persons. In the simplest cultures the producer of food, the strongest hunter, or the most enterprising farmer is perceived by other members of his group as possessing power and on this basis is awarded a position of social dominance. But a distinct attribute of all human societies is some perception that power is also possessed by, and dominance awarded to, individuals who demonstrate some prowess in contact with what Durkheim termed the sacred or the supernatural. There are those who are seen to have a gift of religious or supernatural power which enables them, on behalf of the community, to deal with the unknown forces in nature. This form of power can be distinguished from the temporal powers possessed by those manifesting simple profane physical or intellectual force. Homo sapiens became a religious animal as he increased in his capacity to conceptualize and to share symbolic collective representations of the supernatural, as well as the profane, in patterns of social communication.

Force or power becomes an internal subjective human experience: it can only be shared within the conceptual means available within the cultural community. Only with a culturally induced objectification of this experience, through the experiences of socialization from childhood to adulthood, can distinctions be made between changes in the natural world due to will or motivation and simple sequences of mechanical occurrences.

Man throughout his history has tended, therefore, to personalize nature by conceptualizing a supernatural possessed of supermechanical and superpersonal forces which for him form an integral part of the social and natural environment.[4] Supernatural forces are presumed to govern man's life cycle. They regulate birth, fecundity, and food supply, illnesses taking place in his body, and the time and manner of his inescapable death and dissolution. Similarly, the changeability of the natural environment is easily equated with the changeability of human motivations as guided by the emotions of love or rage. In every human culture one finds some developed system of magic and religion to deal with the control of supernatural forces by manipulation or placation. The cogency of these introductory remarks concerning religious power will become clearer when I give further consideration to the basic instrumental-expressive dichotomy in human relationships which governs two distinguishable systems of dominance and subordination in human society.

For purposes of clarity, in the following discussion I would like to distinguish between systems of social stratification which are based on the possession of material power, as institutionalized in political or economic status positions, and those based on the possession of spiritual power which occurs in "hierarchy," the ranking in society according to the relation to the sacred or in more secularized times an affect-laden derivative of a system of expressive social values.[5] I shall return later to this basic distinction between instrumental and expressive dominance or exploitation in society. This distinction is necessary to understand the basic differentiation between social structures based on class or caste.

Before we begin our examination of the instrumental-expressive dichotomy in stabilized dominant-subordinate social systems, it is necessary to consider briefly another side to the internal experience of power resulting from man's uniquely developed psychological structure. Man has a developed capacity to internalize constraint as part of his learning of culture. This internalized feeling of constraint is also basic to the two systems of instrumental social stratification and expressive hierarchy in which man lives.[6] The social pecking order is defined not only by individual dominance patterns but also by group patterns defined by age, sex, occupation, class, and caste. Yet in most instances no overt conflict arises in assuming one's "proper" place in even fairly complex human social systems. The socialization process in human childhood, when properly tuned to adult status structures, usually leads to a fairly automatic assumption of what can be termed proper attitudes of respect by subordinates and responsibility by authorities, which obviates open conflict. In order to understand those occasions where overt conflict arises in human society one therefore has not only to examine problems relevant to adequate analysis of the social structure, but to ask how such problems occur on the psychological level in disrupted patterns of constraint or acceptance of moral authority that result in the appearance of overt conflict between individuals or groups.

If we take a rather overall evolutionary perspective on human conflict, as it relates to man's psychological evolution of an ability to internalize and symbolize his social experiences, two further considerations occur. First, man has developed a fearful capacity to identify with the victims of his own acts of aggression or destruction, whether they be animal or human. He therefore needs to find social and psychological means of escape from this kind of identification by secondary processes of distantiation, which symbolically place his victims at a distance from him. Equipped with an emerging sense of common humanity, he must find in others particular traits abhorrent to his own group's values, in order to feel justified in killing or exploiting them. Second, he has developed a disturbing capacity to internalize conflict itself so that he can become at war within himself. What can be said syncretically about the common aspects of human conflict in caste or class or relationships between the sexes derives from these uniquely human psychological traits of incorporating the environment symbolically and at the same time separating out a developing sense of social self.

The resulting development of a human conscience from these dual processes of taking in and separating out has two disturbing effects on simple biological evolution and the automatic functioning of forces of dominance in nature. Man, a Promethean rebel, interferes with nature through his capacity to identify. For instance, he has learned to protect the weak because he has tendencies to identify with passive victims and therefore has a need to act as a protector or preserver. He has the disconcerting need to engage himself in the impossible task of preserving life and preventing death. He also continually attempts to harness the human capacity for destruction within the bounds set by a given society. The religious systems he has created help him deny death. As part of his uneasy conscience, he has a continual need for self-justification and finds it much more acceptable to define his own behavior as basically defensive rather than as wantonly destructive. He can, through the psychological mechanisms available to him, project his own motives toward destruction on to forces or beings in his external environment, to remove himself or his social group from culpability. The development of symbols related to the experience of force is inescapably linked to religious symbolism as well as to a sense of process between means and ends or to representations of natural causality.

In short, religiously sanctioned systems of belief help men to deny socially, through the sanctions of collective representations, the immutable facts of nature as they are. Culture creates consistent distortions in perception which curiously serve to direct men toward the attainment of social goals. Cultures regulate basic psychological mechanisms which permit internalized experience and ensure a continuity of social identity on the one hand and on the other determine how the various members of a segmented society project unacceptable feelings or emotions that are cognitively dissonant with acceptable role definitions of self.[7]

Societies define specified behavior as acceptable or dissonant within particular roles and statuses. Since potentials for learning social roles are greater than the dimensions for action afforded by any particular role, man has a much greater potential than can be realized in concrete behavior. Sanctioning systems, partially internalized, are necessary to contain behavioral tendencies within socially acceptable patterns. Sanctioning systems are controlled and manipulated by the dominant power segments of the society toward the realization of their own purposes; but it must be recognized that the dominant members themselves become subject to such sanctioning systems and social values guiding social behavior. The needs and fears of the dominant group itself are structured by cultural traditions. They cannot escape internalized patterns which limit their freedom of action.

The capacity to internalize feelings and identify with the

needs of others can, in some instances, lead to a source of tension and dissension within a dominant segment of the society. On the one hand, there are those who become directed by the universalizing of moral imperatives and thereby seek to protect the weak and helpless with whom they identify and thus artificially to prolong their survival. On the other hand, many members of a dominant group will seek to increase the gains to be derived from the prerogatives of dominant status and continue to exploit those who are individually or collectively the weaker segments of the society.

Sociologically, one must study societies in terms of processes of group inclusion and exclusion. On a psychological level, one examines the processes of identification and of maintaining distance from alien groups. Psychologically, one has not only to learn to identify with one's own group but in a segmented society one has selectively to avoid any strong identification with other segments of the society to which one owes lesser allegiance. There is a constant tension in social identity between belonging and alienation. The processes of socialization taking place during childhood are selective and help to determine the relative impermeability of the individual not only to extracultural aliens but also to meaningful experiences with members of his own society belonging to other social segments. On the part of members of the socially dominant group there is a need to maintain one's self and one's status by symbolically maintaining distance from those who are perceived as inferior. There is a proneness to resort to inflexible automatic psychological defenses to maintain the security of a selective identity, through symbols which maintain this distance.

Being sensitive to some inner awareness of the motivations attributable to socially submerged groups, it is difficult for men in dominant positions to avoid feelings of possible retribution from exploited segments of their own society. To illustrate briefly, W. N. Stephens, in a . . . cross-cultural analysis of the institutionalization of severe menstrual taboos,[8] finds that institutionalized restrictive practices against women are significantly more pronounced in polygamous societies in which the social status of women is low. One can interpret his results as suggesting that the greater the political dominance of men over women, the greater the fear of women, and consequently the greater the need to maintain barriers securing the social status of men. Generally, the greater the exploitation of subordinate groups, the greater the social need to maintain external symbols of status differentiation.

There are two forms of exploitation practiced by dominant groups upon the vulnerable lower segments of a society. The first of these, rationally goal-directed or "instrumental" exploitation, the use of subordinates to realize one's own goals or desires, has become well recognized as playing a central role in the drama of human history. Marxist theory of class stratification is built round an analysis of the various forms taken by goal-oriented, exploitative relationships between dominant and subordinate groups in society. Class conflict resulting from instrumental exploitation has been well described. There is no need for repetition here. Instead, I would like to draw more specific attention to a second general form of social exploitation found in systems of social segregation related to caste or sexual division. This second form of social exploitation I term "expressive" exploitation. Social science theory, with the exception of theories derived in part at least from some form of dynamic psychology, tends to have an instrumental bias in analyzing the determinants of social relationships. Therefore, what I term expressive exploitation has not received the attention it deserves, although various forms of human conflict can be traced to the operation of such a system in particular societies.[9]

As I define it, expressive exploitation is related directly to the irrational and unconscious psychological processes and motives characteristic of man's complex mental structure. The motives behind such exploitation are less readily perceived than those leading to instrumental exploitation. It is much more apparent when socially dominant members of a society make instrumental use of others for enhancement of direct pleasure or material advantage than when indirect use is made of others for a psychological advantage. Nevertheless, one finds institutionalized forms of exploitation, as practiced by politically dominant groups—such as those that have evolved into definable caste structures—whose social functioning cannot be understood simply on a utilitarian basis. Further implications thus exist in such situations, and a theoretical explanation in terms of psychological processes becomes necessary for further understanding in a dimension not yet sufficiently considered.

Expressive exploitation, although universal in one form or other, is most visibly institutionalized in societies that are rigidly segregated by birth into occupational groupings. Inherent is a biological and/or a religious concept of unalterable inferiority which distinguishes one group of men from another. In external group or cultural relationships this patterning of belief is apparent in the justification of wars. Within a society, it justifies maintaining a fixed social order of dominance and subordination from birth to death.

The relative presence of institutionalized forms of expressive exploitation in social hierarchy is what distinguishes caste from class, a distinction that cannot be clearly held if one analyzes exploitation and conflict solely within a Marxist social-theoretical framework. The Marxist examination of complex, highly stratified societies stresses the fact that in such social systems, with their high degrees of occupational specialization, the economically dominant groups are able to exploit the primary production of workers or agricultural laborers for the exercise of economic and political power by which to maintain or increase their dominant status.

This line of analysis overlooks sources of expressive gratification derived from social stratification by both the dominant and subordinate groups. First, this analysis overlooks the continual presence to some degree in everyone of feelings of helplessness and dependency which become related to some sense of belonging to a particular society. If one examines the actual organization of any society, simple or complex, it is not found to be necessary to exert direct coercion since, as we have already noted, human beings are prone to internalize constraint so that each can find a place with minimal conflict within some stable system of social stratification. Individuals voluntarily place themselves with fair certainty and regularity within a particular social segment of the society without experiencing any continual sense of rebellion or coercion. On the contrary, there is found in most stable societies gratification of particular needs and expectations by the system, based on divisions made for the realization of mutual obligations as well as an alleviation of feelings of dependency and helplessness.

The Marxist interpretation of history overlooks a second aspect of stratification, that related to the literal sense of the term *hierarchy*, a religious-value ordering of status in society—that is to say, a system of status stratification based on social values or religious criteria that have to do both with a sense of social self-identity that is part of the particular history of the group or society and with the supernatural. The presence within society of social hierarchy related to expressive social value can become functionally independent of political or economic considerations for fairly long periods of history.

Religious criteria of hierarchy have to do with two fundamental concerns. The first is a characteristic concern for the proper exercise of religious power as distinct from political power. Religious power is expressed in relationships to supernatural forces which are an integral part of most social systems. The second is that in value hierarchies there appears concern with relative degrees of purity and contamination among the members of the society as they influence relationships with the supernatural or express in specialized behavior the supposedly unchangeable values of the group. In societies with a strong sense of hierarchy, concepts of purity and contamination can become as prepotent in determining social status as political or economic prowess. Such societies are apt to become organized into some form of caste structure. In more modern times feelings of relative degrees of purity or contamination can become linked to pseudoscientific concepts of racial superiority. Although caste structures can become elaborated, as in the case of India, caste in essence is the institutionalizing of a self-perpetuating, endogamous, and elevated or degraded segment of the population separated off as uniquely different from the majority of the people. This difference relates to a sense of hierarchy felt to be natural and proper in maintaining distinct segments within a society.

In many societies there is a tendency to fuse in one dominant status position the possession of political and religious power. A hereditary kingship usually involves hierarchical as well as political dominance. One finds numerous anthropological examples of the presence of a divine king.[10] One finds, for example, in ancient Chinese or Japanese culture in their early forms that the king or emperor also served as a principal high priest in the performance of religious ritual. One finds throughout J. Frazer's *Golden Bough* [11] a compilation of evidence from Europe and Africa to the same effect, that political and religious systems of dominance tended in many instances to be unified in the person of a single individual. There are readily ascertainable psychological reasons for attributing all forms of power to single dominant individuals.

Sebastian De Grazia in his perceptive volume *The Political Community* [12] discusses the magical and religious expectations usually held by members of the society in respect to their leader.

The tendency toward hereditary kingship stems from the attribution of magicoreligious powers to the ruler. The sacred functions of kingship made it essential to ensure the continuity of blood in the kingly line, in order not to jeopardize the wellbeing of the entire group.

Continuity of ritual purity makes it incumbent that marriage and reproduction be regulated. Such systems of social regulation of reproduction within specialized occupational segments of the society enter into any operational definition of caste.[13]

Endogamy, important as it is from the standpoint of social structure, is not by itself sufficient to produce caste even when it is linked directly to occupational specialization within a society. In traditional societies, caste begins to appear as institutionally operative only if sacrificial ritual has to be performed by a specially elevated group or ritually polluting activities must be performed by a debased social group. In examining the appearance of types of endogamy related to the concept of a sacred or ritual function in society (compare Durkheim's discussion of the "sacred"), one can note that there are numerous instances in which there are types of social interaction which tend to lead to the creation of a ritually endogamous, elevated sacred group as well as the converse type of relationships which lead toward the formation of a ritually polluted out-caste group. In a unified theory of caste, both of these tendencies toward institutionalizing a social hierarchy in terms of innate purity must be considered. In societies in which social hierarchy is defined in sacred rather than secular terms, there is a need to separate off and elevate certain groups of individuals who deal with the supernatural. Conversely, there is the need to maintain the degraded position of any social segment whose behavior personifies the reprehensible or unclean, the polluting or dangerous.

The study of caste in various cultures seems to suggest that there are fewer instances of the continued stability of an in-breeding elevated caste than of the persistence of degraded or pariah out-caste groups. For example, efforts in European societies to establish the divine right of kings by maintaining an endogamous nobility were continually vitiated by the sexual proclivities of the nobility themselves, whose interests strayed beyond that directed to women of a sufficiently elevated nature. On the other hand, the type of ritual specialization which occurs when a priestly caste becomes separated off from the rest of the society is often marked by a lack of continuity by means of endogamous reproduction. There are relatively few recorded historical instances of self-perpetuating social segments such as the priests of early judaism or those of Hindu India. Since religious asceticism is more often an act of adult will and the exercise of self-imposed constraints on behavior or, in some instances, the appearance of special "talents" which are nonhereditary in nature, rather than the result simply of birth into a specific group of pure individuals, there is perhaps less cultural occasion for the formation of a successfully maintained endogamous elevated group than for the occurrence of the opposite, a polluted and debased out-caste minority whose members are reprehensible from the standpoint of marriage. The fixed establishment of a social caste such as the Brahmans in India, who maintain a dominant position from the Kshtryas, or warrior caste, is a relatively rare cultural or social structural development.

There are more numerous examples of the persistence of socially exploited pariahs who are also separated off by "sacred" considerations. These individuals are debased by their continued close contact to the demonic or the uncanny in some instances.[14] In most instances pariah castes perform innately polluted acts as part of their occupation, but the inherent pollution becomes something from which they cannot be cleansed. It persists by blood continuity into their offspring whether they practice the demeaning occupation or not.

One can point out the psychological equivalents of caste in more recent racialist attitudes in Europe and America in which particular cultural or ethnic groups are considered to be of biologically different—inferior—"racial" origins from the majority of the society. Cultural, racial, or religious minorities are viewed as indigestible elements in the body politics, as witnessed in Nazi Germany, the American South, or, more recently, in Great Britain. Although of seeming diverse cultural origins, present-day racialist attitudes share a common element in that they are direct psychological equivalents to caste attitudes and that when they are allowed to become institutionalized they serve to segment the society into a caste hierarchy.

It is the persistence of socially debased groups in spite of a change in the political and economic structure of a society that brings out the essential difference between a class and a caste structure. The irrational-expressive exploitation involved in caste differs radically from the utilitarian usage of subordinate individuals in a class structure or in slavery as an institution. In a class society shifts in economic distribution or an increase in the power of a particular previously submerged group result with time in a social readjustment making for greater consistency in the economic, social, and political aspects of ascribed social position. In a caste society, however, such readjustment does not occur. Increased economic or political power does not lead to the dropping of sanctions against intermarriage.

In our volume on caste in Japan [15] we describe how the religious and occupational justification for the maintenance of an untouchable caste has disappeared, but, nevertheless, vague feelings concerning the possible contaminating effects of contact, the supposed inherent uncleanliness, and the supposed biological inferiority of the former officially designated out-castes not only serve to maintain, sub rosa, their caste status, but have resulted since 1871 in an actual proportionate eightfold increase in the percentage of the out-caste population to be found in present-day Japan. No amount of wealth or occupational or professional prestige removes the out-caste stigma. Similarly, F. Barth[16] reports how in Swat, in spite of the Muslim egalitarian ideology in opposition to caste, one finds "holy men" forming an elevated caste, and sweepers and other untouchables forming a pariah group in which hypergamy (marrying up from one social stratum to the next on the part of women) does not occur. Whereas in the middle ranges of the stratification system of Swat there is a positive correlation between ritual status and political-economic status, this correlation does not extend to the debased group of sweeper origin. Harold Isaacs, in his book on India's exuntouchables,[17] illustrates in detail the same phenomena continuing in modern India, where the professional or other accomplishments of an out-caste do not lead to mobility, as would occur in a class society.

The maintenance of caste, in spite of social change, cannot be traced to instrumental reasons, although, naturally, there will be a continued economic exploitation of any vulnerable submerged group. The maintenance of caste depends on the transmission from one generation to the next of functionally autonomous psychophysiologically based attitudes and aversions which depend upon the continued presence of a disparaged group for their expression. There is strong resistance to change in the institution which permits the expressive exploitation of a submerged group who represent the socially and personally disavowed in a society. The caste hierarchy can therefore be distinguished from forms of class stratification by the persistence of socialized feelings of aversion, revulsion, and disgust directed toward a group of despised, inferior beings who are separated off from "good people" by a contaminated blood lineage. Sanctions preventing intermarriage are most strongly invoked against the two extremes of any caste hierarchy and are generally not subject to exceptions. In the intermediate ranges of an evolved caste hierarchy, on the other hand, hierarchical position will tend to be congruent with the instrumentally organized political and economic determinants of social stratification.

It has often been pointed out how a society can externalize

its internal tensions by going to war to "defend itself" from its neighbor. The use of groups of individuals outside the society is a fairly well recognized form of displacement of internal tensions. As such, war can be as much or more an expressive act as a means of instrumental gain at the expense of others.

So, too, the peopling of the external world with super-natural, malevolent forces, demons, witches, and warlocks permits a displacement of tensions from within the person or social group on to outside sources of malevolence or pollution.[18] Such behavior is obviously far more expressive in nature than instrumental in intent.

Similar forms of expressive exploitation are found in the scapegoating of vulnerable social segments within the society itself. The scapegoating or projective function of an out-caste group or in some societies of women who are held in lower status is more subtle and less direct.

First, the disparaged group within does have instrumental utility and the dominant groups have a continuing feeling of dependency toward this group and toward the functions that it performs, both those of a menial, instrumental nature and those of an expressive, psychological nature. The dominant members therefore want the out-caste group to continue the exercise of its functions and cannot practice irretrievable violence upon it.

Second, the out-caste or disparaged group is necessary for the maintenance of a secure definition of superior social status on the part of the dominant groups. It fits on the bottom of a hier-archy of virtue by examplifying inferiority in its varying forms.[19] For those individuals who have some source of continuing in-security relative to their status either as men vis-à-vis women or as members of a dominant social group, a sense of threat is coun-tered by some symbolic affirmation of their status demanded of those in the legally and socially subordinate group. Any diminu-tion in deference can result in immediate sensitivity and in the use of coercion or even violence to reaffirm dominance. Periodi-cally, when there are sources of increased tension or insecurity, the individual, in concert with others of his group undergoing a similar sense of tension, may seek alleviation by recourse to culturally or institutionally available acts of scapegoating involving particular members of a subordinate group. As a collective act the scapegoating can also serve to reaffirm dominance and to intimidate the subordinate group, to prevent overt challenge or manifest conflict.

The psychic energy necessary to maintain a projective system is continual in those individuals bedeviled by processes with which they cannot cope internally, and the need for some form of external projection remains unceasing. B. Bettleheim and M. Janowitz, in a systematic psychological and sociological study of both anti-Semitism and anti-Negro attitudes in the United States,[20] find that prejudice in individuals is inversely related to the strength of integration of the ego. Individuals who manifest relatively weak integration of the ego do not seem to be able to manage inner conflicts without resorting to some form of projection or displacement. Individuals who cannot well manage sources of intrapsychic tension are especially prone, therefore, to continual recourse to institutionalized scapegoating.

Collectively held and socially reinforced representations help to sustain individual psychic structures. By resorting to historically available sustaining group beliefs, whether they be of a positive or a negative nature, the individual can gain some relief from his own tensions since the energy demanded to believe in a collectively held social myth is much less than that necessary to create and maintain an individual projective system. The true believer in some form of socially accepted prejudice is less threatened and can maintain a level of acceptable social adjustment and solidarity with others who may also be faced with similar internal stresses. Whereas the weight of maintaining individual projections might be unbearable and lead to a form of behavior defined as psychopathological, social projections shared collectively within a group permit some form of psychic balance to be maintained without any overt social malfunctioning. Under ordinary conditions overt conflict does not appear. However, when stress becomes unmanageable, some overt form of violence may erupt.

To the degree to which the system of dominance in society, be it hierarchical in castes or stratified into class segments, is internalized and to the degree that systems of social self-identity are mutually accommodating, conflict remains minimal. Given situations of social change and the possibilities of taking on new definitions of social self-identity, either from cultural incursions from outside the traditional society or on the basis of internal social changes, situations of conflict become more evident. In the modern age with its rapid social change one may predict an increasing tempo of internal social conflicts becoming visible in segmented social orders.

[In summary,] there are two forms of exploitation by dominant groups within human society. The first of these, rationally goal-directed or "instrumental" exploitation—the use of subordinates to realize one's own goals or desires—has been well recognized as playing a central role in the drama of human history. The Marxist theory of class stratification is built round the various forms taken by goal-orientated exploitative relationships between dominant and subordinate groups.

The second form of exploitation, which I term "expressive" exploitation, has not received the attention it deserves in relation to human social systems. It derives from the irrational and unconscious psychological processes that are a characteristic of man's complex mental structure. This form of exploitation, also practiced by politically dominant groups, is periodically found institutionalized in societies with a definable caste structure or in some societies stressing the basic social inferiority of women. The presence of this form of exploitation is what distinguishes class from caste, a distinction which cannot be clearly made solely within a Marxist theoretical framework.

Man's capacity to identify brings human conflict within him. Man experiences conflict intrapsychically. Potentially permeable to the feelings and experiences of others, given also to the projection of his feelings into objects and beings about him, he find that his culture only imperfectly helps him attain, with relative degrees of assuredness, a secure social self-identity. This social self-identity tends to be somewhat less secure in situations in which a pronounced continuous dependence upon an exploited group cannot be resolved. Some societies which put stress on positions difficult to attain or maintain in a status hierarchy also often provide, for purposes of expressive exploitation, a particular group or segregated segment which personifies the socially or personally disavowed. In times of social stress, this group may be scapegoated as an expression of general social tension.

PART III

If war is too important to be left to the generals, perhaps evil, ordinarily the province of theologians, deserves more attention than it now receives from students of society. Ideas about evil (as well as the absence of ideas about it) offer clues to the ways a society may deal with anxiety and with deviants. In a suggestive historical sketch, Robert N. Bellah shows how traditional American understandings of evil may accelerate social destructiveness in which harsh and brutal exclusions exist side by side with a universal conception of man. Bellah traces this duality with special reference to blacks and to communists. In looking to the future he sketches a new image of man—a theme to which Sanford later returns. In a long chapter that deals with many of the themes so far raised in the book, Charles Drekmeier explores preconditions for and failures of moral sensitivity, asking how men come to see one another as things to be used or destroyed. In his discussion of two ways of knowing and their rela-

174

THE NATURE
OF EVIL

*tion to destructiveness, Drekmeier offers a variety of perspectives—
phenomenological, behavioral, and philosophical—not often
found in a single author. He asks whether a form of reason has
emerged which impedes, perhaps makes impossible, our ability
to see destructive behavior for what it is. The chapter concerns
separation in all its variety, whether between man and things, a
person and his fellows, a society and its "outsiders," or behavior
and understanding. Whenever man ill uses his powers as extended
by technology, we hear that moral development has lagged behind
scientific advances, but what meaning can we tease out of this
cliche? How is moral knowledge related to the kinds of knowledge that are creating a second, man-made nature? Morality is
often regarded as a vaguely impractical set of maxims, but in exploring the relation between evil and our society, both Bellah and
Drekmeier stress the survival value of moral sensitivity.*

175

CHAPTER **12**

Evil and the American Ethos

Robert N. Bellah

I would like to define the perimeters
of our problem with two quotations. The first is from the Rev-
erend Samuel Purchas, one of the first Englishmen to describe the
New World opened up by the great explorations. In 1614, when
Britain was on the verge of imperial and colonial expansion on a
worldwide scale, he wrote the following panegyric to the unity
of mankind religiously conceived:

*The tawney Moore, blacke Negro, duskie Libyan, ash-col-
oured Indian, olive-coloured American should with the whiter
European become* one sheep-fold, *under* one great Sheepheard,
till this mortalitie being swallowed up of Life, *wee may all* be one,
as he and the father are one . . . *without any more distinction*

177

of Colour, Nation, Language, Sexe, Condition, all may bee One
in him that is One, and onely blessed for ever.[1]*

The other quotation is from the nineteen-year-old infantryman in
Vietnam mentioned in Chapter Five:

*I think someone ought to kill those long-haired, queer bastards
back in the world. Anyone who demonstrates against the war
ought to be lined up and killed, just like any gook here.*[2]

Unfortunately both the assertion of the fundamental unity of man
and the assertion that whole groups of people are defective and
justly subject to extreme aggression are genuinely part of our
tradition. Only five years after Purchas wrote, the first group of
Negro slaves landed at Jamestown, Virginia, and the commonest
way in seventeenth century America to indicate the distinction
between black and white was to speak of Negroes and Christians.
On the one hand being a Christian meant having a deep commitment to the oneness of man; on the other it meant acknowledging
the right of Christian Europeans to enslave any who differed radically from them in belief, custom, and complexion. The dialectic
between inclusion and exclusion is found among all peoples. But
nowhere more than in America has a universal conception of man
existed side by side with such harsh and brutal exclusions. Nor
can we argue for the existence of two American traditions, a good
and a bad. As Thomas Mann had sadly to remind his fellow exiles
thirty years ago, there are not two Germanys but one. The
demonic and the supremely creative are deeply intermixed in the
German soul. It is the same with America. The best and
the worst go hand in hand. Only, perhaps, by understanding that
can we begin to move beyond our customary murderousness to
accept both ourselves and others in a universal community.

In this connection it may be well to point out that William
Calley, the other American soldiers at My Lai, Spiro T. Agnew,
and the whole silent majority are, for better and for worse, our
brothers. If we deny that they too are Americans, or worse, if we

deny that they too are men, then we exemplify our problem and have no point of leverage from which to overcome it. The first place to look if we are to understand the deeply human need to reject others in order to define ourselves is in our own hearts. Then if we have to point the finger at others, as we must, it will be with charity and forgiveness and not with murderous rejection.

A historical sketch of the development of a sense of national community in America can provide a helpful background for understanding the meaning of evil in the American ethos. Our nation began with the convenant communities of the early settlers, of which the Plymouth Colony and its Mayflower Compact have become an archetype but of which the much larger Massachusetts Bay Colony was a more decisive example. From the beginning our society or important segments of it were based on the voluntaristic compact of equals and were governed democratically. But remember what kind of democratic voluntaristic society this was. In early Massachusetts church membership was a prerequisite for voting. This was a community of saints, a gathering of the elect. And there was a sharp dichotomy not only between the elect who had come to the New World and those sunk in sin and left behind, but also between the elect and the reprobate in the New World. The reprobates, those not morally upright or religiously orthodox, were excluded from full membership in the community and were forcibly controlled and repressed by the elect. There was indeed a close relation between the inner repression of the Puritan Protestant character, which guaranteed the responsible behavior of the elect (the full members of the community), and the outer repression of the nonconformists who did not behave as the community expected. From the beginning this relation between a democratic social order and personal and social repression resulted in a peculiarly sharp distinction between the saved and the damned, not only religiously but socially.

It is worth contrasting this social order with that of hierarchical societies which remained Catholic. From one view such societies remained authoritarian, nondemocratic, and nonvoluntaristic. Everyone had his place in an infinite series of gradations both in the church and in the civil society. No one was free, though all had some degrees of freedom, but no one was excluded.

Indeed the Catholics kept a sense of total community which the Protestants had shattered, and even though this community was upheld in conservative or even reactionary ways, it remained a living ideal which Protestants are only now beginning to rediscover. The Protestant notions of individual saintliness and the rule of the elect provided no basis for a genuinely inclusive community.

The original Protestant position, however, was gradually modified. The early Calvinists held that God alone decided in the mystery of predestination who was saved and who damned and a man could do nothing whatsoever about it. If God gave a man a sign of his salvation, that sign was the basis for admission to church membership, and a man could achieve that status no other way. The eighteenth century saw a gradual erosion of that position by Arminianism, a late form of the old Christian heresy of Pelagianism, which argued that man can save himself through his own good works. The Arminians did not put it so bluntly, but they did interpose a strong element of pulling oneself up to salvation by one's own bootstraps. The Great Awakening, the beginning of American revivalism in the 1740s, was not entirely Arminian in theology, but it helped to spread the doctrine which later became basic in American pietism and revivalism. Arminianism greatly expanded the community of the elect by providing religious freedom of opportunity. Admission to the elect was still contingent on strict adherence to high standards of moral conduct, but in principle no one who conformed could be excluded.

Many have seen the Great Awakening as the religious forerunner of the American Revolution, which established a society that in certain respects was a secular version of the elect community of old New England. Certainly the imagery that America was a New Israel was strong in the early years of the republic. America was supposed to give birth to a new man in contrast to the old man of Europe. In the great upsurge attending the formation of the new nation, the idea of an exemplary role, of a city set on a hill, was extremely prominent. But full membership in the society was not open to everyone. There was a strong expectation of a certain level of moral behavior (which

Benjamin Franklin describes very well how to simulate, for those
not entirely comfortable with it), and a substantial economic
standing in the community was essential. Both were presumably
available to anyone who displayed the necessary plain living and
hard work. But even in those days some were defined by their
very nature as deficient and therefore incapable of gaining full
admission—namely, Indians and Negroes. One need not roman-
ticize the treatment of these groups in Latin America to realize
that they were never so drastically excluded as they were here. The
process then and still today operates with a peculiar double bind
in a Protestant society. First it asserts that a certain group of
people lacks the qualities that would allow its members as individuals to rise, and then it systematically deprives that group of
all the resources necessary for its members indeed to rise.

The nineteenth century saw for the first time in America
the large-scale immigration of non-Protestant and non-English
speaking peoples, which toward the end of the century and the
early years of the next turned into a vast flood of millions of
human beings. They were mainly Catholics and Jews from southern and eastern Europe, and their arrival profoundly challenged
the American national community. At that point a new conception
of community based on cultural pluralism might have developed,
and indeed some Americans proposed such a solution. But the
main line was quite different. The demand was for assimilation,
the end of hyphenated Americans, 100 per cent Americanization,
all summed up in the image of the melting pot. This image took
on graphic form in an event described by Robert Michaelson.[3]
For a festival sponsored by Henry Ford during the early 1920s a
giant pot was built outside the gates of his factory. Into this pot
danced groups of gaily dressed immigrants dancing and singing
their native songs. From the other side of the pot emerged a single
stream of Americans dressed alike in the contemporary standard
dress and singing the national anthem. As the tarantellas and the
polkas at last faded away only the rising strains of the national
anthem could be heard as all the immigrants finally emerged. The
enormous pressures which created this vast transformation
amounted almost to a forced conversion.

By and large a literal melting pot did not develop. Major non-Protestant groups have neither abandoned their separate religious organizations nor massively intermarried with the majority population. While one ought not to underestimate the external pressures for cultural accommodation in the heyday of Americanization, the massive adoption of basic American values by new immigrant groups seems to have been largely voluntary. It was even, in spite of many traumas, liberating insofar as the new cultural values were much more open than were the narrow conceptions brought over from the peasant or ghetto past in the old country. And yet all too often the liberating induction into new values, and the new opportunities that never existed in the old country amounted in the end only to conversion to the now fully secularized version of American Arminianism, namely the worship of what William James called the bitch goddess, success.

In order to indicate what the dominance of the success ideal did to the national community I quote two of our greatest twentieth century American prophets, Henry Miller and James Baldwin. Miller shows us the almost maniacal upward sweep of the quest for success, Baldwin its inevitably accompanying fear of the downward fall. In the 1920s Miller worked as personnel manager for the telegraph company in New York City, where his main job was hiring messengers. One day the vice-president bawled him out and said he would like to see someone write a Horatio Alger book about the messengers. Of this event Miller writes:

I thought to myself—you poor old futzer, you, just wait until I get it off my chest. . . . I'll give you an Horatio Alger book . . . . My head was in a whirl to leave his office. I saw the army of men, women and children that had passed through my hands, saw them weeping, begging, beseeching, imploring, cursing, spitting, fuming, threatening. I saw the tracks they left on the highways, lying on the floor of freight trains, the parents in rags, the coal box empty, the sink running over, the walls sweating and between the cold beads of sweat the cockroaches running like mad; I saw them hobbling along like twisted gnomes or falling backwards in the epileptic frenzy. . . . I saw the walls giving way and

*the pest pouring out like a winged fluid, and the men higher up
with their iron-clad logic, waiting for it to blow over, waiting for
everything to be patched up, waiting, waiting contentedly . . .
saying that things were temporarily out of order. I saw the Horatio
Alger hero, the dream of a sick America, mounting higher and
higher, first messenger, then operator, then manager, then chief,
then superintendent, then vice-president, then president, then
trust magnate, then beer baron, then Lord of all the Americas,
the money god, the god of gods, the clay of clay, nullity on high,
zero with ninety-seven thousand decimals fore and aft. . . . I will
give you Horatio Alger as he looks the day after the Apocalypse,
when all the stink has cleared away.*[4]

Baldwin shows us the other side of the Horatio Alger myth:

*Now I think there is a very good reason why the Negro in this
country has been treated for such a long time in such a cruel way,
and some of the reasons are economic and some of them are political. . . . Some of them are social, and these reasons are somewhat more important because they have to do with our social
panic, with our fear of losing status. This really amounts sometimes to a kind of social paranoia. One cannot afford to lose status
on this peculiar ladder, for the prevailing notion of American life
seems to involve a kind of rung-by-rung ascension to some hid-
eously desirable state. If this is one's concept of life, obviously one
cannot afford to slip back one rung. When one slips, one slips
back not a rung but back into chaos and no longer knows who
he is. And this reason, this fear, suggests to me one of the real
reasons for the status of the Negro in this country. In a way, the
Negro tells us where the bottom is: because he is there, and where
he is, beneath us, we know where the limits are and how far we
must not fall. We must not fall beneath him. We must never allow
ourselves to fall that low, and I am not trying to be cynical or
sardonic. I think if one examines the myths which have proliferated in this country concerning the Negro, one discovers beneath these myths a kind of sleeping terror of some condition
which we refuse to imagine. In a way, if the Negro were not here,*

we might be forced to deal within ourselves and our own person-
alities, with all those vices, all those conundrums, and all those
mysteries with which we have invested the Negro race.[5]

Let us recapitulate the argument so far. From the beginnings of our history American society has been based on a community of voluntary participants and has realized more genuine
democracy and equality than was usually the case in Europe or
the rest of the world. But also from the beginning that community
was based on exclusion and repression—first, the intrapsychic
repression of rejected impulse and, second, the repression of those
members of the society who represented those rejected impulses
and had to be controlled and denied full membership. Originally
this distinction was put in religious terms: the elect against the
reprobates. Later, especially after the spread of Arminian piety,
the distinction was between moral, upstanding members of the
community and the lazy and recalcitrant. Finally, after the in-
stallation of the bitch goddess, it was a distinction between the
successful and the failures.

At every stage there has been a tendency to equate these
distinctions with that between good and bad. The best of the
early Puritans, in spite of our stereotypes, recognized the sin in
their own hearts as well as in the hearts of the reprobates and
attributed their election to the sole majesty of God. They carried
out their mission of constructing an orderly and in many ways
repressive society with a heavy sense of responsibility to a higher
power. It was, however, difficult to maintain the tension and complexity of the Reformation view of man, and, especially with the
rise of Arminianism, the doctrine that man's salvation resulted
from his own good deeds, those who felt themselves saved tended
to forget the evil in their own hearts and to attribute it all to the
reprobates and ne'er-do-wells. And it has been hard indeed for
the successful in secular terms not to feel that they have earned
their position, that they deserve it because they are somehow good
and those who have failed are bad. This position leads naturally
to Richard Nixon's statement in his inaugural address that "I
know the heart of America is good." By America we can be sure
he meant the silent majority and not the communists, criminals,

hippies, student radicals, and black militants which he leaves to Agnew to attack.

Another consequence of this primitive form of splitting of good and evil to which Americans have been so prone is the notion that the good, being good, can do no evil. Any action taken against groups seen to be evil is justified, for the good can have only good ends in view. Thus in America the enslavement of blacks, the mass murder of Indians, the lynching of Negroes, the atom bombing of Japanese, and the massacring of Vietnamese have all had their defenders. Other Americans have condemned these actions and have worked to make America in many ways a humane society. But just as the army has not established an effective sanction system which would prevent My Lai and the many small My Lais that take place every day, so more generally in America we have not been able to establish effective controls over aggression against a variety of powerless out-groups.

Two groups have been particular victims of the American tendency to project evil and then to inflict aggression on the allegedly evil group. The first is the American Negro, who has received more brutality and aggression from the majority population over a longer period of time than have all other groups combined. All rejected unconscious tendencies have been projected onto the Negro, in particular sexuality, aggression, dirtiness, and sloth—precisely those things which do not fit the stereotype of the Protestant Ethic and which therefore most need to be controlled in white Americans. The Negro is punished, restricted, and reviled in order symbolically to help the white man keep his self-control.

From the beginning of contact white Americans have been fascinated and horrified by the blackness of the black man's skin. Here they found an objective symbolization of their inner propensity for moral splitting, for black and white thinking. Some of the greatest of the Puritans were aware of the superficiality of this equation. Cotton Mather went out of his way to deny that skin color had any ultimate significance: "Their *complexion* sometimes is made an Argument why nothing should be done for them. A *Gay* sort of argument! As if the great God went by the Complexion of men, in His Favours to them! As if none but *Whites* might hope to be Favoured and Accepted with God! . . . Away

with such Trifles! The God who *looks on the Heart,* is not moved
by the colour of the *Skin;* is not more propitious to one *Colour*
than another." [6] But even Mather thought that the black skin,
though ultimately unimportant, was in this world a handicap, to
say the least, and he exhorted his white listeners to "be the Happy
Instruments, of Converting, the *Blackest* Instances of *Blindness*
and Baseness, into admirable *Candidates* of Eternal Blessedness." [7]
What exactly the blackness meant to the white man is indicated
by the lurid sexual and aggressive fantasies that he early invented
about the Negro and which circulate to this day.[8] The deepest
fear of the slaveholding population was that the blacks would rise
up, kill the white men, and ravish the white women. This fantasy
is still alive in those involved in the so-called white backlash. It is
understandable only in terms of deep inner problems in the white
psyche and in white culture and society. To the extent that the
black population has been treated so miserably that the fantasy
has some slight justification in fact, it is a self-fulfilling prophecy
brought on by centuries-long treatment of Negroes as instruments
for the working out of white interests and fears rather than as
autonomous human beings in their own right. I dwell on this
issue because it is the deepest trauma in the American soul and
because it underlies all our current problems both domestic and
international.

A second group which has more recently become a representative of our negative identity is the Communists. The Communists seem to stand not so much for general id impulses, though
there is some of that, as for the deep-seated dependency needs that
strong, self-reliant, free enterprisers are not supposed to have.
While we in America are free and independent, in Russia a massive
government takes care of everyone. But those so horrified by big
government and creeping socialism may have unconscious dependency needs they dare not admit. Communism can also stand for
a motive which is almost the opposite of dependency, namely
antiauthoritarian rebelliousness. Being against all constituted authority is symbolized by the opposition of communism to the
Most High, namely its denial of God. But those to whom the
constant reiteration of the phrase *atheistic Communism* or *Godless
Communism* gives such pleasure may themselves be unconscious

atheists, revolutionaries, and father murderers. In such persons the struggle against Communism takes on a bitter intensity, for it is also a struggle against inner impulses which threaten the integrity of their self-images. Under these circumstances they can easily feel that no means are too horrible if they effectively oppose Communism. All the consequences of the American's need to be good and to project evil on others are summed up in our treatment of the Viet Cong, who are both gooks (nonwhites) and Communists. Naturally nothing is too bad for them, and so we have with little compunction, in spite of much bitter protest, conducted in Vietnam one of the most barbaric wars in history.

If this analysis of the place of evil in the American ethos is at all accurate, it calls for a fundamental restructuring of American values. Every society is based on a dialectic of inclusion and exclusion. Every person and every society must have a sense of identity and boundary which defines him or it in relation to others, but that sense of difference does not have to lead to projection and aggression. Difficult though it may be, we must create a society in America which includes all its members and is open toward other societies. Such a goal must not be dismissed as utopian, for our survival and perhaps the survival of the world depend on our ability to realize it. The propensity to identify one's own group as good and to project evil on outsiders is a general human problem that other societies as well need to work on. But our sense of mission, which is part of our dynamism and success, has expressed itself in particularly demanding standards of purity, which, relative to those of many other peoples, have made it exceptionally hard for us to admit our own shortcomings.

If we begin to specify what needs to change, perhaps the most fundamental thing is our view of man. We have lived for a long time with a model of man as one charged by a stern God to carry out his commands, a man who must be up and doing, a man in quest of mastery and success. On the basis of that model we have built a remarkably dynamic society, and we have created resources for vast enterprises such as the conquest of space. But the limitations of that activistic, achieving image of man are now our greatest problem. The man narrowly pursuing mastery and success has to repress too much of himself, to narrow his sympathies too drastically to be able to respond adequately to the deepening problems of the twentieth century. We need to be able to accept and use creatively much in our personalities which we have had to deny during the long upward climb. We need a conception of a God who is not only external and commanding but also deeply inner and who speaks from depths of ourselves of which we are scarcely aware. That conception of God implies a new conception of man.

There has been a long history of thought about a new man in America. Let me describe what I see as some of the traits that we need if we are to face our problems and to overcome our destructiveness. This new man will be able to accept his darker side better than we have usually been able to do. He will be able to accept his id impulses, his sexuality, his dependency, and his rebelliousness without being overwhelmed by them and without having to deny them, but he will be able to combine them in an integrated and creative personality. Since he will not have to be lily white in his self-estimation, the symbolic meaning of another's black skin will not terrify him. He will enjoy his brother's blackness as an enrichment and extension of his own humanity rather than being fascinated and frightened by it. The new man will have a strong dose of the Protestant Ethic, for he will still be an American, but he will see that achievement is not the only basis for human dignity and he will value in himself and others much that has no direct connection with the struggle for success. His broadly inclusive conception of humanity will allow him to accept a genuine cultural pluralism which can make America a model for international cultural pluralism.[9] Most of all the new man will not be able to accept a society which condemns any group to a permanently inferior status. Whatever other goals the society will have, the first priority will be to guarantee a floor below which no person and no group will be allowed to fall. A fundamental anxiety about achievement and a deep fear of failure may be understandable in a society of precarious scarcity, but they are wholly unacceptable in a society of material abundance. Internationally the new man will be much less likely to act as an international judge and policeman than Americans have been. He will see that the deepest problem in the world is guaranteeing security and dignity to all people. While we cannot expect such a new man to be perfect or to keep perfect control of his aggression, we can expect that such a new man and the society he creates will have much firmer restraints against the unleashing of brutal aggression against helpless out-groups than Americans have had—a restraint possible only if the aggression formerly expressed in intergroup tensions finds a creative outlet in the conquest of social problems.

The use of the phrase *firmer restraints* may seem to go against the spirit of this chapter. Certainly unthinking admiration of firmness, strength, and hardness and anxious rejection of anything suggestive of weakness, softness, and slackness are part of the syndrome which creates harsh repressiveness. But openness and sensitivity to the widest range of feelings and meanings do not imply the abandonment of all limits and restraints. For example I think it is important to understand the many pressures that the soldiers at My Lai were under and to accept the fact that we too might have acted the same way under certain extreme conditions. There is no need to scapegoat Medina, Calley, or the others, to condemn them as human beings and reject them from the human race. We do have a right, however, to condemn those who have failed to create sanctions so that a My Lai would not happen or to ensure swift and public justice if it did. One can understand the feelings that may lead to the most terrible acts, but that does not justify the acts which in themselves are unqualifiably wrong. Where unjust and inhuman actions occur, we must demand controls and restraint so that they will not happen again. This does not mean extreme and vindictive punishment of a few scapegoats but an entire reorientation of the offending system whether it be the police, national guard, or army. Similarly it may be necessary to use force to defend university buildings against violent attack from outraged students and to institute clear judicial procedures to indicate what are the limits of acceptable political behavior on campus. Here too basic structural reform of the institution may be the only viable long-run solution, but even in that reform some limits and restraints will be necessary. There are no easy recipes for moral action in the world in which we live, but a genuine moral imagination involves both sensitivity to the feelings and aspirations of all persons in question and the ability to make moral judgments of right and wrong.

This new man is not wholly a dream. Chapter Seventeen outlines the conditions for his development, and I think we can see him coming into being around us. Never before has a generation challenged so profoundly our achievement ethic, demanded more strongly the full inclusion of the poor and the oppressed, or sought more fully to express aspects of personality long suppressed in America. Many in this generation have a deeper sense of what it means to be human than has been common in our past. But, and this is not surprising to an American of Calvinist descent, we also see many in this generation who abandon the old splitting of good and evil for a new one. Once again we have a notion of those whose hearts are inherently good as opposed to those against whom any aggression is justified. Often this new mode of splitting uses the rhetoric of revolution, of "the People" and their "enemies," who may be dehumanized by calling them "pigs," and draws on Marxism, which is itself a version of the old-fashioned moralistic splitting and projected aggression that we most need to escape from. The victory of such an ideology could easily lead not to an open and humane society but to one even more repressive and narrow than it is at present. The other side of this coin is that hippies and student radicals seem now to be joining Negroes and Communists as the most convenient target for middle America's hostility, for reasons that should now be clear.

In spite of this depressing tendency toward polarization, the tendencies in the direction of the new man may be deeper and more persistent than are our current pathological eruptions of student violence and police repression, in part because these tendencies, however strengthened by cultural influences from European philosophies or Oriental religions, are also genuine expressions of the American ethos. They are in one sense a later phase of that American experiment that so deeply concerned Thomas Jefferson, Ralph Waldo Emerson, Abraham Lincoln, Walt Whitman, William James, and John Dewey.[10]

I am fully aware that deep structural problems, political and economic, stand in the way of the radical change in American society which I feel is necessary. I have concentrated on the level of conceptions of man not because I underestimate the seriousness and difficulty of those structural problems but because I think in the long run the outcome may be determined more by what image grips the souls of men than by particular institutional rearrangements. The present requires action, but it also requires moral sensitivity and moral imagination, the subject of Chapter Thirteen. Unless we begin to think in ways we have not thought in before we may have no future to think in at all.

CHAPTER **13**

Knowledge as Virtue, Knowledge as Power

Charles Drekmeier

          "**T**hese people are not civilized," remarked General Hughes when queried by Senator Rawlins as to whether the destruction of village shacks in the Philippines was considered to be within the ordinary rules of civilized warfare.[1]* This century, in which it is estimated that fifty million persons have been killed in wars, murderous attacks, and other deadly quarrels, opened with an uneasiness in the minds of many Americans about the manner in which Filipino insurgency had been

* Notes for this chapter start on p. 346.

put down and atrocities committed against women and children rationalized. The incidental killing of civilians had, however, become acceptable military strategy when, in World War II, area bombings of cities with industrial plants were sanctioned; in 1944 the bombing of civilians became an end in itself, the object being to break the will of the enemy. In one night 135,000 citizens of Dresden were killed, twice the number later destroyed at Hiroshima. If one accepts the testimony of a former director of psychiatric research for the Army in Vietnam, the "body count" of slain Viet Cong usually included noncombatants, among them women and children.[2] A high count brings a commendation from the commander. Those familiar in a professional capacity with combat therapy tell us that unrestrained behavior by troops expresses the authorization (generally tacit) of such behavior by commanding officers who may simply convey the impression that certain conduct will not be punished. In military courts soldiers have testified that they were advised by their officers to regard the Vietnamese as "not really people."

When, twenty months after the events of My Lai, it became clear that the incident would soon be public knowledge, an official investigation was launched in an effort to convince the nation that the killing was contrary to policy. The subsequent trial may or may not succeed in obfuscating the issue of ultimate responsibility for the kinds of behavior manifested at My Lai, but we may be almost certain that the crimes against civilians which *are* a part of official policy come to trial only when the offending nation is a defeated power. Indeed, as Chapter Five points out, My Lai deflects our attention from the far more massive—albeit less cold-blooded—civilian destruction represented by the search-and-destroy missions, Operation Phoenix, the B-52 raids and the burning of habitations, the crop destruction, the forcible transfer of civilian populations ("urbanization" policies), the chemical and gas warfare, and the use of other weapons prohibited by conventions to which the United States is a signatory. Should not the outrage engendered by the razing of Ben Suc and the massacre at My Lai extend to actions condemned in international law and custom? Perhaps we perceive, at some level of our minds, that responsibility is more broadly shared; the fact that a fellow countryman can shoot a small child crawling from a ditch in My Lai may indicate that our civilization has a more fragile base than we have been prepared to admit, while the accepted tactics of the war in Indochina are an indictment of the civilization itself.[3]

The killing in Vietnam, and probably in any war, requires the soldier to regard the enemy as something less than human. This image is systematically encouraged by governments and military authorities. The correct choice of strategy is the all-important consideration in a war. The same can be said of modern industrial societies, characterized as they are by a rationality which reduces to a correct choice among strategies as the institutional framework loses its significance. Since productive relationships require no ethical justification, the technical imperative replaces concepts of legitimacy. Rationality itself becomes no more than a corrective within the system and loses its function as a critical standard.[4] The fabric of social interaction, of nondominative communication in which legitimacy is rooted and in which the self is negotiated as it comes to recognize and define itself in relations with others, wears thin as instrumental action preempts the human stage. This chapter suggests the nature of an attitude of mind that finds expression (one would hope an extreme expression) in the argument of the American diplomat in Laos quoted in *Le Monde:* "To make progress in this country, it is necessary to level everything. The inhabitants must go back to zero, lose their traditional culture, for it blocks everything." The potential for evil in collective irrationality does not concern me so much as the dehumanization we have come to accept as a part of our lives and the fact that the reaction samplings taken shortly after the My Lai disclosures revealed that almost two-thirds of the Americans interviewed felt no shock.

What follows is an essay on reason and the construction of meaning, using where they seem appropriate behavioral, philosophical, and phenomenological approaches. The question that dominates these pages is "How do men come to see one another as things to be used or destroyed?" Man and thing, it appears, are born together, and I begin with the prior question pertaining to the nature of the object and the types of perception through which the object is known. Unavoidable is the further question, darker than the first, "Has there emerged a reason which impedes, perhaps makes impossible, our ability to see criminal behavior for what it is?" Has ethics itself been suppressed? Reason, in the tradition of our culture, has had an evaluating function and has depended on concepts that enabled judgment and did not simply function to summarize characteristics. The reasonable man of the law of torts was a man of prudent action the bases of which were recognized standards tested by time in the preservation of human well-being. Reason was insight into the structures of the universe and experience. Reason was contrasted with emotional response but never consistently so, for emotion and sentiment are a large part of the definition of man, and mankind constituted the measure that made reason a normative quality.

Today, however, reason has different functions. The calculations of marketing, the computations of technology, have proven irresistible. Reason has for us become a tool to be employed in the domination of man and nature. The cost-effectiveness calculus refuses to take into account such classic concerns of reason as the long-range consideration, resources like trust or material goods which no one owns (the air we breathe), or the consequences of a policy for the spirit and character of those who execute it. Ends no longer dictate means. My theme is separation: separations within society and separations within the individual himself. I begin with the problem of man's separation from the object world.

Object and meaning. Learning appears to be more than the habituation of certain gestures after a series of trials. Gestaltists hold that learning presupposes a general "attitude" regarding the structure of the context in which the creature operates. Maurice Merleau-Ponty, commenting on Koehler's studies of ape mentality, argues that the broken bit of branch becomes an instrument of the primate only where the pressures of a context indicate its usefulness; as the object is removed from the goal, it loses its instrumental values, "which is to say that it is not made up of precise mechanical properties which would be independent of its position." The chimpanzee cannot vary its points of view, "just as it cannot recognize something in different perspective as the same *thing*. . . . What is really lacking in the animal is the symbolic behavior which it would have to possess in order to find an invariant in the external object, under the diversity of its aspects, comparable to the immediately given invariant of the body proper and in order to treat, reciprocally, its own body as an object among objects." [5] The chimpanzee is unable to treat the field as a field of things.

The power of varying his points of view makes it possible for man to create instruments and to view his own body as an instrument. As man became proficient at manipulating and transforming his environment, we may suppose that he became increasingly conscious of his purposes and eventually able to pose the problem of his own condition. But man cannot discover himself completely in his actions, and his ability to control his body makes possible concealment behind the mask of appearance. In this same process the thing, that object which maintains its integrity while entering into a variety of relations, is born. That "invariant under the diversity of its aspects" sets the mind on a philosophical path from Parmenides to the moral philosophy of Kant and beyond; and, on the darker side, it makes possible the treatment of man himself as an object to be used and destroyed. The tool provides a sense of control and a means for calculating the significance of the external world. But modern technology, which may be viewed as an organizational phenomenon, has had the effect of making man himself a tool and has obliterated this sense of control. The tool, which at first may have been understood as an extension of the body, seems in our day almost to have absorbed the man, making him its object. Tools and techniques form our environment for us. They no longer stand out against a background of nature and man's natural activities, allowing him a fuller comprehension of his own condition; technology obscures that primordial nature. Tools have populated our world with man-made things, and yet few of us can say "I made this."

Ours is a postmaterialist rather than a materialist society— a collection of lives in which the world of objects has lost much of its meaning, much of its value. The object-in-use perspective leads us, like Procrustes, to cut off those aspects of the object that cannot be used. We come to see everything from the perspective of our need satisfaction. Meaning comes to be equated with satisfaction. For all peoples in all times this has no doubt been true in some degree, but, as an ecologist has recently written, "using and loving a few things long and carefully leads to a different kind of experience, a more profoundly fulfilling one, than does the careless use and abandonment of many things in rapid succession." [6]

In the development of the child the self- or subject-centered perceptual mode, described in the psychological literature as autocentric, gradually makes way for the allocentric, or object-centered, mode. In the former there is little objectification; the feeling state of the subject eclipses the object, and sensations of pleasure and discomfort or aversion fuse with the specific sensory quality. In the allocentric mode the perceiver opens himself to the object or attempts to "grasp" it. [7] Autocentric perception returns, however, in illness, weariness, anxiety. And when, in these states, the world is felt as impinging upon us, pleasure comes to be sensed primarily as the release of tension. In this state of enhanced subjectivity the object world loses the sharpness of its delineation. The consequences are similar when consumption becomes the characteristic activity of individuals, when objects exist to be consumed and serve less and less as points of orientation and reassurance. Our scheme of order begins to disintegrate. When, as in the classical conception of alienation, the things men made stood apart from them and against them, at least the problem could be seen, the oppressor located. Today, as Richard Means has so well put it, the things of our worlds do not demand a value response from us. "The sine qua non of the truly alienated man is to be so awash in his own subjectivity, so self-centered (and without a self as true object) that the world has no structure, no order, no objectivity." [8] This disintegration of the object world and consequent fading of the self-concept turns the individual to others for his cues and results in the "objectless craving" of which David Riesman speaks —the craving not for specific objects so much as for satisfactions available to others and desirable because others have them. [9]

The events of our lives have meaning insofar as we are able to place them within a certain order. In terms of this scheme we arrange and classify and describe the things of our world. Knowledge is ultimately the understanding of where something fits in this fundamental structure. And thus openness to the object world, allocentric perception, provides a control that the autocentric beast, whose objects are known only in terms of need satisfaction, cannot have. Theorists of society, personality, and cognition have concerned themselves with the mechanisms through which these structures, this meaning system, come to be established. Perhaps it may be said that the evil of our time is the loss of the awareness of evil, for to be conscious of evil is a dimension of the understanding of what one does and what the meaning of those actions are. The problem, as I shall later argue, is also political and social in an ideological sense because the system of production emphasizes a competence rooted in a highly specialized knowledge, bought often at the price of understanding, and it does not place a high value on autonomy and critical intelligence. And in this system power now includes the prerogative of defining reality itself.

There is another side to this phenomenology of the object. The object, we may be fairly certain, was first encountered not as a thing but only as a resistance because objects are given significance by shared meaning. This shared meaning readily fetishizes or overinvests the object, transforming it into demon or deity. If and when these meanings are challenged by those who do not share our particular concept of order, by those who speak the language of another civilization, then, as Kurt Riezler comments, "the nature of the thing itself will be whatever no one can deny to the thing. The thing itself *is* no longer sacred; it is we who made it sacred." Where this coexistence of meanings must be tolerated (and toleration begins where there is no viable alternative), there develops the distinction between subjective meaning and objective reality. But men are reluctant to develop this capacity, and historically they have preferred to kill rather than tolerate. "When the 'objective' nature of this thing is divested of its 'subjective' meanings, something happens to both man and thing. The thing loses its nearness to man and its deference to life and becomes flat." [10] The individual, however, as the source of subjectivity, acquires a value in his own right; the ego emerges along with the objective thing. In this process, man becomes aware of separations, of distances, and of what will be called evil or sin. The resistance that confronted him loses its mystery and becomes objectified—becomes the thing itself.

Divergent cultural perspectives may thus be accommodated on a cognitive level in a process in which the subjective self not only makes its appearance but also becomes the basis for detachment from the object world. Social differentiation and social conflict also increase the awareness of an individual self and a sense of the capacity for asserting the claims of this self (the will). This control may be directed toward internal objects as well as external (will power). Will is a morally ambiguous phenomenon because, in the assertive act, it so easily overvalues the past and devalues the present and the world around us. When will jeopardizes the resources on which the self depends, threatening to destroy the self, we are confronted with the problem of pride—that is, pride considered as a sin. This is the pride that "goeth before destruction," arrogance, the pride without humility which reduces future ability to learn. It stands opposed to that other pride which respects the self.

Emotion and motivation. In the modern era the most influential currents of Western religious thought have represented a reaction to the teleological position of Aristotle, an immanentalist argument which was thought to have destroyed or at least seriously compromised the mystique of evil based in a theology of revelation. The upshot of these developments, the curious convolution of which has been described by Ernst Troeltsch, Max Weber, Herbert Luethy, and others, was the provision of a symbolic leverage by which the world could be moved. According to Weber, the "plebian god" and his associated form of "ethical" prophecy makes man his instrument. This version of deity reflects the view that the world, because it is characterized by suffering and injustice, must be transcended. The influence of Nietzsche is evidenced in this emphasis on the distinction between commoner and aristocrat. The latter is more likely to be associated with exemplary (as opposed to ethical) prophecy and mysticism (being as opposed to function), less concerned with transcendence and the overcoming of the world. The plebian god tends to punish man not only for his pride, which is associated with the aristocracy, but also for his joy in existence. (And individuals ready to punish themselves are often more ready to punish the rest of nature.) By reviving a theology of good and evil in which man depends for his salvation on God alone, the Calvinist is prepared to see the world as being of secondary importance and the body along with it. Religion provides the strength necessary to resist the seductions of the world, to garner the energy freed from expenditure in gratification along with the capital freed from expenditure in consumption. Expanding production requires an expanding market, and attitudes toward consumption would become ambiguous. If it did not follow from the logic of this argument, it did follow from the logic of economics that in the seventeenth century the good would be associated with that which was desired. Anything that facilitated the satisfaction of man's wants could be justified as good. Freedom came to mean freedom to adapt the world to our needs and wants. But the world includes other men, and freedom thus stands in an equivocal relationship to the freedom of others.

Despite the hedonic overtones, this freeing of the individual for unlimited appropriation and gratification was not intended to elevate the status of his emotional life. The classical legacy was not completely forsaken. If the golden mean had become somewhat tarnished, reason continued to be understood as the means of comprehending the moral law, and emotion continued to be understood as a blurring of judgment. Impulse control was crucial to the building of a capital base and had functional advantages for society. Emotion, that "abrupt drop into the magical," [11] remained closely associated with evil. Complexly organized societies believe they can ill afford departures from standard cause-and-effect cognition. But today it is hard to resist the thought that the equation of evil with irrational violence deflects our attention from the highly calculated, indeed rational, forms that evil may take. We may find ourselves forced to the conclusion that rational organization, the principle of efficient coordination of acts pursuant to the achievement of some goal, has limited our individual capacities to see causal and structural relationships; in other words, that one kind of rationality is threatened by another. Automatic submission to authority may produce greater evils than does animal aggression.

Emotion, as we usually use the term, is aroused by external (occasionally by internal) stimuli and is directed toward the environment. It generally refers to an object, but it need not be related to behavior. It may simply affect belief or judgment. In contrast, biological need (a deficiency or imbalance which, if not corrected by input from the external environment, leads to disturbance or death) originates internally and is related only indirectly to the environment. Affect and biological need are both regulated by the hypothalamus, and yet they are frequently independent functions; they are not necessarily linked together.

Evidence of an aggressive need or instinct is not very persuasive. In their natural environment, the large primates tend to be docile and affectionate. In nonliterate cultures aggressive expression varies dramatically. Research on electrical stimulation of areas of the brain indicates that the reaction to negative stimuli is violent where the culture teaches such response; aggression remains within the pattern of earlier experience. Children who are frustrated by aggressive treatment commonly respond by becoming aggressive, imitating the parent. And the aggressive parent frequently rewards aggression when it is expressed toward an object outside the family. Child psychologists are convinced that children display considerably more aggression when they have been exposed to an aggressive model. The effect of learning from parental example appears to be particularly strong in this area of human behavior: aggression is essentially a role which is culturally learned.

Affect can develop only when there is adequate sensory stimulation in the early months of life. Deprived of maternal care in the first year and a half, the child cannot develop the capacity to form human bonds. Qualities of self-observation and self-criticism, the conscience itself, all fail to develop, and abstract thinking is also impaired. Such a child in later life is capable of crimes for which there is no motive—that gratuitous act which so fascinated the French novelists.[12]

D. O. Hebb and W. R. Thompson view emotion as being in some sense a disruption or breakdown of the thought process, which leads them to surmise that emotionality becomes more marked as thinking becomes more complex; the operation of the machine can be disturbed in more ways as the mechanism becomes more elaborate. A higher level of intelligence would thus be more vulnerable to emotional disturbance. "There are certain primitive causes of avoidance and aggression that seem to work equally well at all levels of mammalian development, . . . but as we go from rat to man there is a progressive increase in the range of effective stimuli to avoidance and aggression and in the duration and complexity of the response." The causes of aggression are more varied in the dog than in the rat, and when we reach the chimpanzee the variation has increased greatly. Fear susceptibilities have also increased. This enhanced excitability may be expected to pose severe problems for the social stability of human groups. Hebb and Thompson claim that the abundance of ghosts and evil spirits in primitive societies must be understood as a device to encourage conformity. Civilization, however, does not have to rely on counter-stimuli to the same degree; uniformity of appearance and behavior reduces those encounters which cause strong emotional disturbance. In this theory it is argued that a major function of society, perhaps more important than control of the environment, is the control of man's own behavior. Men are trained to act so as not to overexcite their fellows.[13]

It can be questioned whether uniformity may not make small deviations appear more strange and whether emotional intolerability is reduced. Americans, according to the surveys, are more incensed by campus unrest than they are concerned about the war. The more secure the world in terms of rules and routines the more likely people are to magnify the significance of a disruptive act. Then, too, the society that denies the existence of a very real social problem by removing it from sight or by directing attention elsewhere has not solved that problem and more often than not exacerbates it. We often deny a problem by concentrating on certain negative stimuli (considerations such as the hair, dress, and language of young people) which are only superficially related to the issue.[14]

It is the Hebb-Thompson thesis that social uniformities that aid in the control of behavior can replace the symbolic representation of evil forces. Sigmund Freud could be expected to counter with the argument that the demon is moved from the cultural realm to the individual psychic structure. Civilization demands an internalization that makes emotional release difficult. Forms of repression and other such mechanisms sacrifice the individual to society as he turns his hostility against himself. Aggression comes to be used by the superego against the ego, taking the form of guilt. However, the Freudian model does not take adequate account of the ways in which object cognition is shaped by cultural patterns. Freud often makes the object more independent of the internalized culture than can actually be the case, and this independence of the object gives the superego a seeming arbitrariness.[15] But in the Freudian model external stimuli are less important than the consequences of the ego's attempts to cope with the problems of personality development as it struggles for autonomy. Freud believed that the untamed impulse experiences a more intense satisfaction when it manages to achieve its goal than is the case when the drive has been domesticated. There is, however, some indication that the impulses build up their exquisite tensions in the very process of man's self-taming [16] and that pleasure is not simply tension release.

The psychoanalytic theory provides us with a model in which ego autonomy is understood as a successful balance of internal and external stimuli, which checks the tyranny of both the environment and the contents of the unconscious. Uniformity in the environment, in terms of this model, may produce a type of fantasizing which supplies demons where they did not exist before. It is not the provision of uniformity that should be sought, but rather the conditions encouraging the formation of meaning structures essential to personality integration. Hebb, in earlier research, established that fear and anxiety are induced by variations in the familiar, which threaten our sense of the order of meaning. Because anxiety and fear are thus rooted in challenges to the meaning structure, the control of these destructive energies requires a broadened and flexible scheme of order rather than the reduction of multiplicity.

The reduction of environmental stimuli may result in a desensitizing which in turn facilitates dehumanization. Konrad Lorenz suggests that modern weaponry screens the killer from whatever stimulus activates those inhibitions which serve to con-

trol aggression toward members of the same species. These inhibitions were never particularly strong in the first place because
man is one of those animals who cannot, in their natural state, do
great damage to others of their own kind. Lorenz locates the extreme nature of human destructiveness in depersonalized remote-
ness: "No sane man would even go rabbit hunting for pleasure if
the necessity of killing his prey with his natural weapons [hands
and teeth] brought home to him the full, emotional realization
of what he is actually doing." [17] Less is known empirically about
such "qualitative" screening of stimuli than about the consequences of sensory deprivation. Studies have demonstrated that
apathy results from poverty of sense stimulation and that, in the
child, sensory deprivation may have irreversible effects after a
year; it is then known as autism, the lack of affective expression
and communication and the desire to avoid a stimulating environment. There is also the point to be made, and Hebb himself makes
it, that mammals seek out situations that produce a mild degree of
emotional disturbance. When things are dull, the primate is all
too ready to become the troublemaker.[18]

Hebb and Thompson are not the only psychologists inclined to see emotion as disruptive behavior. R. W. Leeper, in a
well known essay, criticizes this view, arguing that the terms *organization* and *disorganization* (when used with reference to emotion) have not been adequately considered and that usually the
negative emotions are emphasized. He contends that the person
experiencing fear or anger is viscerally organized so that he can
act consistently with this emotion and that the replacement of preceding activities by other activities does not mean that behavior is
disorganized when shaped by emotion. Emotional processes, according to Leeper, operate primarily as motives because they arouse,
sustain, and direct activity. Such processes are one of the basic
means of motivation in the higher animals, who need motives
which supplement the merely physiological. "The animal that did
not make avoiding responses until it was grabbed by an enemy was
less likely to survive than an animal capable of reactions of fear
that would be set off by relatively slight stimuli. . . . The primate that had an almost insatiable urge to explore was more
likely to get the maximum benefit out of its chief asset—its great

potential learning capacity—than [was] the animal lacking such motivation." [19] In line with this interpretation, we may hold that Western man is saddled with an emotional development that is decreasingly functional in a highly rationalized and bureaucratized civilization which no longer has a need for the kind of motivation provided by the emotions. It can be argued that the world has become too uniform. Leeper comments that Nazism "was not just an appeal to unhealthy emotional reactions but . . . was probably partly a consequence of the emotional poverty of modern life." [20] Hannah Arendt, in *Eichmann in Jerusalem,* remarks at some length on Adolf Eichmann's visceral response the first time he saw with his own eyes what was being done to the Jews. Eichmann, confronted directly with the horror, forced himself to fight back an emotional reaction close to a swoon and to proceed with the task.

R. S. Peters, embroidering on this theme, points out (contrary to Leeper) that the most natural use of the term *emotion* is to account for our passivity, as when we are overcome by fear or jealousy. But when emotions are discussed in the context of actions, they become motives, reasons for our actions. When we speak of them as emotions, there is no necessary connection with behavior and action. He agrees with Leeper that normally emotions arouse and invigorate and guide activity, but beyond a certain level of intensity they can be disruptive. Sartre's discussion of emotion, according to Peters, relates emotion more to the wish than to the want. Emotion which is linked to wants involves an appraisal of the situation, so that one may act. When we speak of emotions as motives, this discriminating kind of appraisal is involved. Karl Pribram makes the same equation of motive with action and suggests that emotion is usually the opposite—a state of being possessed. In his discussion he distinguishes those instances in which we perceive more than we can accomplish, where the imbalance in repertories requires the mechanisms of motivation or emotional compensation, from those instances in which we can accomplish more than we can perceive and which require that a "whole new set of techniques must be brought to bear. The consciousness-expanders so popular today are, according to this view, a corollary of our technologically proficient society." [21]

The more developed the nervous system the more likely
are curiosity and exploratory behavior, and exploratory behavior
develops new kinds of rewards, new kinds of stimuli. What is interpreted as destructive activity in children is very often the expression of curiosity and the exercise of developing capacities. In
the neonate, distress is associated only with tension originating in
a biological need. Later, changes in brain activity bring with them
the association of distress with the absence of the mother and the
stimulus she provides. The phenomenon known as eighth-month
anxiety is the distress occasioned by the appearance of a stranger.
At this time affect has become a form of social communication,
and perception has begun to take on an allocentric character,
directed toward objects. As the child explores the strange, always
ambivalent in his investigations, he discovers new rewards. If he
does not encounter hostility, he finds an outlet for positive emotions, which are less intense than negative emotions because their
satisfaction requires that the autonomy of others be preserved. (It
is interesting to note that those most likely to be aroused to joy
are also those most self-assertive, serious, capable of anger, and
heterosexual. Cyril Burt distinguishes the expansive affects from
those which cluster around inhibition and submission. Anger and
joy may be more closely related than anger and fear or grief.[22]
Neurosis means, among other things, a restriction in the breadth
of emotional responsiveness.)

The child explores his world through play—the activity
that merges the real and the imaginary as new experience comes
to be incorporated in his expanding scheme of order. But behind
this emergent world is the figure of the protective mother and the
reassurance she represents. In our society the mother provides
the emotional focus and the first and most significant model, with
the result that masculinity is often a problem for the boy, sometimes to the point of preoccupation. Tenderness is identified with
the female, and toughness is the central trait of the caricature that
develops from this compulsive maleness. Talcott Parsons remarks
that it is not surprising to find goodness unconsciously identified
with feminity and, as a part of the reaction and the attempt
to establish identity, an emphasis on antisocial behavior in the
definition of masculinity. The mother may encourage such a role

image and its accompanying behavior. We can expect the military ideal and, generally, the authoritative role to be valued. The military ideal is considered by Parsons to be the most dangerous potential of this reservoir of repressed aggression, which, because it cannot be directly expressed, assumes the form of antisocial mobilization.

This repressed aggression is the consequence of a dialectic of frustration. The competitive relationship tends to characterize almost all childhood associations apart from the immediate family, although it can be found there too. Parsons claims:

Doing well . . . is highly valued in the society, and this attitude is likely to be shared by the mother, so that her own love and approval tend to become contingent on the child's objective performance rather than unconditional as it is in many societies. This love is therefore more acutely needed than in most societies and more precarious. The situation is favorable to a high level of anxiety and hence of aggression. But because of the very acuteness of the need for affection and approval, direct expression of aggression is more than normally dangerous and hence likely to be repressed.[23]

The problem centers in the fact that if the family is to prepare the child for the skills and social relationships that modern economic organization requires, the parent cannot provide a definite role model for the child.[24] The erosion of trust begins in childhood experiences of disillusionment—the betrayal of expectations permitted him. There develops a suspicion of the motives of those with whom he has to deal and thus a fertile ground for the projection of repressed impulses in himself.

In preindustrial society the household or estate exercised coercive pressures and probably produced strong personal hatred along with close emotional attachment. Changes in the economic system have separated the household from the occupational organization and, in the interest of compatibility with the occupational structure, have limited the size of the kinship unit to the conjugal minimum. Differentiation may damage normative bonds and group solidarity, but it also may modify certain personalized oppressions rooted in the lack of privacy.[25] The contemporary nuclear family is capable of providing both an intense emotional bond and, where relationships produce a sense of rejection, severe traumatic effects and the schizophrenic adopting of a false self as protection against a threatening world. Children from homes in which control tends to take the form of the threat of withholding love are not likely to direct their anger outward but to turn it inward, producing feelings of guilt. This moral structure characterized by internalized controls facilitates life in an impersonal environment where many strangers are encountered and the rate of social change makes it difficult to rely on external cues. Self-control is at a premium.

In modern industrial societies people protect themselves by learning how not to express emotion, how to deny the existence of a problem, or at least how to overlook the other person's vulnerability. Or emotions are limited to certain times and places deemed appropriate to their expression. Emotional expression is thus inhibited. And when impersonal institutions annoy and harass us but provide no focal point at which our irritation can be directed, emotional expression is rendered simply ridiculous, and the result is a sense of helplessness and a diffuse need for revenge. The entertainment media furnish a means for vicarious acting out and partial emotional release. Our enjoyment is rooted in identification with behavior which is for the most part acceptable only in fantasy.

Rich as we are in goods and services, we have become a population (particularly true of the female half) with very few opportunities for the stimulation that creative and exciting activities provide—activities which are satisfying in themselves and which challenge our skills and talents. So much of what we do is done as a means to some end which lies outside the activity. When the meaning structure has dissolved to the extent that men cannot hope to share basic assumptions and be understood, those many devices such as humor that soften the edges of our relationships can no longer be employed. They are possible only where men feel secure enough to detach themselves from their own egos to some degree.

Psychiatrists comment on the inability of many people to

act out their emotional feelings—or, for that matter, to experience anything on an other than cognitive level. The intellectualist bias of modern culture obscures the creative, active side of man's nature, which reveals itself in decision and valuation, the order of praxis. It is this allocentric self that mediates between the shared base of subjectivity (the perceptual infrastructure that affords meaning) and the transcendent order we call the social structure, which arises from the interactions of individuals. When the infrastructure (in this modification of Claude Lévi-Strauss) continually threatens to collapse into autocentricity, sensation replacing emotion and fusing with the sensory qualities of objects, then shared meaning is reduced to passive responses or to a fetishizing of the social structure, which comes to be seen as a jural structure of rights rather than a political structure of communicative interaction. When shared meaning is reduced in this way, the intervening order of praxis and the creation of value—sentient man seeking his own solutions—has little reality or meaning apart from the practical and the expedient. The social structure is objectified in the manner of the descriptions of British social anthropologists, and the infrastructure amounts to little more than a collective unconscious.[26] The categorical and the abstract replace learning rooted in the perception of structures, thinking takes on a schizophrenic quality as the concept precedes the knowledge that comes from direct experience, and language becomes more and more metaphorical. It is not only that reality testing has become difficult. Fantasy has an important function in itself when objects exist primarily to be exploited and when the market must artificially stimulate demand. The overinflated image produces a population always preparing itself for a disappointing reality.

Sensory overload. Through trial and error, by means of behaviors that seek out sources and intensifications of stimulation (exploratory responses), and through the development of symbolic structures, the individual gathers information. Survival depends on our possession of a good deal of information. But most of the information we receive through our senses is superfluous, and if we are to keep our sanity, the superfluous must be separated out. Sherrington long ago made the point that messages from outside the system have to compete for efferent pathways. The motor equipment is capable of only a fraction of the responses to which stimuli give rise.[27]

Stimulations, whether internal or external, break the unity of patterns that have built up in the brain. And then, as one theorist speculates, the brain selects that input which promises to reestablish the rhythmic pattern.[28] Information irrelevant to what psychologists call the optimal response is frequently termed *noise,* and noise represents most of the stimulus situation. For this reason it is argued that biological adaptation depends as much on rejection of information as on transmission of information. Qualitative considerations must be taken into account. A case in point is the discovery of Hebb that the model of a chimpanzee's body without the head or even a research assistant wearing a coat borrowed from an associate can induce terror in a chimpanzee. In certain pathologies any kind of unfamiliar stimulus may be very threatening. Studies of brain damage in German soldiers wounded in World War I indicated that the compensatory techniques that enabled these men to function at all depended on routine and a completely predictable environment.[29] Hebb and Thompson, as discussed in the preceding section, extrapolate a general theory of society based on this and similar research. The implied policy consequences of their view would probably not be acceptable to the modern progressive. In the present section, given the theme of the chapters in this volume, the central point is that individuals themselves work out strategies for coping with stimulus input (which by sheer volume has a damaging potential) and that in certain kinds of strategy can be found the roots of the legitimation of evil or at least the delegitimation of the good.

Where the social environment assaults the individual with many and varied stimuli, he may be forced to disregard or at least to discount the claims of those who are not immediately relevant to his own needs and interests. Survival in the city appears to require a large measure of indifference. And very often what passes for tolerance in our world is little more than indifference. Indifference prepares the way for violence, for sometimes violence may be the only way to get any attention; and indifference is itself a type of violation. Where, as in the Catherine Genovese case, the cry for help is not directed at a specific person, those within hearing are likely to assume that someone else will inform the police. There is also, in our kind of society, a general reluctance to interfere, to meddle in the affairs of others,[30] which may extend even to reluctance to assist a person in mortal danger.

Stanley Milgram [31] links individual experience to demographic circumstance by means of a concept drawn from systems analysis and cybernetics, the concept of overload: "a system's inability to process inputs from the environment because there are too many inputs for the system to cope with or because successive inputs come so fast that input A cannot be processed when input B is presented. When overload is present, adaptations occur. The system must set priorities and make choices." This line of analysis has certain affinities with that of Georg Simmel in his description of the metropolitan type of personality. Simmel emphasizes the constant and rapid change of both outer and inner stimuli, which, as he sees it, results in the intensification of neurotic agitation.[32]

In daily life the pattern of information flow that is the mind may be so seriously disrupted as to produce functional mental disturbance. The individual may have to decide which inputs must be sacrificed, which parts of the self must be suppressed, how he is to protect that which he considers the core of his being. And as significant as the quantity of stimulation is its quality; especially harmful is the kind of paradoxical information which produces what Gregory Bateson terms the *double bind,* a message that holds within itself its own contradiction.

The blasé attitude developed in an urban context prevents the stimulus input from the environment from overwhelming the constitutionally given drives, which, in the psychoanalytic model, may be understood as guarantors of ego autonomy. This effort to escape what David Rapaport terms *stimulus-response slavery* is a tricky game. It may produce a relatively emotionless condition. "This situation occurs only when the organism restricts his perception to a limited, relatively 'closed system' part of his universe. To deal with this inversion he must 'open' himself to variety—in today's language he must take a 'trip'." [33] If the city-dweller seems to be continually seeking new forms of stimulation, this may mean only that the boredom or anxiety resulting from a blurred or damaged scheme of order (where meaning is too much for him to bear) leads him to the frantic attempt to substitute titillations for the old structures. Familiar elements are rearranged to provide an element of surprise, but such experiences very seldom provide insights or give substance to his life. He may find himself developing those characteristics—orderliness, stubbornness, and parsimony —that marked an early phase of his psychosexual maturation and prevented him from being pushed around by the environment. Such an anal character has come to mistrust his environment.[34]

The problem of stimulus overload is unquestionably related to the reduction of social distance, to democratization. Coping with this overload frequently takes the form of individual and group attempts to reestablish social distance by creating pariahs and other out-groups. The physical distance from the victim that modern weapons allow and that Lorenz makes responsible for carnage has its cognate in the social distance produced by redefining the species so that some men come to be considered subhuman and so that the inhibition against their violation or destruction is reduced. Hero worship is also a means of coping—as for that matter, is the uncritical acceptance of authority. "The horrors which we have seen, the still greater horrors which we will presently see," wrote Bernanos, "are not signs that rebels, insubordinate, untamable men, are increasing in constant numbers but rather that there is a constant increase, a stupendously rapid increase, in the number of obedient, docile men." Our cognitive processes may be clouded by an overload of information, much of it extraneous, in the calculated attempt of authorities to disguise their handling of a problem or to handicap critical response. What qualifies as overload is culturally conditioned to a significant degree. For instance, modes of thinking rooted in scarcity and the corollary emphasis on postponement of gratification discourage any arousal that has a high stimulus effect: four letter words, nudity, intense visual and auditory effects.

Man and the higher primates seek moderate amounts of unpredictable change and an environment that includes surprises. The nervous system in higher animals is not capable of optimal functioning when the demands on it are too exacting, but we generally do not experience too much stimulation; if anything there is not enough. It would seem that the best way of viewing the problem of stimulus overload is to see the modern world as abundant with situations and experiences that are difficult to fit into a consistent scheme, experiences that we must either interpret out of existence or refuse to perceive. The more rigid and limited our scheme of order, the more difficult it is to make things fit and the more vulnerable we are to that fear we call anxiety. We demand conformity and a simpler world. Experiences that do not fit must be repressed, problems that do not fit must be shoved out of sight, men who do not fit must be discarded. If stimulation is felt as intolerable, perhaps it is because we sense our experiences as not being ours: "We know that experiences we have not succeeded in expressing for ourselves continue to victimize us; laws which are not ours, disciplines which are not self-taught—all these dehumanize us: we know they make us the instruments of nature or of others." [35] Stimulation without meaning, impersonal mechanisms for relating without conflict, messages that damn us if we do and damn us if we don't, all produce circumstances that make it almost impossible to know or feel that what we do has moral significance. When trust diminishes, the large part of our factual beliefs, which are held at secondhand on the basis of trust in others, is in jeopardy. All the easier, then, for the state to supply the facts that serve its purposes.

Studies in the consequences of stimulus deprivation attest to our dependence on objects and on others for psychic balance, a finding consistent with the basic psychoanalytic model. In order to obtain an adequate input, the individual, when he perceives his world as threatening, may have to supercharge certain objects. Social philosophers point out that fetishism in the most fundamental sense is a relationship to a world seen as fragmented, in which objects lose dimension, lose depth and variation, a world in which the individual with a limited behavioral repertoire but with the wish for fuller gratification seeks to contrive a relationship that excites while protecting him from full commitment.[36] In such an object relationship meaning is highly concentrated, as though to compensate for the impoverishment of the lover, worshipper, or killer. As such, this relationship is the obverse of what we generally consider art to be, a relationship which seeks to reveal new possibilities in what is to be known and to provide new opportunities for response in both the actor and the object. Or a comparison with love is relevant. Sex without that mutuality which is essential to love makes the partner an observer. The attempt to procure satisfaction without giving of oneself creates the voyeur; this attempt is the essence of pornography.

Lack of mutuality—whether this lack is expressed as violation or fetishism, for both involve treatment of the person so as to reduce his humanity and disparage his uniqueness—is the ultimate source of shame. In our time shame is associated with failure to achieve and with a lack of confidence, but, in its foundation, shame is the inability to fulfill oneself in a relationship with others. Fetishism, then, is the refusal of potentiality, the reduction of the world in order to find at least a modicum of meaning and a shred of gratification without increasing one's vulnerability. (We are never so vulnerable as when we love, said Freud.) This phenomenon is akin to Herbert Marcuse's "repressive desublimation"— satisfaction of a passive, essentially masturbatory, nature. Scapegoating may be a reverse fetishism, in that one concentrates the threat in a single object or set of objects. Racism is similar to that part relationship that characterizes fetishism. It reduces a man to a caricature in the effort to avoid knowing him in his full humanity and diversity.

Excluding. Some forms of racism and other prejudice are grounded in the idea that if you can remove evil (which tends to be personified), the good will automatically flourish. The good is already given, and there is thus no need for an anguished search. The naive dualism which has always been something of a problem in Protestant America encourages such a way of looking at things. Such a simplification is one way of managing the overload problem, and, as Milgram suggests, overload can be controlled if one limits his "span of sympathy" to those who, for instance, are of the same ethnic group. A world that can otherwise not be understood requires an orientation such as that which the scapegoat provides. Its byproducts are a kind of security, an object on which to vent generalized resentment, and an opportunity for actions that are not otherwise sanctioned. The scapegoat allows us to project psychological contents which are threatening because they are not adequately understood, often because they are not admitted to consciousness. This displacement of aggression onto out-groups typically represents the failure to comprehend and locate the real cause of frustration. Such a displacement, according to E. C. Tolman, is a narrowing of the cognitive map.[37] Where inner conflicts can be externalized and projected onto others, one can then fight them in others rather than in himself. But there still has to be a justification for maltreatment. Scruples are weakened by making the victim a part of a powerful conspiracy. (The conspirators need be no more than two, as witness laws under which dissenters have been tried.) Resentment often focuses on those who have not been willing to conform, to regulate gratification in standard ways, and to accept the standard rewards.

The artificial creation of meaning through stereotyping, scapegoating, and the whipping-up of anxiety is more easily achieved where the experience of change and of the new is felt as disturbing—what was earlier described as the autocentric perceptual mode. Anxiety about one's capacity may be allayed by fantasies about national superiority. The individual in his self-doubts may find security in the larger identification. What brutish men like to think of as toughness in themselves is frequently the deep desire for conformity and the approval of others. At Nuremberg no Nazi had the courage to defend the ideology of the Third Reich. We may be tempted to think of racism as the downgrading of others in order to exalt oneself, but it can also be seen as the negating of another man's humanity in order to negate one's own —to avoid responsibility and freedom.

When no goal values are articulated, the quality of the life shared by members of a community is known indirectly through an understanding of what lies beyond the boundaries. This understanding may take the form of what may be called transcendent knowledge—knowledge of transcendent values or of the sacred. In other cultures the deviant, the enemy, or the barbarian defines the parameters of the community. The word deviant suggests a standard or norm from which such a person or group deviates, but frequently only the existence of the deviant can provide the sense of shared standards and sentiments. And this he does not by the values and ideas he espouses but by the resentment and fears he inspires.[38]

Sartre argues that prejudice attaches one to a community of men who reinforce one another in their attitudes. Where opportunities for fellowship diminish, such communities of the frustrated may be expected to assume increasing importance. Prejudice is a way of escaping loneliness as well as a means of providing certainty. Such a temper, which requires victims as well as enemies, is easily mobilized by the state that requires solidarity. Today the backlash has become politically useful for consolidating the support of that portion of the populace threatened by the young, the black, and the poor. And in this sense socially disastrous policies that build disaffection among the latter groups may have a political advantage insofar as they stimulate a reaction which can then be used to develop a conservative coalition. Law and order thus comes to disguise injustice. Social cleavage reaches the point where there is insufficient moral unity to make effective communication possible, and expedience replaces argument. At first leaders pretend that a consensus still exists, and this pretense more often than not entails the argument that differences of opinion stem from the influence of "outsiders."

The mechanism of displacement which requires the scapegoat in the larger society helps also to create the schizophrenic in the family. R. D. Laing argues that the schizophrenic provides a device for holding a family together, just as the deviant may perform a similar service for society. The schizophrenic contrives a second self in order to protect his "real" self and to allow him to negotiate to some extent with an environment too bewildering or too menacing to confront directly. The false self that faces the world absorbs stimuli that in the healthy person hold in check the flow of unconscious contents into the ego; insulated, the other (real) self is free to build a private world out of the materials of fantasy. The schizophrenic's casual regard for a self which he does not consider the real self, when that mask-self comes to be associated with the body, makes possible types of expression which are not liberating, expression not truly experienced, in which the individual remains on the outside looking in.

The number of Americans crippled by schizoid-type disorders would fill a city the size of Philadelphia, but most of us, while functioning adequately from day to day find it necessary to close off a part of our nature, to repress more of ourselves than is necessary for societal life. One way of coping with an overload of incongruent vocabularies and double-binding messages is to hold a part of life in abeyance. Another and related strategy is to assign the parts of a contradiction to two parts of the self. When the self is divided, one part of it may be allowed to destroy without our having to accept full responsibility for such an act. After "barbecuing" civilians from a distance of forty thousand feet, the airborne soldier leaves his role of killer, leaves his "false" self. In such an act of destruction or degradation there remains some sense of decency and responsibility, but it is confined to one of the selves, freeing the other to destroy. There are also individuals in whom the self is not divided and who do not sacrifice themselves by restructuring mechanisms for dealing with reality, although their world makes insufficient sense to allow them to act effectively or feel deeply. Such persons may charge ahead in perverse and aggressive reality testing, attaining a pitch of excitement that offers the self a momentary unity. Such sensation (Sade's "l'isolisme") is devoid of compassion and goes no deeper than the flesh.

From the vantage point of information theory, acts of destruction are attempts to eradicate parts of the environment which challenge distorted, severely restricted, or brittle systems of meaning. One chooses to destroy rather than to learn. From this same perspective, which has produced a number of revealing insights into human relationships, violence can also be interpreted as a means of communication for those without status—a way of surfacing in an ocean of messages. Status-ambition is, accordingly, the striving, often also desperate, for a privileged position for one's "messages." [39] Such consideration of status, however, presupposes a society which describes its values as available to those willing to enter the competitive fray. The competitive market requires a system of civil rights which provides each man with a status that makes it possible for him to enter the struggle as an independent entity—and also makes it possible to justify the withholding of social protection from him on the theory that he now has the means to take care of himself. [40] Empirical studies indicate, however, that discontent is not concentrated in those denied the rewards of a competitive system. Discontent appears to be greatest among those who have attained positions of status possessing at least a limited authority.[41] In such instances resentment contains a large component of frustration; even a modest investment in the system limits the ways in which aggression can be expressed. Generally, the supportive ideologies, such as equality of opportunity, deflect hostility from those who apply the standards, those individuals of wealth and status. Frustrations then find their outlet against those whom the system defines as outsiders.

Individual competition takes the place of collective solidarity, status replaces class as the significant sociological concept, society is atomized. And where competition pervades the whole life of a man, where cohesive attachments are of value only as solace, and where the struggle for status is strenuous, moral principle becomes a luxury that the junior executive, the lower-echelon bureaucrat, can ill afford. Ugly and petty behavior attenuates a man's self-respect. Montesquieu was only the first of modern social commentators to observe that when men begin to develop contempt for themselves, they easily become instruments for hurting others.

Organizing the ego. Role and status organize and locate men in interactive systems. The role concept allows us to enclose one another in metaphors which condition behavior. Such metaphors facilitate our dealings with people because they are no longer regarded as unique individuals.[42] The more mutuality a relationship requires, the more necessary to define a man in terms of his being rather than in terms of his function. Where spontaneity and personal decision are important, as in friendship, love, and intimacy (or their obverse), good and evil are relevant concepts. But where men relate only in terms of segments of their personalities such categories seem beside the point. In the modern literature on social interaction we rarely encounter the terms *good* and *evil*. The role requires role distance, and the effective playing of roles requires the learning of an assortment of defensive devices—wit, cynicism, and the spectator position—to establish and maintain this distance. These devices are different from those, humor for instance, which allow us to drop our defenses and permit the ego to relax. Still, we do manage to get by and to find relationships that are satisfying in some degree.

But the maintenance of this surface of agreement, this veneer of consensus, is facilitated by each participant's concealing his own wants behind statements which assert values to which everyone present feels obliged to give lip service. . . . [Each participant] remains silent or noncommittal on matters important to others but not immediately important to him. We have then a kind of interactional modus vivendi. *Together the participants contribute to a single overall definition of the situation which involves not so much a real agreement as to what exists but rather a real agreement as to whose claims concerning what issues will be temporarily honored.*[43]

In the modern enterprise formal decisions are also made by groups. And such decision-making undoubtedly makes it easy to avoid the consideration of moral issues. No one person has to consider himself responsible. Some writers see the corporation as a device to solve moral as well as economic problems. As an early nineteenth-century historian of money and banking commented, "A crime that would press quite heavily on the conscience of one man becomes quite endurable when divided among men."[44] Sutherland was willing to go further: "A director loses his personal identity in this corporate behavior, and in this respect, but in no other, corporate behavior is like the behavior of a mob.[45] The organization encourages the individual who is willing to accept the policy of the moment, to accept what he may find repugnant to his moral sense, in order to preserve a position of influence so that at some future date he can promote policies to which he is committed. Those in positions of influence and power have those positions to lose if they take a moral stand; others are more free to follow their consciences. But standing firm on moral principle may cost them appointments and promotions.

Organization is administration, and administration in turn

translates into relations of subordination and superordination. Old images of bargaining and citizenship may be retained for ideological purposes, but they have lost their reality. And because organizations exist to accomplish some goal, responsibility loses its old meaning of accountability downward and has its reference instead to the assembly of resources needed for the accomplishment of a task. Words like *public, citizen, support,* and *participation* give way in a model that finds its appropriate terminology in *function, subject, duty* and *power.* Behind it all is a rationality that assumes a scarcity of means in order to justify efficiency. But that rationality itself contributes to the creation of scarcity by stressing wants rather than needs and by assuming that wants will never be satisfied. (True, the theory of marginal utility did stress need, but when the radical, egalitarian implications of that particular theory were appreciated, it was modified to serve the ideology of the market.) This scarcity model also induces in individuals a general attitude of defense and offense.

The system of rationalized control of man and machine in which tasks are divided according to defined areas of expertise is known as technology. Technology has invaded our lives to a degree that makes it extremely difficult for us to view it critically. Our basic values have been shaped by a conception of progress rooted deeply in technological development, but in obscuring the very idea of humanity, technology has rendered ambiguous that tradition of enlightened values from which the concept of progress emerged. Only recently has it been understood that the system that advertises itself as the most efficient set of devices for satisfying human wants must also be seen as an extremely effective means of accommodating men to its own needs. The tool of the man-ape made it possible for him to develop, over the eons, a moral vision, by allowing him both to see things in their contexts and to see invariances that remain when things are abstracted from their contexts. But now that the relation of man and tool appears almost to have reversed itself, we may speculate that man has started on the path back to the stupor of a world known only through the mediation of his drives and the fantasies that substitute for their expression.

In 1906, Weber wrote:

Those American workers who were against the "Civil Service Reform" knew what they were about. They wished to be governed by parvenus of doubtful morals rather than by a certified caste of mandarins. But their protest was in vain. . . . If only material conditions and interest constellations directly or indirectly created by them mattered, then every sober reflection would convince us that all economic weathercocks point in the direction of increasing servitude. It is utterly ridiculous to see any connection between the high capitalism of today—as it is now being imported into Russia and as it exists in America—with democracy or with freedom in any sense of these words.[46]

In the two-thirds of a century that separate us from these words, although the plutocracy and the machine bosses have become less brazen and the corporation has elaborated a managerial ideology, technology and international involvements have had consequences beyond those Weber foresaw. Formal education has become preoccupied with training in the development of the skills required by the system, and a significant sector of the population has found itself increasingly superfluous. Since World War I this country has witnessed an increasing exercise of authority by private groups in the public areas that concern them,[47] although direct and vastly lucrative concessions to private business concerns reach far back into the nineteenth century. A defense budget of massive proportions has amplified the power of defense corporations, the Pentagon, and the military—an influence very little inhibited by responsibilities to the electorate. The Cold War may not be the invention of the industrial system, but the great corporation is certainly the beneficiary of mass sentiment based on vague fears of foreign aggression.

In these developments, one perceives a trend toward the reduction of the rational element in authority—a tendency to justify the need for restricting information and to avoid giving the underlying reasons for an order. In the public bureaucracies the security interests of the country are used to justify the withholding of information, even when the relation of an organization to foreign policy is tenuous, but the possibility of embarrassment is substantial. As though it were not enough that policies are formulated in such a way as to make difficult their public debate and that no attempt is made to justify these policies, we find the public prepared for the belief that authority should not be questioned because those in positions of power must surely have the facts. Such a belief does violence not only to a conception of authority based on the ability to give reasons which relate ultimately to communal values but also to history. If history is clear on anything it is that the leaders of men are frequently and even monumentally wrong and that their vanity often comes before the well-being of their peoples. Those authorities most likely to invoke the concept of privileged information are also most inclined to isolate themselves behind a cordon of yes-sayers. Distortion in perception and judgment is often as widespread among public officials as it is in the general population. (See Chapter Six.)

Mass apathy and fear are sometimes the basis of authority when it cannot afford rational legitimation. Authorities frustrate rational criticism by denying, concealing, and mystifying the facts which are needed to discuss policy intelligently. While justifying the restriction of information, public agencies deny that right to others and have tapped telephones of anyone under the shadow of suspicion, have accepted evidence from anonymous informers, have protected perjurers, and have stolen documents. At one time undercover agents of the FBI were so numerous in the Communist Party that they found themselves informing on one another. Members of Congress are themselves intimidated.[48] Today many hundreds of thousands of dossiers exist in computerized and microfilmed files—information that can be instantly retrieved. The files are not confined to members of the Communist Party or those who have tried to burn a bank; they include those perceived as malcontents and a potential embarrassment to public officials. The data banks now being compiled are totalitarian instruments.

Although authority rests in trust, today militarism, along with economic colonialism, requires increasingly a management of consensus and of information. Institutions begin to take on a paramilitary character. Every tactical goal comes to be represented as greatly important in order to elicit commitment in situations where it is not otherwise easy to get the proper response. Some-

times such tactics are intended to provoke dissent and to provide
a pretext for coming down hard on those who protest. It should
go without saying that when a society relies increasingly on the
use of negative sanctions to secure conformity, it is experiencing
a weakening of authority. But the employment of police and other
agencies of control may also be an indication that the principle
of legitimacy is changing in a direction that may have positive
consequences for that society. Uncritical compliance cannot be
relied on in the same degree, and authority must regain its modern
meaning as communication founded in reason and in shared ideals.

In our day another and older justification of power differ-
entials has made its appearance. It has been pointed out that the
higher echelons of government and business are staffed by individuals who readily view themselves as having sacrificed their own
peace and comfort in the service of the public good. John Mc-
Dermott suggests that this conception of unrewarding eminence
provides almost a mystique.[49] Executives, bureaucrats, and lower
level managers are not to be compared with the nobility that
decorated the Bourbon court. They work a long day, and their
devotion may match that of religious disciples. But such uncom-
plaining effort based in a certain righteousness is possible in many
of these instances only where men have been trained never to consider the larger purposes of their efforts.

Nor can it occur to these men that in their absorbing of
responsibility, selfless as they may be, they compromise democratic principles. This new parentalism assumes that justice may be
incorporated in efficiency and that general social goals are essentially those of the industrial system and of the state—the instrument begins to see itself as the end. Galbraith comments that
members of the corporate system find no problem in identifying
their purposes with those of the larger social system. It is easy to
have a social conscience when that conscience cannot be distinguished from one's own interests. It is evidently not very difficult
even for Dow Chemical: "Simple good citizenship requires that
we supply our government and our military with those goods [in
this case napalm] which they feel they need whenever we have
the technology and capability and have been chosen by the government as a supplier. . . . We will feel deeply gratified if what

we are able to provide helps to protect our fighting men or to speed the day when the fighting will end." [50]

The pluralistic analysis of society rarely considers how the individual has fared within private associations. If those groups claim the right of self-government, challenging the state in the name of liberty, we are entitled to question the condition of freedom within the groups themselves. The modern industrial system locates enormous power in individuals outside any system of effective control, although this power is often disguised by such myths as consumer or shareholder sovereignty; and this is as true within the organization as in the larger society. Decisions on matters of significance are highly concentrated. One would suppose that the distance from decisions would produce feelings of impotence in the typical member of the organization. Studies indicate that those relatively low in the hierarchies find little meaning in the tasks that occupy most of their time. But because they have gained something, perhaps a good deal, by entrusting large parts of their lives to the expert, these individuals are generally willing to accept the system even though areas of personal freedom diminish. The more powerless they become, the more important those who hold the power appear to be. The need to believe—to believe that the managers will look after them—is strengthened. Distance from the managers makes difficult the testing of these beliefs (and helps protect the myth of managerial wisdom).

In the psychological laboratories, experimenters have discovered that those who obey instructions that run counter to moral norms are likely to believe that responsibility for the results rests with the experimenter, the "authority," rather than with themselves. Martin Orne found that subjects who were asked to pretend that they were hypnotized were willing to do dangerous and unpleasant things, willing even to throw acid in the face of a research associate. Milgram found that the hypnosis pretense was unnecessary. Obedience to authority took priority over the moral sense.[51] This unwillingness to question authority, to doubt that the President has the facts, is almost the definition of the silent majority so-called: silent because they refuse to question. In a way, it is hard to criticize a man for wishing to escape autonomy. In the world we know, autonomy can be a handicap; it can make it difficult for him to adjust and adapt as the system requires. We may accept superior merit as an adequate justification of authority in some spheres, but we cannot afford to do so in politics, at least not in democratic politics; when we do, the temptation to feel ourselves relieved of responsibility is difficult to resist. The "good German" is thus reborn. And then, at the other end of the authority structure, the self-sacrificing official may reverse the pity that men normally feel when they witness suffering and say not "What horrible things I had to do!" but, as Himmler said, "What horrible things I had to endure in the pursuit of my duties!"

A democracy requires a knowledgeable public and must to some degree assume the ability of the individual to participate in determining social objectives, but the balance of social knowledge has so shifted that this is becoming a forlorn hope. Karl Mannheim warned of the consequences of what he termed functional rationality, that calculable action which permits the coordination of men but deprives the average man of thought, insight, and responsibility and serves to transfer these capacities to those who direct the process of rationalization.[52] C. Wright Mills reached a similar conclusion: "The expropriation which modern work organization has carried through . . . goes far beyond the expropriation of ownership; rationality itself has been expropriated from work and any total view and understanding of its process." [53] It is almost impossible for certain groups in our population to get an adequate perspective on the structures of social reality and their own position in that reality. Without this knowledge a man cannot know his own interests or act politically. To see this as a personal problem rather than a social problem, to speak of better dissemination of better assembled information, is to participate in the very problem, which is one of social institutions and social priorities: in terms of political philosophy, the problem of the loss of a public realm.

McDermott suggests that we are now experiencing a widening of the gap between the political cultures of the lower and higher orders of society. At the beginning of the modern era, economic developments, religious movements emphasizing personal salvation, demographic changes, and inventions such as the printing press contributed to the narrowing of this cultural divi-

sion and disparity—the reduction of social distance to which I
have earlier referred. Today we see the reverse trend. The quality
of social experience has diminished as the new technology requires
more men to do more things of which they do not comprehend
the character and implications. Social rationality declines when
men are cut off from experiences which train them in distinguishing and then relating and adjusting means and ends. This decline
in popular literacy and in the quality of social experience is conducive to the growth of what McDermott calls social paranoia.[54]

Knowledge of social processes is generally limited to the
range of an individual's experience, and that is at once an increasingly limited experience in terms of possibilities for reality testing
and an increasingly abstracted and passive kind of knowing. The
satisfactions that build confidence and respect for oneself are based
in accomplishment and require the opportunity to put our powers
to the test. When a person feels he has little control over the
objects and events of his world, he may seek substitute satisfactions
by making at least something respond to his power, much as the
child enjoys molesting the kitten. Because it is hard for such a
person to locate the source of his frustrations (and when they can
be located, hard for him to respond), paranoia begins to shape his
thoughts. In such an impersonal world aggression cannot usually
provide the satisfaction that was possible when the frustration or
the perceived injustice could be attributed to a specific person or
group. And this situation also contributes to a weakening of the
sense of guilt as one comes increasingly to feel himself as a thing
reacting against things. If I act as an instrument I cannot be held
responsible. And when we feel that we are instruments for other
persons who can be identified, persons interested in us only insofar
as we are useful to them, trust and confidence cannot develop.
The alienated man senses the world as foreign to his purposes,
and consequently feels no moral responsibility for it.[55]

Richard Christie, pointing out that the research of social
psychology has paid far more attention to the follower, the manipulated man, or the authoritarian personality than to the manipulator, has attempted to construct a character profile of what he
terms the Machiavellian. Such persons, he concludes, share with
the authoritarians a low opinion of others, but, unlike the sub-

jects of those famous studies (and of Chapter Ten), the manipulator is not moralistic. His cynical regard for others, who exist as
an opportunity for his own advantage, is associated with emotional
detachment and the amoral attitude that successful deception
seems to require. Emotional involvement makes it difficult for a
man to treat another as an object. The individual who rated high
on the tests devised by Christie and his associates appears to be
"an effective manipulator *not* because he reads the other person
and takes advantage of his weakness but because his insensitivity
to the other person permits him to bull his way through in pursuit of coolly rational goals." [56]

Whether or not Machiavelli is the locus classicus of this
type of person, a glance at his times may suggest certain linkages
between thought and behavior. It is clear that industrialization,
urbanization, and democratization affect the very ontology of a
civilization, its vision of reality. In the traditional society, although
men were more intimately associated, social entities were viewed
from greater social distance than they now are, and thought was
morphological in that the world was explained in terms of unan-
alyzed given wholes. "The secret was pierced for the first time in
the West during the Renaissance period," writes Mannheim,
"when in the course of social changes new elites penetrated into
the top region and came to see the actual process instead of the
stereotyped symbol." [57] Machiavelli was one of the first to tell
what he had seen on the inside—intrigue, struggles for position
and power, maneuvering, and manipulation. The analytical approach has its roots in the insider's view of things; analysis, however, requires some sense of the *Gestalten,* of patterned wholes, or
at least of the ideal type. But when, as began perhaps in the
eighteenth century, life comes to be felt by many as an overload
of stimuli, burdensome multiplicity, when details come to seem
the strongest reality of all, then, as T. W. Adorno argues, details
blind the eye to genuine perception. The position of Adorno and
a growing number of social theorists is that the resistance of modern society to rational understanding is the result of those very
processes which, in their inception, made analysis possible; this
resistance "should be understood first and foremost as the sign
of relationships between men which have grown increasingly in-

dependent of them, opaque, now standing off against human beings like some different substance." [58] When structural understanding is lost, the insider is no longer "inside" in the sense of being an active participant in a process; he finds his world reified, he remains outside. Since he is discounted as a formulator and creator, little is left for him but the petty scheming and maneuvering, the activities of the inside dopester. Where the world is atomized, so is thought.

Advanced technological systems are unable to tolerate behavior that does not fall within certain categories relevant to research and production. Behavior and techniques of an erratic, self-determining, or improvisory nature are eliminated in the interests of maintaining performance and coordination at a certain level. Whatever gets in the way of the efficient performance of a job has tended to be viewed as an obstacle to be overcome or a disease to be remedied; emotions are seen as disruptive. The popular conception of the child as progressing from emotional to rational responses is based as much on the demand for skills and facts and nonemotional processes in industrial society as it is on empirical observation.[59]

Classical liberalism, in stressing productivity and justifying production with a psychology of unlimited desire and a theory that removed the moral onus from unlimited appropriation, reduced experience to instrumental terms and encouraged a perception of the self which is essentially a self-in-opposition, which defines its boundaries in competitive activity. This conception of the self reveals a side of alienation which Marx, viewing the condition through the eyes of those who are manipulated or oppressed, did not consider, although Hegel did anticipate the problem of a life unworthy of human powers. Modern societies, and technological society in particular, require the development of controls and skills; the ability to respond to rapid change, to move easily from role to role, to adapt and compromise and abstract; the capacity to make subtle discriminations. The technological society requires, in Kenneth Keniston's words, "a dictatorship of the ego." [60] Bureaucracy, says Weber, develops the more perfectly the more it is dehumanized, the more it succeeds in eliminating all the personal, emotional, and irrational elements—those like love and hate, which escape calculation.[61]

Performance values are achieved at the cost of other possibilities of ego development—that "regression" in the service of the ego. "He who takes the ego to bed with him will never get a gold star for genital primacy. The orgastic model has virtue for certain human activities requiring a temporary submergence of self, such as inspiration, creative imagination, and thoroughly relaxed play." [62] In our understanding of the self we give too little consideration to the need for periodic surrender and that kind of self-validation that requires spontaneous relationship and relaxation. And then we discover that the less expression allowed to passion and idealism, the more unruly they become and the more energy is needed to hold them down. We distrust the "vitalist" rejection of ego controls and are appalled by the authoritarian "refusal of freedom." And then, in this confusion of responses, we see conscience degenerating into the narrow expediency that is rationalized today as realism.

Knowledge and being. It is widely held that the major factor in the growth of industrial production is knowledge. Less appreciated is the fact that scientific-technical progress has become the major basis of legitimation in industrial societies. In the remainder of this chapter I suggest that the presuppositions of this knowledge and the tendency for instruments to become confused with purposes have dangerous or at least highly ambiguous consequences. When man is placed in the service of knowledge, the only measure of knowledge is its own development and the growth of the forces of production. But in this process science loses its rationale, its telos, which has been the safeguarding and amelioration of human existence. The technical development of science, divorced from its rational development, is the modern version of an ancient theme intended as a warning to those who know but do not understand. I conclude with an attempt to understand, to bring together elements of the earlier discussion in a consideration of the relationship of consciousness and knowledge to the moral sense.

"The real accomplishment of modern science and technology," as Galbraith sees it, "consists in taking ordinary men, informing them narrowly and deeply, and then, through appropriate organization, arranging to have their knowledge combined with that of other specialized but equally ordinary men." [63] Technology bestows extraordinary power on ordinary men. We think of knowledge as an individual attainment, but knowledge today has become so fragmented and specialized that for the most part it exists only when organized in groups of men.

Knowledge is classified in units for purposes of assemblage, storage, and retrieval, and this classification, among other things, now makes possible government by manipulation and by controls based on the leverage that the files allow. Once men thought that government must be the rule of those who are wise in the knowledge of themselves and in the knowledge of men's needs and aspirations. Now, however, we are governed by specialists in what may better be called counter-knowledge—the kind of manipulation that obliterates the question, that prevents a problem from becoming a public issue, that confuses consciousness, that manages conflict by disguising the intentions of those who hold power. And it may be that in a highly organized and managed social system our freedom depends more and more on a category of knowledge which is a type of counter-power, a knowledge of how to block, deflect, or transform certain initiatives. F. G. Bailey comments on the fact that "the man who correctly understands how a particular structure works can prevent it from working or make it work differently than a man who does not know these things." In his understanding of an institution, he can "find out which roles are crucial . . . and among these roles which are the most vulnerable." [64]

Business control has meant the creating of those desires that can be satisfied within the terms of the system.[65] The emphasis on consumption is related to, perhaps dependent on, a conception of man as a collection of needs and wants and of satisfactions that can be quantified. This view and the psychology that takes man to be a bundle of responses have in turn produced an image of human nature which reduces or disregards the importance of sympathetic understanding of the processes of another person's emotional and mental life.[66] This model is associated with the institutionalization of highly generalized criteria of performance, preeminently with procedures that aim at avoiding unnecessary cost in relation to yield. These generalized criteria have replaced specific standards of conduct.[67]

Thus, technology demands the development of skills and the absorption of considerable information, but the kind of training it encourages discourages the fostering of critical intelligence. Even the university curriculum gives very little emphasis to the consideration of alternative values and objectives. Culture, we have to remind ourselves, has traditionally meant the expansion of perception, appreciation, and comprehension. The developed life of mind and spirit, however, are vaguely subversive of an order of values stressing satisfactions that can be mass produced. As higher education has become more and more costly, the autonomy of universities has declined. Administrators must be fund raisers, and those who provide support, even if they do not name the tune, exercise considerable influence over university policy. Higher education willingly produces the technically trained personnel the industrial system requires, and faculty as well as administrators are often surprised to learn that there may even be an issue here.

Behind all this, the capstone in the ideology, is the concept of toleration. Tolerance has come to be a value more important than any particular social goal. Toleration was born as the grudging acceptance of facts of life—more specifically as acceptance of the fact that political loyalty need not require religious uniformity. Its subsequent history owes much to the competitive model of the market, but what is less appreciated is the reliance of the market on a situation relatively devoid of strong political commitment. Tolerance protects the realities of power from critical examination insofar as it justifies the avoidance of commitment and of the kind of confrontation which seems to be the only available device for revealing the power base of certain social institutions. Tolerance operates best where the issue is a matter of indifference to most people or the major interest groups or where procedural considerations are primary. Where the market principle itself is at stake, there is little toleration. As in the principle of equality of opportunity, the real issue for our time is not equality so much as the very nature of opportunity. Is there a victory for democratic culture when equality means equal chance to participate in a narrowly defined struggle, where only certain aptitudes are relevant, for satisfactions valuable in part because they set a man apart from others in a manner that violates the principle of equality? And so with tolerance, culminating in a situation where all is tolerated because little can be taken seriously. Values reduce to one denominator, diluting the moral quality of life.

Without the existence of choices, we can have no freedom, but in order to choose we need criteria that make it possible to see the alternatives and that provide the basis for preferring one thing to another. There are indications that in our world such principles are dissolving and choice itself is burdensome. The distinction between fact and value allows us the belief that our descriptions of the world are objective. At one time this distinction was intended to fend off the pressures of power and the influence of interests, but it has come to justify the dissociation of the very values that legitimated the free life of the mind. "The very idea that good and bad are subjective preferences removes one possible brake from the triumphant chariot of technology." [68] The loss of the normative, the prescriptive, is the loss of possibility and of the future.

There is the knowledge that aims at self-understanding and the knowledge that brings parts together in a whole (this is what philosophy was traditionally considered to be), but there is also the knowledge that is used to obfuscate and dominate. Knowledge stands in an ambiguous relation to power insofar as power can be seen as the ability to afford not to learn, "the priority of output over intake, the ability to talk instead of listen." [69] Seymour Hersh, in *My Lai 4*, describes the widespread and almost total ignorance among GIs of Vietnamese customs and other aspects of life in that country. Even more appalling was the minimal effort of the army to provide some kind of comprehension. Power, we may say, is driven by its past and readily ignores the present, the context, and the other. Responsibility, by contrast, and here it differs from guilt as well as power, must look ahead and take the form of a commitment.

Specialization of knowledge makes it hard to see the relation of knowing and being, the relation of the self and its context.

Where the nature of the objects that surround us and their effects on us cannot be adequately understood, experience may be felt as a compulsion or, at least, as in the case of Albert Camus' protagonist in *The Stranger,* as something that happens to us, a feeling more like animal experience. In the case of the schizophrenic, the individual may no longer trust his own sense experience. Specialized roles and functions complicate our attempts to build a life around a consistent pattern of values. We live within a variety of groups, each with a certain set of expectations about our conduct. To recall an earlier remark about the concept of a tool, it could be said that while man is, within limits, variable to himself as he moves among roles and in and out of moods, to others he is invariant within the context of the roles through which they know him (through which, in Laing's phrase, they enclose him in a metaphor).

The market system is paralleled in styles of thinking which isolate particulars from their contexts and impede structural comprehension and which reflect the emphasis of the market on quantification over qualitative considerations. The market economy has been devastating to culture considered either in the conservative sense as the symbolic integration of traditions and institutions or in the progressive sense as a qualitative critique. Education becomes training in developing something that can be sold, rather than preparation in either the public or truly private spheres of life. Whereas freedom, as Archibald MacLeish notes, was once something one used, it "has now become something you save—something you put away and protect like your other posessions—like a deed or a bond in a bank." [70]

As technical language becomes increasingly remote from the words of ordinary speech, the gulf between the elite and the popular culture widens. This is not the kind of distantiation essential to the development of knowledge; on the contrary, it threatens the ability to relate data and structure and thus to develop knowledge. Communication and community are closely related. Where we lack a certain fund of shared experience, language loses its evocative function. Technology and the economy and the conception of science that confines it to a few methods of discovery and verification have had the effect of collapsing language into

limited areas of discourse and restricting our very ability to think
in moral and esthetic terms. Experience for some people still remains broader than the possibilities of the concepts at their dis-
posal, and from time to time we hear the remark, "I wish I could
describe what I feel."

Meaning is a comprehension of the structures of our world,
insight into the interrelations of events. It involves the ability to
fit our experiences into patterns and to know the results our behavior will have. Routines may aid the development of meaning
by providing a fabric of expectations, but at the same time life
may be the poorer as routine restricts the ways in which we
relate to objects. Meaning includes the ability both to get beyond
immediate experience (in order to discern the pattern) and to
experience intensely. "He who aims at the experiencing of experience," says Martin Buber, "will necessarily miss the meaning, for
he destroys the spontaneity of the mystery." [71] Objectivity includes
a similar tension. Objectivity is more than passivity and detachment: "It is a particular structure composed of distance and nearness, indifference and involvement. It is the freedom from the
kind of commitment that can prejudice perception and evaluation." [72] In understanding this remark of Simmel's we must appreciate both that objectivations are social (intersubjective) and, as
mentioned earlier, that a desacralizing process must take place.
The individual must detach himself from his ongoing experience
—a process which requires participation in the experience of
others. In a situation shared with others, the individual finds himself having to interpret the subjective processes of his partners,
to attune the experience he has of others to his inner experience.
As this happens a certain detachment develops. As Thomas Luckmann observes, "While detachment from the flux of immediate
experience cannot rise autonomously, it can be 'imported' in the
form of an 'external' point of view. One begins to look at oneself
through the eyes of a fellow man. This is originally possible only
in the reciprocal social processes of a face-to-face situation." [73]
This detachment remains in touch with subjective processes and
may be contrasted with the splitting effect of schizophrenic coping
strategies.

This process of mediation in the face-to-face situation

(which the symbolic interactionists would also see as the negotiation of the self) should not be compared with those social relations governed by such imposed typifications as role and status, which, in our day, may require that a man identify himself as a whole with a particular characteristic as he becomes an interchangeable segment of a typified class. "It is possible," writes Alfred Schutz, "that exactly those features of the individual's personality which are to him of the highest order of relevance are irrelevant from the point of view of any system of relevances taken for granted by the group of which he is a member." [74] Resulting conflicts in the personality encourage the development of a subjectivity which, as we may expect, has had a profound impact on modern esthetic theory—the artist reacting to objectivations and typifications of a society governed by commercial values. This reduction of objects to consumer value has led to a radical questioning of the world of objects and a search for forms of expression free from the language and things of ordinary experience. For those less talented in objectifying the subjective than Baudelaire or Picasso (who said that "with me a picture is a sum of destructions" [75]), for those who remain awash in subjectivity and cope with the loss of meaning and coherence through consumption, ethnocentricity, and other autocentric means, detachment is difficult, for they cannot get an adequate perspective on the self. Intellectuals, scholars, and technicians in pursuit of what Simmel terms "the freedom from the kind of commitment that can prejudice perception and evaluation" may be free of the problem of bias that arises from strong commitment but also deprived of the opportunities for detachment that come of shared experience, in which in knowing others one knows himself (a political life as opposed to an administrative order). This tradition of truth-finding is foreign to our style of thought; rhetoric and the belief that truth can emerge in argumentation and the confrontation of selves have been replaced by the techniques of science—truth as demonstrative proof. The kinds of control of prejudice represented by the dialogic moment of illumination in the dramatic mediations of the Socratic Plato have been replaced by experimental controls. These are all that remain to us.

But to understand what is involved here requires our going

back to a process that phylogentically precedes detachment. This is the concept of abstraction, a concept crucial to modern ideas of objectivity. As suggested earlier, information cannot be gathered without "information" also being rejected. I use the quotation marks because the rejected information is not considered relevant —not true information. But in order for the self to develop and for detachment to occur, there must be an openness to information. We are again back with the problem of the overabundance of stimuli, but now it is a question of knowing what those stimuli are. They have no existence apart from the receptors of the receiving nervous system; stimuli are private events. As Erwin Straus remarks, there is a tendency to understand a stimulus simply as signifying a thing—"yet the relation of stimuli to receptors differs radically from that of experiencing creatures to objects." [76] The detachment process described above is a means of determining what information is authentic and what is not; the reference is the self in relation to others—the environment essential to an open system. Autocentric man is an essentially closed system; this was Freud's model of man until he understood that pleasure could be more than tension release and that it could be projected toward other persons and toward the future. Obviously allocentric perception also blocks a part of the stimulus field, thus favoring one group of receptors, although there is always a sub rosa input, the "tacit knowledge" of which Michael Polanyi speaks. Such perception, however, is far more open to the new patterns that, as Bateson suggests, are to be found only in "noise." A characteristic of what we often think of as the style of learning of the adult person, however, is a competence within established channels, a technical proficiency. But this competence is very readily achieved by limiting possibilities for new combinations of information. The organism or organization screens information allowed to enter or to influence within. The price is a loss of sensitivity.

Increasingly, objectivity has come to mean the selecting out of certain properties of a stimulus pattern (other properties being rejected). This type of learning and knowing we call abstraction.[77] The abstract or the general may be opposed to the concrete, in the sense of an individual or particular case. The concrete, however, may also be understood as requiring a regard for context, in which sense the concrete stands opposed to the thing or fact in isolation. Because concrete has this double sense, the abstract by extension comes to be understood as the fact in isolation.[78] This situation induced the Marxists to reject a mode of analysis that culminated in reification—a way of viewing the world which abstracted capital from its human environment, failing to understand that capital must be understood contextually as social relationships. Man emerges as he abstracts the broken branch (or whatever) from its context, distinguishes its invariance from its variable aspects, and thus comes to create the tool; man and the process of abstraction are born together. The ability to create a distance prepares him for the naming of objects and the symbolic control of his world. This is a large part of what it means to be human, but it is also the root of man's inhumanity to man, for morality requires a knowledge of the context in which action takes place. Only in interaction free of distortion and domination in acts of communication can the crust of typifications be broken and self-awareness develop in a detachment which does not reduce sensibility or place our own experience at a distance.

When we find it hard to make sense of our own experience, it is that much harder to put ourselves in the positions of others in order better to understand their feelings and their values. We are disturbed by our incapacity to feel deeply moved by the destruction of thousands of lives in a Peruvian earthquake or a tidal wave in Pakistan. It seems necessary to witness hardship and suffering and death, to see with our own eyes, or at least to know personally those who are afflicted before we feel stirred by emotion. The intellectual quality which contributes to this sympathy and which is significant to the shaping of the moral sense is the element of imagination. At the most basic level it provides a practical knowledge of risks and dangers that make us wary of certain situations, such as hitchhiking in the Deep South if our life style is both visible and different from that of the natives. It is not always necessary to be victimized, and in such a situation the victim is hardly justified in considering himself a martyr. The imagination that enables us to grasp the meaning of the terror experienced by victims of the Gestapo and the suffering and sense of degradation felt by victims of poverty and cruelty and war is an essential part of the kind of knowledge that must be developed.

This union of cognition and feeling is related to a style of knowing more dependent on concrete images than on the kinds of models we employ in analysis. A model "is a symbolic projection of its object which need not resemble it in appearance at all but must permit one to match the factors of the model with the respective factors of the object, according to some convention. . . . [An image] organizes and enhances the impression directly received. And as most of our awareness of the world is a continual play of impressions, our primitive intellectual equipment is largely a fund of images." [79] In science, as we tend to define it, one works with the model rather than with an image because a model is based on a systematic abstraction ultimately capable of being expressed in mathematical terms, whereas the play of imagery may complicate logical conception.

The disintegration of structures of meaning requires that we prepare ourselves to see with new eyes, to require of knowledge that it cut through old prejudices embodied in our very concepts. It is a knowledge that must begin again with concrete experience and see clearly the uniquenesses. But the unique can be known only by way of general concepts, for something is unique only as it departs from a general rule. The concrete and the abstract are in this sense interdependent. Imagination and the knowledge of contexts demand a change in our relation to the world of objects. Because we have devalued things, seeing them only as objects-in-use, we have come to devalue man. As it is, our definitions of pathology do not allow us to include those individuals incapable of human warmth and playfulness. Half a dozen psychiatrists certified Eichmann as "normal." And perhaps he was, given the dominative attitude toward the environment which makes it difficult for the ego to drop its defenses, to reopen itself to that fantasy which is not protective or compulsive, to uncritical acceptance which is not authoritarian regression, to the erotic which is not fetishistic. A man's health depends on the active expression of his own creative talents. Things are necessary to this expression, and their importance should not be discounted. And creativity typically entails what we call inspiration, which is the vision of new kinds of relationships, the "explanation" that brings more elements together or rearranges them in more gratifying patterns. It involves a playful, experimental, more open attitude toward the world. As Deutsch puts it:

The demobilizaiton of fixed subassemblies, pathways, or routines may . . . [be] creative when it is accompanied by a diffusion of basic resources and, consequently, by an increase in the possible ranges of new connections, new intakes, and new recombinations. In organizations or societies the breaking of the cake of custom is creative if individuals are not merely set free from old restraints but if they are at the same time rendered more capable of communicating and cooperating with the world in which they live. In the absence of these conditions there may be genuine regression; barbarism would then mean the relative dumbness and deafness to which the Greek word barbaros first referred.[80]

That knowledge which is imagination and permits the deeper awareness of other points of view and the ambiguities of every situation may also become an impediment to the expression of moral values in actions. Understanding may only deepen the sense of tragedy; it has to be communicated and made politically effective if it is to mean anything. C. Wright Mills suggests that here distance can help us avoid collapse into self-pity and lamentation.[81] Knowledge as virtue involves a recognition that the collective morality may be (always is in some degree) destructive of individual integrity and virtue. It involves also a recognition that consciousness must be highly developed before the dilemma of contradictory duties can be resolved. Such knowledge requires the virtues of courage and humility, but if courage is to be more than foolhardiness and humility more than weakness, virtue must be informed by mature consciousness.

Daniel Berrigan, priest and poet and burner of draft files, writes that he came to the conclusion that it is better to burn papers in a selective service office than to acquiesce in the burning of children in Vietnam. His words are worth quoting at length:

This was an audacious, arrogant, and finally intolerable form of reasoning, as the loss of appeal will shortly demonstrate. The boxes of paper ash were wheeled into court on the first day of the trial as evidence against us. But the bodies of napalmed children could not be produced; they were abstractions, distant, debatable objects unrelated to the brute facts of the case. . . . Our action was non-violent, careful of human life and well-being, and proceeded as the outcome of a long and lonely social protest, preceded by years of service to our society. But nothing of this was to the point. The jury, borne aloft in airy platonic weightlesness by the judge's instruction, was allowed to consider only "the facts," apart from all moral or social circumstances . . . (the obscene word napalm *never passed the lips of prosecutor or judge).*

Berrigan contrasts his trial with the court-martial of four soldiers who kidnapped, raped, and then killed an unknown Vietnamese girl.

The legal proceedings served . . . only as a charade of justice behind which the most atrocious crimes ensue. Here and there enlisted men, generally cowed by a misbegotten system, sexually starved, lonely, spiritually adrift, pure American products, disposable items to be used and thrown away—such men as the Hill 192 four—pay a price for going to war. Not so heavy a price, either, as things turned out. Of the four court-martialed soldiers two are already at large, and the sentences of the remaining two have been reduced again and again. From this and other instances it becomes clear that military justice acts as a public pacifier, quelling the first storm of outrage, and is in no sense related to civilized justice. No such sunny prospect as a reduction of sentence awaits the Catonsville felons [Berrigan and the others who burned the files]. Two crimes: the burning of hunting licenses issued against humans, and the hunting and slaying of human beings. War, which institutionalizes the second, must with utmost rigor punish the first. Simply translated, the Catonsville nine will undoubtedly spend a longer time in prison than the Hill 192 four. But even the slight and symbolic punishment meted out in wartime to rapists and murderers never threatens those whose decisions make such crimes inevitable.[82]

One question that remains concerns self-righteousness. How is one to distinguish what I take to be the mature consciousness of Berrigan from the variety of moral crusades that punctuates American history? By imposing our values on others we seek to reform the rest of the world. This same propensity for moralism can be found in those who oppose, who resist. Conscience, as William Sloane Coffin says, "is a good servant, but it can be a bad master. One needs more than simply conscience; one needs to have a great deal of information and a great capacity for a rational judgment to take . . . a moral stand." [83] It can be said, however, that conscience alone is more defensible as a justification for refusing to commit what is considered an immoral act than as a justification for committing an act that may have injurious effects on others. The mature consciousness requires information and also that kind of knowledge which can be described as awareness of moral oppositions within oneself. This appears to be what Camus had in mind when, in *The Plague,* he wrote that "the evil that is in the world always comes of ignorance, and good intentions may do as much harm as malevolence if they lack understanding, . . . the most incorrigible vice being that of an ignorance that fancies it knows everything and therefore claims for itself the right to kill. The soul of the murderer is blind; and there can be no true goodness nor true love without the utmost clear-sightedness." [84]

Several schools of psychology and traditions of religious belief interpret evil in the psyche as the separation of the rational or the conscious from the instinctive, the unconscious. G. K. Chesterton described the madman as "the man who has lost everything except his reason." [85] The dark side of the personality must be revealed, seen for what it is. Only then, and when pride is understood as a separating function, can evil be overcome and the ego find its proper place in a self harmonized. The sense of freedom is the sense of freedom to decide, and this freedom in turn requires a knowledge of the moral oppositions, including knowledge of the repressed sides of our own natures. Recognition of our own limits is a part of the experience of freedom.[86]

We move beyond good and evil when we move toward an openness to the sources of creative energy. In so far as the conception of evil represents that which impinges on us, we remain in essence dominated by the embeddedness affect characteristic of autocentric perception. There may be another conception of evil, more congruent with an openness to the world and with that type of transvaluation of which Nietzsche spoke in his call for a transcendence of the herd morality. This conception is the understanding and appreciation of the depths of experience which have been lost or repressed—the sources of that passion which Buber held is evil if it is without direction, just as action without passion is evil. Both are lacking in true decision, which is the true Eros, the movement toward wholeness.

No choice between the creative spontaneity which derives from the unconscious and the ordering achievement of the conscious mind is required; neither is good or evil in itself.[87] Working together they reveal a world objectified but unalienated in which men can relate to objects and others for the joy of the relationship. Objects retain an instrumental value, as they must if we are to grow, given our difference from other creatures in the relation between drive and gratifying object. But the world closes in on us and is felt as a mass of impinging objects when activity is not an end in itself. The creative act helps us to see the world as a world of forms rather than as a flood of impressions. But from this appreciation of form arises the process of abstraction which assists us in ordering our world—and also in separating ourselves from it. Evil is this closure, and evaluation of the past over the present and the present over the future, the reluctance to accept new information. The consequence is a line of conduct which destroys resources necessary for existence: the pollution and destruction of the environment, an emphasis on short-range goals at the expense of larger purposes, the damaging of trust and of legitimating values that results from bigotry and jingoism. Typification becomes prejudice and ultimately the inability to see or feel.

Stimulus overload is a problem when the world is perceived autocentrically; when the environment is experienced as impinging on our senses we must close ourselves to stimuli, we must train ourselves not to feel. This "ignoring" is the essence of modern immorality. Willful ignorance of the systemic nature of our world, this ignoring, is perhaps not so far removed from the classical understanding of evil as ignorance. Sin and evil are the separation of man from man, man from his environment, man's own ego from the other parts of his personality. Of course without separation there is nothing to overcome. The experience of love makes clear the dependence of fulfillment and happiness on the act of overcoming the separation. Love preserves the other (who is both subject and object of love) while seeking union. Evil, then, is best seen as the inability or unwillingness to overcome separation. It is the refusal to see the world as process.

PART **IV**

Having shown how social structure, psychic process, and culture can conspire to sanction evil, we turn in Part Four to some types of resistance, of awareness, and of social change in addition to those suggested or implied in previous chapters. What we outline is more philosophic than directly political in a programmatic sense. For example, we consider the question of how various people somehow involved in social destructiveness discover what is happening and act on that kuowledge—or fail to do so. For example, Philip P. Hallie considers resistance from the viewpoint of the direct victim (in his dominant example, the slave who rebels). As Hallie shows by using Plato's allegory of the cave, victims may long fail to see the injustice of what they suffer. How do they come to see the light? Similarly, Jan M. Howard and Robert H. Somers explore resistance from the viewpoint of the organization member who is led toward participation in destructiveness; and Craig Comstock,

244

RESISTANCE TO
DESTRUCTIVENESS

from that of the citizen, the everyman in whose name so much official violence is being done or prepared. In particular, Comstock examines how systems are often harmed by their own defenses and how awareness of this process may reduce reliance on self-defeating responses to danger. Picking up this theme, Nevitt Sanford tells how sanctions for evil are prevented in the long run not only by specific counter-measures but by a positive vision of what men and their society can become and by broad efforts toward personality development which can sustain such a way of life. After outlining some basic values that sustain a constructive society, Sanford discusses how parents and teachers can help children—and meanwhile help themselves—to live according to these values. Changes in child-training and education, however, are no substitute for other forms of political action, whether directed against a particular source of destructiveness or toward promising social inventions.

CHAPTER 14

Justification and Rebellion

Philip P. Hallie

W. E. B. Du Bois in his biography
of John Brown asked a "riddle of the sphinx": how do we know
the right and the wrong, and how do we know the difference in
time to act? Instead of reciting the old philosophic battles about
the criteria for applying "good" and "evil" to particular situations, Du Bois, one of the greatest American sociologists, made a
point that is an assumption of this chapter: "All men know that
there are in this world here and there and again and again great
partings of the ways—the one way wrong, the other right, in some
vast and eternal sense." [1*] He was thinking of American slavery
and Brown's firm stand on the matter. Let us, like him, put aside

---

* Notes for this chapter start on p. 352.

for a moment the riddle and the book battles on criteria and take advantage of hindsight by considering some instances of momentous harm-doing that are (now) plainly "evil." Whatever the definition we may offer for that archaic, rich term "evil," the enslavement of the black people in America counts as evil and so do the brain-bustings and killings in the Nazi concentration camps. One can find many such clear instances of evil (at least clear now), including the destruction of the Digger Indians in America and the enslavement and killing of millions of Indians in the New World by Spanish missionaries. The riddle of the sphinx may be unanswerable in general, but the domain of the term *"evil"* is all of that nightmare we call "history."

In *The Paradox of Cruelty* [2] I explored part of this domain; in this chapter, however, as in the others in this book, we are studying an epiphenomenon of the nightmare: the self-deception and often the hypocrisy that seek to hide harm-doing under justifications. In that now classic biography of Brown, Du Bois went on to say: "The forcible staying of human uplift by barriers of law, and might, and tradition is the most wicked thing on earth. It is wrong, eternally wrong. . . . It is especially heinous, black, and cruel when it masquerades in the robes of law and justice and patriotism." Du Bois's masquerades is not a rich enough metaphor for use in studying the justifications of harm-doing, and it can be misleading. In a masquerade everybody knows that masks are being worn; the "deception" is playful, the duplicities transparent. The masks are outlandish, and we take them off at midnight with ease and pleasure. As we shall see, none of this is the case in man's concealments of destructiveness.

In one sense these concealments can be thought of as masks. They have a context and a shape; there is a milieu and a surface logic to man's vindication of his "forcible staying of human uplift." Other chapters describe its etiology in the depths of the human mind or in the depths of social processes. Here I try to understand its topology. In this sense I am studying masks, phenomena.

A more useful speculative instrument than Du Bois's for understanding these phenomena is available to us at the beginning of the seventh book of Plato's *Republic,* the "Allegory of the

Cave." In Paul Shorey's lucid translation in the Loeb Library, Socrates says:

Compare our nature in respect of education and its lack to such an experience as this. Picture men dwelling in a sort of subterranean cavern with a long entrance open to the light on its entire width. Conceive them as having their legs and necks fettered from childhood, so that they remain in the same spot, able to look forward only, and prevented by the fetters from turning their heads. Picture further the light from a fire burning higher up and at a distance behind them and between the fire and the prisoners and above them a road along which a low wall has been built, as the exhibitors of puppet shows have partitions before the men themselves, above which they show the puppets.

The fire and the puppet stage are behind them; a blank cave wall is before them; upon this wall appear the shadows of the puppets moving on the puppet stage; on one side is the entrance to the cave into which the light of day is coming. But they cannot see that light, nor can they see the light of the fire that is casting the shadows of puppets onto their wall. The fetters make it impossible and even unthinkable for them to turn their heads. All they know is shadows, and they take these shadows to be reality, not the shadows of artificial objects. After all, they cannot check. The topic of the allegory is education. For Plato the prisoners were kept prisoners, not only by chains but by their own ignorance of the light.

Let us assume that we are standing quietly at the entrance to the cave watching the scene, that we can see the shadows on the wall and that those shadows are the vindications of evil that men find themselves facing. Let us call victimizers those who do great harm by "the forcible staying of human uplift." One often has great difficulty in picking out the one who initiates the harmdoing; he is often obviously a link in a long causal chain of such actions. The victimizers, the Nazis or the compact white majority in America or the Spanish missionaries, may have themselves been, to some degree or other, victimized. However, the momentousness of their own destructive deeds makes etiology not perhaps an irrelevancy but surely a temptation to evade the subject before us. Slavery, the concentration camps, the destruction of millions of Indians, whatever their causes, now concern us because they happened and because their happening itself is of vast human import. Let us look at the victimization that was perpetrated and leave it to others to understand the long causal chain that may have led to the destructiveness.

In the kind of harm-doing that does not appear in the history of nations, it is often extremely difficult also to pick out the victim of another's power and initiative: wives may torture their husbands for financial, sexual, social impotence, and then the husbands may leave them or even kill them. And who is the victim? Problematic. Those who do not accept Du Bois's assumption about the "great partings of the ways—the one way wrong, the other right"—may wish to apply the same spirit of inquiry to the historical events we have mentioned. And certainly Jews, Indians, and blacks have been troublesome. But again, when millions of Jews or blacks or Indians are subtly taught to despise themselves and to despise their own kind and then are tortured and killed in captivity, to talk about their troublesomeness can be an evasion of the topic of evil. Let us call this process victimization—the substantial cruelty that various societies for the prevention of cruelty to animals emphasize, as against superficial, temporary harm-doing upon the weak.

Now standing at the entrance to Plato's Cave, with the sunlight on our backs, let us look at our prisoners. Instead of thinking about those who have imprisoned them, let us consider only the victims. And let us do something that will be very useful for our purposes: let us put the victimizers and their victims together on those benches, together "fettered from childhood." Let us put them on different benches, but have them see the same images from different points of view or see different shadows. They are all restricted to staring at those shadows and are not permitted to arise, to see the fire, or to walk up the long entrance to the mouth of the cave and see the light of day.

If you wish to elaborate on the model, imagine that the destruction of victims is done by speaking words, not by moving about and striking the victims. In the long history of man's "forcible staying of human uplift," dramatic physical harm is often only symptomatic of the destruction going on. Evil is not simply a matter of pain or death but of what people do to each other's minds, to each other's understanding of themselves and of their opposite numbers. In fact, staring at bloody events can render us too callous to understand the unselving of a human being that is at the heart of victimization.

And so those in the cave sit looking at shadows. What do the victimizers see? In general for them the justification of massive harm-doing takes two forms: good ends justifying bad means and, in a more complex way, bad means justifying good ends. The words in this formula change in meaning many times, but the formula with its apparent circularity is basic to their logic: high or valuable goals excuse the doing of harm, and harm done to such racial inferiors as "niggers" or "savages" glorifies their valuable goals by contrast. For the Spanish the end was gold, the expansion into heathen lands of high Spanish civilization and opportunities for salvation. For the compact white majority the end was sometimes stated in terms of profit (a cheap, stable labor force was needed to make a steady profit from indigo, rice, cotton); at other times it was stated in terms of religious benefits to the blacks. For the Nazis it was the Third Reich, the thousand-year Reich. The substance of these justifications is a matter of history. Here we are studying their shapes.

Consider an example of goals justifying means. Frederick Douglass was severely beaten by the Negro-breaker Covey, to whom Douglass had ben lent for a year in order to be made more obedient. He ran away from Covey's farm to his master, Captain Auld, and told Auld about ferocious beatings, begging his master to protect him from Covey. Douglass describes Auld's reaction: [3]

At first Master Thomas seemed somewhat affected by the story of my wrongs, but he soon repressed whatever feeling he may have had and became as cold and hard as iron . . . , I distinctly saw his human nature asserting its conviction against the slave system, which made cases like mine possible; but, as I have said, humanity fell before the systematic tyranny of slavery. He first walked the floor, apparently much agitated by my story, and the spectacle I presented, but soon it was his turn to talk. He began moderately by finding excuses for Covey, and ended with a full justification of him, and a passionate condemnation of me. He had no doubt I deserved the flogging.

Then after a few minutes his ultimate justification for condoning Covey's act appeared. Douglass' "professedly *Christian* master" said: "If you should leave Covey now that your year is but half expired, I should lose your wages for the entire year. You belong to Mr. Covey for one year, and you must go back to him, come what will." [4] This economic motive was not simply selfishness on Auld's part; it was a key rule in the system of slavery: the master's economic advantage justifies any treatment of his slaves. This custom was essential to the system and was built into its laws in many ways. Auld was not being perverse or sadistic; he was being a good slaveholder. The matter was not simply, if at all, a personal one between Auld and young Douglass. The personal aspects almost made Auld relent (and indeed caused him to let Douglass stay the night and rest before he set off for the farm of his tormentor). In sending Douglass back, Auld was following the rules, which justified his economic greed and helped him to brush aside all compassion and pay attention only to the hard facts of property and profit. Such rules, such justifications for abusive action or fatal inaction, made up the system of slavery. Similarly, the concentration camps in Nazi Germany embodied a set of rules which could justify any means to reach the pure goals of the Third Reich. The Spanish missions with their Indians were another such system. Systematic victimization is a set of rules for justifying any destructive means that lead to the goals of the system and of its beneficiaries.

In one form, this kind of justification occurs when people argue, as some public figures seem to do, that the orderly working of the system, peace in the streets, is so high a goal that maintaining it justifies following any laws, no matter how destructive. The law of a country and the order it helps to promote become the ultimate good. In *I Cannot Forgive* Rudolf Vrba and Alan Bestic tell about Yankel Meisel, a prisoner in a Nazi concentration camp. Because he had forgotten to sew his buttons on his uniform before an inspection tour by Heinrich Himmler, he was dragged into the barrack block and beaten to death while the whole camp was standing at attention waiting for Himmler. And while he was being beaten, while he was screaming under those blows, his fellow prisoners "all hated Yankel Meisel, the little old Jew who was spoiling everything, who was causing trouble for us all with his long, lone, futile protest." [5] They were waiting for their chief executioner to appear, waiting with the Germans' love of order, and they did not hate that fatal order—they hated the dying man who was threatening to disrupt it.

Some people are fascinated by orderliness, a fascination frequently seconded if not created by practical considerations of "business as usual" and, when a "duty" is done, by the excuse that "they made me do it." Practicality and this fascination can create a force so great as to justify the most horrendous of deeds. The laws relating to slavery in America were among the most destructive of mind and body that any slaveholding system has devised. Every slave was sheer chattel, animate property. He was not a party to a social or any other kind of contract; he was in absolute slavery (as South Carolina put it in 1740). His marriage was not legally binding, and so any slave family could be ripped apart by the master, the children sent one way and the father another without any recourse. A slave could not learn to read; he could not testify in court against a white man, nor could he testify under any conditions: he was sheer property, not a human being or a person. And manumission was in practice impossible in most southern states. In short, as South Carolina put it: "All Negroes . . . and all their issue and offspring, born or to be born, shall be and they are hereby declared to be and remain forever hereafter absolute slaves." [6] The same provision obtained in various other southern states in the eighteenth and nineteenth centuries.

These laws became the standards for good and evil for whites and for many blacks. To violate them was evil; to accede to them was the minimum that could be expected—even for a subhuman. In fact, one can make a useful distinction between justification and legitimation. Justification involves being aware of a tension (or cognitive strain) between good and evil; one knows two contradictory things and is trying to build a devil's bridge between them to make them consistent, as Auld was doing after Covey had beaten Douglass. Justification is rationalization, the only partially successful smoothing over of a tension: an employee of a bank may thus rationalize embezzling funds. But legitimation is perfected justification and thus a far more effective mask, a stronger mode of defense. In fact, it is so strong that it is not even a defense—not even defensive. To legitimate an action, to make it legal, or to acknowledge its legality is to see its goodness. To violate the law, to be a criminal, is to be evil in our secularized modern world. The laws of slavery did not merely justify making men, women, and children things "forever hereafter"; they acknowledged no tension between legality and evil. Because of this possibility, the law offers a supreme temptation to permit and even to promote the victimization of man. With all its great virtues—and even that last value term pales before the brilliant power of the law—it is the most effective means men have devised for condoning destruction. It is the overarching image on the prisoners' wall in Plato's Cave, the image at which victims and victimizers gaze in fascination and even awe. "Law and order" can legitimate almost any harm-doing. Perhaps all this was what Immanuel Kant meant when he wrote: [7]

There is nothing worse, nothing more abominable, than the artifice that invents a false law to enable us, under the shelter of the true law, to do evil. A man who has transgressed against the moral law, but still recognizes it in its purity, can be improved because he still has a pure law before his eyes; but a man who has invented for himself a favorable and false law has a principle in his wickedness, and in his case we can hope for no improvement.

Aside from the implication that men deliberately invent a false law (I have put the victimizers on benches, fettered from childhood, side by side with their victims), this statement summarizes all I have said about the distinction between justification and legitimation.

And as to the reverse of the formula, that despicable means justify glorious ends, this too, is a matter of history. The Indians are a stinking, lazy, ignorant lot, and so are the blacks, while the

Jews are biologically impure, part of an international conspiracy, and so using them in certain ways shows by contrast how valuable our goals are: Spanish Catholic civilization, white society, or a Nazi master race. Anything that puts such creatures in their proper place, be it a grave, a concentration camp, or a cotton field, must be itself noble and pure. The content or domain of the formulas changes but the pattern remains the same: something else justifies doing this. The justifications are transitive; they carry the mind elsewhere and give innocence by association.

This is what the victimizer sees. The shadows that the victims see exhibit much the same form but with important differences. The justification of evil is not a project only for those with the initiative and the power. It is part of the mental life of their victims as well. There is, running like a leitmotiv through all the victims' rationalizations, a laudatory envy of the power and self-confidence of the victimizer. This envy helps perpetuate the victimization process. Thus some Jews are ashamed of their hooked noses and names and want to be taken for neat-nosed Aryans; blacks form the Brown Fellowship of Charleston in South Carolina, putting light skins in an aristocratic class, and conk their hair to resemble that of Caucasians. And Indians admire the whites as consummately practical men and sometimes even as gods on earth.

It is not as if the slaves chose to admire their white masters and chose to despise themselves as black-assed niggers. Making them believe that they were chattel whose only higher law was the will of their masters was crucial to the mechanisms of slavery. Slaves were trained from the cradle "to think and feel that their masters were superiors and invested with a sort of sacredness" [8] (says Douglass). In this "slaveholding priestcraft," as Douglass describes it, they were taught that they were the black target of God's displeasure. Their highest wisdom was to be found in such phrases as "Servant, obey thy masters" and "Well done, thou good and faithful servant." Their self-despisal was institutionalized by the conventional associations surrounding words like *nigger, Sambo,* and even *black.*

But there were even more deliberate ways of making the black man so contemptible in his own and others' eyes that any

treatment of him was justified. For instance, the slaveholders got
their slaves deplorably drunk [9] by making bets that a certain slave
could drink more than the others. And the slaves were induced
by this moment of pseudoliberty to rival each other in degradation. As a result, many slaves were stretched out after such a cun-
ningly contrived debauch, drunk and sick, "helpless and disgusting" as Douglass put it in his autobiography.[10] And when they
sobered up they saw more clearly than ever how despicable they
were, how kind their masters were, and how they themselves deserved continuing degradation. Their brutishness justified—in
their own minds—any ends their noble masters chose to attain.

Sometimes the victims allowed their victimization to continue because of promises of heaven for obedient servants or
promises of peace and safety and order here and now—ends justifying means. And sometimes both formulas were conflated: we
lowly beings are expendable for such glorious goals and such
beautiful, powerful people.

The physical power of the victimizer over the victim does
not in itself constitute a justification of victimization. Physical
force is more like the fetters on the prisoners than like the shadows on the walls. In American slavery, for instance, the isolation
of the plantations, the poor white patrollers (who trapped runa-
ways), the gun, the bloodhound, and the lash, all in themselves
did not justify slavery—just as the concentration camps with their
modes of physical isolation and the missions with theirs did not
act as justification. These immense physical hindrances kept many
from daring to escape from or to resist the pattern of victimization
in the first place, as when blacks were taken from Africa under
guard. But sheer force itself, physical superiority, was not cited
by slaveholders or slaves as a defense of the institution of slavery.
Vindication, as in Roman law, involves recourse to more than
sheer superior physical force; it involves words vindicating problematic modes of behavior within a set of values. When a slave
says, "I dare not resist," he is not vindicating the system, he is
bowing under threats. This bowing may lead to rationalizations,
may arise from rationalizations, but until these are offered, he is
simply bowing, not justifying. The line between the two kinds
of actions is fine and shifting and hard to draw, but it is an im-

portant one. Fear, whether rationally founded or not, is not vindication, unless it is laced with value arguments like "I'd rather
be a live coward than a dead hero." Such a statement is one of
many instances or rationalized or vindicated fear which causes
the victim to cooperate in the system without resistance or even
mild risk-taking; it works along with the chains but must not be
confused with them.

But not all substantial harm-doing can be readily vindicated for its victims. Justification does not seem to work well in
cases of person-to-person (instead of group-to-group) harm-doing.
It seems to occur most persuasively in institutional victimizations
(genocide, slavery). Consider the personal cruelties unto death that
the Marquis de Sade describes in his essays and novels; though he
tries to vindicate them by reference to ethical skepticism, materi-
alistic indifference to death as a mere change of bodily form, and
sensationalism, those vindications do not work on his victims,
though they may convince some would-be victimizers who are
reading Sade's works. Within the novels, no victim ever begins
to justify her or his victimization. His libertines always fail to
convince their victims that their destruction is justified, and the
victim always defends his or her right to freedom.

That this is so teaches us a great deal about both justifications and the evils that can be palliated by justifications. Institutional victimization has long-term goals and a long-term history,
while Sade's orgies occur in episodic, separate nows, with no history and no goals that could fetter people "from childhood, so
that they remain in the same spot, able to look forward only," as
Plato puts it. Institutional victimization (by no means separable
but often readily distinguishable from personal victimization)
becomes common sensical in time, becomes second nature, even
rises to the level of a supernatural commandment. Moreover,
sadistic victimizers have an honesty about them—they call a victim
a victim and not a "true and faithful servant" or a "poor heathen."
Such victimization usually happen swiftly or with a rather brief
history that does not give them time to be sanctioned by habit or
custom.

If physical force is one of the elements of the fetters on our
prisoners, habit or custom is also an element. As Du Bois put it,

the forcible staying of human uplift by barriers, might, and tradition is wicked. Might and tradition, working together over long periods of time, make our prisoners what they are—dupes of illusions. In personal relationships this seldom happens, at least for the victims. Again, there is something honest about sadistic, personal cruelty compared, say, with the remarkable Requirement that the Spaniards read to the Indians in order to justify the persecution that was soon to follow. The Requirement was read aloud at them in such a way that no Indian had a chance to reply before the onslaught of the slavers and the killers. And sometimes it was read with no Indians present, to trees, to deserted villages, and even to the open sea before coming into a port.[11] Only a long-held, deep institutional commitment could cause men to believe in such a sham.

Sadism, even in its most thoroughly developed philosophical form, has never dreamt of justifying itself to its victims and could not perpetrate such a sham as this. It usually despises the institutional traditions which, for all their accomplishments in sustaining Du Bois's "human uplift," can be Circe's drink, turning us all into swine or, far worse, into willing victimizers and willing victims masquerading their victimization in the robes of law and justice and patriotism. In terms of logic, personal victimization—for example, the sadism defended and practiced in the novels and plays of Sade or in the murder of Leslie Ann Downey in the Dartmoor murders (during which her screams were recorded on tape—is perverse. Its rewards for the victimizer usually involve doing something because it is wrong. Erotic or other thrills rise from violating conventional morality, public custom, even common sense. It trades in irritation. But institutional victimization trades in long-term efficiency, the smooth operation of power with a minimum of conflict or paradox. It is practical; it gets things done in the long run. It seeks efficiency, not self-indulgence, and it pursues publicly acceptable, conventional ideals like the purification of the German folk, the attainment of heaven, or, in the case of the southern planters, the profitable and constitutional use of one's property.

Consequently, the logic of institutional harm-doing is a logic of consistency, of the smooth working together of various elements.

This logic is easily put into statements consistent with each other and with the accepted ideals or conventions of the community. Institutional harm-doing is the most justifiable of all the modes of maiming human beings, the only mode capable of legitimizing massive harm-doing. It alone seriously seeks to convince its victims of its absolute rightness. So powerful is its grip that it reduces us all to righteous murderers and (sometimes) to willing victims.

But where then is that parting of the ways Du Bois promised between a right deed and a wrong one? When do the prisoners in the Cave see that evil is indeed happening? Douglass asserts that one flaw in the system's operation can destroy its efficacy.[12] What happens when that flaw occurs? At first physical and habitual restraints keep the prisoners inactive, in the sense of not changing the situation. Fear and rules combine with the justifications we have been discussing to make the Cave the only plainly conceivable way of life. Escape from the Cave is not only immoral but impossible.

But gradually the victim becomes aware of inconsistencies. The dissonance of means and ends begins to reveal itself; habits are called into question, fears are softened or at least questioned, and then, sometimes, the victim begins to act. Sometimes he breaks his chains, stands up, walks around the parapet, and sees the fire and the artificial devices whose shadows he has been regarding. For example, Douglass found it difficult to see a beautiful young slave whipped mercilessly simply for loving another slave. Such punishment was in conflict with the idea "that God was good and that He knew what was best for everybody. . . . It came point blank against all my notions of goodness."[13] He began to doubt. His eyes had turned from the shadows. And then he discovered that not all black people were slaves and that not all white people were masters. He learned about runaway slaves who had survived, and he learned that some slaves remembered being stolen from Africa, from freedom. Not God or His commandments, but man had made slavery! Not all blacks are "niggers," disgusting means to noble, preordained ends. And he reached a conclusion that in itself, prior to any significant action on his part, released his neck so that he could turn to see the dupery to which he had been subjected: "My faculties and powers of body and soul are not my own but are the property of a fellow mortal in no sense superior to me, except that he has the physical power to compel me to be owned and controlled by him. By the combined physical force of the community I am his slave—a slave for life." [14]

Thus the victim sees the light. And if he is a Douglass, with his mental and physical powers, his moral fervor, and his luck, he finds himself acting to pull clear of the last chains, acting with allies (one thinks of Douglass working with William Lloyd Garrison and black Abolitionists) to break each other's chains. Together they try to turn the heads of the victims and the victimizers to see the dupery in which they have all been caught. Usually the victims are the first to rise; the victimizers have much to lose from this new knowledge, and they resist it with their old vindications. The released victims use what Garrison called "danger and guilt" to show men the contradictions they have been blind to for so long. The justifications the victimizers believe in usually crumble only after the victimizer has been put into some kind of danger, has been coerced. When one's self-interest is at issue, guilt, if it comes at all, frequently follows danger.

This shattering by danger of the victimizer's justifications is well summarized in a story James Farmer, one of the founders of CORE, likes to tell. A black sharecropper plowing his field with his mule was interrupted by a white motorist who rudely asked the direction to the nearest town. When the black man failed to respond and kept on working, the white man commanded: "Boy, I'm askin' you a question!" The black farmer whipped a pistol out of his overall pocket, pointed it at his tormenter, and suggested that the white man might want to kiss his mule. "You know," said the white man, "I've always *wanted* to kiss a mule!" After Abolition many planters piously asserted their long-standing conviction that the slaves should be freed, and many Nazis stated stoutly, after the unconditional surrender, that they always thought destroying Jews was unnecessary or even wrong. Unfortunately for our species, victimizers need to experience contradiction in the form of coercion and moral guilt.

Gunnar Myrdal calls the main contradiction between the consequences of slavery and the democratic creed of all men being created equal "an American dilemma," and he says that Americans are beginning to see this contradiction. But perhaps the blacks are seeing the contradictions that count and the whites are seeing only the conflict between protestors and a peaceful, orderly society. They may not be reexamining their justifications for slavery and its current consequences in employment and housing as much as they are, as Charles Silberman puts it, deploring "that their peace is being shattered and their business interrupted." [15] They may be still using that old legitimation, law and order. In effect for them, the end of peace still justifies the continued harm-doing.

And so danger and guilt do not necessarily go together. The escape of some victims from their chains and images does not entail the escape of the victimizers from their chains and images. Smashing chains and turning from shadows to light do not always have a happy ending. Institutions die hard—a cliché, but at the same time a fact. Kant was thinking of this truism when he held out no hope for the moral improvement of the legitimizer of evil.[16] Plato suggested this possibility when he imagined a prisoner in the Cave freed of his bonds and standing up suddenly, turning his head and lifting his eyes to the firelight: the prisoner would feel great pain looking squarely at the light after all that time in the dark. The prisoner may for a while even prefer to rejoin his fellow prisoners in their chains.

After Douglass had seen the light, had seen that slavery was sheer robbery and murder sanctioned only by superior physical force, not by God or high ideals or the subhuman nature of black people, he found himself

no longer the light-hearted, gleesome boy, full of mirth and play, that I was when I landed in Baltimore [where he learned to read and found books that pointed out the violent contradictions in slavery]. Light had penetrated the moral dungeon where I had lain, and I saw the bloody whip for my back and the iron chain for my feet, and my good, kind master was the author of my situation. The revelation haunted me, stung me, and made me gloomy and miserable. As I writhed under the sting and torment of this knowledge I almost envied my fellow slaves their stupid indifference. . . . Liberty, as the inestimable birthright of every man, converted every object into an asserter of this right. I heard it in

every sound and saw it in every object. It was ever present to tor-
ment me with a sense of my wretchedness. . . . I do not exag-
gerate when I say that it looked at me in every star, smiled in
every calm, breathed in every wind, and moved in every storm.[17]

The point of Plato's allegory is that conversion, turning the soul
about, is not a simple or an easy matter—it is painful, total, and
precarious.

And what of a man who has seen the light and comes back
to his fellow prisoners to tell them about it? Plato put it this way:
"Would he not provoke laughter, and would it not be said of
him that he had returned from his journey aloft with his eyes
ruined? . . . And, if it were possible to lay hands on and to kill
the man who tried to release them and lead them, would they not
kill him?" Compare this to the torment involved in convincing
the victimizers, the white population or the Nazis or the Spanish
missionaries, of the dupery with which they had lived and killed.
Indeed, the story of Douglass' life after his escape from slavery,
the story of his leadership in the Abolitionist movement, is the
story of that torture.[18] When in Eli Wiesel's *Night* Moché the
Beadle comes back to his fellow Jews after having seen the Nazi
bosses, they laugh at him, isolate him, and he disappears.

The awareness of inconsistencies in a society whose machinery works only under law and order is a painful and a dangerous awareness. Plato realized this fact about all learning. It is
even more strikingly the case when momentous victimizations are
interrupted by this awareness, when victims are converted away
from staring at the justifications with which they have learned
to live.

Our interpretation of Plato's allegory limps when pushed
too far. For instance, perhaps it is attributing too much innocence to say that the Nazis or the whites in slave America were as
much imprisoned by physical power and habit as their victims
were. But many whites believed sincerely in the inferiority of
the blacks: self-deception in the service of self-interest can do
much. Moreover, as Wilbur J. Cash put it: [19] "The institution
was brutalizing—to white men. Virtually unlimited power acted
inevitably to call up, in the coarser sort of master, that sadism

which lies concealed in the depths of universal human nature— bred angry impatience and a taste for cruelty for its own sake. . . . And in the common whites it bred a savage and ignoble hate for the Negro, which required only opportunity to break forth in relentless ferocity." Not only did it give rise to personal cruelties, harm-doing for the sheer joy of harm-doing, but for a whole society the lash, as Cash points out, "lurked always in the background," with dragging chains, the bay of hounds, the reports of pistols, and a general brutalization that the superficial amenities of plantation life never adequately covered. Though such considerations can be carried too far, so that they make all plantation owners far more tortured or brutalized than they were, this fact must not be ignored. For example, Douglass says that the slaveholders "had to deal not with earth, wood, and stone, but with men, and by every regard they had for their own safety and prosperity they had need to know the material on which they were to work. So much intellect as that surrounding them required watching. Their safety depended on their vigilance. . . . Knowing what they themselves would do were they the victims of such wrongs, they were constantly looking for the first signs of the dread retribution." [20]

There are important differences among the evils we have been discussing here. The Nazis had not as strikingly as had the whites in America fettered their own minds and the minds of their victims from childhood, although history richly displays the anti-Semitism that preceded the concentration camps. And the Spanish missionaries, according to the eye-witness accounts of Bartolomé de las Casas,[21] had even less time than did the Nazis to fetter their own and their victims' minds. But, with all these differences and others, the justifications of evil and the later contradictions of these justifications can be studied fruitfully by using Plato's allegory. Evil thrives not only on force but on the illusions it creates to distract men from both that force and the destruction they are perpetrating on each other. And that evil is known to be evil only when men learn to see through the illusions—learn it painfully, dangerously, and precariously.

CHAPTER 15

Resisting Institutional Evil from Within

Jan M. Howard, Robert H. Somers

W hen an institution acts so as to reduce the humanity of people, its actions can be resisted not only by the victims or potential victims but also by members of the institution whose work would ordinarily contribute to the dehumanization of others. In this chapter we focus on the latter, on resistance from within. This distinction between victims and victimizers is not entirely clear because participants in dehumanization may themselves be dehumanized. In fact one can argue that this is inherent in the dehumanization process. And, as the Nazis were so shrewdly aware, the best dehumanizers may be the victims themselves. Thus, the "final solution" to the Jewish "problem" was facilitated by their cooptation into the machinery of extermination—by their able, if unwilling, participation in self-destruction and the destruction of other Jews. What happened to the Jews is merely illustrative. We could substitute Negroes or Chicanos or Japanese in relocation centers.[1]* The surest way to dehumanize a person or group is to gain their cooperation in self-debasement. It is also the surest way to quell resistance. Thus, the Black Power and Chicano movements were predicated on the ideal of self-enhancement to combat cooptation of victims into the machinery of their destruction.[2]

In this discussion we are most concerned with resistance within institutions for the purpose of countering the dehumanization of others. These others include clients of the organization, "enemy" soldiers and civilians, and oppressed groups (such as Jews) of which the resister is not a member. He resists on behalf of other persons, and in the process he protects himself against dehumanization.

Sometimes, however, the resister may benefit more directly from his opposition to evil—because he is a member of the subclass of people who are being debased and on whose behalf he is resisting (blacks, Nisei, unorganized laborers); because the whole society or subsociety of which he is a member is being victimized by dehumanizing policies (Nazi Germany, the armed forces, prisons, concentration camps); or because the resister is singled out for special persecution on account of his resistance, and this persecution itself becomes an issue for further opposition. We are not concerned here with which kinds of people are most likely to become resisters and their preparation for it. This aspect has been dealt with elsewhere.[3]

Before considering the various processes of resistance from within an organization, let us look at the concept of resistance. At least two dimensions are important, for resistance can be active or passive and, in either case, visible or invisible. When these distinctions are considered jointly, four types of resistance appear: active-visible, active-invisible, passive-visible, and passive-invisible.

* Notes for this chapter start on p. 353.

We consider each in turn and illustrate its relevance by example. The fact that we link together several illustrations of the concept we are describing does not mean that the same degree of evil is being resisted in each case.

Active-visible resistance is often called open opposition. The resistance is visible to those who are being resisted, and it actively challenges and calls into question dehumanizing behavior. It encompasses demonstrations of draft resisters and GIs in opposition to the Vietnam war, faculty protests in support of the Free Speech Movement at Berkeley, revolts by the Sonderkommando (crematorium workers in German concentration camps), and on at least one level of conceptualization, civil libertarian support for George Lincoln Rockwell's refusal to be silenced.

Active-invisible resistance is comparable to subversion. It includes underground movements in Europe during the Nazi period, sub rosa meetings of medical students and interns for the purpose of undermining the impersonality of out-patient clinics, and maybe some uses of the secret ballot. Even where action is directed toward goals the establishment gives lip service to, it often has to be sub rosa because calling attention to a need for change can itself be threatening to authorities. Governments that institutionalize anonymity in voting recognize that open expression of opposition carries a risk.

By passive resistance, we mean feet-dragging rather than active opposition to particular patterns of behavior. We are not thinking of Mahatma Gandhi or Martin Luther King, Jr., who qualify as activists in this conceptual scheme. The passive-visible resister is the social worker who calls in sick rather than engage in midnight bed checks on his welfare clients.[4] He does not participate in the midnight searches, but he does not actively oppose them. His nonparticipation is masked by legitimate justifications (sickness, conflicting duties, misinterpretation of directives). However, organized passive resistance of the type described can become rather active. Calling in sick may be a mass technique to get around rules regarding insubordination, and for all intents and purposes it can amount to active visible resistance. Passive-invisible resistance is invisible noncompliance. You drag your feet, but only you or your group knows it. Here we put the soldier who shoots to miss or who does not fire at all but never tells anybody about it.[5]

The selection of one or another mode of resistance depends to a large extent on the relative authoritarianism of the system or subsystem in which one operates. Under tyranny one does not shout one's opposition from the palace steps, unless he is prepared to take the consequences. The soldier lives under a form of tyranny. And, accordingly, passive resistance, visible or invisible, is the more likely form of opposition in My Lai or equivalent situations. Some, of course, go further than passivity. Refusing to remain silent, they actively call into question through internal and external protest the dehumanization of enlisted men, stockade prisoners, and enemy civilians.[6]

In a charismatic authority system, resistance also tends to be passive and probably invisible. Where the evil authority is popular and persuasive, it is risky to tip one's hand. But effective resistance in such a case may require removal of the charismatic leader, and removal means active rather than passive opposition. The plot to kill Caesar had to be invisible, but the conspirators were anything but passive. Charisma and tyranny often go hand in hand, making resistance particularly difficult because the leader rules by a combination of popularity and repression. To the extent that his charisma fails to instill allegiance, he rules by force. Where charisma is combined with legitimate authority (rather than tyranny), resistance can be more open and active.[7]

If we consider the degree of responsibility of a person or persons involved in carrying out acts of dehumanization, some interesting things happen to the activity-passivity dimension and to visibility-invisibility. The greater one's responsibility for carrying out the act, the more likely his resistance will be active rather than passive and visible rather than invisible. When an officer drags his feet, he is likely to change the line of march, and his dissent is visible. On the other hand, even if he somehow removes himself from direct participation in acts of dehumanization, he tends to be held responsible for the evil actions of his subordinates.

People in positions of authority are likely to go along with or openly espouse mandates of the establishment even when they oppose them on principle. Opposition among the in-group tends to be a private affair. In public the members continue to appear as a team unanimously committed to promulgated policy, as described in Chapter Six. One can imagine a transition stage during which a potential resister grapples with the possibility of breaking openly with the administration, severing his connection, and either forming an opposition group or drifting into oblivion. During this transition period he may engage in invisible resistance (covertly sharing his views with sympathetic listeners inside and outside the power structure), and he may begin to drag his feet pending a definite decision to stay in or get out.

In the discussion to follow we shall focus on three fundamental processes of resistance: to institutional selection, socialization, and social control. In discussing these processes it is relevant to consider whether the resistant behavior is active or passive and visible or invisible. We begin with the process of selection and counter-selection.

Every system by definition is somewhat closed in the sense that it includes certain people and excludes others. The rules or criteria for inclusion and exclusion depend on the system or organization in question. Participants or potential participants may have varying degrees of control over their selection. They may influence the specification of selection criteria; they may influence who gets looked at with a view to selection and who does not; and if looked at, they may be able to determine whether they personally meet the selection criteria. Thus, a young man who wants to avoid being drafted may try to pose as a homosexual or psychotic.

A person of awareness and principle (some principle) may face the choice of whether to opt in or out of a particular dehumanizing system. Alternatively, if he is already a part of a system engaged in dehumanization, the question may be "Do I stay in or get out?" Do you let yourself be drafted into the army? Do you become a social worker in a public bureaucracy whose practices you abhor? Do you teach in a university that seems to you a factory? Do you remain a citizen and resident of a country that exterminates Jews, or one that drops an atomic bomb on Hiroshima and conducts a body-count war?

The answers to such questions have many facets, and we can be concerned with only a few. Obviously they depend on perceived consequences for self as well as others. Will I go to jail? Will my family go hungry? Will I lose friends? But a rational answer also depends on perceived possibilities for changing the system by working from within as opposed to pressuring from without. This perception, in turn, involves considerations of relative survival time as an insider versus an outsider, expectations of internal and external support from persons sympathetic to the cause, estimates of surplus time and energy that could be devoted to resistance activity beyond normal job requirements, anticipation of the psychic and social effects of guilt by association, and some overall assessment of the probability of doing more good than evil. The dilemma of opting in or out may also apply to an emergent resistance movement. When conflict in an organization or society leads to increasing polarization, there is increasing pressure on participants to declare themselves on one side or the other. A popular song of the labor movement ("Which Side Are You On?") put it succinctly: "They say in Harlan County there are no neutrals there; You'll either be a union man or a thug for J. H. Blair." [8]

In certain situations one may elect to enter an evil organization with the specific intent of leaving at some predefined or indefinite time. The purpose is to learn how the institution works (including its strengths and weaknesses), to gain a reputation as someone who can make it with the opposition, or possibly to build or help support a constituency of resisters within the organization. Another reason and probably the most usual where selection and entry are involuntary (military service) is to avoid penalties for nonpartipation and to bide one's time. A draftee may decide to be drafted but to opt out of combat if he is sent overseas. In essence, the resister draws imaginary limits beyond which he will stop participating. He may also play the situation entirely by ear with no preset notion of the time and place of disengagement.

Ultimately, this approach may lead to resistance or it may

simply remain a face-saving means of avoiding penalties. Among the hazards for the anticipatory resister is the fact that insiders are treated as insiders and begin to define themselves accordingly. Other factors equal, the longer one participates in evil the greater his chance of being depersonalized, coopted, and rendered incapable of severing his connection with the institution. Furthermore, the turncoat carries with him a stigma that breeds distrust. He is more likely to be respected in his dissent if he genuinely changes his values as a result of firsthand experience with evil than if his decision to get out later rather than earlier is a matter of expediency.

One also faces the possibility of diminishing options. In participating at all, one makes certain commitments to the institution. At the minimum, one assumes certain obligations vis à vis others, and the penalties for irresponsibility with respect to these duties can be very severe, much more so than if the obligations had not been assumed in the first place. The soldier in combat who elects not to shoot jeopardizes the lives of his comrades, which cannot be tolerated.

In spite of the potential hazards of deliberately submitting oneself to an evil environment, in many situations this is the only means of successful resistance. The history of the American labor movement clearly demontrates the importance of organizing from the inside. Ready-made communication channels are available. People have been gathered together, have been assigned tasks, and function with predictable regularity. All that is necessary is to organize from within.

Many times no alternative is possible because the evil institution embraces a whole society or subsociety as did Nazism in Germany and oppressive company towns in earlier years of American history. For the miner and his family, it was company job, company house, company store, company pub, and company mortuary. Given this pervasive dependency of employee on employer, advocates of resistance had no option but to work from within company-controlled institutions. They could advocate temporary extrication in the form of a strike and try to lessen dependency by breaking up company control of the total life situation. But they could hardly suggest that their constituents go elsewhere for employment. Free universities and experimental colleges are options for some students and faculty in the academic community. Industrial equivalents are rare indeed.

Even when a resister finds a way to stay on the outside of evil and to organize effective opposition, he is often not completely free of complicity. The conscientious objector, with few exceptions, pays taxes that feed the war. And a more subtle kind of complicity also merits consideration—complicity by nonresistance. The hippie drops out of society as we know it, joins a commune, grows his own corn and potatoes, and absolves himself of participation in evil institutions. But how should we measure abdication of responsibility for evil-doing—by the evil one does not do or by the evil one could have prevented if one had opted in and resisted instead of opting out? The answer again depends, in part, on the degree of totalitarianism in the system one wishes to oppose.

We do not wish to exaggerate the potential for creating and developing effective resistance organizations within institutions in our society. Americans are committed to evolutionary change, and in spite of our revolutionary origins we have a high degree of tolerance for evil. Our history books are not replete with illustrations of successful third party movements among the oppressed, nationalistic movements among blacks and browns, or peace coalitions that stopped wars. The labor movement of the thirties is a notable exception, particularly when we recall that John L. Lewis and the CIO successfully split from the AFL for the express purpose of organizing the unorganized, whom the AFL wanted to ignore.[9]

Because our society is evolutionary in perspective we ought to consider the gradual, almost imperceptible, humanitarian changes that have occurred, without fanfare, without violence, without severe organizational disruption. Health, education, and welfare programs, for all their inadequacies, are a godsend to major segments of our population. Students alternate between classrooms, committee rooms, and the street and leave in their train a wealth of curriculum changes, experimental teaching programs, and novel channels of communication. School boards, nudged and threatened by government bodies, grapple with various techniques of ending segregation. It is, therefore, important to recognize the potential for humanitarian change within American institutions. One is not necessarily capitulating to evil simply because he is a member of a dehumanizing organization—which almost by definition all organizations are to some extent.[10] If one is committed to working from within, he may have considerable impact.

So much for the dilemma of selection and counter-selection. Assuming one joins an organization or remains in it to avoid penalties and to help change its dehumanizing policy, what conditions permit him to persist as a square peg in a round hole without being rounded to fit the hole? This question brings us to the second process of resistance—counter-socialization.

Keeping one's values insulated from conflicting values of the institution in which one participates is no easy task. It requires a stabilizing point of reference and behavior patterns which harmonize to some degree with one's values. We are deliberately specifying two ingredients—a supportive reference system or group [11] and a behavior pattern which offers protection against dehumanization of self and others. A person's values or attitudes may not be consistent with his behavior,[12] and the institutional resister is a ripe candidate for his dissonance, with accompanying tension and a strain toward equilibrium. Unless he is careful, the spy comes in from the cold and forgets being a spy.

Keeping one's private values distinct from the value system in which one participates is especially difficult where the conflict concerns important values of the institution. The individual must somehow remain counter-socialized. All ways of doing this require some outside frame of reference stable enough to resist pressures toward change and flexible enough to permit the individual's survival in the new system. He cannot be so doctrinaire in his position that he quibbles over nonessentials. To some extent his values must be adaptive. It is not enough that the resister be a humanist or a humanitarian. His value system must permit changing definitions of what constitutes humanitarian behavior in different situations. This adaption, however, must be guided by values other than those implicit in the socialization one is supposedly resisting.

To be adaptive without embracing the values of the opposition is an art not easily learned. To stay on guard, resisters should occasionally test the limits of institutional tolerance for deviant behavior. Because they stand opposed to the system and may fear expulsion from it, dissidents or groups of them may too narrowly define the boundaries of freedom and may mentally discard alternatives of action that could be fruitfully pursued. One can be guided by the experience of others but more can be gained from personal testing. One reaffirms a commitment to resistance and nudges oneself out of complacency.[13] We are not suggesting that resistance be ritualistic. This is too rigid a formula for survival and change. But to keep from absorbing new value systems, one may find it useful from time to time to gut-react with automatic responses. If one always thinks about consequences before one expresses his true feeling, the feelings themselves may imperceptibly change. Just as the system limits what it will tolerate by way of opposition, the resister must also limit what he will tolerate by way of cooptation.

To keep antivalues from dying or fading away, it helps (it may even be essential) to have value sharers to whom one can refer for guidance and support. The reference group or individual can be other persons in the institution—a formal or informal counter-group.[14] Such a reference system has the advantages of being accessible, relevant (everyone is in the same institution), and salient in its interpretive scheme. Counter-values can also be sustained through contact with or reference to people outside the system. This support has its own advantages. People not caught up in the same milieu as you may be more objective than you in evaluating alternative courses of action. Furthermore, their existence does not depend on your system—a very important point if the going gets rough and authorities within the system try to weed out dissenters.

To minimize static from outside contacts, some organizations try to learn as much as possible about the various roles potential members play elsewhere before they admit them to membership. Corporations like to look at the wives of potential executives because wives can undermine as well as support their husbands' institutions. When the Communists placed their members in "mass organizations" to influence policy and build constituencies, the party continually faced the problem of losing their allegiance.

Various means of maintaining contact were used such as liaisons, caucuses among persons in the same organization, and informal primary group ties.[15]

One of the most intriguing questions from both a theoretical and practical standpoint is: How long and under what conditions can a person maintain dissonant values without support of any kind from others? Can internal fortitude based on some distant reference system keep one's brain from being washed and one's spirit as free as a bird, and, if so, how? [16] One important ingredient of value preservation under conditions of deprivation and loneliness is a sense of the intrinsic worth of the individual, particularly the self. Colin Franklin, who was hospitalized at the age of twenty-one for tuberculosis, observes: "A form of self-respect is needed in long illness and perhaps . . . in all kinds of imprisonment. One has the impression, reading a book such as *Solitary Confinement*, that Christopher Burney kept self-respect through his experience; and Paul Ignotus writes in *Political Prisoner* about conditions in which this quality might have seemed impossible— yet he made poems in the darkness and preserved some fragment of the truth about himself which he respected." [17]

Maintaining one's integrity under repressive conditions may require some mental separation of the self from the evil institutions in which one participates. Thus, Bruno Bettelheim invoked the scientific stance of the observer and partly separated himself from the concentration camp in which he was a prisoner.[18] He attributes his sanity to this process. In effect, he refused to be coopted into the machinery of self-debasement. Scholars and nonscholars can use similar techniques of disengagement under less extreme conditions of repression. By trying to understand the institution in which he finds himself and his relation to it, the resister attempts to maintain a separate inner life. Just being able to anticipate what is going to happen and having predictions validated by future events can be ego-supporting. In essence the resister acts cognitively with respect to experience. According to Eugene Heimler, preservation of the psyche is also facilitated by exercising freedom of action, however restrictive the limits.

In the work camps of Buchenwald and Berga-Elster I regained some of these freedoms, except of course the freedom of movement.

. . . It seemed that it was absolutely essential to express as many of these freedoms as possible to maintain my sanity. The freedom to express thought is an indication that one is not entirely at the mercy of internal and external forces; it enables one to face the darkness and the enemy. . . . Freedom of action, particularly forbidden action, was also of great importance.[19]

An interesting question concerns the effect of the focus of the New Left on the present. What is their staying power under pressure? Where other youth are available as reference points, the ideology will probably remain intact. But what would happen in solitary confinement or in concentration camps dedicated to human debasement? To the extent that modern rebels eschew an intellectual interest in the origin of their values,[20] they may not be preparing themselves well for commitment under adversity. But the now generation does emphasize the inherent worth of the individual, and it has role models like Eldridge Cleaver and Che Gueverra, which could be a saving grace under the pressure of dehumanization.

Let us now consider how the resister finds a behavior pattern consistent enough with his values to protect him from dehumanization. Obviously the open-active resister can behave in a manner consistent with his values. And the active subversive may commit enough of himself to humanitarianism to counter the evil of his public behavior. Passive resisters are more vulnerable to value change because they are generally unorganized feet draggers, devoid of systematic constituency support and counter-evil role behaviors. If they cop out frequently enough to protect their humanitarian values, they become active resisters almost by definition, lose their jobs, or both.

Within particular institutions, the insider with outside values may play a number of roles that can help insulate and sustain his counter-values. We consider each in turn. First, there is the role of counter-organizer. Democratic institutions often permit and even encourage counter-organizations within them. The right to organize in opposition to the establishment or the right to watchdog protection through ombudsmen may be formally guaranteed through constitutional mandate, legislative act, or contractual arrangement. Totalitarian systems generate antigroups which tend to be unauthorized and illegitimate. Depending on their tactics and legitimacy, the resistant organizations are above-board or undercover. Counter-organizations may be cyclical and transitory, as student movements often are today. Such inter-mittent dissent is obviously not as value-sustaining as is continu-ous struggle.

Occasionally an organization that is an integral part of the system (like an associated student body) may be converted by its leader into a counter-group. Its success depends on institutional freedom and mass support among the appropriate constituency. Functionaries in counter groups can behave at least part of the time in a manner consistent enough with their resistant values to maintain them, but full-time counter-functionaries are rare in-deed. Even students who belong to a multitude of anti-Establish-ment groups and protest dehumanization in the academic factory have to play ball with the system most of the time, attending mass lectures, reading prescribed readings, and competing for grades.

Where counter-groups are subversive, functionaries and members spend much of their time cooperating with the system. Otherwise their counter-activity is exposed. They may even try to be especially good organization men so they can participate in important decisions and be privy to inside information. The im-pact of such duplicity on values has already been alluded to. Or-ganizations are always alert to effective counter-leaders, and where that effectiveness hurts too much, they try to subvert their influence or coopt them into the power structure. Cooptation is often the beginning of the end for viable antivalues.

This discussion of counter-organizers has emphasized for-mal organizations, but effective changes may come about infor-mally. In institutions that are somewhat flexible and that maintain only modest control and surveillance of their members, a presti-gious establishment-type participant may engage in resistant be-haviors that would be considered highly deviant and disruptive if he were not so respectable. An established university professor, for example, may manipulate bureaucratic requirements with impugnity if his hutzpah is properly tempered with aplomb, sophistication, and status. Such rebels may adopt a behavior pat-tern quite consistent with humanitarian values without making themselves causes célèbres or being catalysts for formal resistance.

Second, there is the role of symbolic resister. Some institutions permit or even exploit symbolic resistance from a single person or an organized group such as a black caucus. Stanford could boast of Paul Baran, its Marxist economist, because he exemplified what the institution liked to believe was its ideology: "Let the winds of freedom blow." While authorities quietly tried to scuttle several other faculty radicals, they pointed with pride to Baran whenever they were accused of stifling academic freedom. Baran and other symbolic deviants can resist being socialized by the institution because deviant behavior and values are not only tolerated but expected. In fact, such dissidence can be useful for an institution that is publicly devoted, as a university is, to the concept of free expression.

This is not to suggest that symbolic deviants have free choice of opposition behavior and suffer no consequences for their resistance. In some cases they live according to a formal or informal set of establishment expectations—that they will not preach in the classroom; that they will be candid with the administration regarding organizational affiliations; that they will at least discuss their own political background if subpoenaed by government committees. And a professor such as Baran may be penalized in covert ways: he may be denied salary increases commensurate with his status,[21] may be subjected to private criticism for holding deviant views, or be socially ostracized by colleagues in positions of power.

Establishment tolerance for the symbolic deviant or deviants varies with the tide of public and private opinion and the dependency of the institution on that opinion. When universities are engaged in fund-raising drives and bond campaigns, they may try to temper or silence deviant expression. They may approach the symbolic resister and encourage temporary restraint for the common good. Such agreements are possible because symbolic deviancy signifies some level of expedient or principled accord between the institution and the deviant. Once an institution permits symbolic deviance, it may be stuck with the opposition whether it wants it or not. Invoking a repressive policy can make the deviant or deviants still more symbolic, with more disasterous consequences for the institution than enduring the status quo.

Third, the insider with outside values can play the post office role. If you ask a German over fifty what he did in Germany during World War II, he is supposed to say, "I worked in the post office." Every institution has such roles. Medics in the army can tell themselves, if not others, that they are the humanitarians of the war. Supply clerks and communications personnel may escape the shooting. Traffic cops may avoid wielding billy clubs. Research scholars without teaching responsibilities may escape the task of depersonalizing scholars-to-be.

The resister who wants to protect and remain true to his values may be able to select a post office role in a dehumanizing institution (the electrical engineer who works in a defense industry but not on defense contracts). This choice lessens his sense of complicity and the tension of dissonance and makes it easier for him to survive in the institution without forsaking his ethics. But it may also lessen his motivation to resist since he feels partially separated from evil-doing and its consequences. In this respect we should probably distinguish between post office roles which disengage one from evil and those (like that of medic or clergyman) which permit one to act as a humanitarian amidst the evil. If the latter choice is open, it probably offers the best protection against socialization by the larger group because the humanitarian's behavior is consistent with his values and because the subgroup can offer ideological support. However, being a humanitarian in an institution engaged in dehumanization can produce intolerable dissonance in the individual, especially when his freedom to do humanitarian acts is constricted by the institution (when medics are allowed to treat GIs but not civilians). The humanitarian role player also gives legitimacy to the institution in which he functions, even if he does not approve of its evil-doing. When clergymen and doctors don olive drab, they sanctify killing, even if their mission is to serve the dead and dying.

Fourth, where the resister's values are somewhat in harmony with the stated ideology of the institution or where there is strong inside or outside pressure toward value change, the dissident may be able to play a semiradical, semiconservative broker or advocate role. He may be allowed to lead the loyal opposition or to be a go-between for the establishment and other resisters. To play this role, he has to persuade authorities that permitting some resistance to established values and behavior patterns is an expedient or principled alternative to repression. Illustrative is the Student American Medical Association, which is allowed to deviate from traditional AMA patterns without being as extremist as the nonaffiliated Student Health Organization.

Thus, organizations as well as individuals can be brokers. Legitimate groups occasionally form coalitions with extreme resister organizations to work on specific issues. Representatives of the acceptable groups may serve as intermediaries between the establishment and the alienated factions.

The broker role is intrinsically unstable. Both sides exert tremendous pressure on the intermediary to show greater allegiance to one group than to the other. A number of college presidents are caught in this bind. No matter what they do they cannot please both regents and students. Distrust of the broker is a common response, and very often abating the suspicion of one group exacerbates distrust in the other.

In the process of mediation, the broker's values can change from sheer bombardment and the necessity for open-mindedness. Those whose values remain most stable probably focus on means rather than ends. They may stress the importance of communication for its own sake—the value of confrontation, exchange of ideas, mediation, and an open mind. If this is their perspective, playing the broker role can be value-sustaining, unless the truth of combat is discouraging. But in focusing upon humanitarian procedures, they may forfeit humanitarian ends.

Some institutions permit and encourage advocates (such as lawyers and union business agents) rather than mediators. Advocates are expected to be one-sided, even though negotiation and compromise may be part of their task. Unless the advocate is indiscriminate in representing clients or groups of them, he is in a good position to maintain his values while functioning within the system. There are of course problems. The most downtrodden of clients may not be able to afford his services or the cost of adequate case preparation. If he is paid too well, he risks having his anti-values corrupted by enjoying the perquisites of the establishment.

If he is too strong an advocate, he may be dismissed by the institution, by-passed, transferred, or otherwise divorced from his constituency, and in some cases even punished, like his clients, for contempt. Yet, the advocacy role can be a very satisfying means of combining resistance and participation in the system.[22] If that system recognizes the legitimacy of protest and tenacious representation, dissonance can be minimal. However, if the establishment gives lip service to advocacy without protecting protagonist and client, the advocate may subvert his values by participating in the facade.

The fifth possible role is that of the meshugana. In certain organizations one can play this screwball or mischievous role, which interferes to some extent with the evil activities of the system. One tries to be disruptive without being decapitated in the process. Such resistance is most likely found in involuntary or coercive sytems like the army, prisons, and public schools. The perpetrators are generally low-echelon personnel who are veiled by anonymity. The "good soldier Schweik" qualifies and so do certain Negroes in premilitant days (Langston Hughes' Simple).[23]

If the resistance is not too disruptive, the institution may tolerate or even encourage it as a sop to the troops, allowing them to blow off steam. But it can also have the effect of sand in the machinery. Successful mischief is good for resister morale especially if it is dramatic, like painting a toilet seat in an army latrine pink. Such acts prove that participants in the system still have a perceptible if limited area of autonomy, and this fact can offer hope.

Sixth, the legalistic role is another possibility. Every institution has a formal (usually written) set of rules promulgated and accepted by some authority or group of authorities. In many cases, especially in democracies and humanitarian institutions, these rules protect rights of clients and participants in the organization. The formal rules provide guidelines for behavior, but they are not necessarily governing. Practical reality generates an informal code that may be more important in determining behavior than are the written norms.[24] To the extent that the formal rules offer more protection against dehumanization than the informal ones, employees dedicated to humanitarian values may find it useful to activate the formal codes. Air traffic controllers have invoked this kind of protection during peak flying times, such as holiday weekends. FAA rules recognize that controllers are human beings, incapable of overseeing traffic with the speed of a computer; so the controllers fall back on these rules when work load and pressure from the airlines are overbearing.

Even in authoritarian organizations like the police force, members dedicated to humanitarian values may successfully invoke the protection of the book.[25] Those who promulgate prescriptions and proscriptions governing police behavior often anticipate the pressures that force police to behave in dehumanizing ways. They set forth guidelines for proper behavior—how to control crowds without resorting to violence, how to secure evidence without violating constitutional rights. And, to encourage compliance, they also teach the police that restraint helps to avoid public backlash, mistrials and hung juries, and intrusive investigations. An alert policeman dedicated to preventing violent outbursts may successfully call into play restraining rules and precedents. In essence, he fulfills a legalistic role, getting others to conform to the humanitarian book. Such behavior is not simply ritualistic or bureaucratic in a depersonalizing sense.[26] To be effective the legalistic resister must adapt general rules and regulations to specific situations and defend their relevance. He is not enamored of rules for their own sake but for their content.

There are pitfalls. If the legalistic resister is obviously selective in the rules he chooses to invoke, he may be exposed as a Machiavellian. If he is too rigid, he may exacerbate dehumanization or be ignored as a ritualistic conformist. If he stands in the way of practicality too often, he may be transferred or fired, unless he is protected by an active constituency, by job security such as tenure, or by sympathetic superiors. The character of the rule book is important in its own right. To be more than sporadically useful, it must reflect a spirit of humanitarianism and be logically consistent. Otherwise, it is all things to all sides, and the legalistic resister is trapped into obeying dehumanizing regulations as well as humanizing ones.

An alert legalist can use the rule book in a number of ways. Where codes have been proliferated ad infinitum as in welfare institutions,[27] a studious review of the book or books will probably reveal some rules that offer protection for staff and clientele. How much protection depends on factors extraneous to the rule itself—administrative and judicial procedures, constituency support, and the relative importance of conflicting norms. The legalist can use adjudication itself as a threat. His adversaries can be intimidated by the symbolic significance of visible opposition clothed in legitimacy, the nuisance value of red tape, and the possibility of a precedent-setting adverse decision, however unlikely this may seem.

The legalist can also live by the book for the express purpose of revealing its shortcomings (procedural delays, universal *dos* and *don'ts* which ignore individuality, and seemingly inconsequential loopholes which repeatedly get the institution off the hook). Informal administrative practices may disguise the true evil of formal codes and perpetuate their legitimacy. By forsaking expediency and invoking the formal rules alone, resisters can expose their content and offer grist for the mill of opposition if effective opposition is in fact possible (through a welfare rights organization, for example). In the short run, dehumanization is exacerbated for the long-run purpose of forcing action against the system.

Where socialization is incomplete, sanctions and social control are necessary to deter deviation from institutional values. Resisters who select themselves, or are selected, into a dehumanizing institution and manage somehow to maintain their counter-values risk punishment of one form or another. To keep their resistance meaningful or to give themselves that option, they must avoid punishment, minimize it, or exploit it. This is the process of counter-control.

One way to avoid negative sanctions is to choose the path of invisible resistance. But this choice is not always possible or effective. Engaging in passive rather than active resistance is another alternative because, even if visible, it does not directly call into question the values of the system. If you report to sick call rather than go on patrol on a day you anticipate a possible My Lai, maybe you can cop out without being punished for it. Repeated cop-outs, however, will probably result in punishment.

A third avenue of escape, and a good one if possible, is to build a power base or constituency that supports your resistance. It is difficult to become personally indispensable to an institution unless you have leverage over others. In this respect the active-visible resister may be in a stronger position than those who are invisible or passive because sanctions against open activists are immediately suspect even when the true rationale for punishment is disguised. When the invisible or passive resister is discovered, he is more easily forced out of the institution on false charges, although he may be given the option of quietly resigning.

Democratic or benevolent institutions may protect deviants and dissenters from severe punishment. In our society civil servants, tenured professors, elected officials of various sorts, ambassadors, and judges all have some protection against harassment and punishment for dissidence. Legitimate organizations of resisters (like trade unions) often try to formalize protective procedures. But institutions have many ways to punish those with formal security. Being socially ostracized, not getting travel money, and being forced to teach introductory courses are informal sanctions in the university setting.

If a resister has certain status characteristics, sanctions against him may be minimized. If he is a child, she is a woman, he is a black, questionable behavior may be excused to some extent and punishment lessened. However, the resister may balk at leniency on the ground that he knew full well what he was about and wants his full measure of punishment. The child wants to be treated like an adult, the woman like a man, and the black like a white, for in accepting special consideration from an evil institution the resister helps it achieve a humanitarian image. Those who engage in civil disobedience emphasize the importance of punishment. Purists do not cop pleas or otherwise mitigate penalties. In accepting their punishment, they underscore not only their moral commitment and their alienation from the establishment but also their acceptance of normative order.[28]

The shrewd dissenter may want to exploit sanctions against him. The success of his martyrdom depends to a large extent on the existence of a moral or legal order which makes his resistance legitimate, particular sanctions against him illegitimate, or both.

We have witnessed a decade of exploitation of sanctions in this country. The civil rights movement under King, Jr., the Free Speech Movement at Berkeley, the peace demonstrators at the Oakland induction center, protestors at the Chicago convention, and people practicing civil disobedience in a multitude of settings have all exploited the violent sanctions of the establishment to prove the worthiness of their resistance. At times resisters such as King have even invited and provoked violence (albeit reluctantly) to underscore their legitimacy and the illegitimacy of the opposition.[29] To suggest that King and his followers invited violence is unacceptable to the average liberal. In support of our thesis we quote from King's discussion of the logic behind the Selma march:

The goal of the demonstrations in Selma, as elsewhere, is to drama-tize the existence of injustice and to bring about the presence of justice. . . . Long years of experience indicate to us that Negroes can achieve this goal when four things occur: (1) Nonviolent demonstrators go into the streets to exercise their constitutional rights. (2) Racists resist by unleashing violence against them. (3) Americans of conscience in the name of decency demand federal intervention and legislation. (4) The administration, under mass pressure, initiates measures of immediate intervention and reme-dial legislation.[30]

If the conscience of America is aroused only by violence, then resistance movements will exploit and even provoke it, as hypocritical and self-punishing as this course may seem. One diffi-culty is that the American public appears to have an ever-increas-ing tolerance for violence, and it takes an escalating amount of horror to get the same public reaction. Over the last decade we have also witnessed resister exploitation of sanctions for the pur-pose of invoking support from the legal order or changing the law. Sit-in demonstrators in the South forced the establishment to punish them. Then they contested that punishment in the court and changed the law. This course is possible only where the law and the lawmakers are potentially supportive. Exposing oneself to punishment can be personally functional for resisters, imbuing them "with a sense of courage and dignity that strengthens their personalities." [31] It also lets one test the extent of his commitment and prove to himself and other resisters that he is worthy of their respect.[32] Finally, it can be self-confirming. When people you define as bad hurt you, your evaluation is correct.

Now that we have discussed the processes of resistance, let us consider aspects of time and setting. Quite commonly, people join, remain in, or support institutions with which they disagree, on the premise that eventually they will have the power, prestige, and security to effectively resist its evil-doing. In the meantime, they try to stay out of trouble. Thus, the graduate student begs out of a student strike by arguing that he can do more good if he gets his Ph.D. The assistant professor opts out of signing a petition against the war by arguing that he can do more if he gets tenure. The congressman votes with the caucus because he expects to be appointed to an important post where he will be free to champion the underdog. In all these cases the potential resister postpones his resistance on the premise that the ultimate good he can do justifies temporary cooperation with the establishment. He may well be right, but the risks involved must be considered.

While the postponer bides his time, he is bound to alienate others who share his values but stick their necks out along the way. Devoid of this constituency he is particularly vulnerable to establishment sanctions if his true values are discovered and he is considered a threat. In the process of rationalizing his temporary complicity, the postponer is likely to adopt or accept some of the values he supposedly opposes, if only to say to himself: "What I'm required to do is not really as bad as it may seem." Then, too, the system rewards those who cooperate with it, and some institutions deliberately escalate the value of these rewards over time, with pension and retirement programs, stock options, vacation pay, sick leave, and seniority schemes. As one's marketability goes down, the social economic advantages of playing ball with the system go up. Age may also take its toll in fostering conservatism. One tells himself that he can offer better resistance when he has more power, prestige, and security than he has now. The *more* is infinite, and so may be the postponement. Perhaps most important, in order to perfect any behavior pattern, one must practice it. The resister learns by his mistakes and successes, by watching others succeed and fail. The longer one postpones active or passive resistant behavior, the more difficult it is to prepare oneself for resistance.

We are not totally negating the value of the postponer pattern. We do suggest that its success depends on adequate training for postponement and continuous involvement in resistance behavior, however low key and invisible. While delaying open opposition to the establishment, the postponer may anonymously contribute money to resistance movements or function as an informant, dropping enough hints about the evil-doings of his organization to bring journalists and public authorities to investigate.

Opposition to the establishment can be deferred by a separation of roles as well as by postponment. Resisters continually face the dilemma of determining the context in which opposition will be most effective and least penalizing. A major choice in our society concerns the relationship of resistance to the milieu of employment. Should one take up the banner of defiance only as a citizen or should this involve one's vocation as well? [33] The dimensions of this dilemma are many. Resistance may be more appropriate to one setting than another. If dehumanizing conditions of work are the issue, the vocational tie is obvious. But one still may choose at the beginning to fight on one's own time, remaining affectively neutral in the work situation and organizing, planning, and protesting at night. Contracts of employment may stipulate that certain political activity must take place after hours and off the premises. In the focus of evil is the larger society rather than the work milieu, the citizen role may be the most appropriate context of resistance. But even so, the work role can influence or be influenced by opposition behavior.

In some cases obligations of employment set limits on off-hours activity. The Hatch Act, for example, curtails the political life of government employees. And resisters may be punished, even fired, for unbecoming conduct as citizens. The Board of Regents of the University of California severed the employment of Angela Davis, an avowed Communist, supposedly because she roared her opposition to the establishment instead of letting forth an occasional muted bark.[34]

Particularly among professionals and semiprofessionals the border line between work and private life is blurred at best and is often nonexistent. When one speaks as a citizen (a Democrat, a Republican, a PTA member, a consumer), one's status as a professional is hard to hide and, in fact, is often invoked specifically to add prestige to one's viewpoint. Realization of this fact has prompted certain scholars to warn professionals against exploiting their prestige when functioning in nonprofessional roles. "Keep your hats distinct," they caution,[35] and the caution extends to the question of whether professional associations should take stands on social issues.

Some individuals find such role separation theoretically and operationally impossible and succumb to the necessity of being whole persons who adopt the same posture in a variety of milieus. If they are hard-nosed scientists wedded to objectivity and proof, they are also hard-nosed citizens who close their minds only when they are finally convinced of the righteousness of their cause. If they believe that certain principles and values supersede technique, they invoke these values as scientists as well as citizens. This desire to wear one hat all the time can be a catalyst for protest or a rationalization for silence. Some believe that enjoying the prequisites of high status obligates one to use one's talents and training in the arena of politics and protest. Others feel that protest is a full-time job, not to be engaged in by part-time politicians.

In most occupations, options are available, and some elect to protest through the kind of work they choose to do and not to do. Social scientists study war and conflict, racial tension, poverty programs. Engineers focus on ecology, economical distributions of water and power, and peacetime uses of nuclear energy. On occasion, the whole work organization may take a stand against evil, especially if its orientation is humanitarian (a church, a university, a medical center, a welfare institution). Or groups of workers in particular institutions may refuse to use their talents for evil ends such as engaging in war-related research.

Opposing the status quo within the work milieu may be most effective when one openly plays a dissident role and pays as much attention to the fact of opposition as to the content of it. The resister may appropriately define his task as keeping minds open to alternative viewpoints. He becomes a sophisticated devil's advocate, sensitive to the moral implications of organizational policy and the possible unanticipated consequences of action. In some cases he functions as the conscience of the organization. This role is by no means easy to adopt and play successfully. Chronic complainers readily lose their influence and job security. Pretentious moralists are too reminiscent of little old ladies in tennis shoes. Protection lies in tenure, job expertise, a colleague power base, the symbolic value of organizational tolerance, and the resister's receptivity to the opinions of others.

We have approached the question of resistance here from the standpoint mainly of the individual rather than a collectivity or organized resistance movement. We have done so for a number of reasons. Initially, we were concerned with the possibility of resisting participation in genocide within oppressive societies and subsocieties. The prototype case is Nazi Germany, but, as My Lai demonstrates, our own American army may on occasion provide an illustration. Under tyranny, some degree of individual resistance is almost always found, but organized opposition tends to be nonexistent or transitory and precarious. The rebel is often on his own. Decisions to resist or not can literally mean life or death. Such choices affect individuals to the depths of their psyches and leave in their wake enhanced selves, crippled selves, or beings completely dehumanized by the system.

Since World War II and the Nuremberg trials, the principle of morally based individual resistance to organizational directives is more widely recognized. Resistance organizations themselves may be suspect. Participants in the New Left of the 1960s were realistically aware of the extent to which organizations with humanitarian aims can themselves be oppressive. As Robert Michels theorized in his Iron Law of Oligarchy,[36] they can be transformed into depersonalizing instruments quite like the establishment organizations they were founded to oppose.

The New Left was insightful in another way. They constantly reminded us of our subtle ongoing participation and complicity in dehumanization. Crises like the "incursion" into Cambodia, the Democratic National Convention of 1968, and the beatings at Selma wake us up; we mass or coalesce into ad hoc resistance organizations that live and fight for the moment and pass into oblivion like a thousand organizations before them. And we go on as individuals cooperating or not cooperating with the system.

Even when the Old Left prospered and the labor movement was successfully organizing, antiestablishment rebels were not simply automatons who followed orders. They were forced by circumstances to make moral choices for themselves every day. All systems limit the dissent they tolerate, and the resister must constantly struggle to achieve a proper balance of dissent and conformity, continually testing the limits of his freedom and his capacity to influence the behavior of others. The importance of the single resister should never be underestimated. His voice can break the spell of loneliness which isolates potential comrades. Its echo may be a chorus of voices stirred by example.

To stress the importance of the individual is not to minimize the power of organization. We recognize that effective resistance ultimately lies in counter-action by groups. Charismatic humanitarians with an eye for proper timing and proper issues can stem the tide of evil, but they do so only through the power of persuasion and organized group support. Joe Hill, the folk-hero labor organizer, was starkly aware of this fact. When he was about to be executed for alleged murder, he admonished his followers: "Don't mourn for me—organize!"

When the chips are down, the best of resistant organizations may not be able to protect the rebel. And the best of resisters always faces the possibility of the chips being down because he knows that the potential for combating evil is always present if he and others can only disengage themselves enough from the system to gain perspective while involving themselves enough to be effective.

CHAPTER 16

Avoiding
Pathologies of Defense

Craig Comstock

In many aspects of life we recognize
that harm may come to us as much by the defenses we employ as
by the dangers we seek to avert. In medicine, for example, some
diseases are iatrogenic, caused by efforts at treatment; and according to research on diseases of adaptation, the body may exhaust
itself through excessive response to an irritation.[1]* In either case
the process may be described as a pathology of defense, a situation
in which the mode of protection generated by a system (or put
into it) either corrupts the system from within or stimulates further dangers from outside. The latter effect occurs in an arms

* Notes for this chapter start on p. 356.

race: the weapons procured by one side appear to the other as a threat, stimulating a cycle of deadly extravagance.

Pathologies of defense occur in many areas. Psychologists tell us that certain patterns of adaptation which may defend the personality in a given stage or situation also impair its flexibility or further development, sometimes so severely that when new challenges occur the system breaks down. In the ecosystem man is now learning that defenses such as insecticides may cause more trouble than they prevent. In social life, pathologies of defense occur on all sides. A man keeps a gun in the house for use against burglars and ends by shooting his wife during a quarrel. A motorcycle club is invited to police a rock festival and reportedly kills one of the audience, beating others. A ruler is deposed by his own army. In this sense, a pathology of defense occurs whenever an agent of violence turns against a person whom he was engaged to protect.

Most of our defense is established by the government and paid for out of public funds, in the form of police and military organizations. Harold Lasswell calls these public forces the specialists in coercion, and since World War II he has said they would become the dominant world elite.[2] During the 1960s, however, it occurred to many Americans that at least one campaign of violence being conducted in our name was dubious in its premises and brutal in its methods, that the military was wasting a huge share of the federal budget on weapons we did not need, and that the "balance of terror" between the United States and the Soviet Union was even more delicate than originally feared. In April, 1960, only 18 per cent of a national sample of adults said that defense spending ought to be reduced; in September 1970 that percentage was up to 49 (and among those twenty-one to twenty-nine years old, as among all those with "college background," it was up to 60 per cent).[3] At least part of this emerging majority senses, we may assume, that a pathology of defense has occurred.

In the case of the war in Vietnam, this country has been noticeably weakened, not only by its casualties or by the money spent there or by the inflation, but more seriously by the social effects, by the disgust and the loss of confidence it caused. I do not mention the suffering of Vietnamese people here because the concept of a pathology of defense is reflexive: it refers only to harm suffered by the people in whose name the violence is done. What the concept thus gains in irony it loses in ethical scope. As a self-regarding concept it applies to "outsiders" only insofar as they threaten us in response to our own violence. Thus it offers no direct protection to the weak or peaceful, nor could it help to restrain our defenders except when violence or its preparation would arguably corrupt our own system or stimulate a greater threat from outside.

A flagrant example of the latter situation is the strategic arms competition between the Big Two, a competition so costly and perilous as to lead to negotiations about halting such further developments as the ABM and certain other devices which threaten the mutuality of deterrence. Anxiety generated by our reliance on this system appears in many forms; in young people it has been analyzed most incisively by Kenneth Keniston, who suggests that "the issue of violence is to this generation what the issue of sex was to the Victorian world." [4]

In the 1960s, however, suspicion about pathologies of defense extended beyond the military (whether in its role as deterrent of nuclear attack or as scourge of guerillas) to the police, especially to those who work in ghetto areas or who come into contact with students. Distrust among white students was probably first aroused during the civil rights movement, when southern law enforcement officials either ignored gross violence directed at the "outside agitators" or else took part in it themselves. Few will forget the picture of a sheriff laughing with scorn as he read the indictment accusing him, in effect, of murder.[5] In the course of demonstrations and later in the growth of a widespread counter-culture, many young people became aware of a violence which had long been used against blacks but for which a middle-class upbringing had not prepared them.

To the extent that police humiliate the people they are supposed to serve and to the extent that they meanwhile fail to provide proper services to ghetto residents, we are confronted by another pathology of defense. When leaders regard neglect of ghetto problems as benign and rely instead on preventive detention, midnight murders of black leaders, and no-knock provisions, they support a process of repression, sanctioned perhaps by periodic outbreaks, a process that can lead only to more of the same. In 1968 Congress passed almost unanimously the scandalous Crime Control and Safe Streets Act, a folly described with wit and passion by Richard Harris.[6] Now that rhetoric about cooperation with the Soviet Union is so useful, a politician who began his career by attacking communism and its domestic agents sustains his political ascendency by shifting attention to home-grown enemies. A strategy of domestic repression may benefit the politicians who exploit it, but the social benefits are illusory. Earlier, a pathology of defense was defined, in part, as a mode of protection which corrupts a system from within. No large-scale system of repression can avoid negating our higher ideals as a people.

So far we have touched on three pathologies of defense that many people are coming to recognize as such: the mutual deterrence system which we sustain together with the Soviet Union, the self-righteous intervention in a civil war on behalf of a corrupt regime which only our power keeps in office, and an emerging policy of domestic repression. All these policies involve violence done or threatened in our name. All of them provoke anxiety, which, in turn, serves to sustain the pathological system. The first of these policies may lead to our sudden ruin; the second kind of policy, to a further waste of money and lives plus a deepening gap in our political culture; and the third, to further anxiety about counter-cultures of dissent and resistance, along with the police apparatus which thrives on such a culture and the attendant loss of liberties. Most serious perhaps, to the degree that we rely on these kinds of violence done in our name, we will be unable to move toward policies of cooperation (where possible), disengagement (where necessary), or political development toward a more humane society.

Why do so few people ever strenuously question any of the violence done or threatened in their name? On one level we all know that the medicine may be worse than the disease, but many of us seem reluctant to apply this skepticism about the safety or efficacy of defenses to the public realm. If the danger from any one of the pathologies of defense is even half as great as the

sketches above suggest, we ought to know why so many of us
either fail to notice these reflexive dangers or, when they become
obvious, find them so hard to cope with. Even some rough specu-
lations may help us understand why the defenders and the broader
groups which sanction their policies have such power over us.
This understanding, in turn, may suggest some ways of restricting
the defenders more nearly to their proper role as last resorts when
all other approaches to threatening situations have failed at least
momentarily.

In a classic paper on Nazi Germany,[7] E. C. Hughes noted
that people generally assume that the preservation or success of
a society depends on a certain amount of dirty work, acts which
most "good people" prefer not to think about too closely, including internal repression. Society is organized so that they are not
forced to do so. The dirty work, such as repressing people declared
to be enemies of the state, is done by relatively small corps of men
who are not shocked by killing or brutality and may even enjoy it.
What country can claim to be without such men? If they are organized and sanctioned by the state and if most people regard the
work as necessary or at least excusable (insofar as they think about
it at all), then who is to stop the dirty work? Since the brutality is
described to the public only in attractive metaphors or in bureaucratic euphemisms, the good people are allowed both to keep their
consciences clean and to participate vicariously in the scapegoating. They see any "excesses" as necessary responses forced on a
reluctant staff by the perfidy of the victims.

The reflex of blaming nearly all pathologies of defense on
people we feel threaten us probably offers errant defenders more
protection than any other single response by the public. All but
the most flagrant pathologies of defense thereby increase our
hatred of an enemy or troublemaker so evil as to drive us to such
measures. The reaction of people who prefer not to examine their
own pathologies of defense is, then, we didn't do it and besides
they made us.

Along with insulation from brutality and the device of
blaming the other side for everything, yet another mechanism that
prevents people from recognizing pathologies of defense is a deep
fear, probably going back to infancy, that if we hate the person

on whom we are dependent, that hate will lash back and harm us or leave us defenseless. With regard to the defenders, many of us appear to react like the small boy who feels love for, but also strong resentment toward, his father. In order to relieve this tension, he may develop a set of antithetical images: one of an ideal whom he may love without reserve, and the other composed of all the perceptions of his father which he has come to hate. Hatred of the "bad" father arouses guilt, which is repressed and thus helps to endow the image with "all the merciless hatred and destructive fury which the child feels but dares not fully recognize in himself." [8] When the child grows up he may seek to persecute men who seem to fit this image, but seldom does he choose a person who is actually as powerful or monstrous as the image suggests; instead he probably finds a bad father who can be made to appear terrifying but who is actually without much protection. Jews have often been put in this latter role.

If we assume that the image of the bad father is projected onto a real person, might not the image of the good father also be projected onto a real person or persons—for example, onto the defenders (as I have called them), those who claim to protect us against aggressors or at least to punish them. If this were the case, it might help account for the obdurate reluctance of many people to admit that they may be harmed by the defense they employ and for the link between faith in the defenders and strong projections of evil. The general process of splitting moral complexity into antithetical sets of characteristics and then projecting these sets suggests that the main danger in vituperative denunciation of the enemy may spring from a complementary trust in the defenders, a trust that neglects the dangers posed by an unlimited warrant in the hands of the police or military.

Because of this psychic splitting, the defenders are free to act out our fantasies of exclusion and punishment. When during the Detroit riot police allegedly shot some young black men found in a motel suite with white girls, an incident painstakingly reported by John Hersey, did they perhaps feel they were acting not only on their own behalf but as representatives of a larger sanctioning group? In the case of police, sanction may derive from the occupational attitudes of fellow officers or from politicians representing constituencies bent on punishment. In the Chicago "police riot" of summer 1968 officers eager to swing clubs may have ignored superiors who told them to stop, as reported in some instances, but even the most brutal were doing no more than the mayor had seemed to suggest.[9] A majority of the public approved; and although a majority presumably do not approve of murder by police officers, many appear satisfied by the phrase "justifiable homicide."

The defenders often encourage this process. Part of their job is to be suspicious of the other side, and, in having to prepare for the worst, they institutionalize a degree of paranoia. In the United States and in many other nations, the defenders are regarded as civil servants who specialize in violence or coercion but who, as political neuters, are restrained by law or by civilian leaders. In this sense, the defenders stay out of politics. In a more profound sense, however, their professional advice radically skews the political scene. This is so not alone because their regular prophecies of trouble can be self-fulfilling but because their preparation to fight or coerce the other side, and the psychic aspects of that preparation, prevent them from considering alternate futures. Why do the police not call for the social measures that would eventually reduce the hatred with which they are regarded in some places? Why does the military not support, even welcome, arms control measures that may reduce the risk of their dying (of our all being hurt) by a foolish war? These questions suggest the degree to which the defenders, in spite of being considered politically neutral, behave as an interest group.

Since the defenders are authorized to use violence, they need to be watched, checked, and corrected, more than any other group in our society; but, for the reasons given above and for others, we have regarded them with too little skepticism or vigilance. Indeed, they often seem protected by a hermetic system of approval. Excessive or misdirected violence elicits quick support from large sanctioning groups who feel that what is supposed to defend us can not hurt us. Meanwhile, the views of the defenders are shaped by what John Kenneth Galbraith calls "bureaucratic truth," [10] and our view of what they do is blocked by propaganda, secrecy, and lies. If, as in Vietnam, they blunder or if the situation makes their task impossible, blame falls not on the defenders, much less on the politicians who sent them, but rather on those who failed to unleash the military, who predicted stalemate, who asked what was the point of it, who lacked the will to win.

By their ideology of force, their need for funds, and their stimulation of counter-measures by the other side, the defenders distract us from constructive possibilities. What is worse, they often oppose methods other than their own for dealing with people who seem to threaten us; and when anxiety is high they make it contradictory to pursue policies complementary to their own. In order to meet a violent threat, no society can depend wholly on peaceful initiatives or social reform. Apart from revolutionaries, the argument is thus between those who would rely largely on violence done in our name and those who recognize the value of what Arthur Wascow calls "creative disorder" as a means for social reform.[11]

The defenders and the social reformers compete for scarce resources. The military (if not the police) claim a strikingly large share of our national product, a fact in which representatives of the poor are taking a keen interest. Even the Commission on the Causes and Prevention of Violence, viewing poverty from the outside, declared in its final report that we ought to be as concerned with the antisocial behavior of the deprived as with "any probable combination of external threats."[12] Although the commission found that further police controls were necessary, it warned that "the pyramiding of control measures could turn us into a repressive society, where the peace is kept primarily through official coercion rather than through willing obedience to law." A society dependent on this kind of defense, said the commission (borrowing a phrase from Karl Marx), "nurtures within itself the seeds of its own violent destruction." In other words, this pattern of internal defense is pathological. While the commission did not deal with foreign policy, it did suggest that at the end of the Vietnam war we cut military spending sharply and devote the saving, plus the expected rise in Federal revenues, to social improvements. In order to justify this expenditure, however, the commission relied less on a vision of a decent society than on the threats inherent in the one we now have: "While serious external dangers remain, the graver threats today are internal." This structure of thought leads, at best, to "wars" on poverty and, in general, to a policy based on double negatives, on erecting a defense against every particular threat in place of the positive work of constructing alternative patterns of life.[18]

What can we expect from a society which conducts so much of its public discourse in terms of defense? In passing the National Defense Education Act, a coupling of words which hardly seems odd anymore, Congress implied that even scholastic pursuits merit funds mainly because they help us meet a threat, in this case external. The commission on violence likewise seemed to argue not that voting more money for domestic purposes would sustain social improvements of which we might all be proud, but rather that the funds would buy off trouble. (In reply to this argument, people naturally ask why we should reward those who threaten us.) In foreign relations we may dispense some aid or corrupt whatever leaders we can, but primarily we depend on the capability to threaten harm. In domestic terms, this approach leads to an over-reliance on police control. In terms of direct economic costs, police are cheaper than reform; and whereas the pay-off of reform seems distant and uncertain, the police, like the military, can go to work at once. Leaders can avoid dealing with, much less rewarding, the troublemakers, criminals, or aggressors who upset ordinary patterns of business and make such awkward demands. Instead, the administration and its supporters can bask in their self-righteousness and share a sense of danger; and as the danger grows, so does their insensitivity to pathologies of defense.

In a typical pathology of defense, the danger to the system is felt to be clear and immediate (or else doubly feared for its concealment), and the costs are falsely thought to be only economic; the economic costs are widely shared, and the necessity for them is blamed on the other side. The opposite is true of social reform. Its costs are immediate while the benefits seem distant and dubious; and even worse the benefits seem restricted to those who are feared but the cost is paid by others. Reformers can win support by emphasizing the hidden costs to the whole society of a failure to act, such as a probable rise in crime or rebellious acts. As this chapter argues, they can also show how a society can be corrupted by its own defenses, especially when defenses are used as a substitute for constructive ventures; and they can offer a vision of how society could be changed so that everyone would be better off.

In its narrow sense, the concept of a pathology of defense ignores the fate of opponents or victims outside the system, except insofar as action against them may stimulate dangers to those on the inside or lead to an internal transformation of the system so that its civil values are eroded. If the concept applies only to those on the inside of a system, the question of who is included becomes central. Who are the *we* that we are defending? If our defenders hurt someone, must he not have been an enemy and, in that case, no part of us or else a traitor? In terms of this reasoning, no pathology of defense occurs unless the observer himself is hurt by the defenders (and not even then if the observer has deeply internalized the values of the defenders).

To adopt the occupational values of the military or the police, however, is to shrink the concept of a pathology of defense so far that it means simply a defeat or weakening of the defenders. Logically, a garrison state can hardly be corrupted by military values or a police state by repression. In a civil society, however, questions arise about who is to be defended and who defined as a danger, stigmatized, or set apart. Since every society has built up a tradition of how to sort its members among these categories, we may assume that a particular society notices a pathology of defense only when it is led to define an unusual number of its members as outsiders. Assuming, however, that exclusion of others proceeds in part from repression of aspects of the self, as research on the authoritarian personality has shown,[14] we may argue that any social exclusion creates a presumption that a pathology of defense has begun. Our best alternative to these pathologies is what Erik Erikson calls "the anticipatory development of more inclusive identities."[15] As in the case of Gandhi or those who have learned from him, such identities provide not an escape from necessary conflict but a means for conducting conflict within a larger identification which meanwhile emerges.

In the next chapter Nevitt Sanford describes the kind of personality development that would help people to recognize and avoid what I have called pathologies of defense. This concept itself, as a category of social analysis, may help us to become more aware of self-damaging modes of protection, both in the personality and in political life. Without a widespread sense of how pathologies of defense can harm us, legislators find it hard to vote down funds or powers demanded for "security," no matter how desperately the funds are needed elsewhere, no matter how dangerous the powers might become. Basic to our Constitution is a suspicion of unchecked power, yet the defenders argue that in their hands power harms only the "enemy" or the "criminal," categories that become ever more widely or casually defined. Most of the Congressmen detailed to watch over the Pentagon seem more hawkish than the generals who appear before them. When the defenders control 10 per cent of our total resources, one may be excused for wondering who is controlling whom.[16] Since expert knowledge is essential to intelligent control, I would suggest that we need a better organized source of independent, expert evaluation of the "security" proposals made to Congress by interested parties such as the Pentagon and its affiliates. During the fight against the ABM, we saw the skeleton of such a body.

Some critics have referred to the defenders as nothing more than necessary evils. That phrase admits of several meanings, but insofar as coercion is required, ought the "good people" to call their agents evil? Necessity, however, must be judged by men skeptical of the defenders and imaginative about other approaches based on hope rather than fear. The structure of opportunities for our leaders is now such that reliance on the defenders may seem to offer more reward than do constructive policies; a President can shake the world in foreign affairs but be humbled in trying to rearrange a welfare program. It is often said that until we stop spending so much on defense, social reform must wait; but we ought to invert the proposition and recognize that until we find plausible methods for substantial reform, our anxiety about disorder will probably support a continuation of present defensive pathologies.

Just as we need the anticipatory development of more inclusive identities, so we need lobbies on behalf of future social configurations. Many groups other than "the poor" would benefit from a decent society which was more imaginative in its methods than we have been, but so far these groups have hardly been recognized, much less organized on behalf of their futures. Although popular attention is focused on technological development, the central challenge of this decade is whether we can turn our ingenuity to social inventions.[17] David Riesman long ago observed the need for "utopian" thought on what sort of a society we would like to have; at present nearly all of what passes for thought about the future is either apocalyptic (nothing will help) or projective (more of everything). Until we recover a sense of the future and imagine what we want, we will be left to defend what we have, even when we dislike it; and as a consequence of this defensiveness we will continue to overlook or excuse the violence done in our name.

CHAPTER 17

Going Beyond Prevention

Nevitt Sanford

Our analysis has shown that social destructiveness is highly complex, involving the interaction of deep-seated tendencies in the personality with processes in the immediate situation, in the face-to-face group or organization, and in the larger society and culture. The picture that has been drawn is grim, and it would not be surprising if a mood of pessimism has settled over many of our readers. Yet, as we said at the beginning, our major object has been to learn how acts of social destructiveness can be prevented. We would be less than human if we did not continue our efforts to understand and to counteract the evils that have been described.

Prevent, however, is not an adequate word for what we want to do or for what is needed. It is not enough to prevent dehumanization and destructiveness; a more worthy goal, and one just as obtainable, is to humanize and to develop constructive relationships among people. This is not merely toying with words or reversing emphasis in order to attain an optimistic view. It is in the nature of planned action affecting people, whether singly or collectively, that in order to do more good than harm, it must be guided by positive values because both individuals and social systems are organized complexities, not bundles of isolatable problems. A change in any element of a system, be it a virtue or a fault, a strength or a weakness, brings desirable or undesirable changes in other areas; and actions directed to one feature of the totality are likely to affect others in various ways, some good and some not so good. For example, a mother's attempts to prevent her young son's displays of aggressiveness can impair his sense of masculine identity; the efforts of a school to promote competence in a particular child can reduce his creativity and spontaneity and block his social development; the efforts of a university to prevent militant activism by some of its students may easily promote activism in most of its students or else suppress the spirit of inquiry throughout the institution; what a nation does to prevent its people from thinking the wrong thoughts is likely to impair all their thinking. Actions must be based on an understanding of the whole, and actions concerned with specific features must be consistent with a conception of the well-being of the whole. The best overall strategy is to work with features that have determining relationships with most other features.

These general considerations will be clarified and exemplified as we now proceed to discuss, in turn, the promotion of greater humanity in individuals and improvements in the functioning of social systems. Along with our discussion in Parts One and Three of social and cultural processes in which individuals are caught up, we show in Part Two how personality processes have various roles in the determination of social destructiveness, in particular how differences in personality explain differences in response to the same situation. At the same time, we have seen that the relations between personality and culture are such that it is impossible to tell which comes first. Just as the idea of the individual's incorporating social norms is necessary to an explanation of personality development, so is the formulation of ways in which individuals manage their impulses and inner conflicts necessary to an understanding of how culture is generated and sustained. In this sense, activities to change personality and activities to change culture are related.

Changing personality and culture are, to be sure, relatively long-term processes, but we do not have to wait until the next generation has been raised before humane and constructive personality dispositions can come to exist in our people. Personality-developing activities, affecting adults as well as young people in large numbers, can be undertaken now through well directed actions to improve the institutions (the family and the school) primarily responsible for shaping personality in children. The main thing is to have a clear conception of what we want and an adequate theory of personality development.

This brings us back to the strategy of devoting our energies to promoting psychological well-being in general rather than focusing on particular undesirable tendencies, even so general and deep-seated a tendency as destructiveness. This shift in emphasis is in keeping with important trends in contemporary thought about mental illness and health. Since the mid-fifties Marie Jahoda and others have encouraged a new interest in positive mental health—in defining it and in experimenting with ways to promote it.[1]* Meanwhile the concept of mental disease itself has been called into question. We need not go all the way with Thomas Szasz and with Ernest Becker in their attacks on psychiatry in order to agree with these writers that what is called mental disease may in fact sometimes be ethical conflict and sometimes mere deviance from social norms and that for conceptualizing and attempting to cope with these and other psychological troubles medical models of disease are inappropriate and probably harmful.[2]

Particularly relevant to the argument being advanced here is Karl Menninger's notion that mental illness is all of one piece.[3] He points out that the history of psychiatry could be written as a story of how a long list of categories of mental illness was built up and then gradually reduced to three or four and finally, in his

* Notes for this chapter start on p. 357.

own work, to just one, mental illness. Menninger conceives of a single process underlying diverse manifestations of mental illness and mental health and, hence, of a single dimension extending from serious disruption of "the vital balance" to a condition of being "weller than well." If specific kinds of illness do not exist there is obviously no point in assuming that a diagnosis must be made before people with psychological difficulties can be treated, no point in supposing that illnesses can be prevented by discovering and removing their specific causes. Actions affecting people in the role of patient as well as actions directed to people who may later have psychological difficulties must be guided by conceptions of what, in general, favors individual well-being.

I do not suggest that we define mental illness out of existence or that we go along with Menninger in reducing the number of kinds of mental illness to one; I do urge, however, that we accept fully the organismic view of the person that is fundamental to Menninger's conception of "the vital balance." If we do this last, it will become clear that any planned action affecting a person's welfare must take into account his complexity and potentialities for further development and that the goal of full development should take precedence over goals of preventing particular ills or failings.

To see what this view means in practice let us consider some of those personality trends that have important roles in collective destructiveness. Talcott Parsons has suggested that a group leader's compulsive need to display his masculinity can be crucial in determining the direction of group activity; Stanley Milgram has shown that the tendency to obey without question—which in some cases may have roots deep within the personality—may allow individuals to commit any sort of evil act that authorities are believed to favor; [4] and John Hersey assembled much evidence to show that some of the men who took the lead in the Algiers Motel incident had extraordinary needs to punish sexual deviance.[5] Should we then seek to work out programs for overcoming or preventing supermasculinity, overobedience, and punitiveness toward deviants? If we do we are likely to find ourselves doing much the same things in all three cases, for these personality dispositions tend to go together, to be integral features of the authoritarian personality

syndrome. We would be better advised, then, to set about preventing authoritarianism in personality. This course has much to rec-
ommend it, but it would not avoid the difficulties that have been
mentioned. It would almost inevitably lead us to diagnose authoritarian trends, to identify individuals in whom this trend was
marked, and to label these people as authoritarian personalities.
In clinical work these practices may have a place, and they can
certainly be controlled, but in the everyday business of child training, education, and public enlightenment they may easily become
self-defeating if not harmful. It would be better to put the emphasis on promoting the opposites of authoritarian trends: secure
sexual identity, independence of thought and action, and acceptance of diversity in people. Better still, we should devote ourselves
to developing the whole personalities in which authoritarian
trends and their opposites have places.

In order to promote full development we need, as Robert
N. Bellah argues in Chapter Twelve, "a conception of man which
allows us to accept our darker side, to use creatively our id impulses, our dependency needs, and our rebelliousness rather than
projecting them on others and then murderously repressing them."
Broadly inclusive humanism not only counters directly the evil
we have been discussing but is a vision of fulfilled human potential.

Other, not dissimilar, visions have been offered by such
psychologists as Erik Erikson, R. W. White, Abraham Maslow,
Frank Barron, Marie Jahoda, and Gordon Allport.[6] I base my
thinking about human potential and how it may be developed
mainly on a study of education beyond high school, but I agree
with what others have written about earlier development and also
about growth outside of formal institutions of learning. I would
say that a high level of development in personality is characterized
most essentially by complexity and by wholeness. In general terms
I mean that a large number of different parts or features have different and specialized functions and also that communication
among these parts is great enough so that, without losing their
essential identity, they become organized into wholes in order to
serve the larger purposes of the person. The highly developed

person enjoys a rich and varied impulse life. His feelings and emotions are differentiated and civilized; and his conscience is enlightened and individualized. It operates in accord with his best thought and judgment. The processes by which he judges events and manages actions are strong and flexible, being adaptively responsive to the multitudinous aspects of the environment and at the same time in close enough touch with the deeper sources of emotion and will so that there is freedom of imagination. This highly developed structure underlies the individual's sense of direction, his freedom of thought and action, and his capacity to fulfill commitments to others and to himself. But the structure is not fixed once and for all. The highly developed individal is always open to new experience and capable of further learning; his stability is fundamental in the sense that he can go on developing while remaining essentially himself.

Particular value orientations of this kind are easy to criticize, for they are frequently bound by culture, social class, or historical era. The answer to this criticism is not ethical neutrality but a fresh attempt to think well about values. The search for worthy values must go on, and if social scientists are to assist in designing plans for the upbringing and education of children, they must be guided by open-ended conceptions of what people can become. Even while committing themselves tentatively to particular systems of value, they can continue their efforts to improve thinking about values by showing how values are arrived at and what the consequences of holding particular values are.

A reasonable course for the scientist or educator who wishes to avoid dogmatism is to start with some attribute of the person that no one denies is a value and to set about promoting it without immediately raising questions about its place in a hierarchy of values. He would be on safe ground today if he began with competence, for example. If he accepted the view that virtues, like illness and weakness, are not isolated in the person, he would soon discover that actions to promote competence had consequences for other qualities. Although competence is often attained at the expense of other desirable qualities, is this sacrifice necessary? Intellectual and emotional development can be regarded as aspects of the same process; and it ought not to be beyond our competence as educators to arrange for various aspects of the person to develop in concert.

How people develop is less a subject for controversy than what they may become. Psychologists generally agree that people develop when they are confronted with challenges that require new adaptive responses and are freed from the necessity of maintaining unconscious defensive devices. However, the challenge must be within the limits of the individual's adaptive capacities; too much strain induces a falling back upon primitive, antidevelopmental responses. Except in cases of severe disturbance in childhood, however, we can help to make the unconscious conscious or increase self-awareness without resorting to special psychotherapeutic action. Educational procedure can help make people aware of their impulses and defenses, and these procedures are the more effective the more the personality as a whole has been expanded through appropriate challenges. These general principles hold for adults as well as for children and adolescents. People can develop at any age if the right conditions are introduced.

The authors of *The Authoritarian Personality* were not backward about making proposals for child training that could help to prevent the development of authoritarian personality trends. "All that is really essential," they wrote, "is that children be genuinely loved and treated as individual humans." [7] They assumed that lack of love is a fundamental cause of aggression and that authoritarian discipline is a formidable barrier to ego development. They argued that discipline that is strict and rigid and, from the child's point of view, unjust or unreasonable may be submitted to, but it is not fully accepted—the child does not eventually apply it himself in the absence of external authority. Where the child is not allowed to question anything, to participate in decisions affecting him, or to feel that his own will counts for something, the stunting of the ego is an inevitable consequence.

These perspectives on upbringing have long been shared by most professional people who in various formal and informal ways are involved in the education of parents. Furthermore, a vast American literature on child development, much of it addressed directly to parents, goes far beyond cautions about authoritarianism in setting forth general conditions for healthy development. It is possible to summarize much of this literature by saying that children need to be brought up in an atmosphere of trust, love, justice, freedom, and truth. Trust in someone is absolutely necessary if the child is to learn the most elementary facts about the social world and to establish those stable relationships upon which basic inner stability depends. The child must be loved if he is to develop the self-esteem and sense of identity that enable him to love others in a genuine way. Justice is the cornerstone of faith in the human community; its denial to a child is a major stimulus for aggression and unbridled self-seeking. If a child or young person does not feel that he is justly treated he does not care about freedom; and he must have freedom, in amounts suited to his stage of development, if he is to experience making choices. This experience is requisite to his becoming an autonomous person. Truth is the overriding value. The child must learn to appreciate it and live according to it if he is to gain any understanding of and therefore some control over himself and if he is to work with others in gaining control over his environment. He can be taught only by example.

How these values can guide the day-to-day behavior of parents toward their children has been the subject of innumerable books, pamphlets, articles, and newspaper columns. The great trouble is that everything that can be specifically recommended has the aspect of being more easily said than done. Parents have problems of their own which stand in the way of giving their children what they need. Many parents are highly authoritarian and bring to their relations with their children the same moralistically punitive attitudes that they express toward out-groups and toward their own impulses. And these attitudes are constantly reinforced by the culture in which they live. Many parents are so taken up with getting love or justice or freedom for themselves that they have neither the inclination nor the ability to give these things to their children; others are capable of love and know what they should do but are prevented by the pressures of everyday life in our society—to get money, status, respectability—from taking effective action.

The authors of *The Authoritarian Personality,* aware of

situation of parents in our society, expressed the view that the authoritarian personality syndrome is a product of the total organization of society and is to be changed only as that society is changed. This was not a counsel of despair, however. These authors saw that ascribing all our ills to the system was foolish and that changing society all at once was impossible; any effort at social change has to begin somewhere, and large-scale change is a matter of attaining a multiplicity of subgoals. "Any act, however limited in time and place, that serves to counter or diminish destructiveness can be regarded as a microcosm, as it were, of a total effective program." [8]

One way to begin an effort at social and cultural change, to build a microcosm of a larger effective program, is to help parents to do a better job with their children. As suggested above, such an effort need not be limited to producing a better future generation; it would, properly carried out, have beneficial effects for the parents and at the same time would be likely to improve those who carried it out.

Let us consider an example. Community colleges that are fully to serve people of the inner city must have facilities on the campus for taking care of the children of mothers who need and want to attend those colleges. Some of these mothers and other students could work in these centers, and this work could be integrated with formal and informal instruction in child development and child care. Instructors would assume, and it would soon be taken for granted by all concerned, that mothers or other students who wanted to understand and do what was needed for the children would first have to understand themselves and change some of their value orientations. This understanding and change would be furthered by the fact that they had community support. And the mere presence of children on campus would help to make the whole college more of a human community. All hands would be reminded of what they were and what they might become. The mere fact of being in college would be a boost to the self-esteem of the mothers and an important step toward their liberation from men; and this would be for the latter a crucial step toward their liberation from male chauvinism and authoritarianism.

Some say that for these changes to occur our culture would

need to have changed already, but we have to start somewhere, and it seems more reasonable and more hopeful to set about instituting a child care center at a community college than to set about changing our culture. If, however, what was done at this college became a model for a hundred other colleges, there probably would be some impact on culture; and even if it did not become a model, it would still be worth doing because of its intrinsic values.

Programs such as this should aim at personality development in general and be guided by a theory of development such as that suggested above. However, further conceptual clarification is needed. For example, our culture abounds with confusion and disagreement about the nature of man and of human aggression and about the role of authority in personality development. Psychologists and social scientists have not done all that they might to clear up these difficult issues.

Concerning the first issue, it appears that these scientists have added to the confusion. The idea of the whole personality, of personality as an internally coherent system, is fundamental to our whole conception of destructiveness and of dehumanization, and obversely we need such a concept in order to guide programs for the development of personality. Yet, we must face the fact that this idea—the concept of personality itself—is sadly neglected in scientific work. Psychologists, in their research and theoretical work, tend to focus on finer and finer analyses of part functions with a minimum of attention to the personality contexts in which these functions occur and become meaningful; in the work of most sociologists the person tends to get lost in an aggregate of social roles, social group memberships, and interpersonal relationships. This conceptual failing parallels the fact that institutions designed to promote health, education, and welfare rarely treat people as individuals but focus on particular symptoms, functions, or problems with a minimum of concern about connecting what is done by one specialist with what is done by another. Both science and practice have probably been influenced by the same processes in society, chiefly the technological pressure toward increasing specialization in productive work. But, since practice is ordinarily based in some kind of theory, scientists have to accept the larger share of the blame for not resisting the pressure. Blame-worthy or not, we now have to reconstruct the concept of the person.

The concept of the person is also necessary in order to see aggression in proper perspective and to find the best way to man-age aggression in children. The element of aggression in social destructiveness is extremely remote from any instinctual aggres-sion or the aggressive propensity that a child brings into the world; aggression by an adult is always a result of much shaping through experience and always interacts with other learned ten-dencies such as obedience, conformity, striving for sexual identity, and defining victims as less than human.

The anger of the frustrated young child, largely an expres-sion of an inborn potential, is not in itself something for the parent to worry about. We do not want children to be incapable of anger or fear to express any; we want them to learn to be angry about the right things (human exploitation, for example) and to express their anger in ways that help to counter destructiveness. The passionately nonviolent mother fails her child when she re-sponds with horror to any display of anger by him and sets herself the task of totally suppressing his aggression. She forces the child to direct his aggression against himself and thus to bear guilt that properly belongs to her.

The child's natural potential for aggression does not be-come a source of destructiveness toward himself or others until aggressive impulses having specific objects and modes have been built up through experience. The crucially important experiences are losses or denials of love, weakness and humiliation, unjust punishment, threats of bodily harm—experiences which the child interprets as having catastrophic implications. Love and gentleness and firmness are the counters to such experiences, but such are the exigencies of childhood that the generation of some aggressive impulses is virtually unavoidable. The child still needs the par-ents' help in learning to control these impulses, to express them in relatively nondestructive ways.

However we may conceive of the contributions of nature and of experience to the generation of the child's aggression, there is no store of aggression which has to be drained off in one way or another. Even in children noted for their meanness, who seem ready to be aggressive on slight provocation, this does not seem to be the right formulation. Aggression, far from being drained off, is likely to become its own stimulus, for aggressive behavior leads to feelings of guilt, which may be suppressed by more aggression. Aggressive behavior has many meanings. Various (often quite specific) internal readinesses to be aggressive are triggered by external events which are not so much obviously frustrating in themselves as evocative of long-standing susceptibilities to humiliation or to feelings of powerlessness or of being catastrophically threatened. An observer can hardly hope to find the meaning in every case—nor can the subject himself. The best strategy for coping with this state of affairs on a long-term basis is to build self-confidence, competence, adequate sexual identity, and self-awareness.

A major stimulus for the generation of aggressive impulses in children is unjust punishment at the hands of repressive authority. Yet, children brought up by stern or carelessly punitive parents rarely become courageous rebels; instead, they are likely to become authoritarian. For the young child such parents are seen as dangerous, and he learns quickly enough to suppress his aggression against them, even to tell himself that they are not bad but good, and to redirect his aggression to people who do what he would like to do but cannot. Should parents then never punish or forcibly restrain their children? If not, how are they to distinguish between the use of force that is wise or just or at least necessary and that which leads to authoritarianism? Must they be either sternly punitive or permissive?

Here it is necessary to distinguish among styles of authority and to consider parental control in relation to the child's stage of development. Parents by law and custom are in a position of authority; they are vested with the right to command obedience, respect, and confidence. How they go about carrying out the responsibilities of this position varies widely from one family to another. Many parents, unfortunately, are not well qualified for the position they have seized or had thrust upon them. Out of indifference or neglect or ignorance, they offer the child too little authority or regime; this behavior is experienced by the child as a lack of love and as untrustworthiness in the world at large, and hence it is a major source not of authoritarianism but of the most serious kinds of psychological disturbance. Other parents practice an authoritarian style of discipline; unsure of themselves, afraid of their own impulses, overeager to have their children conform to conventional standards, they make many rules, try desperately to stick to them, overreact to the child's failures to conform. In general, they conduct themselves as parents more in accord with their own unrecognized psychological needs than in accord with the needs of the child. This behavior is very different from the flexible use of authority to supply guidance and support as needed.

Young children need authority, but as they grow older this need diminishes gradually. Parents, it seems, have great difficulty in adapting themselves to the changing needs of the child. Strong believers in authority tend to favor authority in all times and places, regardless of the needs or the circumstances of the developing individual; strong believers in freedom, in respect for the child's individuality, tend also to develop a total ideology and to underestimate the young child's need for authority. It will help parents to find the right approach if we ask, once again, what, in a positive sense, we desire for our children and how do children in fact develop.

In a democratic society we value independence of judgment. We want people to grow up to become their own authorities. We recognize, however, that this is a difficult accomplishment, for everybody at some time experiences a need for some authority. Young children need it most and can tolerate it best, adolescents need a lot of authority but have very little tolerance for it, while the ideally developed person needs relatively little and can tolerate it well.

The young child needs authority because his own impulses lead him to imagine punishments of the most terrible kind, and he is very glad to have external controls that protect him, as it were, from his own impulses and fantasies. Parents who aspire to be liberal have to recognize that the child who too early is left to make his own decisions about when to go to bed becomes increasingly active and troublesome, thereby making an implicit plea for external control. Believers in strong authority have to recognize that as soon as a child says "I won't" in response to a parental command, he is asking for a little respect and that the time has come to allow him some role in decisions affecting him. The child who says "I won't" is developing normally, and parents who can adapt their use of authority to such strivings for autonomy find that the child gradually internalizes their prohibitions and sanctions. (This internalization does not occur if the parents make themselves hated and feared or if they never offer the child any standards at all.) As the child grows older, internalized prohibitions and sanctions—with their occasional reinforcements from outside—are gradually replaced by his own judgments. This latter process goes on for a long time however, longer than adolescence; and even college students sometimes need authority, reluctant though they are to recognize this need.

Whatever parents may do—to generate authoritarian personality trends or to set the child on the road to full development —can be profoundly altered, favorably or unfavorably, by the schools. This point seems generally understood, for in America almost everybody is willing, even eager, to offer his opinion about what the schools should do and how they should go about it. About the only thing that seems generally agreed is that schools should produce good democratic citizens—informed, useful, concerned, and loyal Americans. How this is to be done is a subject of much controversy, and official statements of policy are often contradicted in practice.

Such controversy seems inevitable, for educational institutions, which involve nearly a third of our people as students, teachers, and administrators, are fully expressive of our culture, with all its conflicts and contradictions. What the public schools do seems, on the whole, quite in line with what most people of the great middle class think they want them to do. Education is thought of as a scarce commodity, and access to it is according to a system of merit, usually based on degree of conformity with middle class values and ways. The process of education is defined as the acquisition of skills and knowledge and is to be accomplished in the most efficient way possible; achievement is the highest value, and it is measured in terms of performance within the system of prearranged goals and tasks.

Yet almost nobody is happy about the schools. Most unhappy, no doubt, are the students, who in 1969 brought about serious disruptions in two-thirds of city and suburban and one-half of rural schools in the country. These disruptions upset a large segment of the tax-paying public, who demand more of the repression which makes the students unhappy in the first place. Caught in the middle and severely frustrated are most teachers and administrators and all parents who have some understanding of what education for democracy means.

The trouble is surely connected with the fact that the public schools are guided mainly by the belief that their task is efficiently to impart knowledge and skills; children are to learn how to be democratic citizens, presumably by learning the facts about democracy. This belief and the procedures based on it have had some success in the past, not because the skills and knowledge imparted had much to do with democratic behavior—though they were useful in other ways—but because schools were more or less democratic institutions and were manned by men and women of humanity and goodwill, as they to a large extent still are. In times of rapid social change and great controversy, however, teaching the facts becomes the only defense against involvement in controversy, yet it is precisely such involvement—relevance—that students and many parents demand. Today, schools are confronted not only with conflicting ideological pressures from without and within but with enormously expanded enrollments and greatly increased diversity of students in the same school and the same class. The reaction has been greater organizational rigidity—more and more rules, which are more and more rigidly enforced.

Presumably what goes on in the schools is still called education for democracy. Yet the basic requirements of such education (trust, love, justice, freedom, and truth) are largely sacrificed to a desperate need for immediate order. Students are still acquiring some prescribed knowledge and skills, but much of their learning is, as always, by the example of their elders. Thus, it is not surprising to find, as we do, that students who do not rebel arrive at college with marked dispositions to authoritarianism.

For turning our culture in the direction of humane and democratic values nothing is more important than reform of our schools. Nobody knows how this reform is to be accomplished, but we can offer some suggestions. Although schools probably need some structure, they certainly do not have to be authoritarian. The authoritarian style, as we have seen, is not inherent in human nature but is a patterned reaction to circumstances. Likewise, an organization tightens up in response to external (or internal) threats, and as it does individual teachers and administrators exhibit more and more authoritarian behavior, thus affecting directly the young people in their charge. The classroom teacher need not be more authoritarian by disposition or more incompetent than the average in order to be provoked into totalitarian behavior by a class that seems about to get out of hand or by a principal who insists upon order at any cost. That principal may behave as he does because of his fear of the superintendent, who, in turn, is afraid of the school board. But if a school system as a whole is moved in an authoritarian direction in this way, it can also be turned in a democratic direction by strong leadership from the top—by the superintendent or the board.

At the same time, individuals, though heavily influenced by the system, are not totally determined by it. A principal with courage and resourcefulness can still do much to determine the climate of his school, and a teacher of high competence and determination can still have a class that is democratic in spirit. Indeed, largely because of such people in the schools, these institutions, in spite of everything, are turning out some of the best young people that this country has known.

In such people as these we also find expression of truly impressive counter-forces to authoritarianism. If the present is a time of great tension and rigidity in the schools, it is also a time of much soul-searching and innovation. Not only students but teachers, researchers, and administrators complain of impersonality, lack of relevance, and stultifying bureaucratic processes. For reform to occur students and their parents have to keep up the pressure, but a substantial proportion of educators are ready to respond, and from time to time the balance shifts in their favor. Thus it is that recent years have seen more than a few stunning innovations in public schools: experimental schools within schools, student participation in decision-making, use of the school as a laboratory for social and political studies, use of new kinds of reward systems for lower-class children, field studies and work-study programs for high school students, involvement of people from the community—students, parents, citizens—as tutors and assistants to teachers, use of social scientists for crisis intervention and for training everybody connected with schools in crisis intervention.

Most of these innovations have not required any great pouring of money into the schools. Other reforms, such as better teacher training, better teacher-student ratios, and better facilities, particularly for ghetto schools, are, however, very expensive, and needed funds are not likely to be forthcoming until an aroused citizenry becomes actively aware of the crisis in education and is inspired by a new vision of education for democracy. Such awareness and inspiration is possible. In Cleveland, for example, a group of citizens committed themselves to share the blame for education in the urban setting, organized themselves as Programs for Action by Citizens in Education, and worked effectively as a catalytic agent.[9] This group saw clearly that it is up to our citizens to say what education in our society should be and to provide a climate in which educators can do their work. But citizens and educators, however close their cooperation, can not do all that needs to be done. The problems and the prospects of the schools call for all the moral and intellectual resources our society can muster.

All these proposals will not meet the need, however, unless the effort is inspired by a rededication to the humanistic goals of education. There was a great upswing of public interest in education in the early 1960s and a great outlay of federal funds. Unfortunately they came when national spokesmen for education were fascinated by a so-called explosion in knowledge, and most educators, still defining their field as the learning of content, felt bound to use all possible means to speed the process. They opened the way for educational technologists who, with their systems analysis and computerized instruction, not only left a trail of confusion and disappointment but contributed to the fragmentation and impersonality from which the schools suffer.

Once again, however, counter-forces have been at work. Devotion to humanistic education has been persistent, though rarely dominant, in America, and this development has been strengthened by reaction to the new technological thrust. However, many educators who favor liberating, or developmental, education have despaired of making progress within the public school system. Hence, a large number of experimental schools, free schools, in-community schools, and after school schools have been springing up, started either by educators who have been turned off by the public school system or by educators with a special concern for young people who have been turned off by that system. These schools vary widely in philosophy and specific aims, but all have conceptions of what young people need for their development and some kind of theory, however implicit, about how these needs are to be met by a new program. W. Soskin and S. Korchin, for example, started with the aim of developing a therapeutic program for reducing "the incidence and prevalence of the use of hallucinogens and stimulants among high school and junior high school students." They are now operating an after school school which is the very model of a personality-developing institution.[10] Their program is designed to promote three personal outcomes: to improve one's sense of self-identity; to promote a strong sense of personal competence; to effect a commitment to one's personal goals, community, fellow men. They undertake to achieve these outcomes through group therapy, seminars, small group activities, retreats, work projects, individual consultations, parent-youth consultations, and sessions with groups of parents—all designed in accord with hypotheses concerning ways in which these procedures work to promote development.

Many of the new schools give particular attention to the needs of ethnic minorities and thus are part of a movement to oppose those forms of legitimized evil which destroy cultures. The black, brown, and red minority groups that seek to preserve, to reconstruct, and to build up their own cultures see that for reaching these goals the education of their children and youth is crucial. This education may well make use of the developmental approach being advocated here.

Young people of ethnic minorities (like all others), need cultural identity, a sense of having roots or a tradition of which they may hope to be worthy; but their case is special, for they live in a predominantly white society which tells them in one breath that they must conform with its superior culture but that they cannot fully do so because by its standards they are inferior and must remain so. How, in these circumstances, are they to acquire the self-respect necessary to the development of their personalities? People can attain a suitable degree of self-love only if they live during their most formative years in a culture that affirms them as they are, whatever their color, and that is relatively free of conflicts respecting basic values. This knowledge, one may believe, persuaded American Indians that they had to preserve their cultures, which they have done in the face of almost inconceivable odds; they have seen too many of their children corrupted by a dominant society that neither respected their differences nor permitted them full membership in it. This belief is consistent with the report of G. Ortega [11] that Spanish-speaking Americans who emerged as leaders in the Southwest lived during their formative years—before the advent of television—in Chicano enclaves, where they were relatively untroubled by the intrusions of Anglo culture, until they had enough security in their identity to cope with the surrounding dominant culture. In this light, the efforts of black people to build solidarity and pride around a cultural heritage of their own are in accord with the present emphasis on personality development.

Membership in a culture must, however, be seen in a developmental perspective. Cultural identity is by no means all that a person needs in order to participate fully in a society such as ours, and what is at one time necessary for self-definition can at another stage be restrictive. People whose personalities develop securely in one culture can learn without great difficulty to live in one or more other cultures; they can become citizens of the world. But first they must have a secure sense of identity in one culture. Everybody is familiar with the white, middle-class adolescent who goes abroad and compares everything unfavorably with what he has known at home. We sympathize with him in his need to be sure of himself and what he belongs to before he can appreciate differences or adapt himself to foreign ways. We ought to consider in this light the young black militant who is striving for a sense of identity with a newly conscious black community and to recognize that it is imperative for him to accomplish this phase of personality development before he can be fully open to an education that can prepare him for a creative role in a wider and more pluralistic community.

Community-run schools and ethnic studies programs within schools and colleges are thus highly significant as personality-developing institutions; they should be supported and then carefully evaluated. Although members of ethnic minorities are, as individuals, no less susceptible to ethnic prejudice than are other people, it seems unfair to label as racism in reverse or as separatism the efforts of black, brown, or red minorities to establish some basis for cultural identity and pride. When these minorities have what they want and need, namely, their own cultural identity and the freedom to go where they please, we will find them mingling freely with white people in all places where the good things of our society are to be had. Educational programs for ethnic identity can very well be carried out in integrated schools, provided these schools are not run by white people for the benefit of white people and provided white people do not say, in effect, "we'll accept them when they become like us" or feel guilty or anxious every time minority students are observed to stick together—in the cafeteria or on the playground or in classes of their own.

The efforts of minority groups to gain admission to college and to institute ethnic studies programs and Third World colleges have helped to focus attention upon the developmental approach to higher education in general. Not only do these efforts put the student at the center of the educational enterprise but the changes being urged in admissions policy, in curriculum, in methods of teaching, and in the structure of institutions would, if fully instituted, serve the needs of all students.

What these needs are and how they can be met in institutions of higher education make up the essential substance of the developmental approach to higher education. This approach has been the subject of an outpouring of literature in recent years.[12] And the developmental approach is having a significant impact in practice. Numerous new programs and some new institutions, such as the Santa Cruz campus of the University of California and Johnston College of the University of Redlands, have been planned and set going largely in accord with it.[13]

Once educators accept the basic fact, now well established,

that personality can and does develop during the college years, they have to ask how the various resources of the college may best serve developmental goals. They have to look at admissions with attention to various qualities and potentials in addition to cognitive ability, at governance with attention to what forms best encourage the student to become his own authority, at the teaching of literature with a view to what methods favor growth in self-awareness, and so on for other educational policies, arrangements, and procedures.

To turn to widely agreed developmental goals such as independence of thinking—to name a trait that stands in direct opposition to authoritarianism—educators will see that almost all the resources of the college can be brought into its service: not only governance that helps the student become his own authority and course content that helps him become aware of his own impulses but teaching that challenges preconceptions and gives practice in criticism, faculty members who are models of independent thinkers, and a general climate of freedom and respect for the individual.

This developmental approach to higher education is in its essentials the same as that advocated for child training in the home and for education in elementary and high schools. If we adopt this positive approach and become used to working within the framework it provides, the concept and the ideology of prevention will appear to be not only restricting but irrelevant. The aims of preventing specific evils are embraced by the larger aim of promoting human development, and preventive activities that do not keep this aim in view may set up barriers to its achievement. More, if we adopt the general theoretical approach advocated here but still cling to the idea of prevention, we will find ourselves speaking of preventing failures in development. It seems less awkward and, far more important, more stimulating, more hopeful, more worthy, and in the long run more practical to be explicit about promoting development toward full humanity.

CHAPTER 18

Epilogue: Social Destructiveness as Disposition and as Act

Nevitt Sanford, Craig Comstock

In order to help prepare the way for further study of social destructiveness, we here draw together some themes developed in other chapters, adding new thoughts that occurred to us while editing this book. First we discuss the process of sanction-giving, with special attention to institutional sanctions, and we expand on the theme of dehumanization, distinguishing its several forms. We then discuss destructiveness as a psychological disposition—a concept not previously mentioned. Finally, we explain some ways in which these ideas could be tested and some reasons why the topic calls for a new mode of research.

If most social destructiveness is done by people who feel they have some permission for what they do, we need to know more about what questions are raised by the paradigm of X telling Y that he may act in such a way that Z is harmed. The giving of such a sanction is not necessarily criminal; as we have seen in previous chapters, the state may take the role of X. It may convey that certain behavior ordinarily prohibited is, for some reason, excusable, permissible, unavoidable, or even mandatory. For example, it may order a program of genocide, as Adolf Hitler did, or may engage in a war that kills civilians on a scale otherwise associated with genocide. It may fail to punish or may even encourage the degradation of groups defined as inferior, as in the enforcement of a racist order. In these cases, we could not easily regard the acts as criminal in the strict sense, except perhaps by invoking international law. Similarly, the state may respond in such a way as to suggest that certain previous "excesses" were wrong but somehow unavoidable or understandable. In each of these otherwise very different cases, those who commit the acts sense at least a tacit approval of, or tolerance for, what they are doing; and often the sanction is given openly, sometimes even under color of law.

Sanctions for social destructiveness, however, may come from many groups other than the men who represent the state. Some of the resulting acts may remain beyond official notice, while others, especially when they involve violence, are treated as criminal. Social destructiveness, in short, is distinguished not by whether it is illegal, but by whether a sanctioning group has given permission, encouragement, or possibly orders. This definition leaves aside destructiveness done by a person who is truly acting alone, to recall the phrase applied to several recent assassins, though even a lone assassin may feel that his act is sanctioned by some cause or body of opinion, if not by a group on whose behalf he acts. We would not wish to suggest that any group is responsible for a free-lance psychotic acting in its name, but as observers we must note that sanctions have their effect not in the form they are given but in the way they are perceived.

In studying social destructiveness, we may start with whatever sanctions various people feel they have been given and proceed to examine the sources and distortions. Otherwise, how can we deal with groups which deny any ill intent but which act in ways that lead some people to feel they have been given a sanction for destructiveness? In this sense we begin with a perception, sometimes exaggerated or even fantastic, in the mind of a potential harm-doer—a perception that a relevant group or authority has given permission to do acts which, if done in other circumstances or to other victims, would be prohibited or at least disapproved of.

Sanctions for destructiveness are sometimes supplied not by a special group but rather by the prevailing form of social organization. In such a case, the sanction appears not as a special event or announcement but as a set of norms. Thus it is hard to isolate. Instead of proclaiming an exception to a general rule, the sanction has, as it were, been absorbed into the very structure. In such a situation people who act normally or who merely do their jobs contribute to destructiveness, often unconsciously, as in the case of institutional racism. Sanctions that pervade the system allow what Hannah Arendt has called the banality of evil, which occurs when an official is absorbed more by the functional rationality of doing his assigned part than by the probable result to which his actions contribute.[1]*

In genocide, the destructive result is clear at least to those able to focus on it. In many other situations, however, a bureaucracy is set up not to kill people or to harm them but to control them benignly or to provide services. For example, the police (among their bewildering range of duties) are supposed to protect people from assault; the welfare department is intended to support the destitute in a variety of ways; and schools are meant to educate people. Nonetheless, as segments of both middle-class and ghetto residents are coming to realize, these agencies often may function less as helpers than as parts of a system that oppresses people. Although some of those who staff these agencies may consciously wish to keep the people they are supposed to help "in their place," much of the destructiveness probably occurs because the terms of the work make it hard to act in any other way. In this sense, the

* Notes for this chapter start on p. 359.

very pattern of human relationships contains its own sanctions; nobody has to give them.

We believe that it would be helpful to make a comparative study of all these kinds of sanctioning and of others mentioned in this book. To do so is not to equate them in a moral sense. A bloodthirsty cry for the murder of people called vermin or pigs or mad dogs or apes differs considerably from bureaucratic imperatives that cause harm to people; but behind both these sanctions may lie a feeling, sometimes unconscious, that the people who are suffering or complaining somehow deserve less than other people, such as those who act upon them. Either they are bad or they do not count. In this sense, they are dehumanized. Whether such an attitude toward others is seen as a psychological defense or as a mark of exploitation or simply as a way of dismissing what are felt to be irrelevant complaints, dehumanization has consequences. In essence it excludes people from the protection of moral prohibitions recognized by a certain group (and often from receiving the material benefits that group enjoys as well); and thus it serves as a sanction for destructive acts or at least for a denial that a pattern of relationships is destructive.

This point raises the question of the visibility of social destructiveness.[2] When it takes the form of an outbreak or an atrocity, most of us pay attention at least briefly, as when television news showed pictures of Watts or My Lai or Kent State. When destructiveness occurs as part of a routine, however, we quite easily ignore it. In fact, we commonly define news as an event which is happening for the first time or which otherwise disrupts routine. The daily round of ghetto life calls for no coverage, and even the Vietnam war may lapse into a statistical pattern less irregular than the stock market. Superficial familiarity may serve as an even more effective defense than denial.

Faced with this resistance, those who suffer (or identify with those who do) are sometimes tempted to draw attention to neglected and routine destructiveness by eliciting (or even engaging in) the kind of destructiveness that society does not so easily ignore. Thus, nonviolent civil rights marches elicited some of the official violence which outsiders had been ignoring and caused it to be displayed on television. Revelations of social destructiveness call for great skill because its violent forms usually occur in secret and its nonviolent forms lack the drama that arouses quick outrage. For example, the experience of poor people with government officials or other establishment figures, such as policemen, welfare workers, landlords, political hacks, and school officials, would undoubtedly also frustrate and outrage any middle-class person, but these encounters lack the social visibility of cattle prods or nightsticks used on peaceful demonstrators.

A further difficulty is that sometimes even the direct victims of social destructiveness may fail to realize what is being done to them. They are socialized into accepting destructiveness as gradually and inevitably as an official learns to contribute to it. They are taught to blame themselves for their "failure" or to accept fate and meanwhile to turn their rage against one another, producing crime among the victims instead of protest against the system.[3] No informed person can doubt that destructiveness within the ghetto far exceeds destructiveness done to outsiders by residents of the ghetto, yet the former remains largely invisible to those outside; and to those inside the ghetto it may appear as evidence of their own "badness," not as a result of sanctions in the system.

A number of contributors to this book have noted a link between social destructiveness and the dehumanization of others. Of course, dehumanization of a vituperative kind is not necessary for great destructiveness to occur; nor do denigratory images of other people necessarily lead to physical acts against them. Destructiveness, however, is caused no less by social arrangements than by easily visible physical blows, and dehumanization takes many forms other than fearful abuse. For example, we may regard members of a particular group less as demons or germ carriers or beasts of prey than as machines or statistical units or children who need to be taken care of. We do not respect the autonomy of someone defined as incompetent, nor do we consider the feelings of people who are seen as machines with inputs and outputs and maintenance problems. This latter image of man may seem natural to those who identify with a "technetronic" future and who hope to stay on the right side of the control panel,[4] but we would argue that a mechanical or electronic image of man, if taken seriously, may lead to straitened forms of life.

To some extent our concept of dehumanization stems from the complex tradition of thought concerning alienation.[5] When people are regarded as less than human by the dominant society, of course they feel alienated from it; and those who see this dehumanization even without being direct victims of it share with the victims a sense of alienation. However, dehumanization can refer not only to a perception of others but also to a way of life suffered by those taught to treat others as less than human. Those who do this harm to others (or who contribute to a system that does it) may themselves be regarded as dehumanized in that they lack wholeness or a chance to develop aspects of themselves. In spite of their own dehumanization, some of these people identify strongly with the system, blaming their anxieties not on the hidden failures of their society but on threats posed by those who appear to be attacking it. A dehumanized person may thus exemplify his society rather than being alienated from it. Similarly, he may avoid the discomforts of anomie (in the simple sense of lacking norms) by holding tightly to a set of norms which, for example, may attribute all good to his own group and all bad to others. This belief, too, sustains his own dehumanization.

Although the process of splitting and projecting accounts for much of the dehumanization around us, another kind may arise from corrupted images of man which the dominant group applies to itself and strives to fulfill. If, for example, a dominant group devotes itself overwhelmingly to achieving control and possession, it may slight other aspects of life and other ways of relating to people and thus deprive itself of human values which it may eventually forget the possibility of seeking. If dissatisfactions felt by members of such a group are attributed to individual failure within its terms or to weakness caused by dissidents in the system or simply to a momentary lack of goods which that system may eventually provide, members will probably resist any change or expansion of their image of man, in spite of their own infelicity. In a system such as this, members are dehumanized by their own way of life, even if nobody on the outside deprives them of significant human possibilities.

If dehumanization can refer both to a view taken and to a life lived, what is the relation between these two senses of the word? Each of them can refer either to the self (or one's own group) and to others. Thus, we may learn or fashion denigatory images of ourselves as well as of other people, and others may instill in us a bad self-image, which (as noted above in the case of ghetto blacks) serves as a means of social control. Dehumanization as a view taken, either of the self or of another, could be revealed and measured in a number of ways. Scales developed for the study of authoritarianism, necrophilia, and Machiavellianism, together with clinical studies, measures of ego growth, of self-esteem, and of moral development, and instruments for eliciting basic images of man, all suggest methods for a detailed study of dehumanization as a perception or attitude.[6]

Dehumanization as a condition of life, apart from perceptions by the participants, calls for additional kinds of observation or measurement. Such research is necessary if we are to examine the links between images and actuality and if we are to avoid suggesting that the problem is solely psychological. For example, one person may wrongly blame all his troubles on a society he believes dehumanizes him; and another who actually is dehumanized by his conditions may fail to realize it. Thus a study limited to these perceptions would fail to describe adequately the problems of either man.

Moreover, perceptions of one group can help to perpetuate another group's dehumanized way of life. If a significant group of white people regard black people as shiftless, dangerous, stupid, or immoral, and if these perceptions have any influence on public policy or private behavior, the blacks suffer and lose opportunities to develop as full human beings within our society. Further, whites who engage in such defensive and condemnatory thought are themselves dehumanized by their absorption into a world peopled by stereotypes. Thus, both black victims and white victimizers suffer a diminishment of their humanity.

To formulate and study the kind of human reduction they experience, we need an image of man such as the one sketched in Chapter Twelve and a model of human development such as the one outlined in Chapter Seventeen. Our model can remain loose, inclusive, and open, but in order to see the deprivations that people suffer we need a working image of what man can at best become, of salutary kinds of development. We would include ideas of self-actualization and of psychic integration, of diversity and wholeness. Dehumanization denies this potential, impairs its realization, or even induces regression. Correspondingly through humanization a person approaches at each stage of his life the best of which he is capable.

With an open model of human development in mind, we want to ask, for example, in what ways a failure of development may lead to behavior that impairs the development of others (or to denigratory attitudes toward them)? Which experiences lead to reliance on a psychological disposition that we may call destructiveness? We would define the disposition of destructiveness by naming its object, its motive, and the way it operates. Destructiveness has human beings as its main object; its aim is, in some sense, to get rid of them; it does so by means of psychological mechanisms and social practices which make certain people disappear or lose their humanity. This disposition differs both from the so-called instinct of aggression and, in its scope, from violent behavior. Acts of violence defined in the ordinary sense [7] are easy to recognize, to classify under a single heading, and even to count, but the motivational sources of violence are extremely diverse. According to a long-standing psychological proposition supported by numerous experiments, aggression (and resultant violence) is provoked by frustrations; and everyone can think of many frustrations he encounters. In the case of destructiveness, in contrast, the acts are diverse, while the motivational source is a single complex disposition. As we have argued above, destructiveness can occur through symbols or through social arrangements as well as by violence; it can thus appear in forms as diverse as polite social discrimination or a massacre of the innocents.

Unlike "instincts" such as the aggression described by some popular writers, the disposition of destructiveness is not inborn but is generated out of experience and learning in a social environment (especially out of the punishments, terrors, and "final solutions" of childhood). Fundamentally, its source is inner conflict, which leads to a need to get rid of what is all too human in oneself. If this badness is felt to be located in the self, a person may become self-destructive; but often he may ascribe the badness to other people upon whom the conflict is then played out. Although this process may induce a moralistic sense of rightness, it can never free a person from the lurking sense of his own badness, which is continually visited upon others. As an adaptation to the problems that many of us face, the disposition of destructiveness is a dangerous failure; but in seeking alternatives we may derive hope from its status as a learned adaptation, not an instinct.

In order to build empirical support for this conception of destructiveness, it will be necessary to develop an internally consistent scale made up of items expressive of both self- and other-directed destructiveness, of a disposition to do psychological or physical damage to people, and also of items expressive of the opposite disposition—reverence for life, appreciation of human development, tolerance, compassion, and so forth. If this scale were reliable and valid, the next question would be whether it measured something different from what is measured by existing instruments. Closest in their content to what we have in mind are the F scale for measuring authoritarianism, and a biophilia vs. necrophilia scale based on the works of Erich Fromm.[8] Doubtless the F scale includes expressions of destructiveness; but it also includes other dispositions as well, such as conventionality and submissiveness toward authority. Moreover, the F scale does not touch upon self-destructiveness (although clinical studies have suggested that self-contempt is a feature of the authoritarian syndrome), nor does it include any items which express the opposite of destructiveness. It is our view that any scale for measuring destructiveness will correlate positively with the F scale, but that, given the culture of today, many people would score high on destructiveness but not on the F scale. Only a great deal of empirical work can show the interrelationships among these scales and, more important, which of the hypothetical variables mentioned here are truly independent and how they relate to the others.

In addition to measurements and analysis of this psychological disposition, a study of social destructiveness might investigate situations in which ordinary, decent people may nonetheless do great harm to others. Here we have in mind not only atrocities in Vietnam but a series of experiments run by Stanley Milgram on what he called obedience.[9] Milgram was surprised to discover that a large fraction of university students and townspeople in his samples would push switches which they thought gave severe and dangerous shocks to subjects who failed to supply correct answers in what was described as a learning experiment. Even when the learners simulated pain, announced that they had heart conditions, and demanded to be let out of the experiment, most of those seated at the control panel continued to follow the direction of the psychologist to complete the experiment; they accepted such comments as "you have no choice." In this case, they could simply have walked out, as some did, but most obeyed. We must assume either that an extraordinary percentage of the sample were highly disposed to destructiveness or that severe social destructiveness may be carried out by people who respond less to hatred toward the victims than to the guidance or commands of superiors. To the extent that the latter is true, we must investigate the disposition to submit to what others ask or at least to acquiesce in what they are doing and meanwhile look at the social structures which helped to create the disposition and which later make use of it. In each case, we must also study exceptions, such as dispositions to question an authority whose commands violate important values, to seek changes in the system, and to resist if necessary.

Creative resistance against organizations which are being destructive, including resistance from within, can sometimes forestall great evils; and at the least it can help to preserve the resisters from absorption. In order to deal with the pervasive danger of destructiveness by organizations, however, we clearly need ways of changing their structures. We must face the problem that certain kinds of organization in all advanced countries, whether socialist or capitalist, seem to contribute inadvertently to various forms of social destructiveness. Some critics refer to size as the main source of trouble, but all of us can think of fairly small organizations that may do considerable harm, including the nuclear family. It would be rewarding to study a number of organizations which are doing harm to (or at least failing to benefit) their clients, their staff, or others who are affected. We are especially interested in organizations whose basic aim is not to make a profit but to provide various basic services or which administer social controls. We are curious, for example, about the relation between the way the organization treats its members and the way they deal with other people. If an official is dehumanized by the role he is asked to fill, does that process have an effect on those over whom he has power (or on those with whom he lives)?

It might be hypothesized, for example, that welfare workers often suffer losses of humanity under the pressures and temptations of the welfare system and that this dehumanization leads them to treat their clients as less than human—something which in time leads to the actual dehumanization of these clients. In order to test this hypothesis it would be necessary to develop measures of such human qualities as autonomy, empathy, and maturity of ego and such manifestations of dehumanization as bad conscience, cynicism, and sense of powerlessness; to select or develop independent measures of prejudice toward ethnic minorities and of dehumanizing imagery of clients; and then by means of longitudinal or panel studies to note changes in these measures in relation to length of time in the agency or system. We would predict that, in general, both signs of loss of humanity and negative attitudes toward (and imagery of) clients would increase with length of service in the agency or system and—most important for our purposes—that the greater the dehumanization experienced by the welfare workers the greater their tendency to regard clients and others like them as less than human. If we were able to make careful and extended observations of the behavior of the welfare workers, we could probably show that dehumanization in them was associated with a corresponding treatment of their clients; and similar studies of these clients would probably show that as a result of the treatment they received, they suffered actual dehumanization.

For studying the dehumanization of clients by an agency that is supposed to help or studying the failure of such clients to develop toward full humanity, a school or college would offer the researcher advantages over a welfare system. Here changes in students over time are relatively easy to observe and to measure, and since they spend most of their waking hours within the educational system, the researcher might discover which features or processes of the system had given effects. It is well known that the overall effect of formal education in America is humanizing; numerous studies have pointed to a correlation between level of education and such qualities as autonomy, flexibility, tolerance, sense of identity, and capacity for self-expression. Schools, however, are justly charged with failure to do all that they might to promote development toward full humanity and even with actions (and inactions) that tend to dehumanize the students. A quarter of American youth drop out of school before completing the twelfth grade, and many become psychologically disengaged, lapsing into passivity, self-contempt, even overt destructiveness and despair. In studying the processes that lead to these unfavorable outcomes, we would predict that the schools in which teachers suffer the greatest loss of their humanity will also show the highest rates of developmental failure on the part of the students.

As the discussion of social workers and teachers has made clear, sanctions for destructiveness may derive from occupational norms. Sometimes these sanctions are consciously recognized and are kept secret from outsiders. William A. Westley relates how police arrogate to themselves a right to use violence in ways of which the courts and perhaps even large segments of the public would not necessarily approve.[10] Some officers argue, however, that it is they, not the courts, who face the dangers, and they who know how bad people must be dealt with. Especially in a country where the police are known colloquially as "the law," some officers may feel a sanction, if only from their peers, for punishing bad people instead of merely apprehending them.[11] And in some cases no discretion is required; the punishment may be given in public. When the public grows especially anxious about a perceived threat to its security, such as black criminality or student radicalism, police can direct considerable violence at offenders who fall into these categories. Even homicide by police or other armed officials is often defined as justifiable or at least understandable; a commission may regret it but seldom are the gunmen prosecuted.

We expect that a comparative study of various sanctioning processes will yield certain regularities modified by the social structure in which the particular process occurs. One obvious variable is the degree to which the relevant structure is insulated from outside criticism by its ability to operate in secret, to retaliate against critics, or to ignore outsiders. Another variable is the degree to which the harm is apparent to those who sanction the acts that contribute to it; often, for example, officials are simply insensitive to certain effects which seem irrelevant to their work. A third variable is the specificity of the sanction; although certain acts are expressly ordered or allowed, many others take place simply because of the way the organization happens to work. Such effects are often referred to as unintended, but from the viewpoint of victims they may seem sanctioned at least by neglect if not by design. Experience in several fields of public policy suggests that we need a good early warning system against the destructiveness later blamed on the inadvertency of large organizations. A failure to observe the effects of policies as they are carried out is itself a mark of dehumanization; in the process of caring for one group of people or for a single aspect of people, bureaucrats or professionals may in effect ignore other groups affected by the action or may come to see the people with whom they *do* interact as nothing more than a set of part-functions. (A similar difficulty may arise in certain styles of social science or psychological research.)

Just as we need a positive model of human development to help in the study of dehumanization because it both alerts us to failures and suggests alternatives, so we also need examples of organizations which avoid acting on or issuing sanctions for destructiveness because they find other ways to deal with problems of security and fears of change. Given the rather high level of anxiety now prevalent, we are especially concerned to discover ways in which organizations may avoid what one of us has called pathologies of defense, in which the mode of protection generated by or introduced into the system either corrupts it from within or stimulates further dangers from outside.

When we have talked with enlightened teachers and welfare workers about these problems and about doing studies of them, their response has been: "But everybody knows welfare workers and teachers are dehumanized by the systems in which they have to work, and we have no doubt that their attitudes toward clients or pupils often change in the way you suggest; the question is how to prevent the dehumanization from occurring. You have to look at the system itself."

Although we take this response very seriously, we nonetheless think that studies such as the ones proposed above ought to be undertaken. What seems clear to enlightened welfare workers or teachers is certainly not clear to all who are concerned with the welfare or educational systems or even to all teachers or case workers. We would argue, too, that in order to find out which features of the system do what kinds of damage to whom, it is necessary to obtain estimates from the people involved and to relate their reports to various features of the organization.

It would be highly ironical, however, if a study of dehumanization were to contribute to the further dehumanization of welfare workers or teachers, something that may easily happen if they are observed, interviewed, and asked to fill out questionnaires without their knowing the implications of the questions and if the results are then passed along not to them but to their administrators, presumably in order to change management procedures. A humanistic approach to the study of people in the lower ranks of an organization should begin by regarding them as clients, not only as subjects. They should take part in the planning of the inquiry and in the framing of the questions; and they should be the first to be told of the results. Research carried out in this spirit would counter dehumanization at the same time that it yielded knowledge of its nature and causes, for individuals who were interviewed in this manner would find their capacity to resist dehumanization increased through their awareness of what had been happening to them. And, as a study of graduate students has shown,[12] when this awareness is shared by other people in the same situation, a process of change begins in the organization. If certain parts of the organization then act to resist change, they thereby reveal, as nothing else could, major features of its dynamic structure. That would be the time to study, by means of interviews, members of the management, for they would then be faced with the necessity of making new policy. If at this time they could become aware of their own processes in relation to those of the organization, the new policy might be similarly enlightened.

Although we have used teachers and welfare workers to illustrate one kind of study, dehumanization and social destructiveness obviously call for research in many other populations and in several different modes, ranging from the historical to the clinical. Various contributors have illustrated and alluded to some of these modes for further work, and we have tried here to summarize an approach to social destructiveness which may help to focus a number of disciplines on a common topic of concern to us all.

Notes

CHAPTER 1: *Sanctions for Evil*

1. *Nuremberg and Vietnam: An American Tragedy,* as excerpted in the *San Francisco Chronicle,* November 20, 1970, p. 12.
2. See his brilliant and far-ranging philosophical essay entitled *The Paradox of Cruelty* (Middletown, Conn.: Wesleyan University Press, 1969).
3. Although lawyers use the word *sanction* to refer to a penalty enacted to enforce obedience, we use the word in its more general, positive sense to mean something that supports, authorizes, justifies, or legitimates an action, including encouragement given to an opinion or practice by custom, public sentiment, or the like.
4. W. H. Grier and P. M. Cobbs, *Black Rage* (New York: Bantam, 1969).
5. For an account of the damage that may be done to the victimizer, see J. Kovel, *White Racism: A Psychohistory* (New York: Pantheon, 1970).
6. See K. H. Wolff, "For a Sociology of Evil," *Journal of Social Issues,* 1969, *25,* 111–25.

7. Various hunting parties such as this were reported in the *San Francisco Bulletin* in the 1860s.

8. For an outstanding, psychologically sensitive account of anti-Semitic imagery associated with the so-called *Protocols of the Elders of Zion*, see N. Cohn, *Warrant for Genocide* (New York: Harper and Row, 1967).

9. D. Lang, *Casualties of War* (New York: McGraw-Hill, 1969).

10. Y. Rogat, *The Eichmann Trial and the Rule of Law* (Santa Barbara, Calif.: Center for the Study of Democratic Institutions, 1961).

CHAPTER 3: *Conditions for Guilt-Free Massacre*

1. *American Journal of Sociology*, 1956, *61*, 420–424.

2. J. Skolnick, *Justice Without Trial* (New York: Wiley, 1966).

CHAPTER 4: *Existential Evil*

1. R. Hammer, *One Morning in the War: The Tragedy at Son My* (New York: Coward-McCann, 1970); and S. M. Hersh, *My Lai 4: A Report on the Massacre and Its Aftermath* (New York: Random House, 1970).

2. *On Genocide* (Boston: Beacon Press, 1968).

3. R. J. Lifton, *Death in Life: Survivors of Hiroshima* (New York: Random House, 1967).

4. Quoted in M. Polner, "Vietnam War Stories," *Transaction*, November 1968, *6*, 8–20.

5. "Neither Victims nor Executioners," *Liberation*, February 1960.

CHAPTER 5: *It Never Happened and Besides They Deserved It*

1. *Foreign Affairs*, July 1968, 650. Huntington's internal quote is from R. Thompson, "Squaring the Error," *Foreign Affairs*, April 1968, 447.

2. Statement by A. W. Galston, professor of biology, Yale University, to the Subcommittee on National Security Policy and Scientific Developments of the House of Representatives Committee on Foreign

Affairs, December 1969, as quoted by T. Whiteside, *Defoliation* (New York: Ballantine, 1970), p. 108.

3. "The Best Way to Kill People," *San Francisco Chronicle,* December 1, 1969, p. 41.
4. *The Military Half* (New York: Random House, 1968), pp. 42–43, 139, 142.
5. "Vet Condemned for Atrocity Stories," *San Francisco Chronicle,* December 1, 1969, p. 10.
6. Quoted in "GIs Question Massacre Story," *San Francisco Chronicle,* December 1, 1969, pp. 1, 26. This article first appeared in the *New York Times.*
7. T. Adorno, E. Frenkel-Brunswik, D. J. Levinson, and N. Sanford, *The Authoritarian Personality* (New York: Harper and Row, 1950).
8. "The Day the War Became a Personal Thing," *San Francisco Examiner and Chronicle,* November 23, 1969, editorial section, p. 2.
9. *The Wall Street Journal,* December 1, 1969, pp. 1, 14.
10. "Many Disbelieve My Lai Reports," *The Minneapolis Tribune,* December 21, 1969.
11. "General reaction to the reports of the massacre at My Lai, as recorded in a Harris poll in January [1970], can perhaps best be described as bland." P. E. Converse and H. Schurman, "Silent Majorities and the Vietnam War," *Scientific American,* June 1970, 222, 24.
12. "The War: New Support for Nixon," *Time,* January 12, 1970, pp. 10–11.
13. "On Disbelieving Atrocities," *The New York Times Magazine,* January 1944.
14. R. L. Haeberle (photographer), "The Massacre at Mylai," *Life,* December 5, 1969, pp. 36–45.
15. "The Germans and the Jews: Postwar Report," *Commentary,* July 1946.
16. "German Reactions to Nazi Atrocities," *American Journal of Sociology,* 1946, 52, 141–146.
17. *San Francisco Chronicle,* December 18, 1969, p. 14.
18. Moskowitz, *loc. cit.*
19. All American quotes from the *Wall Street Journal,* December 1, 1969, pp. 1, 14.
20. Schell, *op. cit.,* p. 144.
21. Quoted by J. Lelyveld, "How Civilians Get Killed in Vietnam," *New York Times,* also printed in the *San Francisco Chronicle,* December 16, 1969, pp. 1, 26. Bernhardt was one of the members of Company C who refused to take part in the My Lai massacre.
22. Lelyveld, *loc. cit.*
23. W. Buckley, *San Francisco Examiner,* December 4, 1969, p. 36.

24. J. H. Howard, letter to the *New Haven* (Connecticut) *Register,* February 16, 1970. Incidentally, the *Life* photographs do jibe with the appearance of coastal Quang Ngai Province, where My Lai was located, according to my memory and my photographs of the area.

25. Chublarian's paper is available from the author at 236 West Walnut St., Philadelphia, Pa. Wilson's actual words, according to Tom Wicker, *New York Times,* December 2, 1969, were: "Once lead this people into war and they'll forget there ever was such a thing as tolerance. To fight you must be brutal and ruthless and the spirit of ruthless brutality will enter into the very fiber of our national life, infecting Congress, the courts, the policeman on the beat, the man in the street."

26. *They Thought They Were Free* (Chicago: University of Chicago Press, 1955), p. 76.

CHAPTER 6: *Groupthink Among Policy Makers*

1. This chapter is based on a series of case studies of policy-making groups, to be presented in a forthcoming book entitled *Victims of Groupthink: A Psychological Analysis of Foreign Policy Decisions and Fiascos* (New York: Harcourt Brace Jovanovich).

2. J. Thomson, "How Could Vietnam Happen: An Autopsy," *The Atlantic,* April 1968, pp. 47–53.

3. D. Kraslow and S. Loory, *The Secret Search for Peace in Vietnam* (New York: Vintage, 1968).

4. T. Hoopes, *The Limits of Intervention* (New York: McKay, 1969).

CHAPTER 8: *Dehumanization*

1. Adaptive and maladaptive refer to a person's modes of coping with internal and external stress. The distinction hinges on the extent to which such coping is successful with respect to the optimal overall balance of the individual's realistic interests and goals.

2. These occupations, therefore, carry the extra risk of their requisite dehumanization becoming maladaptive if it is carried to an extreme or used inappropriately.

3. *Portrait of Myself* (New York: Simon and Schuster, 1963).

4. "Psychological Effects of the Atomic Bomb in Hiroshima; the Theme of Death," *Daedalus, Journal of the American Academy of Arts and Sciences,* 1963, *92,* 462–497.

5. Because of this primary emphasis, we shall refrain from exploring many important facets of dehumanization which seem less directly relevant to the threat of nuclear warfare. Yet, it permeates so many aspects of modern life that, for clarity in describing it, our discussion must ramify, to some extent, beyond its war-connected context. Still, we have purposely neglected areas of great interest to us, especially with regard to psychopathology, psychotherapy, and community psychiatry, which we think warrant fuller discussion elsewhere.

6. No doubt, when the phenomenon is part of a mental disorder, it has been dealt with therapeutically, to some degree, under the names of other defense mechanisms.

7. "On Disbelieving Atrocities," in *The Yogi and the Commissar* (New York: Macmillan, 1945).

8. "How the Poor Die," in *Shooting an Elephant* (New York: Harcourt Brace Jovanovich, 1945).

9. *Yank, the Army Weekly* (New York: Duell, Sloan, and Pearce, 1947), p. 282.

10. M. J. Kahne, "Bureaucratic Structure and Impersonal Experience in Mental Hospitals," *Psychiatry*, 1959, 22 (4), 363–375.

11. Within our own discipline this is all too likely to occur when thousands of sick individuals are converted into "cases" in some of our understaffed and oversized mental hospitals. Bureaucratic hospital structure favors impersonal experience. In an enlightening study, Kahne points up how this accentuation of automatic and formalized milieu propensities thwarts the specific therapeutic need of psychiatric patients for opportunities to improve their sense of involvement with people (see note 10).

12. This has been particularly well described in novels by Franz Kafka and Albert Camus.

13. *Thirty-Eight Witnesses* (New York: McGraw-Hill, 1964).

14. The news of President John Kennedy's assassination circled the earth with unparalleled speed and evoked a profound worldwide response.

15. *Das Sogenannte Böse—Zur Naturgeschichte der Aggression* (Vienna: Dr. G. Borotha-Schoeler Verlag, 1963).

CHAPTER 9: *Failures of Identification and Sociopathic Behavior*

1. R. Ardrey, *African Genesis* (New York: Delta, 1961).
2. M. Desmond, *The Naked Ape* (New York: Dell, 1969).
3. *Insight and Responsibility* (New York: Norton, 1964), p. 224.

CHAPTER 10: *Authoritarianism and Social Destructiveness*

1. T. W. Adorno, E. Frenkel-Brunswik, D. J. Levinson, and N. Sanford, *The Authoritarian Personality* (New York: Harper and Row, 1950). For evaluations of *The Authoritarian Personality* in the light of more recent research see R. Brown, *Social Psychology* (New York: Free Press, 1967); J. P. Kirscht and R. C. Dillehay, *Dimensions of Authoritarianism: A Review of Research and Theory* (Lexington, Ky.: University of Kentucky Press, 1967); and O. Klineberg, "Prejudice: The Concept," in *International Encyclopedia of the Social Sciences* (New York: Macmillan and Free Press, 1968); F. Greenstein, *Personality and Politics* (Chicago: Markham, 1969), pp. 94–119.
2. *San Francisco Chronicle,* April 22, 1969.
3. *Social Psychology* (New York: Free Press, 1967), p. 525.
4. *Warrant for Genocide* (New York: Harper and Row, 1967).
5. *The Tenacity of Prejudice* (New York: Harper and Row, 1969).
6. "Religion and Attitudes Toward Negroes," unpublished paper, The Wright Institute, Berkeley, Calif., 1969.
7. D.D. Harris, H. G. Gough, and W. E. Martin, "Children's Ethnic Attitudes: II: Relationship to Parental Beliefs Concerning Child Training," *Child Development,* 1950, *21,* 169–181.
8. E. Frenkel-Brunswik, "Further Explorations by a Contributor," in R. Christie and M. Jahoda (Eds.), *Studies in the Scope and Method of the Authoritarian Personality* (New York: Free Press, 1954), p. 236.
9. *The Impact of College on Students* (San Francisco: Jossey-Bass, 1969).
10. "Motown Justice," *New York Review of Books,* August 1, 1968, pp. 24–28.
11. *Time,* Nov. 23, 1970, p. 81.
12. "The Concepts of Culture and of Social System," *American Sociological Review,* 1958, *23,* 582–583.
13. E. Jacques, *The Changing Culture of a Factory* (New York: Dryden, 1952).
14. J. Bushnell, "Student Culture at Vassar," in N. Sanford (Ed.), *The American College* (New York: Wiley, 1962).
15. E. Hughes, H. Becker, and B. Geer, "Student Culture and Academic Effort," in Sanford, *The American College.*
16. K. Keniston, *The Uncommitted* (New York: Harcourt Brace Jovanovich, 1965).

CHAPTER 11: *Conflict, Dominance, and Exploitation*

1. *The Elementary Forms of the Religious Life* (New York: Free Press, 1947).
2. O. Fenichel, *Psychoanalytic Theory of Neurosis* (New York: Norton, 1945).
3. V. C. Wynne-Edwards, *Animal Dispersion in Relation to Social Behaviour* (Edinburgh: Oliver and Boyd; New York: Hafner, 1962).
4. It is even difficult for modern man with his very recent heritage of scientific objectivity to keep distinct the laws that govern natural causality and the laws of social morality. Compare discussion on the distinctions and similarities in B. Malinowski, *Magic, Science and Religion, and Other Essays* (New York: Free Press, 1948).
5. The word *hierarchical* in recent social science literature has tended to lose the original meaning, which was that a hierarch is one who rules or has authority in sacred things and a hierarchy is a ranking of sacred beings.
6. Durkheim in his analysis of socialization within society has helped resolve the dilemma faced by previous social theoreticians, such as Thomas Hobbes, Jean-Jacques Rousseau, and John Locke, in explaining the integrative processes that keep society together by discussing how it is the very essence of man's social nature itself for him to experience a strong sense of inner constraint. This constraint keeps societies integrated without the need to resort to the fiction of the social contract or to rely on the use of instrumental power or coercion. Compare T. Parsons, *The Structure of Social Action* (New York: Free Press, 1949).
7. L. Festinger, *The Theory of Cognitive Dissonance* (Palo Alto, Calif.: Stanford University Press, 1957).
8. *The Oedipus Complex* (New York: Free Press, 1962). Compare a review in G. De Vos, "Menstrual Taboos and Chi Square," *Contemporary Psychology*, 1963, *8*, 434–438.
9. The instrumental-expressive dichotomy in human social role relations has been applied cogently to an understanding of human behavior in the primary family organization by T. Parsons and R. Bales, *Family Socialization and Interaction Process* (New York: Free Press, 1955). Here I am applying these terms to general forms of social dominance in class and caste.
10. A. H. Hocart, *Caste—A Comparative Study* (London: Methuen, 1950).
11. *The Golden Bough: A Study in Magic and Religion* (New York: Criterion, 1959).

12. (Chicago: University of Chicago Press, 1948.) De Grazia writes (p. 19): "Political authority accumulates in the hands of those who are believed to have outstanding skill in the most hazardous and fortuitous elements of provisioning the community. Success in extracting nutriment from the particular conditions of land, sea, and air is the supernatural quality of kings be it called mana as in Polynesia, iddhi as in India, or wakan wanitow or orenda as in Indian North America. The ancient Babylonians looked to their kings for abundance. In Fiji, kings carry the title of sri, which means both prosperity and food. In Polynesia the word *sau* signifies king, peace, or prosperity. Homeric mythology held kings responsible for the food supply. The Burgundians held their king responsible for the fortunes of war. Under the Roman Empire, power over crops and prosperity became especially connected with the emperor. From the time of Augustus, Roman coins bore such inscriptions as 'The Prosperity of Augustus.' The Malays have faith that their king possesses a personal influence over the works of nature such as the growth of crops and the bearing of fruit trees. Drought, dearth, or defeat in war notified the czars of southern Russia that the natural powers of the king were on the wane."

13. It is beyond the scope of this particular [chapter], which is concerned with the nature of conflict and dominance, to go into any detailed theoretical discussion of the structure or origin or persistence of caste in society. This is discussed at length in G. De Vos and H. Wagatsuma, *Japan's Invisible Race: Caste in Culture and Personality* (Berkeley, Calif.: University of California Press, 1966).

14. S. F. Nagle, "Caste and Government in Primitive Society," *Journal of the Anthropological Society of Bombay*, 1954, *8*, 9–22.

15. De Vos and Wagatsuma, *op. cit.*

16. "The System of Social Stratification in Swat, North Pakistan," in E. R. Leach (Ed.), *Aspects of Caste in South India, Ceylon and Northwest Pakistan,* Cambridge Papers on Social Anthropology (London: Cambridge University Press, 1960), pp. 113–146.

17. *India's Ex-Untouchables* (New York: Day, 1965).

18. C. Kluckhohn, *Navajo Witchcraft* (Boston: Beacon, 1962), for an analysis of the social functioning of belief in witchcraft.

19. It is interesting to note that a mythology of contentment with one's status is attributed to a continuously disparaged group. It is claimed of such groups that they "like to be where they are" or that they realize themselves by the proper exercise of their functions. When conflict appears, it is often attributable to outside sources of agitation. For example, among American Negroes today communists or northern radicals are those that bring about dissension rather than the Negroes, who would remain contented if they were left to themselves. See, for example, a paper by Gerald

Berreman, who demonstrates very cogently that the alleged contentment of the Indian untouchables and lower castes is similarly a myth when one actually examines the true feelings of these submerged groups: "Caste in India and the United States," *American Journal of Sociology*, 1960, *66*, 120–127.
20. *Social Change and Prejudice Including Dynamics of Prejudice* (New York: Free Press, 1964).

CHAPTER 12: *Evil and the American Ethos*

1. W. D. Jordan, *White over Black* (Chapel Hill, N. C.: University of North Carolina Press, 1968), pp. 12–13.
2. Quoted by H. Emmerich in the *San Francisco Examiner*, November 23, 1969.
3. "Americanization: Sacred or Profane Phenonemon?" unpublished paper, prepared for the American Academy of Religion, October 25, 1969.
4. Quoted by K. Shapiro, "Introduction," in H. Miller, *Tropic of Cancer* (New York: Grove Press, 1961), p. viii.
5. J. Baldwin, *Nobody Knows My Name* (New York: Dell, 1963), pp. 111–112.
6. Quoted in Jordan, *op. cit.*, p. 258.
7. *Ibid.*, p. 200.
8. *Ibid.*, Chapters 3 and 4.
9. The theoretical issues involved in the question of cultural pluralism are many and complex and cannot begin to be dealt with in this chapter. For a sociologist the central problem is how cultural diversity can be combined with the common values which are necessary for the integration of any society. The evident solution is to build openness and flexibility into the value system as central values themselves. This would involve the ability to accept not only multiple cultural groups as fully belonging to the larger society but multiple cultural identities in oneself and others. We have long come to accept the Zionist Jew as a good American. We must be able to do the same with the Black or Chicano nationalist. Randolph S. Bourne was one of the most persuasive proponents of multiple cultural identities in an earlier generation. Indeed he felt America could be the first nation to become genuinely transnational. Although he was a voice in the wilderness at the time (during World War I), he still has much to teach us. See his essays collected in C. Resek (Ed.), *War and the Intellectuals* (New York: Harper and Row, 1964), especially pp. 107–133. More recently a leading black intellectual, Harold Cruse, has contributed

much to the discussion of cultural pluralism in his book *The Crisis of the Negro Intellectual* (New York: Morrow, 1967).
10. On this point see some suggestions in my "Civil Religion in America," *Daedalus*, Winter 1967, reprinted in my collection of essays *Beyond Belief* (New York: Harper and Row, 1970). The chapters in Part III of the book deal with some of the current cultural resources for new directions in American society.

CHAPTER 13: *Knowledge as Virtue, Knowledge as Power*

1. Senate Document No. 331, 57th Congress, 1st Session; cited by Tran Van Dinh, *Saturday Review*, May 30, 1970.
2. P. Bourne, *Men, Stress, and Vietnam* (Boston: Little, Brown, 1970).
3. It will be argued by some that there have been atrocities and war crimes committed by both sides and that the enemy forces us to respond in kind. There are, however, quantitative differences: American bombing and shelling of villages has caused a loss of civilian life of a magnitude that defies comparison with the consequences of Viet Cong terrorism. There is also the question of whether terroristic actions of Vietnamese against Vietnamese should be equated with the violence of a foreign power employed against the Vietnamese and the question of the responsibility of every American for inhuman acts performed in the name of his country. The My Lai disclosures, according to one expert in the field of international law, indicate responsibilities which "range beyond the idea of criminal liability to encompass all Americans and, indeed, all peoples and governments in the world." R. Falk, "War Crimes and Individual Responsibility," *Trans-action*, 1970, 7 (3).
4. See J. Habermas, *Toward a Rational Society* (Boston: Beacon, 1970), pp. 81ff.
5. *The Structure of Behavior* (Boston: Beacon, 1967), pp. 114ff.
6. S. Paradise, "The Vandal Ideology," *The Nation*, December 29, 1969.
7. E. Schachtel, *Metamorphosis* (New York: Basic Books, 1959), p. 83.
8. *The Ethical Imperative* (Garden City, N.Y.: Doubleday, 1970), p. 241.
9. *The Lonely Crowd* (New Haven, Conn.: Yale University Press, 1950), p. 80.
10. *Man: Mutable and Immutable* (Chicago: Regnery, 1950), p. 58.
11. J. P. Sartre, *The Emotions* (New York: Philosophical Library, 1948), p. 90.

12. See Chapter Nine on the inability of psychopaths to identify with other people.
13. "The Social Significance of Animal Studies," in G. Lindzey and E. Aronson (Eds.), *The Handbook of Social Psychology* (2nd ed.) (Reading, Mass.: Addison-Wesley, 1968), pp. 729–774.
14. See P. Slater, *The Pursuit of Loneliness* (Boston: Beacon, 1970), pp. 53ff.
15. On this problem, see T. Parsons, "The Superego and the Theory of Social Systems," *Working Papers in the Theory of Action* (New York: Free Press, 1953), p. 19.
16. Phylogenetically, the most recent brain area, the part most highly developed in the primates, is the neocortex. When connections from the association centers in the prefrontal lobes to the thalamus and hypothalamus are severed, two major changes result —a loss of inhibition in sexual and oral behavior and a diminished number of sexual impulses. Could one not then argue that as the neocortex developed, civilization itself enhanced the sexual impulse, which it then had to control?
17. *On Aggression* (New York: Harcourt Brace Jovanovich, 1966), p. 242.
18. Hebb and Thompson, *op. cit.*, p. 759. See also D. E. Berlyne, "Conflict and Arousal," *Scientific American*, 1966, *215* (2).
19. "A Motivational Theory of Emotion to Replace 'Emotion as a Disorganized Response,'" in K. H. Pribram (Ed.), *Brain and Behavior*. Vol. 4: *Adaptation* (Harmondsworth, England: Penguin, 1969), pp. 349–372.
20. *Ibid.*, pp. 370f.
21. R. S. Peters, "Emotion, Passivity and the Place of Freud's Theory in Psychology," K. H. Pribram, "The New Neurology and the Biology of Emotion: A Structural Approach," both in Pribram, *op. cit.*, pp. 373–394, 452–466.
22. Reported in R. Plutchik, *The Emotions* (New York: Random House, 1962).
23. "Certain Primary Sources and Patterns of Aggression in the Social Structure of the Western World," in *Essays in Sociological Theory* (Rev. ed.) (New York: Free Press, 1954), p. 304.
24. T. Parsons, "The Link Between Character and Society," in *Social Structure and Personality* (New York: Free Press, 1964), pp. 216f.
25. See N. J. Smelser, *The Sociology of Economic Life* (Englewood Cliffs, N.J.: Prentice-Hall, 1963), p. 110, and R. Bendix, "Tradition and Modernity Reconsidered," *Comparative Studies in Society and History*, 1966–1967, *9*.
26. These structural levels are discussed by N. Dyson-Hudson, "Structure and Infrastructure in Primitive Society: Lévi-Strauss and Radcliffe-Brown," in R. Macksey and E. Donato (Eds.), *The Languages*

of *Criticism and the Sciences of Man* (Baltimore: Johns Hopkins Press, 1970). See also the discussion which follows the essay.

27. *Integrative Action of the Nervous System* (New Haven: Yale University Press, 1911).

28. J. Z. Young, *Doubt and Certainty in Science* (Oxford: Oxford University Press, 1960), p. 67.

29. The phenomenological psychologist may have a different interpretation of such behavior. See, for example, Merleau-Ponty's discussion of Kurt Goldstein's famous patient, Schneider—a victim of brain damage. *Phénoménologie de la Perception* (Paris: Librairie Gallimard, 1945), pp. 114ff.

30. Anglo-American law is impatient with the "altruistic intermeddler"—a type not exactly rare but probably incongruent with an ideology based on the market and individual competition.

31. "The Experience of Living in Cities," *Science*, 1970, *167* (3924).

32. "The Metropolis and Mental Life," in C. W. Mills (Ed.), *Images of Man* (New York: Braziller, 1960). Simmel suggests that the blasé attitude that the city-dweller develops in dealing with his environment has its roots in the money economy as well as in physiology. "The essence of the blasé attitude consists in the blunting of discrimination. This does not mean that the objects are not perceived, as in the case of the half-wit, but rather that the meaning and differing values of things, and thereby the things themselves, are experienced as insubstantial. They appear to the blasé person in an evenly flat and gray tone; no one object deserves preference over any other. This mood is the faithful reflection of the completely internalized money economy. . . . Money expresses all qualitative differences of things in terms of 'how much?'" (p. 441).

33. Pribram, "The New Neurology and the Biology of Emotion," p. 463. See also R. Laing, *The Politics of Experience* (New York: Ballantine, 1967).

34. R. W. White, "Competence and the Psychosexual Stages of Development," in M. R. Jones (Ed.), *Nebraska Symposium on Motivation* (Lincoln, Neb.: University of Nebraska Press, 1960), pp. 120f.

35. H. S. Kariel, *Open Systems: Arenas for Political Action* (Itasca, Ill.: Peacock, 1969), p. 7. "Our constant self-imposed assignment must be to test the degree of tolerable disruption. It must be to incorporate new perceptions and experiences and to maintain our balance in the process."

36. See E. Becker, *Angel in Armor* (New York: Braziller, 1969).

37. *Behavior and Psychological Man* (Berkeley, Calif.: University of California Press, 1961), p. 263. The major study of this phenomenon is T. W. Adorno, E. Frenkel-Brunswik, D. Levinson, and N. Sanford, *The Authoritarian Personality* (New York: Harper and Row, 1950).

38. The current literature on deviance stresses the functional importance to society of acts which defy community standards. Before the beginning of this century, Durkheim interested himself in the righteous reaction to scandal, a response which united the townspeople, producing a temper "which is everybody's without being anybody's in particular. This is the public temper." *The Division of Labor in Society* (New York: Free Press, 1960), p. 192. One is reminded of conceptions of class which hold that a class exists only insofar as there exists a class enemy.

39. See K. Deutsch, *The Nerves of Government* (New York: Free Press, 1963), p. 162.

40. T. H. Marshall, *Class, Citizenship, and Social Development* (Garden City, N.Y.: Doubleday, 1965), p. 96.

41. See, for example, J. Lopreato, "Authority Relations and Class Conflict," *Social Forces*, 1968, *47* (1).

42. On the metaphor, see R. D. Laing, "The Obvious," in D. Cooper (Ed.), *The Dialectics of Liberation* (Harmondsworth, England: Penguin, 1968).

43. E. Goffman, *The Presentation of Self in Everyday Life* (Garden City, N.Y.: Doubleday, 1959), p. 9.

44. Quoted by A. M. Schlesinger, Jr., *The Vital Center* (Boston: Houghton, Mifflin, 1949), Chapter 1.

45. "Crime and Corporate Organization," in R. K. Merton and others (Eds.), *Reader in Bureaucracy* (New York: Free Press, 1952), p. 419.

46. H. H. Gerth and C. W. Mills (Eds.), *From Max Weber* (New York: Oxford University Press, 1946), p. 71.

47. "The process amounts in some situations to the capture of government. However, it is not 'rule' as this is normally conceived; it is a fragmentation of rule and the conquest of pieces of governmental authority by different groups." G. McConnell, *Private Power and American Democracy* (New York: Knopf, 1966), p. 7.

48. H. Wilensky, *Organizational Intelligence* (New York: Basic Books, 1967), pp. 133ff.

49. "Technology and the Intellectuals," *New York Review of Books*, July 31, 1969.

50. D. Whitehead, *The Dow Story* (New York: McGraw-Hill, 1968), p. 264, quoted in G. Wald, "Corporate Responsibility for War Crimes," *New York Review of Books*, July 2, 1970. Wald argues that if the individual soldier must accept responsibility for his role in a war crime, even though he has been ordered to commit these acts, the industrial concern manufacturing napalm or other genocidal agents should likewise be made to accept responsibility.

51. M. Orne, "On the Social Psychology of the Psychological Experiment," *American Psychologist*, 1962, *17*; for the Milgram ex-

periments see *Human Relations,* 1965, *18* (1), and R. Crawshaw, *Medical Opinion and Research, 3* (1).

52. *Man and Society in the Age of Reconstruction* (New York: Harcourt Brace Jovanovich, 1950), p. 58.

53. *White Collar* (New York: Oxford University Press, 1956), p. 56.

54. *Loc. cit.* McDermott observed widespread fantasizing among GIs in Vietnam and concluded that fantasizing is the only way to prevent the atrophying of intellectual capacities in men to whom nothing much has been explained, who simply received their daily orders. Seymour Hersh writes that the belief that mines and booby traps were often placed by women and children was prevalent among GIs in Vietnam, yet no one in Charlie Company (the soldiers involved in My Lai) was ever able to cite an act of terror by a child or a woman.

55. Not that a weakened sense of social responsibility need imply alienation in this sense—as witness the statistical revelations of E. H. Sutherland pertaining to the extent of middle-class crime in America. *White Collar Crime* (New York: Dryden, 1949).

56. "The Machiavellis Among Us," *Psychology Today,* 1970, *4* (6).

57. *Essays on the Sociology of Culture* (London: Routledge and Kegan Paul, 1956), p. 214.

58. "Society," *Salmagundi,* 1969 (10–11). "Almost everyone knows from his own personal experience that his social existence can scarcely be said to have resulted from his own personal initiative; rather he has had to search for gaps, 'openings,' jobs from which to make a living, irrespective of what seem to him his own human possibilities or talents, should he indeed still have any kind of vague inkling of the latter."

59. There is an important exception here, and that relates to consumer behavior, where the market has far less interest in rational behavior.

60. See his discussion of the technological ego in *The Uncommitted* (New York: Harcourt Brace Jovanovich, 1965), pp. 354ff.

61. Gerth and Mills, *op. cit.,* pp. 215f.

62. White, *op. cit.,* p. 135. White intends no radical critique along the lines of Herbert Marcuse's *Eros and Civilization;* he continues with the remark that the orgastic model "will never do for the serious, stable, lasting concerns of human life, the realm that I am trying to designate as work. This is the sphere in which the ego must always keep a firm hand on the helm." We may wonder whether creativity, sex, and a playful relation to the environment are not more fundamental to what it means to be human than the statement implies. White, in his emphasis on competence and mastery, provides a corrective to the autocentric and closed-system psycho-

logical models, but he does not develop a conceptual frame that does justice to the implications of his theory.

63. *Op. cit.,* p. 73.

64. *Stratagems and Spoils* (New York: Schocken, 1969), p. 187; see also M. Crozier, *The Bureaucratic Phenomenon* (Chicago: University of Chicago Press, 1967).

65. See G. Seldes, "Public Entertainment and the Subversion of Ethical Standards," *The Annals,* 1966, *363.* Those "love it or leave it" (the flag or the country) prescriptions that confront us increasingly are a product of the same mentality as that of the television producer who answers his critics with "If they don't like it, they can turn it off." This is the denial of aspiration, of the hope of the true patriot that his fellow citizens are capable of greater justice, of greater spiritual development. It is, rather, the voice of tyranny.

66. "It is the very essence of violence to think of man as a machine. The act of violence is made possible by assuming that man *is* a machine. Machines do not show pain or dream or smile or laugh." Means, *op. cit.,* p. 155. Means points out that in the animated cartoon the viewer more often than not is treated to a series of violent acts which never seem to hurt. The same could be said for the old slapstick movies.

67. See the discussion in Parsons, "The Link Between Character and Society," pp. 199ff.

68. G. Grant, *Technology and Empire* (Toronto: Anansi, 1969), p. 119.

69. Deutsch, *op. cit.,* p. 111.

70. Quoted in C. W. Mills, "On Knowledge and Power," in *Dissent,* 1955, 2 (3).

71. *Eclipse of God* (New York: Harper and Row, 1957), p. 35. See also C. S. Lewis, *Surprised by Joy* (New York: Harcourt Brace Jovanovich, 1955), pp. 218f.

72. G. Simmel, "The Stranger," in K. Wolff (Ed.), *The Sociology of Georg Simmel* (New York: Free Press, 1950), pp. 402ff.

73. *The Invisible Religion* (New York: Crowell Collier and Macmillan, 1967), p. 47.

74. *Collected Papers,* Vol. 2 (The Hague: Nijhoff, 1964), p. 254. Men are sometimes willing to identify their own personalities with a particular character trait, but they do this on their own terms, acknowledging the trait as the organizing element in their own characters. Problematic, from the moral point of view, is the situation where the typification is imposed and the integrity of the personality is broken by identifying the whole with the particular.

75. Quoted in R. Bendix, "Sociology and the Distrust of Reason," *American Sociological Review,* 1970, *35* (5). This essay traces the change in esthetic sensibility alluded to here.

76. *Phenomenological Psychology* (New York: Basic Books, 1966), p. ix.
77. For a discussion of abstraction and attention, see D. E. Berlyne, *Structure and Direction in Thinking* (New York: Wiley, 1965), pp. 43ff.
78. "The two senses of 'concrete' and 'abstract' spring from different, even opposite, points of view: in the first, in which the particular is called concrete and the universal abstract, we start from the assumption that reality is a multiplicity of given entities to be ordered in classes and subclasses; in the second, we assume the unity of a context whose constituent elements are 'grown together' and can subsist only together and with respect to one another, not alone—and by the way not even in thought." Riezler, *op. cit.*, p. 321.
79. S. K. Langer, *Mind: An Essay of Human Feeling*, Vol. 1 (Baltimore: Johns Hopkins University Press, 1967), pp. 59, 68f.
80. *Op. cit.*, p. 171.
81. "The Social Role of Intellectuals," *Politics*, 1944, *1* (3).
82. "The New Man: 'The Compleat Soldier,'" *Saturday Review*, February 14, 1970.
83. Quoted in *Playboy*, August 1968.
84. (New York: Knopf, 1950), pp. 120f.
85. *Orthodoxy* (London, 1908), p. 19.
86. L. Frey-Rohn, "Evil from the Psychological Point of View," in The Curatorium of the C. G. Jung Institute (Ed.), *Evil* (Evanston, Ill.: Northwestern University Press, 1967).
87. K. Schmid, "Aspects of Evil in the Creative," in Jung Institute, *op. cit.*, p. 250. See also P. Tillich, *Love, Power, and Justice* (New York: Oxford University Press, 1954), pp. 67ff.

CHAPTER 14: *Justification and Rebellion*

1. *John Brown* (New York: International, 1962), pp. 339–340.
2. (Middletown, Conn.: Wesleyan University Press, 1969).
3. *Life and Times of Frederick Douglass, Written by Himself* (New York: Crowell Collier and Macmillan, 1962), pp. 131–132.
4. *Ibid.*, p. 133.
5. (London: Sidgwick, Jackson, Gibbs and Phillips, 1963), p. 12.
6. Quoted in Hallie, *op. cit.*, p. 104.
7. *Lectures on Ethics* (New York: Harper and Row, 1963), p. 137.
8. Douglass, *op. cit.*, p. 145.
9. *Ibid.*, pp. 147–148.
10. *Ibid.*

11. L. Hanke, *The Spanish Struggle for Justice in the Conquest of America* (Boston: Little, Brown, 1965), p. 32.
12. *Op. cit.*, pp. 79–87.
13. *Ibid.*, pp. 50–57.
14. *Ibid.*, pp. 155, 84–102.
15. *Crisis in Black and White* (New York: Random House, 1964), pp. 9–10.
16. *Op. cit.*
17. *Op. cit.*, p. 86.
18. P. S. Foner (Ed.), *The Life and Writings of Frederick Douglass*, Vol. 2 (New York: International, 1950), pp. 571–572.
19. *The Mind of the South* (New York: Knopf, 1941), p. 84.
20. *Op. cit.*, p. 158.
21. "The 'Black Legend' of Spanish Cruelty," in W. E. Washburn (Ed.), *The Indian and the White Man* (Garden City, N.Y.: Doubleday, 1964).

CHAPTER 15: *Resisting Institutional Evil from Within*

1. For a rich discussion of cooptation and revolt in Japanese relocation centers, see D. S. Thomas and R. S. Nishimoto, *The Spoilage* (Berkeley and Los Angeles: University of California Press, 1946); D. S. Thomas, *The Salvage* (Berkeley and Los Angeles: University of California Press, 1952); L. Broom and J. I. Kitsuse, *The Managed Casualty: The Japanese-American Family in World War II*, University of California Publications in Culture and Society, Vol. 6 (Berkeley and Los Angeles: University of California Press, 1956).
2. S. Carmichael and C. V. Hamilton, *Black Power: The Politics of Liberation in America* (New York: Vantage, 1967) ; R. F. Williams, *Negroes with Guns* (New York: Marzani and Munsell, 1962).
3. See, for example, D. Clemmer, *The Prison Community* (New York: Holt, Rinehart, and Winston, 1958); D. R. Cressey (Ed.), *The Prison: Studies in Institutional Organization and Change* (New York: Holt, Rinehart, and Winston, 1961), see especially two articles by R. McCleery, "The Governmental Process and Informal Social Control," pp. 149–188, and "Authoritarianism and the Belief System of Incorrigibles," pp. 260–308; R. A. Cloward and others, *Theoretical Studies in Social Organization of the Prison* (New York: Social Science Research Council, 1960); E. Kinkead, *In Every War but One* (New York: Norton, 1959); J. Segal, "Correlates of Collaboration and Resistance Behavior Among U.S. Army POW's in Korea," *Journal of Social Issues*, 1957, *13* (3), 31–40; A. D. Biderman, "Communist Indoctrination Attempts," *Social*

Problems, 1959, *6*, 304–313; R. K. Merton, "Role of the Intellectual in Public Bureaucracy," in R. K. Merton (Ed.), *Social Theory and Social Structure* (New York: Free Press, 1957), pp. 207–224; A. Downs, *Inside Bureaucracy* (Boston: Little, Brown, 1967); V. Thompson, *Bureaucracy and Innovation* (University, Ala.: University of Alabama Press, 1969); W. R. Scott, "Professional Employees in a Bureaucratic Structure: Social Work," in A. Etzioni (Ed.), *The Semi-Professions and Their Organization* (New York: Free Press, 1969), pp. 82–140; G. Stewart, *The Year of the Oath* (Garden City, N.Y.: Doubleday, 1950); K. Keniston, *Young Radicals: Notes on Committed Youth* (New York: Harcourt Brace Jovanovich, 1968) ; D. M. Heckman, *World Views of Students Who Take Risks for Ethical Convictions*, doctoral dissertation, Graduate Theological Union, 1970; International Conferences on the History of the Resistance Movement, First Liege, 1958, *European Resistance Movement, 1939–1945* (New York: Pergamon, 1960); B. Ehrlich, *Resistance: France 1940–1945* (New York: New American Library, 1965).

4. See C. Reich, "Midnight Welfare Searches and the Social Security Act," *Yale Law Journal*, 1963, *72*, 1347–1359; E. V. Sparer, "The New Public Law: The Relationship of the State Administration to the Legal Problems of the Poor," paper presented at the Conference on the Extension of Legal Services to the Poor, sponsored by the U. S. Department of Health, Education, and Welfare, Washington, D.C., November 1964.

5. S. L. A. Marshall, *Men Against Fire: The Problem of Battle Command in Future War* (New York: Morrow, 1947), pp. 50–56.

6. See *San Francisco Chronicle*, July 20, 1970, p. 12; *San Francisco Chronicle*, June 26, 1970, p. 1; D. Lang, *Casualties of War* (New York: McGraw-Hill, 1969) ; and S. M. Hersh, "My Lai 4: A Report on the Massacre and Its Aftermath," *Harpers*, 1970, *240*, 53–84.

7. For an appropriate definition of charisma, see A. Etzioni, *A Comparative Analysis of Complex Organization* (New York: Free Press, 1966), p. 203.

8. See *Talking Union*, Keynote Recordings, Album No. 106, The Almanac Singers.

9. "Congress of Industrial Organizations (C.I.O.)," in *Collier's Encyclopedia*, Vol. 7 (New York: Crowell Collier and Macmillan, 1969), pp. 158–159.

10. On this point, see C. Bay, "Political and Apolitical Students: Facts in Search of a Theory," *Journal of Social Issues*, 1967, *23*, 76–91, especially p. 90.

11. See R. K. Merton, *Social Theory and Social Structure* (New York: Free Press, 1957), pp. 255–386.

12. I. Rosow, "Forms and Functions of Adult Socialization," *Social Forces,* 1965, *44,* 35–45.

13. E. Heimler, "Children of Auschwitz," in G. Mikes (Ed.), *Prison: A Symposium* (London: Routledge and Kegan Paul, 1963), pp. 19–20.

14. See J. Saar, "You Can't Just Hand Out Orders: A Company Commander in Vietnam Confronts the New-Style Draftees," *Life,* October 23, 1970, *69,* 30–37.

15. See P. Selznick, *The Organization Weapon: A Study of Bolshevik Strategy and Tactics* (New York: Free Press, 1960), pp. 25–28, 171.

16. Thoreau provides an engaging description of freedom of spirit in his essay on civil disobedience. *Walden and Selected Essays* (Chicago: Packard, 1947), p. 408.

17. C. Franklin, "Hospital Sentence," in Mikes *op. cit.,* pp. 182–183..

18. B. Bettelheim, "Individual and Mass Behavior in Extreme Situations," in T. M. Newcomb and E. L. Hartley (Eds.), *Readings in Social Psychology* (New York: Holt, Rinehart, and Winston, 1947), pp. 628–638.

19. E. Heimler, *op. cit.,* pp. 19–20.

20. N. Adler, "The Antinomian Personality: The Hippie Character Type," *Psychiatry,* 1968, *31,* 325–338, especially, p. 330.

21. A. Bauer, "Attempted Purge of Paul Baran," *Chaparral,* 1969, *70,* 7.

22. See E. V. Sparer, "The Role of the Welfare Client's Lawyer," *UCLA Law Review,* 1965, *12,* 361–380; J. E. Carlin and J. Howard, "Legal Representation and Class Justice," *UCLA Law Review,* 1965, *12,* 381–437; I. R. Kaufman, "In Defense of the Advocate," *UCLA Law Review,* 1965, *12,* 351–360.

23. J. Hasek, *The Good Soldier Schweik* (New York: Frederick Ungar, 1962); L. Hughes, *Simple Stakes a Claim* (New York: Holt, Rinehart, and Winston, 1957); L. Hughes, *The Best of Simple* (New York: Hill and Wang, 1961); L. Hughes, *Simple's Uncle Sam* (New York: Hill and Wang, 1965).

24. See, for example, P. M. Blau, "Organizations. I. Theories of Organization," in D. L. Sills (Ed.), *International Encyclopedia of the Social Sciences* (New York: Macmillan, 1968), p. 301.

25. See "How to Keep Order Without Killing," *Time,* May 25, 1970, *95,* 25–26; *Rights in Conflict: The Violent Confrontation of Demonstrators and Police in the Parks and Streets of Chicago During the Week of the Democratic National Convention of 1968,* a report submitted by D. Walker, director of the Chicago Study Team, to the National Commission on the Causes and Prevention of Violence (New York: Bantam, 1968), p. 1; *Report of the National Advisory Commission on Civil Disorders,* O. Kerner, chairman (New York: Bantam, 1968), p. 329.

26. On ritualistic conformity, see R. K. Merton, "Bureaucratic Structure and Personality," in *Social Theory and Social Structure* (New York: Free Press, 1957), pp. 195–206.

27. See J. Ten Broek, "California's Dual System of Family Law: Its Origin, Development and Present Status," Part 3, *Stanford Law Review*, 1965, *17*, 615–616.

28. C. Cohen, "The Ethics of Civil Disobedience," *The Nation*, 1964, *198*, 257–262; C. Cohen, "The Fruits of Protest: Law, Speech and Disobedience," *The Nation*, 1966, *202*, 357–362; R. A. Wasserstrom, "The Obligation to Obey the Law," *UCLA Law Review*, 1963, *10*, 780–807, 791n.

29. J. Howard, "The Provocation of Violence: A Civil Rights Tactic?" *Dissent*, January–February 1966, *13*, 94–99.

30. "Behind the Selma March," *Saturday Review*, April 3, 1965, *48*, 16.

31. M. L. King, Jr., "Let Justice Roll Down," *The Nation*, March 15, 1965, *200*, 270.

32. J. Howard, *op. cit.;* R. Adler, "Letter from Selma," *The New Yorker*, April 19, 1965, *41*, 138.

33. See, illustratively, G. A. Lundberg, *Can Science Save Us?* (New York: Longmans, Green, 1961), p. 33; G. A. Lundberg, "Science, Scientists, and Values," *Social Forces*, 1952, *30*, 373–379; R. S. Lynd, *Knowledge for What* (New York: Grove, 1964); R. Jungk, *Brighter Than a Thousand Suns: A Personal History of the Atomic Scientists* (New York: Harcourt Brace Jovanovich, 1958), especially pp. 221–238; D. Easton, "The New Revolution in Political Science," *American Political Science Review*, 1969, *63*, 1051–1061; "Introduction," in T. Roszak (Ed.), *The Dissenting Academy* (New York: Random House, 1968); R. H. Somers, "On Problem-Finding in the Social Sciences: A Concept of Active Social Science," *Berkeley Journal of Sociology*, 1970, *15*.

34. *San Francisco Chronicle*, June 20, 1970, p. 14.

35. Lundberg, *op. cit.*

36. R. Michels, *Political Parties: A Sociological Study of the Oligarchical Tendencies of Modern Democracy* (New York: Hearst's International Library, 1915).

CHAPTER 16: *Avoiding Pathologies of Defense*

1. H. Selye, *The Stress of Life* (New York: McGraw-Hill, 1956). See also D. Bakan, *Disease, Pain and Sacrifice* (Chicago: University of Chicago Press, 1968), pp. 19–31.

2. H. Lasswell, "The Garrison State," *American Journal of Sociology,* 1941, *46,* 455–68; and "The Garrison-State Hypothesis Today," in S. P. Huntington (Ed.), *Changing Patterns of Military Politics* (New York: Free Press, 1962), pp. 51–70.
3. Gallup Poll, reported in *San Francisco Chronicle,* September 25, 1970.
4. K. Keniston, *Young Radicals: Notes on Committed Youth* (New York: Harcourt Brace Jovanovich, 1968), p. 248.
5. A photograph of this scene appears in J. H. Skolnick, *The Politics of Protest* (New York: Ballantine, 1969), after p. 196.
6. R. Harris, *The Fear of Crime* (New York: Praeger, 1969).
7. E. C. Hughes, "Good People and Dirty Work," *Social Problems,* 1962, *10,* 3–11.
8. N. Cohn, *Warrant for Genocide* (New York: Harper and Row, 1967), p. 258.
9. D. Walker, *Rights in Conflict* (New York: Signet, 1968).
10. J. K. Galbraith, "Who Needs the Democrats?" *Harper's,* July 1970, see especially pp. 57–61.
11. A. I. Wascow, *From Race Riot to Sit-In* (Garden City, N.Y.: Doubleday, 1966).
12. National Commission on the Causes and Prevention of Violence, *To Establish Justice, To Insure Domestic Tranquility* (New York: Bantam, 1970); all quotations appear in the Introduction.
13. For an analysis of this general problem, see N. Sanford, "Is the Concept of Prevention Necessary or Useful?" in S. Golann and C. Eisdorfer (Eds.), *Handbook of Community Psychology* (Washington, D.C.: American Psychological Association, 1970).
14. See Chapter Ten in this volume.
15. E. H. Erikson, *Gandhi's Truth* (New York: Norton, 1969), p. 433.
16. See S. Melman, *Pentagon Capitalism: The Political Economy of War* (New York: McGraw-Hill, 1970).
17. For a brief analysis which relates technological development and social inventions, though with a rather narrow view of the latter, see J. Platt, "What We Must Do," *Science,* November 28, 1969.

CHAPTER 17: *Going Beyond Prevention*

1. M. Jahoda, *Current Concepts of Positive Mental Health* (New York: Basic Books, 1958); N. Sanford, "The Findings of the Commission on Psychology," *Annals of the New York Academy of Science,* 1955, *63,* 341–364; K. Menninger (with M. Mayman and

P. Pruyser), *The Vital Balance: The Life Process in Mental Health and Illness* (New York: Viking Press, 1963); N. Sanford, *Self and Society* (New York, Atherton, 1966).

2. T. Szasz, *The Myth of Mental Illness: Foundations for a Theory of Personal Conduct* (New York: Hoeber-Harper, 1961); E. Becker, *The Revolution in Psychiatry* (New York: Free Press, 1964).

3. *Op. cit.*

4. T. Parsons, "Some Primary Sources and Patterns of Aggression in the Social Structure of the Western World," *Psychiatry*, 1947, *10*, 167–181; S. Milgram, "Some Conditions of Obedience and Disobedience to Authority," *Human Relations*, 1965, *18*, 57–75.

5. *The Algiers Motel Incident* (New York: Bantam, 1968), especially pp. 75–76, 79, 107–108.

6. E. H. Erikson, *Childhood and Society* (rev. ed.) (New York: Norton, 1964); R. W. White, *Lives in Progress* (New York: Dryden, 1952); A. H. Maslow, *Motivation and Personality* (New York: Harper and Row, 1954); F. Barron, "What Is Psychological Health," *California Monthly*, 1957, *68*, 22–25; Jahoda, *op. cit.*; G. W. Allport, *Pattern and Growth in Personality* (New York: Holt, Rinehart, and Winston, 1961).

7. T. W. Adorno, E. Frenkel-Brunswik, D. J. Levinson, and N. Sanford, *The Authoritarian Personality* (New York: Harper and Row, 1950), p. 975.

8. *Ibid.*, p. 974.

9. W. L. Smith, "Cleveland's Experiment in Mutual Respect," in The Danforth Foundation and The Ford Foundation, *The School and the Democratic Environment* (New York: Columbia University Press, 1970), pp. 83–93.

10. "Therapeutic Explorations with Adolescent Drug Users," unpublished manuscript, Psychology Clinic, University of California, Berkeley, 1967.

11. Speech before the annual meeting of the Association of Governing Boards of Colleges and Universities, Washington, D.C., Nov. 6, 1969.

12. N. Sanford (Ed.), *The American College* (New York: Wiley, 1962); K. A. Feldman and T. M. Newcomb, *The Impact of College on Students* (San Francisco: Jossey-Bass, 1969); J. Axelrod, M. B. Freedman, W. R. Hatch, J. Katz, and N. Sanford, *Search for Relevance: The Campus in Crisis* (San Francisco: Jossey-Bass, 1969).

13. D. McHenry, "Institutions of Higher Education in the USA: Some Recent Developments," in W. R. Niblett (Ed.), *Higher Education: Demand and Response* (San Francisco: Jossey-Bass, 1970); J. N. Bell, "Campus Revolution, Johnston College Style," *THINK Magazine*, September–October 1970, 32–36.

CHAPTER 18: *Social Destructiveness as Disposition and as Act*

1. *Eichmann in Jerusalem* (New York: Viking, 1965). For an imaginative approach which overlaps with a number of our themes but which emphasizes the dangers of chaos rather than the substantive irrationality of certain kinds of "order," see P. G. Zimbardo, "The Human Choice: Individuation, Reason, and Order versus Deindividuation, Impulse, and Chaos," in *Nebraska Symposium on Motivation, 1969* (Lincoln, Neb.: University of Nebraska Press, 1969), pp. 237–307.
2. See I. Coser, "The Visibility of Evil," *Journal of Social Issues,* 1969, *25,* 101–109.
3. For a gifted analysis of the psychology of victims, see F. Fanon, *The Wretched of the Earth* (New York: Grove, 1966).
4. For a brief portrayal, see Z. Brzezinski, "America in the Technetronic Age," *Encounter,* January 1968, *30,* 16–26.
5. For a provocative analysis of this tradition, see J. Horton, "The Dehumanization of Anomie and Alienation: A Problem in the Ideology of Sociology," *British Journal of Sociology,* 1963, *14,* 283–300.
6. T. Adorno, E. Frenkel-Brunswik, D. Levinson, and N. Sanford, *The Authoritarian Personality* (New York: Harper and Row, 1950); E. Fromm (see note 9 below); R. Christie and F. L. Geis, *Studies in Machiavellianism* (New York: Academic, 1970); J. Loevinger, R. Wessler, C. Redmore, *Measuring Ego Development: Construction and Use of a Sentence Completion Test* (San Francisco: Jossey-Bass, 1970); L. Kohlberg, *Stages in the Development of Moral Thought and Action* (New York: Holt, Rinehart, and Winston, in press).
7. Although Newton Garver stretches the word *violence* to cover nonphysical acts of violation, such as violations of dignity, we hope to avoid confusion by using the word in its ordinary, narrower sense. For an analysis of violence in the extended sense, see his article, "What Violence Is," *Nation,* June 24, 1968, *206,* 819–822.
8. In particular, see E. Fromm, *The Heart of Man* (New York: Harper and Row, 1964), and *The Revolution of Hope* (1968). For a preliminary report of findings based on the use of a biophilia vs. necrophilia scale of a dozen items, see M. Maccoby, "Emotional Attitudes and the Future" (Washington, D.C.: Institute for Policy Studies, 1970). At The Wright Institute, Robert Duckles and others are now developing a more elaborate scale based on the same theory.

9. "Behavioral Study of Obedience," *Journal of Abnormal and Social Psychology,* 1963, *67,* 371–78; and "Some Conditions of Obedience and Disobedience to Authority," *Human Relations,* 1965, *18,* 57–75.

10. See "Violence and the Police," *American Journal of Sociology,* 1953, *59,* 34–41; and *The Police: A Sociological Study of Law, Custom, and Morality* (Cambridge, Mass.: MIT Press, 1970).

11. On the militancy of police, see J. H. Skolnick and associates, *The Politics of Protest* (New York: Ballantine, 1969), Chapter 7.

12. N. Sanford, "Research with Students as Action and Education," *American Psychologist,* 1969, *24,* 544–46; and on the more general question see "Whatever Happened to Action Research?" *Journal of Social Issues,* December 1970, *26.*

Bibliography

ADLER, N. "The Antinomian Personality: The Hippie Character Type." *Psychiatry*, 1968, *31*, 325–338.

ADLER, R. "Letter from Selma." *The New Yorker*, April 10, 1965, *41*, 121–122.

ADORNO, T. W. "Society." *Salmagundi*, 1969–1970 (10–11), 144–153.

ADORNO, T. W., FRENKEL-BRUNSWIK, E., LEVINSON, D. J., and SANFORD, N. *The Authoritarian Personality*. New York: Harper and Row, 1950.

ALLPORT, G. W. *Pattern and Growth in Personality*. New York: Holt, Rinehart, and Winston, 1961.

ALLPORT, G. W. and POSTMAN, L. *The Psychology of Rumor*. New York: Holt, Rinehart, and Winston, 1947.

ALMANAC SINGERS, *Talking Union*, Keynote Recordings, Album No. 106.

ARDREY, R. *African Genesis*. New York: Delta, 1961.

ARENDT, H. *Eichmann in Jerusalem: A Report on the Banality of Evil*. New York: Viking, 1965.

AXELROD, J., FREEDMAN, M. B., HATCH, W., KATZ, J., and SANFORD, N. *Search for Relevance: The Campus in Crisis*. San Francisco: Jossey-Bass, 1969.

BAILEY, F. G. *Stratagems and Spoils*. New York: Schocken, 1969.

BAKAN, D. *Disease, Pain, and Sacrifice*. Chicago: University of Chicago Press, 1968.

361

BALDWIN, J. *Nobody Knows My Name*. New York: Dell, 1963.

BARRON, F. "What Is Psychological Health." *California Monthly*, 1957, *68*, 22–25.

BARTH, F. "The System of Social Segregation in Swat, North Pakistan," pp. 113–146 in Leach, E. R. (Ed.).

BAUER, A. "Attempted Purge of Paul Baran." *Chaparral*, 1969, *70*, 7.

BAY, C. "Political and Apolitical Students: Facts in Search of a Theory." *Journal of Social Issues*, 1967, *23*, 76–91.

BECKER, E. *The Revolution in Psychiatry*. New York: Free Press, 1964.

BECKER, E. *Angel in Armor*. New York: Braziller, 1969.

BELL, J. N. "Campus Revolution, Johnston College Style." *THINK Magazine*, September–October 1970, 32–36.

BELLAH, R. N. "Civil Religion in America." *Daedalus*, Winter 1967, *96*, 1–21.

BELLAH, R. N. *Beyond Belief*. New York: Harper and Row, 1970.

BENDIX, R. "Tradition and Modernity Reconsidered." *Comparative Studies in Society and History*, 1966, *9*, 292–346.

BENDIX, R. "Sociology and the Distrust of Reason." *American Sociological Review*, 1970, *35* (5).

BERLYNE, D. E. *Structure and Direction in Thinking*. New York: Wiley, 1965.

BERLYNE, D. E. "Conflict and Arousal." *Scientific American*, 1966, *215*, 82–87.

BERREMAN, G. "Caste in India and the United States." *American Journal of Sociology*, 1960, *66*, 120–127.

BERRIGAN, D. "The New Man: The Compleat Soldier." *Saturday Review*, 1970, *53*, 31–34.

BETTELHEIM, B. "Individual and Mass Behavior in Extreme Situations," pp. 628–638 in Newcomb, T. M. and Hartley, E. L. (Eds.)

BETTELHEIM, B. *The Informed Heart: Autonomy in a Mass Age*. New York: Free Press, 1960.

BETTELHEIM, B. and JANOWITZ, M. *Social Change and Prejudice Including Dynamics of Prejudice*. New York: Free Press, 1964.

BIDERMAN, A. D. "Communist Indoctrination Attempts." *Social Problems*, 1959, *6*, 304–313.

BLAU, P. M. "Organizations. I. Theories of Organization," p. 301 in Sils, D. L. (Ed.).

BOURKE-WHITE, M. *Portrait of Myself*. New York: Simon and Schuster, 1963.

BOURNE, P. *Men, Stress, and Vietnam*. Boston: Little, Brown, 1970.

BOURNE, R. Essays in Resek, C. (Ed.).

BROOM, L. and KITSUSE, J. I. *The Managed Casualty: The Japanese-American Family in World War II*, University of California Publications in Culture and Society, Vol. 6. Berkeley and Los Angeles: University of California Press, 1956.

BROWN, R. *Social Psychology.* New York: Free Press, 1967.
BRZEZINSKI, Z. "America in the Technetronic Age." *Encounter,* 1968, *30,* 16–26.
BUBER, M. *Eclipse of God.* New York: Harper and Row, 1957.
BUCKLEY, W. F. JR. Column, *San Francisco Examiner,* December 4, 1969, p. 36.
BUSHNELL, J. "Student Culture at Vassar," in Sanford, N. (Ed.).
CAMUS, A. *The Plague.* New York: Knopf, 1950.
CAMUS, A. "Neither Victims Nor Executioners." *Liberation,* February 1960.
CARLIN, J. E. and HOWARD, J. "Legal Representation and Class Justice." *UCLA Law Review,* 1965, *12,* 381–437.
CARMICHAEL, S. and HAMILTON, C. V. *Black Power: The Politics of Liberation in America.* New York: Vintage, 1967.
CASH, W. J. *The Mind of the South.* New York: Knopf, 1941.
CHESTERTON, G. K. *Orthodoxy.* London, 1908
CHRISTIE, R. and GEIS, F. *Studies in Machiavellianism.* London and New York: Academic Press, 1970.
CHRISTIE, R. and JAHODA, M. (Eds.) *Studies in the Scope and Method of The Authoritarian Personality.* New York: Free Press, 1954.
CLEMMER, D. *The Prison Community.* New York: Holt, Rinehart, and Winston, 1958.
CLOWARD, R. A. and others. *Theoretical Studies in the Social Organization of the Prison.* New York: Social Science Research Council, 1960.
COHEN, C. "The Ethics of Civil Disobedience." *The Nation,* 1964, *198,* 257–262.
COHEN, C. "The Fruits of Protest." *The Nation,* 1966, *202,* 357–362.
COHN, N. *Warrant for Genocide.* New York: Harper and Row, 1967.
CONVERSE, P. E. and SCHUMAN, H. "Silent Majorities and the Vietnam War." *Scientific American,* 1970, *222,* 17–25.
COOPER, D. (Ed.) *The Dialectics of Liberation.* Harmondsworth, England: Penguin, 1968.
COSER, I. "The Visibility of Evil." *Journal of Social Issues,* 1969, *25,* 101–109.
CRESSEY, D. R. (Ed.) *The Prison: Studies in Institutional Organization and Change.* New York: Holt, Rinehart, and Winston, 1961.
CROZIER, M. *The Bureaucratic Phenomenon.* Chicago: University of Chicago Press, 1967.
CRUSE, H. *The Crisis of the Negro Intellectual.* New York: Morrow, 1967.
CURATORIUM OF THE C. G. JUNG INSTITUTE (Ed.) *Evil.* Evanston, Ill.: Northwestern University Press, 1967.
DE GRAZIA, S. *The Political Community.* Chicago: University of Chicago Press, 1948.

DE LAS CASAS, B. "The 'Black Legend' of Spanish Cruelty," in Washburn, W. E. (Ed.).

DE REUCK, A. and KNIGHT, J. (Eds.) *Conflict in Society.* London: Churchill, 1966.

DESMOND, M. *The Naked Ape.* New York: Dell, 1969.

DE VOS, G. and WAGATSUMA, H. *Japan's Invisible Race: Caste in Culture and Personality.* Berkeley and Los Angeles: University of California Press, 1966.

DOUGLASS, F. *Life and Times of Frederick Douglass, Written by Himself.* New York: Crowell Collier and Macmillan, 1962.

DOWNS, A. *Inside Bureaucracy.* Boston: Little, Brown, 1967.

DU BOIS, W. E. B. *John Brown.* New York: International Publishers, 1962.

DURKHEIM, E. *The Elementary Forms of the Religious Life.* New York: Free Press, 1947.

DURKHEIM, E. *The Division of Labor in Society.* New York: Free Press, 1960.

DYSON-HUDSON, N. "Structure and Infrastructure in Primitive Society: Lévi-Strauss and Radcliffe Brown," in Macksey, R. and Donato, E. (Eds.).

EASTON, D. "The New Revolution in Political Science." *American Political Science Review,* 1969, *63,* 1051–1061.

EHRLICH, B. *Resistance: France, 1940–1945.* New York: New American Library, 1965.

EMMERICH, H. Article in *San Francisco Examiner,* November 23, 1969.

ERIKSON, E. H. *Childhood and Society* (rev. ed.). New York: Norton, 1964.

ERIKSON, E. H. *Insight and Responsibility.* New York: Norton, 1964.

ERIKSON, E. H. *Gandhi's Truth.* New York: Norton, 1969.

ETZIONI, A. *A Comparative Analysis of Complex Organizations.* New York: Free Press, 1966.

ETZIONI, A. (Ed.) *The Semi-Professions and Their Organizations.* New York: Free Press, 1969.

FALK, R. "Songmy: War Crimes and Individual Responsibility: A Legal Memorandum." *Transaction,* 1970, *7,* 33–40.

FANON, F. *The Wretched of the Earth.* New York: Grove Press, 1966.

FELDMAN, K. A. and NEWCOMB, T. M. *The Impact of College on Students.* San Francisco: Jossey-Bass, 1969.

FENICHEL, O. *Psychoanalytic Theory of Neurosis.* New York: Norton, 1945.

FESTINGER, L. *The Theory of Cognitive Dissonance.* Palo Alto, Calif.: Stanford University Press, 1957.

FONER, P. S. (Ed.) *The Life and Writings of Frederick Douglass,* Vol. 2. New York: International, 1950.

FRANKLIN, C. "Hospital Sentence," in Mikes, G. (Ed.).

FRAZER, J. *The Golden Bough: A Study in Magic and Religion.* New York: Criterion, 1959.

FRENKEL-BRUNSWIK, E. "Further Explorations by a Contributor," in Christie, R. and Jahoda, M. (Eds.).

FREY-ROHN, L. "Evil from the Psychological Point of View," in Curatorium of the C. G. Jung Institute (Ed.).

FRIEDENBERG, E. "Motown Justice." *New York Review of Books,* August 1, 1968, pp. 24–28.

FROMM, E. *The Heart of Man: Its Genius for Good and Evil.* New York: Harper and Row, 1964.

FROMM, E. *The Revolution of Hope.* New York: Harper and Row, 1968.

GALBRAITH, J. K. "Who Needs the Democrats?" *Harper's,* 1970, pp. 43–62.

GARFINKEL, H. "Conditions of Successful Degradation Ceremonies." *American Journal of Sociology,* 1956, *61,* 420–424.

GARVER, N. "What Violence Is." *The Nation,* 1968, *206,* 819–822.

GERTH, H. H. and MILLS, C. W. (Eds.) *From Max Weber.* New York: Oxford University Press, 1946.

GOFFMAN, E. *The Presentation of Self in Everyday Life.* Garden City, N.Y.: Doubleday, 1959.

GOLANN, S. and EISDORFER, C. (Eds.) *Handbook of Community Psychology.* Washington, D.C.: American Psychological Association, 1970.

GRAHAM, H. D. and GURR, T. R. *Violence in America.* New York: Signet, 1969.

GRANT, G. *Technology and Empire.* Toronto: Anansi, 1969.

GREENSTEIN, F. *Personality and Politics.* Chicago: Markham, 1969.

GRIER, W. H. and COBBS, P. M. *Black Rage.* New York: Bantam, 1969.

HABERMAS, J. *Toward a Rational Society.* Boston: Beacon, 1970.

HAEBERLE, R. L. (photographer) "The Massacre at My Lai." *Life,* December 5, 1969, pp. 36–45.

HALLIE, P. *The Paradox of Cruelty.* Middletown, Conn.: Wesleyan University Press, 1969.

HAMMER, R. *One Morning in the War: The Tragedy at Son My.* New York: Coward-McCann, 1970.

HANKE, L. *The Spanish Struggle for Justice in the Conquest of America.* Boston: Little, Brown, 1965.

HARRIS, D. D., GOUGH, H. G. and MARTIN, W. E. "Children's Ethnic Attitudes: II: Relationship to Parental Beliefs Concerning Child Training." *Child Development,* 1950, *21,* 169–181.

HARRIS, R. *The Fear of Crime.* New York: Praeger, 1969.

HASEK, J. *The Good Soldier Schweik.* New York: Frederick Ungar, 1962.

HEBB, D. O. and THOMPSON, W. R. "The Social Significance of Animal Studies," pp. 729–774 in Lindzey, G. and Aronson, E. (Eds.).

HECKMAN, D. M. *World Views of Students Who Take Risks for Ethical Convictions,* doctoral dissertation, Graduate Theological Union, Berkeley, Calif., 1970.

HEIMLER, E. "Children of Auschwitz," in Mikes, G. (Ed.).

HERSEY, J. *The Algiers Motel Incident.* New York: Bantam, 1968.

HERSH, S. M. *My Lai 4: A Report on the Massacre and Its Aftermath.* New York: Random House, 1970.

HILBERG, R. *The Destruction of the European Jews.* Chicago: Quadrangle Books, 1961.

HOCART, A. H. *Caste—A Comparative Study.* London: Methuen, 1950.

HOOPES, T. *The Limits of Intervention.* New York: McKay, 1969.

HOPPE, A. "The Best Way to Kill People." *San Francisco Chronicle,* December 1, 1969, p. 41.

HORTON, J. "The Dehumanization of Anomie and Alienation: A Problem in the Ideology of Sociology." *British Journal of Sociology,* 1963, *14,* 283–300.

HOWARD, J. "The Provocation of Violence: A Civil Rights Tactic?" *Dissent,* January–February 1966, *13,* 94–99.

HUGHES, E. C. "Good People and Dirty Work." *Social Problems,* 1962, *10,* 3–11.

HUGHES, E. C., BECKER, H. and GEER, B. "Student Culture and Academic Effort," in Sanford, N. (Ed.), 1962.

HUGHES, L. *Simple Stakes a Claim.* New York: Holt, Rinehart, and Winston, 1957.

HUGHES, L. *The Best of Simple.* New York: Hill and Wang, 1961.

HUGHES, L. *Simple's Uncle Sam.* New York: Hill and Wang, 1965.

HUNTINGTON, S. P. (Ed.) *Changing Patterns of Military Politics.* New York: Free Press, 1962.

HUNTINGTON, S. P. "Bases of Accommodation." *Foreign Affairs,* 1968, *46,* 642–656.

INTERNATIONAL CONFERENCE ON THE HISTORY OF THE RESISTANCE MOVEMENT, FIRST LIEGE, 1958, *European Resistance Movement, 1939–1945.* New York: Pergamon, 1960.

ISAACS, H. *India's Ex-Untouchables.* New York: Day, 1965.

JACQUES, E. *The Changing Culture of a Factory.* New York: Dryden, 1952.

JAHODA, M. *Current Concepts of Positive Mental Health.* New York: Basic Books, 1958.

JANIS, I. L. *Victims of Groupthink: A Psychological Analysis of Foreign Policy Decisions and Fiascos.* New York: Harcourt Brace Jovanovich (in press).

JANOWITZ, M. "German Reactions to Nazi Atrocities." *American Journal of Sociology,* 1946, *52,* 141–146.

JONES, M. R. (Ed.) *Nebraska Symposium on Motivation.* Lincoln, Neb.: University of Nebraska Press, 1960.

JORDAN, W. D. *White over Black.* Chapel Hill, N.C.: University of North Carolina Press, 1968.

JUNGK, R. *Brighter Than a Thousand Suns: A Personal History of the Atomic Scientists.* New York: Harcourt Brace Jovanovich, 1958.

JUST, W. *Military Men.* New York: Knopf, 1970.

KAHNE, M. J. "Bureaucratic Structure and Impersonal Experience in Mental Hospitals." *Psychiatry,* 1959, *22,* 363–375.

KANT, I. *Lectures on Ethics.* New York: Harper and Row, 1963.

KARIEL, H. S. *Open Systems: Arenas for Political Action.* Itasca, Ill.: Peacock, 1969.

KAUFMAN, I. R. "In Defense of the Advocate." *UCLA Law Review,* 1965; *12,* 351–360.

KENISTON, K. *The Uncommitted.* New York: Harcourt Brace Jovanovich, 1965.

KENISTON, K. *Young Radicals.* New York: Harcourt Brace Jovanovich, 1968.

KERNER, O. *Rights in Conflict.* New York: Bantam, 1968.

KING, M. L., JR. "Let Justice Roll Down." *The Nation,* March 15, 1965, *200,* 270; and "Behind the Selma March." *Saturday Review,* 1965, *48,* 16.

KINKEAD, E. *In Every War but One.* New York: Norton, 1959.

KIRSCHT, J. P. and DILLEHAY, R. C. *Dimensions of Authoritarianism: A Review of Research and Theory.* Lexington, Ky.: University of Kentucky Press, 1967.

KLINEBERG, O. "Prejudice: The Concept," in *International Encyclopedia of the Social Sciences.* New York: Macmillan and Free Press, 1968.

KLUCKHOHN, C. *Navajo Witchcraft.* Boston: Beacon, 1962.

KOESTLER, A. "On Disbelieving Atrocities," in *The Yogi and the Commissar.* New York: Macmillan, 1945.

KOHLBERG, L. *Stages in the Development of Moral Thought and Action.* New York: Holt, Rinehart, and Winston (in press).

KOVEL, J. *White Racism: A Psychohistory.* New York: Pantheon, 1970.

KRASLOW, D. and LOORY, S. *The Secret Search for Peace in Vietnam.* New York: Vintage, 1968.

KROEBER, A. L. and PARSONS, T. "The Concepts of Culture and of Social System." *American Sociological Review,* 1958, *23,* 582–583.

LAING, R. D. *The Politics of Experience.* New York: Ballantine, 1967.

LAING, R. D. "The Obvious," in Cooper, D. (Ed.).

LANG, D. *Casualties of War.* New York: McGraw-Hill, 1969.

LANGER, S. K. *Mind: An Essay on Human Feeling,* Vol. 1. Baltimore: Johns Hopkins University Press, 1967.

LASSWELL, H. "The Garrison State." *American Journal of Sociology,* 1941, *46,* 455–468.

LASSWELL, H. "The Garrison State Hypothesis Today," in Huntington, S. P. (Ed.).

LEACH, E. R. (Ed.) *Aspects of Caste in South India, Ceylon, and Northwest Pakistan,* Cambridge Papers on Social Anthropology. London: Cambridge University Press, 1960.

LEEPER, R. W. "A Motivational Theory of Emotion to Replace 'Emotion as a Disorganized Response,'" in Pribram, K. H. (Ed.).

LELYVELD, J. "How Civilians Get Killed in Vietnam." *San Francisco Chronicle,* December 16, 1969, pp. 1, 26.

LEWIS, C. S. *Surprised by Joy.* New York: Harcourt Brace Jovanovich, 1955.

LIFTON, R. J. "Psychological Effects of the Atomic Bomb in Hiroshima; the Theme of Death." *Daedalus,* 1963, *92,* 462–497.

LIFTON, R. J. *Death in Life: Survivors of Hiroshima.* New York: Random House, 1967.

LINDZEY, G. and ARONSON, E. (Eds.) *The Handbook of Social Psychology* (2nd ed.). Reading, Mass.: Addison-Wesley, 1968.

LOEVINGER, J., WESSLER, R. and REDMORE, C. *Measuring Ego Development: Construction and Use of a Sentence Completion Test.* San Francisco: Jossey-Bass, 1970.

LOPREATO, J. "Authority Relations and Class Conflict." *Social Forces,* 1968, *47,* 70–79.

LORENZ, K. *Das Sogenannte Böse—Zur Naturgeschichte der Aggression.* Vienna: Dr. G. Borotha-Schoeler Verlag, 1963.

LORENZ, K. *On Aggression.* New York: Harcourt Brace Jovanovich, 1966.

LOWENTHAL, L. and GUTERMAN, N. *Prophets of Deceit.* New York: Harper and Row, 1949.

LUCKMANN, T. *The Invisible Religion.* New York: Crowell Collier and Macmillan, 1967.

LUNDBERG, F. A. "Science, Scientists, and Values." *Social Forces,* 1952, *30,* 373–379.

LUNDBERG, F. A. *Can Science Save Us?* New York: Longmans Green, 1961.

LYND, R. S. *Knowledge for What.* New York: Grove Press, 1964.

MC CLEERY, R. "The Governmental Process and Informal Social Control," and "Authoritarianism and the Belief System of Incorrigibles," pp. 149–188 and pp. 260–308, respectively, in Cressey, D. R. (Ed.).

MACCOBY, M. "Emotional Attitudes and the Future," unpublished paper written at Institute for Policy Studies, Washington, D.C., 1970.

MC CONNELL, G. *Private Power and American Democracy.* New York: Knopf, 1966.

MC DERMOTT, J. "Technology and the Intellectuals." *New York Review of Books,* July 31, 1969.

MC HENRY, D. "Institutions of Higher Education in the USA: Some Recent Developments," in Niblett, W. R. (Ed.).

MACKSEY, R. and DONATO, E. (Eds.) *The Languages of Criticism and the Sciences of Man.* Baltimore: Johns Hopkins University Press, 1970.

MALINOWSKI, B. *Magic, Science and Religion, and Other Essays.* New York: Free Press, 1948.

MANNHEIM, K. *Man and Society in the Age of Reconstruction.* New York: Harcourt Brace Jovanovich, 1950.

MANNHEIM, K. *Essays on the Sociology of Culture.* London: Routledge and Kegan, Paul, 1956.

MARCUSE, H. *Eros and Civilization.* Boston: Beacon Press, 1955.

MARSHALL, S. L. A. *Men Against Fire: The Problem of Battle Command in Future War.* New York: Morrow, 1947.

MARSHALL, T. H. *Class, Citizenship, and Social Development.* Garden City, N.Y.: Doubleday, 1965.

MASLOW, A. H. *Motivation and Personality.* New York: Harper and Row, 1954.

MAY, M. "Religion and Attitudes Toward Negroes," unpublished paper written at The Wright Institute, Berkeley, Calif., 1969.

MAYER, M. *They Thought They Were Free.* Chicago: University of Chicago Press, 1955.

MEANS, R. *The Ethical Imperative.* Garden City, N.Y.: Doubleday, 1970.

MELMAN, S. *Pentagon Capitalism: The Political Economy of War.* New York: McGraw-Hill, 1970.

MENNINGER, K., with MAYMAN, M. and PRUYSER, P. *The Vital Balance: The Life Process in Mental Health and Illness.* New York: Viking Press, 1963.

MERLEAU-PONTY, M. *Phénoménologie de la Perception.* Paris: Librarie Gallimard, 1945.

MERLEAU-PONTY, M. *The Structure of Behavior.* Boston: Beacon Press, 1967.

MERTON, R. K. *Social Theory and Social Structure.* New York: Free Press, 1968.

MERTON, R. K. and others (Eds.) *Reader in Bureaucracy.* New York: Free Press, 1952.

MICHAELSON, R. "Americanization: Sacred or Profane Phenomenon?" unpublished paper, prepared for the American Academy of Religion, October 25, 1969.

MICHELS, R. *Political Parties: A Sociological Study of the Oligarchical Tendencies of Modern Democracy.* New York: Hearst's International Library, 1915.

MIKES, G. (Ed.) *Prison: A Symposium*. London: Routledge and Kegan, Paul, 1963.

MILGRAM, S. "Behavioral Study of Obedience." *Journal of Abnormal and Social Psychology*, 1963, *67*, 371–378.

MILGRAM, S. "Some Conditions of Obedience and Disobedience to Authority," *Human Relations*, 1965, *18*, 57–75.

MILGRAM, S. "The Experience of Living in Cities." *Science*, 1970, *167*, 1461–1468.

MILLS, C. W. "The Social Role of Intellectuals." *Politics*, 1944, *1* (3).

MILLS, C. W. "On Knowledge and Power." *Dissent*, 1955, *2* (3).

MILLS, C. W. *White Collar*. New York: Oxford University Press, 1956.

MILLS, C. W. (Ed.) *Images of Man*. New York: Braziller, 1960.

MORRIS, D. *The Naked Ape*. New York: Dell, 1969.

MOSKOWITZ, M. "The Germans and the Jews: Postwar Report." *Commentary*, July 1946.

MUMFORD, L. *The Pentagon of Power*. New York: Harcourt Brace Jovanovich, 1970.

NAGLE, S. F. "Caste and Government in Primitive Society." *Journal of the Anthropological Society of Bombay*, 1954, *8*, 9–22.

NATIONAL COMMISSION ON THE CAUSES AND PREVENTION OF VIOLENCE. *To Establish Justice, To Insure Domestic Tranquility*. New York: Bantam, 1970.

NEWCOMB, T. M. and HARTLEY, E. L. (Eds.) *Readings in Social Psychology*. New York: Holt, Rinehart, and Winston, 1947.

NIBLETT, W. R. (Ed.) *Higher Education: Demand and Response*. San Francisco: Jossey-Bass, 1970.

ORNE, M. "On the Social Psychology of the Psychological Experiment." *American Psychologist*, 1962, *17*, 776–783.

ORTEGA, G. Speech before the annual meeting of the Association of Governing Boards of Colleges and Universities, Washington, D.C., November 1969.

ORWELL, G. "How the Poor Die," in *Shooting an Elephant*. New York: Harcourt Brace Jovanovich, 1945.

PARADISE, S. "The Vandal Ideology." *The Nation*, December 29, 1969.

PARSONS, T. "Certain Primary Sources and Patterns of Aggression in the Social Structure of the Western World." *Psychiatry*, 1947, *10*, 167–181.

PARSONS, T. *The Structure of Social Action*. New York: Free Press, 1949.

PARSONS, T. "The Superego and the Theory of Social Systems," in *Working Papers in the Theory of Action*. New York: Free Press, 1953.

PARSONS, T. *Essays in Sociological Theory*. New York: Free Press, 1954.

PARSONS, T. and BALES, R. *Family Socialization and Interaction Process*. New York: Free Press, 1955.

PETERS, R. S. "Emotion, Passivity and the Place of Freud's Theory in Psychology," in Pribram, K. H. (Ed.).

PLATT, J. "What We Must Do." *Science,* 1969, *166,* 1115–1121.

PLUTCHIK, R. *The Emotions.* New York: Random House, 1962.

POLNER, M. "Vietnam War Stories." *Transaction,* 1968, *6,* 8–20.

PRIBRAM, K. H. (Ed.) *Brain and Behavior.* Vol. 4: *Adaptation.* Harmondsworth, England: Penguin, 1969.

REICH, C. "Midnight Welfare Searches and the Social Security Act." *Yale Law Journal,* 1963, 72, 1347–1359.

REICH, W. *The Mass Psychology of Fascism.* New York: Orgone Institute Press, 1946.

RESEK, C. (Ed.) *War and the Intellectuals.* New York: Harper and Row, 1964.

RIESMAN, D., with GLAZER, N. and DENNEY, R. *The Lonely Crowd: A Study of the Changing American Character.* New Haven: Yale University Press, 1950.

RIEZLER, K. *Man: Mutable and Immutable.* Chicago: Regnery, 1950.

ROGAT, Y. *The Eichmann Trial and the Rule of Law.* Santa Barbara, Calif.: Center for the Study of Democratic Institutions, 1961.

ROSENTHAL, A. M. *Thirty-Eight Witnesses.* New York: McGraw-Hill, 1964.

ROSOW, I. "Forms and Functions of Adult Socialization." *Social Forces,* 1965, *44,* 35–45.

ROSZAK, T. (Ed.) *The Dissenting Academy.* New York: Random House, 1968.

SAAR, J. "You Can't Just Hand Out Orders: A Company Commander in Vietnam Confronts the New-Style Draftees." *Life,* 1970, *69,* 30–37.

SANFORD, N. "The Findings of the Commission on Psychology." *Annals of the New York Academy of Science,* 1955, *63,* 341–364.

SANFORD, N. (Ed.) *The American College.* New York: Wiley, 1962.

SANFORD, N. *Self and Society.* New York: Atherton, 1966.

SANFORD, N. "Research with Students as Action and Education." *American Psychologist,* 1969, *24,* 544–546.

SANFORD, N. "Whatever Happened to Action Research?" *Journal of Social Issues,* 1970, *26.*

SANFORD, N. "Is the Concept of Prevention Necessary or Useful?" in Golann, S. and Eisdorfer, C. (Eds.).

SARTRE, J.-P. *The Emotions.* New York: Philosophical Library, 1948.

SARTRE, J.-P. *On Genocide.* Boston: Beacon Press, 1968.

SCHACHTEL, E. *Metamorphosis.* New York: Basic Books, 1959.

SCHAFFNER, B. *Fatherland.* New York: Columbia University Press, 1948.

SCHELL, J. *The Military Half.* New York: Vintage, 1968.

SCHLESINGER, A. M., JR. *The Vital Center.* Boston: Houghton, Mifflin, 1949.

SCHMID, K. "Aspects of Evil in the Creative," in Curatorium of the
C. G. Jung Institute (Ed.).

SCHUTZ, A. *Collected Papers*, Vol. 2. The Hague: Nijhoff, 1964.

SCHWEBEL, M. (Ed.) *Behavioral Science and Human Survival*. Palo Alto,
Calif.: Science and Behavior Books, 1965.

SCOTT, W. R. "Professional Employees in a Bureaucratic Structure:
Social Work," in Etzioni, A. (Ed.).

SEGAL, J. "Correlates of Collaboration and Resistance Behavior Among
U.S. Army POW's in Korea." *Journal of Social Issues*, 1957, *13*,
31–40.

SELDES, G. "Public Entertainment and the Subversion of Ethical Standards." *The Annals*, 1966, *363*, 87–94.

SELYE, H. *The Stress of Life*. New York: McGraw-Hill, 1965.

SELZNICK, G. and STEINBERG, P. *The Tenacity of Prejudice*. New York:
Harper and Row, 1969.

SELZNICK, P. *The Organizational Weapon: A Study of Bolshevik Strategy and Tactics*. New York: Free Press, 1960.

SHAPIRO, K. "Introduction," in Miller, H. *Tropic of Cancer*. New York:
Grove Press, 1961.

SHERRINGTON, C. S. *The Integrative Action of the Nervous System*. New
Haven: Yale University Press, 1911.

SILBERMAN, C. *Crisis in Black and White*. New York: Random House,
1964.

SILLS, D. L. (Ed.) *International Encyclopedia of the Social Sciences*. New
York: Macmillan, 1968.

SIMMEL, G. "The Stranger," in Wolff, K. (Ed.).

SIMMEL, G. "The Metropolis and Mental Life," in Mills, C. W. (Ed.).

SKOLNICK, J. *Justice Without Trial*. New York: Wiley, 1966.

SKOLNICK, J. *The Politics of Protest*. New York: Ballantine, 1969.

SLATER, P. *The Pursuit of Loneliness*. Boston: Beacon Press, 1970.

SMELSER, N. J. *The Sociology of Economic Life*. Englewood Cliffs, N.J.:
Prentice-Hall, 1963.

SMITH, W. L. "Cleveland's Experiment in Mutual Respect," in The
Danforth Foundation and the Ford Foundation, *The School
and the Democratic Environment*. New York: Columbia University Press, 1970.

SOMERS, R. H. "On Problem-Finding in the Social Sciences: A Concept
of Active Social Science." *Berkeley Journal of Sociology*, 1970,
15.

SOSKIN, S. and KORCHIN, S. "Therapeutic Explorations with Adolescent
Drug Users," unpublished paper, Psychology Clinic, University
of California, Berkeley, 1967.

SPARER, E. V. "The New Public Law: The Relationship of the State
Administration to the Legal Problems of the Poor," paper presented at the Conference on the Extension of Legal Services to

the Poor, sponsored by the U.S. Department of Health, Education, and Welfare, Washington, D.C., November 1964.

SPARER, E. V. "The Role of the Welfare Client's Lawyer." *UCLA Law Review,* 1965, *12,* 361–380.

STEPHENS, W. N. *The Oedipus Complex.* New York: Free Press, 1962.

STEWART, G. *The Year of the Oath.* Garden City, N.Y.: Doubleday, 1950.

STRAUS, E. *Phenomenological Psychology.* New York: Basic Books, 1966.

SUTHERLAND, E. H. *White Collar Crime.* New York: Dryden, 1949.

SUTHERLAND, E. H. "Crime and Corporate Organization," in Merton, R. K. and others (Eds.).

SZASZ, T. *The Myth of Mental Illness: Foundations for a Theory of Personal Conduct.* New York: Hoeber-Harper, 1961.

TAYLOR, T. *Nuremberg and Vietnam: An American Tragedy.* Chicago: Quadrangle Books, 1970.

TEN BROEK, J. "California's Duel System of Family Law: Its Origin, Development and Present Status," Part 3. *Stanford Law Review,* 1965, *17.*

THOMAS, D. S. *The Salvage.* Berkeley and Los Angeles: University of California Press, 1952.

THOMAS, D. S. and NISHIMOTO, R. S. *The Spoilage.* Berkeley and Los Angeles: University of California Press, 1946.

THOMPSON, J. C., JR. "How Could Vietnam Happen: An Autopsy." *Atlantic,* April 1968, pp. 47–53.

THOMPSON, V. *Bureaucracy and Innovation.* University, Ala.: University of Alabama Press, 1969.

THOREAU, H. D. *Walden.*

TILLICH, P. *Love, Power, and Justice.* New York: Oxford University Press, 1954.

TOLMAN, E. C. *Behavior and Psychological Man.* Berkeley and Los Angeles: University of California Press, 1961.

TRAN VAN DINH. Article in *Saturday Review,* May 30, 1970.

VRBA, R. and BESTIC, A. *I Cannot Forgive.* London: Sidgwick, Jackson, Gibbs, and Phillips, 1963.

WALD, G. "Corporate Responsibility for War Crimes." *New York Review of Books,* July 2, 1970.

WALKER, D. *Rights in Conflict.* New York: Signet, 1968.

WASCOW, A. I. *From Race-Riot to Sit-In.* Garden City, N.Y.: Doubleday, 1966.

WASHBURN, W. E. (Ed.) *The Indian and the White Man.* Garden City, N.Y.: Doubleday, 1964.

WASSERSTROM, R. A. "The Obligation to Obey the Law." *UCLA Law Review,* 1963, *10,* 780–807.

WESTLEY, W. A. "Violence and the Police." *American Journal of Sociology,* 1953, *59,* 34–41.

WESTLEY, W. A. *The Police: A Sociological Study of Law, Custom, and Morality.* Cambridge, Mass.: MIT Press, 1970.

WHITE, R. W. *Lives in Progress.* New York: Holt, Rinehart, and Winston, 1952.

WHITE, R. W. "Competence and the Psychosexual Stages of Development," in Jones, M. R. (Ed.).

WHITEHEAD, D. *The Dow Story.* New York: McGraw-Hill, 1968.

WHITESIDE, T. *Defoliation.* New York: Ballantine, 1970.

WILENSKY, H. *Organizational Intelligence.* New York: Basic Books, 1967.

WILLIAMS, R. F. *Negroes with Guns.* New York: Marzani and Munsell, 1962.

WOLFF, K. (Ed.) *The Sociology of Georg Simmel.* New York: Free Press, 1950.

WOLFF, K. "For a Sociology of Evil." *Journal of Social Issues,* 1969, *25,* 111–125.

WYNNE-EDWARDS, V. C. *Animal Dispersion in Relation to Social Behavior.* Edinburgh: Oliver and Boyd; New York: Hafner, 1962.

YOUNG, J. Z. *Doubt and Certainty in Science.* New York: Oxford University Press, 1960.

ZIMBARDO, P. G. "The Human Choice: Individuation, Reason, and Order versus Deindividuation, Impulse, and Chaos," *Nebraska Symposium on Motivation, 1969.* Lincoln, Neb.: University of Nebraska Press, 1969.

Index

375